New Challenges for Maturing Democracies in Korea and Taiwan

THE WALTER H. SHORENSTEIN
ASIA-PACIFIC RESEARCH CENTER

Studies of the Walter H. Shorenstein Asia-Pacific Research Center

Andrew G. Walder, General Editor

The Walter H. Shorenstein Asia-Pacific Research Center in the Freeman Spogli Institute for International Studies at Stanford University sponsors interdisciplinary research on the politics, economies, and societies of contemporary Asia. This monograph series features academic and policy-oriented research by Stanford faculty and other scholars associated with the Center.

New Challenges for Maturing Democracies in Korea and Taiwan

Edited by Larry Diamond and Gi-Wook Shin

Stanford University Press

Stanford, California

Stanford University Press
Stanford, California

Printed in the United States of America on acid-free, archival-quality paper

Library of Congress Cataloging-in-Publication Data

New challenges for maturing democracies in Korea and Taiwan / edited by Larry Diamond and Gi-Wook Shin.
     pages cm — (Studies of the Walter H. Shorenstein Asia-Pacific Research Center)
     Includes index.
   ISBN 978-0-8047-8743-7 (cloth : alk. paper) —
ISBN 978-0-8047-8918-9 (pbk. : alk. paper)
     1. Democracy—Korea (South)   2. Democracy—Taiwan.   3. Korea (South)—Politics and government.   4. Taiwan—Politics and government.   I. Diamond, Larry Jay, editor of compilation.   II. Shin, Gi-Wook, editor of compilation.
III. Series: Studies of the Walter H. Shorenstein Asia-Pacific Research Center.
   JQ1729.A15N49 2014
   320.951249—dc23

                                                                    2013032079

Typeset by Newgen in 11/14 Garamond

Contents

Figures and Tables

TABLES

Acknowledgments

This book is the product of vigorous collaboration among scholars and supporters in three countries, the United States, South Korea, and Taiwan, and between two centers within the Freeman Spogli Institute for International Studies (FSI) at Stanford University: the Center on Democracy, Development, and the Rule of Law (CDDRL) and the Walter H. Shorenstein Asia-Pacific Research Center (S-APARC). As directors of the respective centers, we want to express our sincere appreciation to the many individuals at our centers and at FSI who support our research and conferences.

This volume was made possible by the ongoing support provided by the Taipei Economic and Cultural Office in San Francisco to the Taiwan Democracy Program at CDDRL, and by a generous grant from the Academy of Korean Studies and the Ministry of Education, Science and Technology, South Korea (AKS-2007-CA-2001). We express our deep gratitude to these institutions.

For helping us develop the conceptual structure of the conference and identify some of the Taiwan participants, we thank Professor Yun-han Chu, who has been an active partner in the Taiwan Democracy Program since its inception eight years ago. We thank Hee-yeon Cho, Hsin-Hsing Chen, and Ki-Soo Eun for the very helpful papers they contributed to the May 2011 conference, which we regret that we were not able to include in this volume. We also thank Alice Carter for her steadfast support of the program and of the conference at which initial drafts of the chapters for this book were presented. We are grateful to Heather Ahn (program manager) and David

Straub (associate director) of S-APARC's Korean Studies Program for their help in organizing the conference and managing the subsequent communications with the authors. And we express our appreciation to Joyce Lee for her meticulous work in preparing the manuscript for publication, and to Lukas Friedemann for his energetic research assistance in support of the introduction to this volume.

Finally, we extend our gratitude to our colleague, Andrew Walder, editor of the Stanford University Press Series on the Studies of the Walter H. Shorenstein Asia-Pacific Research Center, in which this book appears, and Geoffrey Burn, Executive Editor at Stanford University Press, as well as two anonymous reviewers. Their critical but sympathetic comments and suggestions helped considerably to improve this book.

We have found it an intellectually invigorating experience to cooperate in this project and compare these two vibrant and important democracies. We hope this work will inspire other such comparisons in the years to come.

Larry Diamond and Gi-Wook Shin

Acronyms

1C2S	one country, two systems
ABS	Asian Barometer Survey
BBS	bulletin board station
CCP	Chinese Communist Party
CEPD	Council for Economic Planning and Development
CSS	Committee for Social Security
DJP	Democratic Justice Party
DLP	Democratic Liberal Party
DPP	Democratic Progressive Party
DRG	Diagnosis-Related Group
ECFA	Economic Cooperation Framework Agreement
FDI	foreign direct investment
FKTU	Federation of Korea Trade Unions
GNP	Grand National Party
ICT	information communications technology
IT	information technology
KCTU	Korea Confederation of Trade Unions
KDB	Korea Democracy Barometer
KMT	Kuomintang
KW	Korean Won
LALIE	Living Allowance for the Low-Income Elderly
MDP	New Millennium Democratic Party
MRT	Mass Rapid Transit

NHI   National Health Insurance
NHIC   National Health Insurance Corporation
NP   New Party
OBM   own-brand manufacturing
ODM   own-design manufacturing
OECD   Organisation for Economic Co-operation and Development
OOP   Out-of-pocket payments
PDA   personal digital assistant
PDP   Peace Democratic Party
PRC   People's Republic of China
R&D   research and development
RDP   Reunification Democratic Party
ROC   Republic of China
SEF   Straits Exchange Foundation
SNTV   single, nontransferable voting
TAIP   Taiwan Independence Party
TEDS   Taiwan Election and Democracy Survey
TFR   total fertility rate
TSMC   Taiwan Semiconductor Manufacturing Company
TSU   Taiwan Solidarity Union
WTO   World Trade Organization

Contributors

Larry Diamond is a senior fellow at the Hoover Institution and at the Freeman Spogli Institute for International Studies, where he directs the Center for Democracy, Development, and the Rule of Law (CDDRL). At CDDRL, he is also one of the principal investigators in the programs on Arab Reform and Democracy and on Liberation Technology. He is also founding co-editor of the *Journal of Democracy* and a senior consultant to the International Forum for Democratic Studies of the National Endowment for Democracy. His latest book, *The Spirit of Democracy: The Struggle to Build Free Societies Throughout the World* (2008), explores the sources of global democratic progress and stress and the prospects for future democratic expansion.

Gi-Wook Shin is director of the Walter H. Shorenstein Asia-Pacific Research Center; the Tong Yang, Korea Foundation, and Korea Stanford Alumni Chair of Korean Studies; the founding director of the Korean Studies Program; a senior fellow of the Freeman Spogli Institute for International Studies; and a professor of sociology, all at Stanford University. Shin is the author/ editor of a dozen books and numerous articles. His recent books include *Troubled Transition: North Korea's Politics, Economy and External Relations* (2013); *History Textbooks and the Wars in Asia: Divided Memories* (2011); *South Korean Social Movements: From Democracy to Civil Society* (2011); and *One Alliance, Two Lenses: U.S.-Korea Relations in a New Era* (2010). Because of the wide popularity of his publications, many of them have been translated and distributed to Korean audiences. As a historical-comparative and political sociologist, his research has concentrated on social movements, nationalism, development, and international relations.

Chong-Min Park is dean of the College of Political Science and Economics and professor of public administration at Korea University. He currently directs the Asian Barometer Survey in South Korea. Park has published articles examining Asian values, social capital, institutional trust, and local governance.

Yun-han Chu is a distinguished research fellow of the Institute of Political Science at Academia Sinica and professor of political science at National Taiwan University. He also serves as the coordinator of the Asian Barometer Survey. Chu specializes in politics of greater China, East Asian political economy, international political economy, and democratization. Among his recent English publications are *How East Asians View Democracy* (2008) and *The New Chinese Leadership: Challenges and Opportunities After the 16th Party Congress* (2004).

Jiyoon Kim is a research fellow and the director of the Public Opinion Studies Center at the Asan Institute for Policy Studies. Her recent publications include "Political Judgments, Perceptions of Facts, and Partisan Effects" (*Electoral Studies*, 2010) and "Public Spending, Public Deficits, and Government Coalition" (*Political Studies*, 2010). She also co-edited the volume of *The Choice of Korean Electorates: National Assembly Election 2012*.

Shelley Rigger is the Brown Professor of East Asian Politics and chair of political science at Davidson College in Davidson, North Carolina. She is the author of two books on Taiwan's domestic politics, *Politics in Taiwan: Voting for Democracy* (1999) and *From Opposition to Power: Taiwan's Democratic Progressive Party* (2001). In 2011 she published *Why Taiwan Matters: Small Island, Global Powerhouse*, a book for general readers.

Minjeong Kim is associate professor of journalism and technical communication at Colorado State University. Minjeong studies communication law and policy and digital media. Her research has been published in scholarly journals such as *Communication Law and Policy, Journal of the Copyright Society of the U.S.A., Journal of Computer-Mediated Communication*, and *Telecommunications Policy*.

Han Woo Park is associate professor in the department of media and communication at Yeungnam University in South Korea. Formerly, he was director of the World Class University Webometrics Institute funded by the Korean government (2009–2011). Since 2007, he has served as co-editor of *Journal of Contemporary Eastern Asia*. He also sits on the editorial boards of *Scientometrics, International Journal of Internet Science, Quality & Quantity*, and *CollNet Journal of Scientometrics and Information Management*.

Chen-Dong Tso is associate professor in the department of political science at National Taiwan University, and also serves as senior adviser to the Asia Foundation, a non-government organization based in San Francisco. His research interests lie in the areas of East Asian regionalism, industrial policy, and Internet society. Tso has published a number of articles in local and international journals, including *Journal of East Asian Studies, Issues & Studies*, and *Australian Journal of Public Administration*.

Yoonkyung Lee is associate professor of sociology and Asian and Asian American studies at the State University of New York at Binghamton. She has been working on research areas of democracy, labor politics, political parties, social movements, and political economy of development. She is the author of *Militants or Partisans: Labor Unions and Democratic Politics in Korea and Taiwan* (2011), and her articles have appeared in *Studies in Comparative International Development, Asian Survey, Critical Asian Studies*, and *Korea Observer*.

Wan-wen Chu is a research fellow at the Research Center for Humanities and Social Sciences, Academia Sinica, and adjunct professor of economics at National Taiwan University. She has published studies on East Asian economic development, especially regarding industrial policy, and is the co-author of *Beyond Late Development: Taiwan's Upgrading Policies* (2003, with Alice Amsden). Other books include *Engine of Economic Growth* (2002) and *Globalization and the Taiwan Economy* (2003).

Sangho Moon is professor at the Graduate School of Governance and department of public administration at Sungkyunkwan University (SKKU). Before coming to SKKU, Moon taught at Tennessee State University. As a public economist, his research has concentrated on income inequality, health-care utilization, and economic well-being of disadvantaged populations. Moon's publications appear in *Applied Economics, Economic Inquiry*, and *Health Policy*.

Wan-I Lin is professor of social work at National Taiwan University. He is president of the Taiwan Association of Gerontology (TAG) and the New Frontier Foundation (the think tank of the Democratic Progressive Party). Since 2004, he has served as editor-in-chief of *Taiwanese Social Work*. He publishes widely on social work, social welfare, and welfare politics. His recent publications include *Social Welfare* (2010), *The Handbook of Disaster Management and Social Work* (2011), *School Social Work Practice* (2012), and *Social Welfare in Taiwan: A Historical and Institutional Analysis* (2012).

Katharine H. S. Moon is professor in the department of political science at Wellesley College. She has served in the Office of the Senior Coordinator for Women's Issues in the U.S. Department of State and as a trustee of Smith College. Moon is the author of *Sex Among Allies: Military Prostitution in U.S.–Korea Relations* (1997; Korean edition 2002) and other publications on the U.S.–Korea alliance and social movements in Korea and Asia (e.g., democratization, women's movements, migrant workers, human rights).

Richard Bush is a senior fellow at the Brookings Institution and director of its Center for Northeast Asian Policy Studies. His scholarly work focuses on China's relations with its neighbors. His most recent books are *Perils of Proximity: China–Japan Security Relations* and *Uncharted Strait: The Future of China–Taiwan Relations*. Prior to arriving at Brookings in 2002, he served for nineteen years in the government, in Congress, in the intelligence community, and as chairman and managing director of the American Institute in Taiwan.

New Challenges for Maturing
Democracies in Korea and Taiwan

Korea and Taiwan
New Challenges for Maturing Democracies

Larry Diamond and Gi-Wook Shin

Over the past four decades, a period in world political history known as the "third wave" of global democratization, more than eighty countries have made transitions to democracy.[1] Outside of Europe, few countries have consolidated democracy—and established a relatively liberal form of it—more quickly and successfully than South Korea (Korea hereafter unless specified otherwise) and Taiwan. These two "Asian tigers" were long known for their developmental authoritarian regimes—non-democratic regimes that sharply restricted political rights and civil liberties but delivered astonishing rates of economic development that transformed very poor countries into middle-class societies in less than two generations. But during the heyday of their economic miracles in the 1970s and '80s, each country experienced growing societal mobilization for democracy, with particularly dramatic expression in the form of popular protests in Korea. By the time military rule was forced to give way to electoral democracy in 1987, under pressure of mass demonstrations, Korea had a robust civil society and very popular figures in the political opposition.[2] Taiwan's democratization proceeded more gradually, crossing one threshold with the legalization of opposition parties and the end of martial law in 1986, then another with the first free and competitive presidential election in Taiwan a decade later.

Both Korea and Taiwan emerged as relatively liberal democracies and made various political reforms in their early years to extend civil liberties, create a still more open and competitive political system, strengthen the rule of law, and improve civilian control of the military.[3] In each case, the once

powerful military and national security establishment is no longer a significant player in domestic politics. With the rise of a more competitive party
system, both countries have twice made peaceful transfers of power from
the ruling to the opposition party. Among peer third-wave democracies that
made transitions during this era, only a few established liberal democracy
so quickly, and only a few achieved such rapid democratic consolidation,
in the sense that democratic institutions became so deeply rooted that they
were relatively immune to breakdown for any internal reason. That was not
the case with a number of other third-wave democracies, however. In fact,
during the period of the third wave, nearly one-third of all the democracies
that have existed have broken down.[4]

In this introductory chapter, we compare Korea and Taiwan not only to
each other but also to a larger set of nine other third-wave democracies that
are now categorized by the World Bank as high-income or upper-middle-
income countries (according to their per capita gross national income). These
other countries are from Southern Europe (Greece and Spain), postcommunist Europe (Hungary, the Czech Republic, and Poland), Latin America
(Argentina, Chile, and Mexico), and the Middle East (Turkey). As shown in
Table INT.I, within five years of their transitions, Korea and Taiwan each met

TABLE INT.I
Democratic trends in selected third-wave democracies

Country	Year of transition	FH score in transition year	FH score + 5 years	FH score + 10 years	FH score + 15 years	Democratic break-down?
South Korea	**1988**	**2, 3**	**2, 2**	**2, 2**	**2, 2**	**No**
Taiwan	**1996**	**2, 2**	**1, 2**	**2, 1**	**1, 2**	**No**
Greece	1974	2, 2	2, 2	1, 2	1, 2	No
Spain	1977	2, 3	1, 2	1, 2	1, 1	No
Argentina	1983	3, 3	2, 1	2, 3	3, 3	No
Turkey	1983	3, 5	2, 4	4, 4	4, 5	Almost
Hungary	1990	2, 2	1, 2	1, 2	1, 1	No
Czech Republic	1990	2, 2	1, 2	1, 2	1, 1	No
Poland	1990	2, 2	1, 2	1, 2	1, 1	No
Chile	1990	2, 2	2, 2	2, 2	1, 1	No
Mexico	2000	2, 3	2, 2	3, 3	—	No

SOURCE: Freedom House, www.freedomhouse.org/.

a reasonable test of liberal democracy—a score of no worse than 2 on each of the Freedom House scales of political rights and civil liberties, where 1 signifies most free or democratic and 7 most repressive. Moreover, they have continuously remained liberal democracies after they crossed this threshold. The same has been the case for the third-wave democracies of Southern Europe and postcommunist Europe, as well as Chile. However, Argentina, Turkey, and Mexico show that the consolidation of liberal democracy is not inevitable when democracy emerges in countries at relatively high levels of economic development (though these three countries, to be sure, were not as rich as Korea and Taiwan). In Argentina, Turkey, and Mexico, democracy regressed after the transition, and liberal democracy has yet to be achieved.

This is not to say that either Korea or Taiwan is a perfect democracy. Each political system still has some distance to go in terms of improving civil liberties and the rule of law (as measured annually by Freedom House). In each case, the total scores on civil liberties (at the end of 2011) rank well behind the most liberal third-wave democracies of postcommunist Europe and Chile (Table INT.2), though they are about equal with Japan. This is mainly because Korea and Taiwan trail Spain, the Czech Republic, and Chile in three areas: freedom of expression, the rule of law, and individual

TABLE INT.2
Freedom House raw point scores on political rights and civil liberties, 2012

Country	PR, CL	Political rights raw points, 40 maximum	Civil liberties raw points, 60 maximum
South Korea	**1, 2**	**36**	**50**
Taiwan	**1, 2**	**36**	**52**
Greece	2, 2	35	50
Spain	1, 2	40	57
Czech Republic	1, 1	38	57
Hungary	1, 2	36	52
Poland	1, 1	38	55
Chile	1, 1	39	58
Argentina	2, 2	32	49
Mexico	3, 3	29	37
Turkey	3, 3	28	35

SOURCE: Freedom House, www.freedomhouse.org/report/freedom-world-aggregate-and-subcategory-scores.

rights. On political rights, Korea and Taiwan fare somewhat better, trailing the most liberal European countries only slightly and achieving 90 percent of the maximum score.

Governance

Not only have Korea and Taiwan been success stories democratically, but also they have sustained comparatively good governance. This is an important observation, because some pundits contend that political democracy may not improve governance of the state. Figure INT.1 shows the average percentile rankings of the eleven third-wave democracies on a composite of four World Bank measures of the quality of governance in these countries: Government Effectiveness (the quality of the civil service, public services, and public policy formulation), Regulatory Quality (in implementing sound policies that foster private-sector development), Rule of Law (compliance with rules, extent of crime, quality of contract enforcement, the police, and the courts), and Control of Corruption.[5] While these measures have been criticized because they are based on a compilation of perceptions (mainly from international ratings agencies, and sometimes from domestic surveys), their effort to average a wide range of relevant indicators gives them greater reliability than any one index. We take the average of these four governance measures as an indicator of the overall quality of the state. As we see in Figure INT.1, Korea steadily and rather dramatically improved its percentile score on this combined measure of state quality from 1996 to 2011, while Taiwan also made significant progress. By 2011, only Chile (among developing countries) exhibited higher overall state quality than Korea and Taiwan.

In fact, both Korea and Taiwan have significantly improved their scores on all four dimensions of state quality since the World Bank began measuring governance in 1996. Korea went from the 73rd percentile in Government Effectiveness in 1996 to 86th in 2011; from 66th in Regulatory Quality to 79th; from 69th in Rule of Law to 81st; and from 65th in Corruption Control to 70th. Moreover, as we see in Figure INT.2, these changes in Korea have mostly involved steady incremental improvement over time. Taiwan has also seen improvement in each of these four measures of state quality, from the 77th percentile in Government Effectiveness to the 83rd; from 79th in Regulatory Quality to 84th; from 68th in Rule of Law to 83rd; and

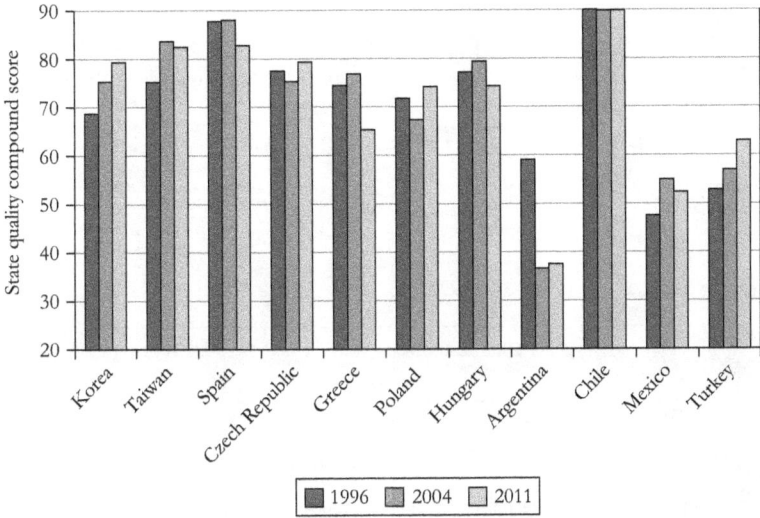

FIGURE INT.1 Trends in state quality in third-wave democracies

SOURCE: World Bank, *Worldwide Governance Indicators*, http://info.worldbank.org/governance/wgi/index.asp.

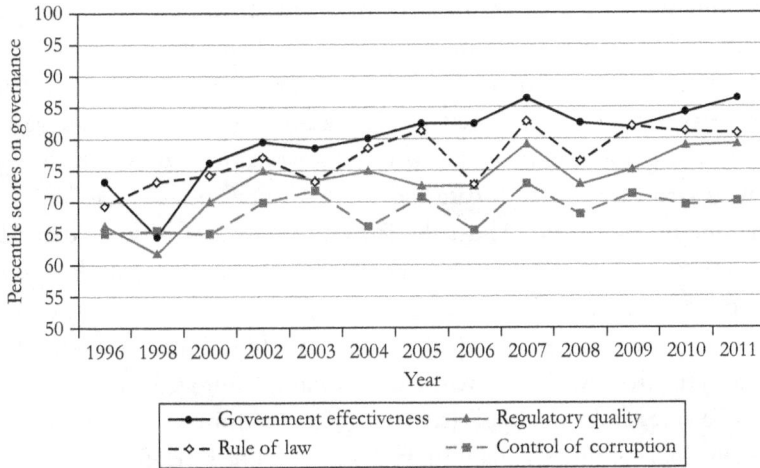

FIGURE INT.2 Trends in governance in Korea, 1996–2011

SOURCE: World Bank, *Worldwide Governance Indicators*, http://info.worldbank.org/governance/wgi/index.asp.

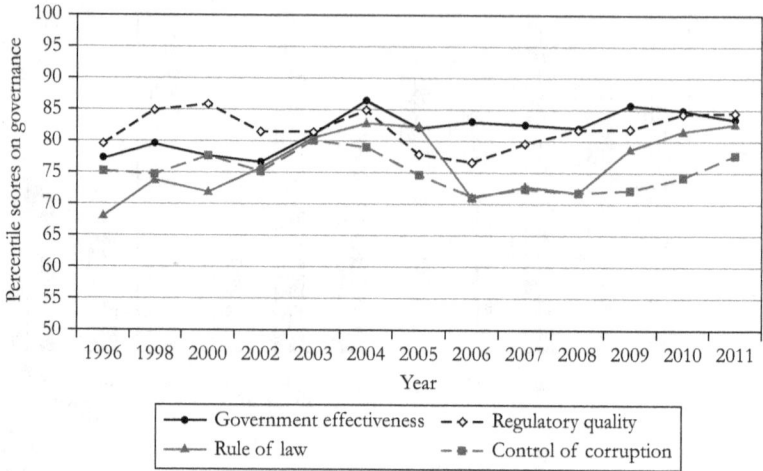

FIGURE INT.3 Trends in governance in Taiwan, 1996–2011
SOURCE: World Bank, *Worldwide Governance Indicators*, http://info.worldbank.org/governance/wgi/index.asp.

from 75th in Corruption Control to 78th. In Taiwan's case, there has been a leveling off or slight regression in some of these measures in recent years (Figure INT.3). But for both countries, the improvements in their percentile scores in governance have not been due to broad global deterioration (such that the two countries look better only because other countries are getting worse). If we examine their standardized governance scores (which range from −2.5 to +2.5), in each case the country's performance has improved over time or leveled off. Thus, the fears and warnings of some defenders of the "Asian values" thesis—that democracy would bring a decline in the quality of governance—have not been realized. Instead, as these two democracies have matured, the quality and neutrality of their state structures and the effectiveness of governance have steadily improved.

To be sure, addressing political corruption continues to be challenging, as recent high-profile scandals attest. Former South Korean President Roh Moo-hyun, who was investigated on the charges of political corruption, committed suicide in 2009, and the former Taiwanese President Chen Shui-bian was sentenced to life in prison for similar charges after leaving office in 2008 (in 2010 his sentence was commuted to twenty years, and in mid-2013 he attempted suicide). Both Korea and Taiwan still score lower on Control of Corruption than on any of the other three World Bank measures of state quality. Each country has also seen discussions about curtailing the power of presidency in order to ensure a better balance of power in the state. Nonetheless, while they suffer such shortcomings in terms of rule of law, Taiwan and Korea are clearly vigorous and comparatively well-governed democracies.

Economy

One consequence of reasonably (and increasingly) effective governance under democracy in Korea and Taiwan has been continued economic growth. As Table INT.3 details, both Korea and Taiwan sustained relatively robust economic growth rates after democratization, though each country (and especially Taiwan) experienced some slowing of economic growth after democratization. It should be noted that interpreting this reduction in growth rates is difficult, because economic growth inevitably slows once countries reach more-advanced levels of development. The economic performance of these two Asian tigers *as* democracies has nevertheless been impressive. Although growth slowed somewhat from the torrid pace of the early and intermediate phases of industrialization (a common pattern), Korea and Taiwan have continued to perform well economically and mature societally *as* democracies. Indeed, in 1996 Korea was inducted into the club of advanced industrial democracies, the Organisation for Economic Co-operation and Development (OECD); and Taiwan would have been inducted were it not for its sensitive geopolitical status vis-à-vis the mainland. Both had become by the mid to late 1990s—and are even more so today—high-income, maturing industrial societies, rather than "developing countries." And to put their growth performances in perspective, Taiwan's 4.3 percent average annual rate of economic growth in the period from 1997 to 2011 may seem modest relative to its predemocratization average growth rate of 7.6 percent. But it was several times larger than the average annual economic growth of Japan in the same period (0.7 percent). As a result, Taiwan surged ahead of Japan in per capita income (in purchasing power parity dollars), and Korea is not far behind Japan. During the 2000–2010 period, the average annual economic growth rates of Korea (4.00 percent) and Taiwan (3.65 percent) were matched only by Poland (which grew at the same rate as Korea). All eight other third-wave democracies in this comparison set—including prominent emerging market economies like Mexico and Turkey—grew at a notably slower pace (see Figure INT.4).

TABLE INT.3

Annual GDP (PPP) growth rates of Korea and Taiwan (fifteen years before and after democratization)

Korea (± 15 yrs. from democratization)	GDP (PPP) growth rate (%)	Taiwan (± 15 yrs. from democratization)	GDP (PPP) growth rate (%)
1973	14.8	1981	6.5
1974	9.4	1982	4.0
1975	7.3	1983	8.3
1976	13.5	1984	9.3
1977	11.8	1985	4.1
1978	10.3	1986	11.0
1979	8.4	1987	10.7
1980	−1.9	1988	7.3
1981	7.4	1989	10.3
1982	8.3	1990	6.9
1983	12.2	1991	7.9
1984	9.9	1992	7.6
1985	7.5	1993	6.7
1986	12.2	1994	7.6
1987	12.3	1995	6.4
1988	**11.7**	**1996**	**5.5**
1989	6.8	1997	5.5
1990	9.3	1998	3.5
1991	9.7	1999	6.0
1992	5.8	2000	5.8
1993	6.3	2001	−1.7
1994	8.8	2002	5.3
1995	8.9	2003	3.7
1996	7.2	2004	6.2
1997	5.8	2005	4.7
1998	−5.7	2006	5.4
1999	10.7	2007	6.0
2000	8.8	2008	0.7
2001	4.0	2009	−1.8
2002	7.2	2010	10.7
2003	2.8	2011	4.0
−15 yrs. average	**9.6**	**−15 yrs. average**	**7.6**
+15 yrs. average	**6.4**	**+15 yrs. average**	**4.3**

SOURCE: International Monetary Fund, *World Economic Outlook Report*, various years, www.imf.org/external/pubs/ft/weo/2012/01/weodata/index.aspx.

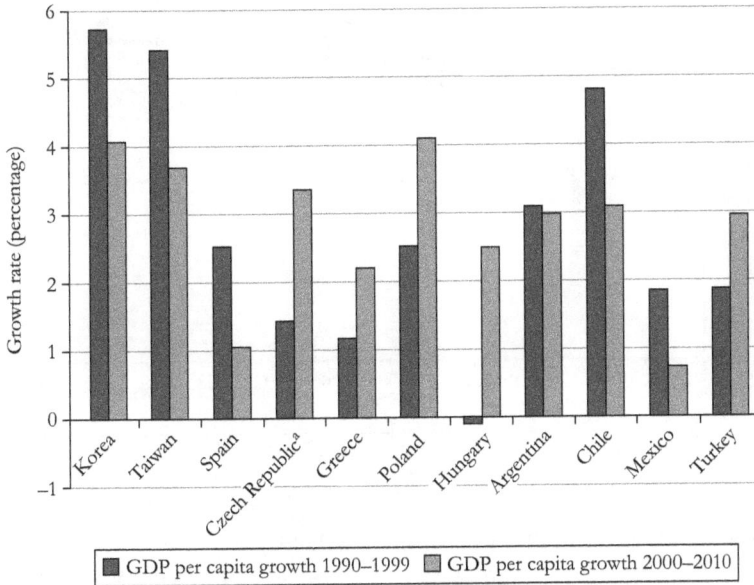

FIGURE INT.4 Average annual economic growth rates in eleven third-wave democracies, 1990–1999 and 2000–2010

SOURCE: International Monetary Fund, *World Economic Outlook Database*, www.imf.org/external/pubs/ft/weo/2012/02/weodata/index.aspx.

ᵃThe GDP growth rates for the Czech Republic are calculated for the period 1996–1999 and 1996–2010, respectively.

Both Korea and Taiwan have continued to perform impressively in improving human well-being, as well, since they became democracies in the late 1980s and early 1990s. In the latest U.N. Human Development Report (covering 2011), Korea ranked 15th on the Human Development Index (HDI), which measures development as a composite of life expectancy, levels of education, and per capita gross national income.[6] In that same year, the government of Taiwan estimated that Taiwan would have placed 18th if it had been included in the survey. Thus, both countries placed in the topmost category of "very high human development," and ahead of many Western European countries, including France, Britain, Italy, Spain, and Portugal. Both Korea and Taiwan reached this pinnacle of development through continued socioeconomic progress *after democratization*; in 1990, Korea ranked 33rd out of 130 countries, near Argentina and Poland; today it is 15th out of 187 countries. Figure INT.5 displays the comparative trends in human development scores among the eleven third-wave democracies.

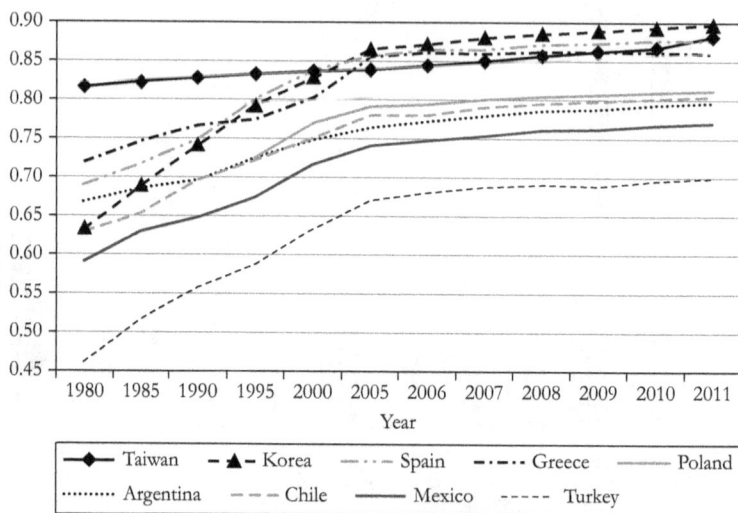

FIGURE INT.5 Trends in the Human Development Index, 1980–2011
SOURCE: UNDP, *International Human Development Indicators*, http://hdr.undp.org/en/data/profiles/.

During the period from 1990 to 2010, Korea registered one of the two fastest rates of improvement on the HDI of all countries now considered "very high" in human development, and among our comparison set it was exceeded only by Turkey (Figure INT.6).[7] Taiwan also improved, but mainly it remained at a very high level.[8]

In short, in discussing the political trajectories and governance challenges of Taiwan and Korea, we are no longer dealing with developing or even emerging-market countries, but now some of the richest, healthiest, best educated, and most technologically advanced countries in the world. Yet an economy's global ascendance comes with a price. As Chapters 6 and 7 in this volume show, the looming stratification between regular and non-regular employment and the growing unemployment among college graduates have emerged as the most serious plagues that undermine the sustainability of socioeconomic cohesion in both societies. Korea and Taiwan are beginning to struggle with many of the issues that confront other advanced industrial democracies: growing social disparities and popular demand for expanded social welfare expenses, in a period of increasing global economic competitiveness and rapidly increasing income inequality within and between countries.

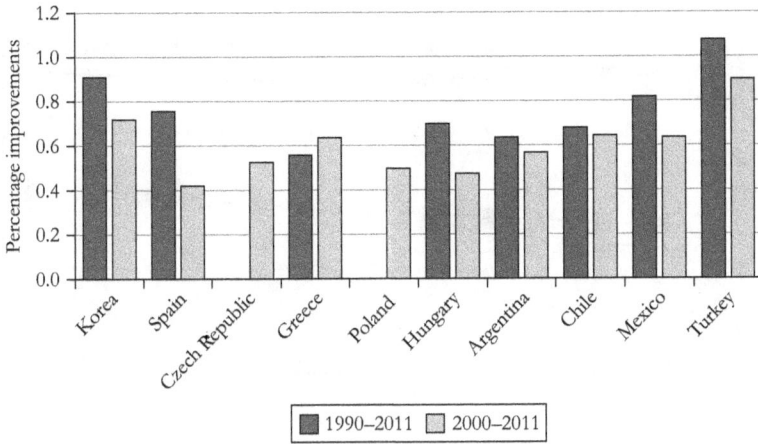

FIGURE INT.6 Average annual percentage improvements in Human Development Index, 1990–2011
SOURCE: UNDP, *International Human Development Indicators*, http://hdr.undp.org/en/data/profiles/.
NOTE: Data not available for Taiwan.

Society

The above economic and political achievements have been extraordinary, marking Korea and Taiwan as two of the most successful developing countries of the post–World War II era. But with success comes new challenges. High levels of development bring changes in culture, lifestyle, family relations, and expectations that can generate new societal burdens. Both Korea and Taiwan are undergoing a demographic transition like that gripping Japan and Europe. All of these societies are rapidly aging, as the birth rate plunges and a smaller number of working-age citizens will increasingly have to bear some of the social costs of health and retirement of an elderly, dependent population. During the five-year period to 2015, the United Nations Development Program (UNDP) estimates that Korea's population growth rate will fall from its already low level of 0.8 percent (during the 1990–1995 period) to 0.4 percent. The median age has risen to 38 years, compared to 28 years in Indonesia. And while Korea's dependency ratio (the ratio of those age 0–14 and age 65 and older to those of working age, i.e., 15–64) is lower than most highly developed countries, it is rising rapidly, as is Taiwan's. The particular concern is the ratio of elderly retirees to those of working age. As we see in Figure INT.7, the ratios are not nearly as high as

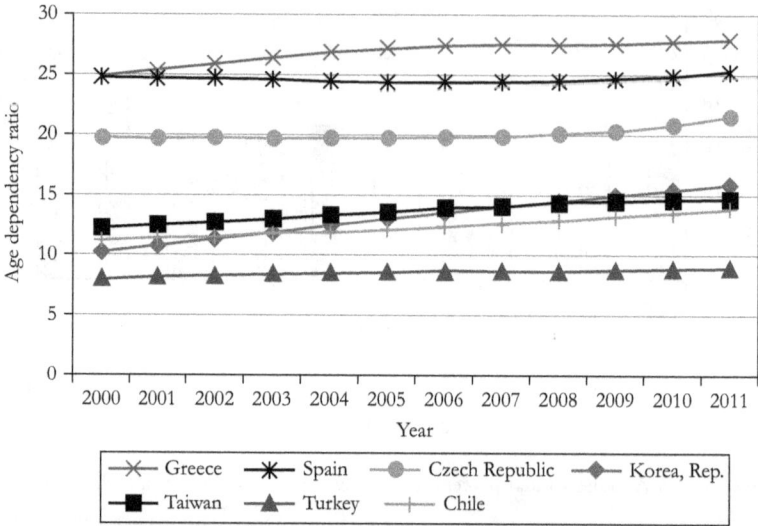

FIGURE INT.7 Age dependency ratios in third-wave democracies
SOURCES: World Bank, *World DataBank*, http://databank.worldbank.org/ddp/home.do; Council for Economic Planning and Development, *Taiwan Statistical Data Book 2012*, www.cepd.gov.tw/encontent/m1.aspx?sNo=0017349.
NOTE: Lines show the ratio of older dependents (people older than 64) to the working-age population (those ages 15–64).

for the European third-wave democracies, but the trend since 2000 and the inevitable future increase are something to worry about.

Political leaders and policy makers face an unanticipated challenge: how to sustain some level of population growth in order to sustain economic dynamism. Related to this, and examined in Part V, are the fiscal implications of aging populations and rising dependency ratios, which result in exploding education and health-care costs, rising demands for other social services, and increased fiscal pressures on the state. Both Korea and Taiwan have seen growing demands for expanded social welfare in recent years. All of this is happening at a time of unprecedented international economic competitiveness, which presents new potential opportunities but also less margin for error, as many more countries are now competing for the same niches in international production chains.

Moreover, each society is confronting—for the first time since land reforms helped to launch their economic miracles—growing economic and social inequality, an increasingly pervasive global trend, no doubt a consequence of accelerating globalization, which no one has yet figured out how to address. In Korea, big business has been doing surprisingly well, but small and medium-sized businesses have been struggling, and many young people, even those with college degrees, are unemployed. Taiwan has experienced similar problems and frustrations. The Korean government has been criticized for ignoring economic disparities, and popular demand for increased social welfare spending has been on the rise. "Economic democracy" was a key campaign slogan for both ruling and opposition party candidates during the December 2012 presidential election in Korea. Similar issues arose in the January 2012 presidential election campaign in Taiwan, although the incumbent, Ma Ying-jeou, was comfortably reelected.

Public Attitudes and Values

How do the people of Korea and Taiwan feel about their democracies? This is an important question, given continued political corruption and criticism of the way democracy works in both societies. To address this important question, we draw from the third round of the Asian Barometer to craft an average level of democratic legitimacy, based on the responses to three different questions, such as whether respondents believe that "Democracy is always preferable to any other kind of government."[9] The average favorable response to these three items during the period 2010 to 2012 varied from 62 percent in the Philippines to 77 percent in Thailand. Taiwan was slightly at the lower end with 66 percent (mainly due to the low response to the first question about whether democracy is *always* preferable) and Korea was toward the high end with 73 percent. Yet Korea and Taiwan ranked first in Asia in the proportions of the public (74 percent in each country) who rejected all three authoritarian options put to them: one-person rule, one-party rule, and military rule. The less economically developed democracies of East Asia ranked dramatically lower on this measure (see Figure INT.8).

People in Korea and Taiwan also manifest surprisingly high levels of satisfaction with their democracy, despite their cynicism about politicians and parties. Two-thirds in Taiwan and nearly 60 percent in Korea said they were satisfied with the way their democracy was working (though this level had been noticeably lower in some previous surveys). Strong majorities also said they perceived the political system in the country to be a full democracy or a democracy with only minor problems (compared to two far more negative categories of response; see Figure INT.9). In fact, as Park and Chu show in

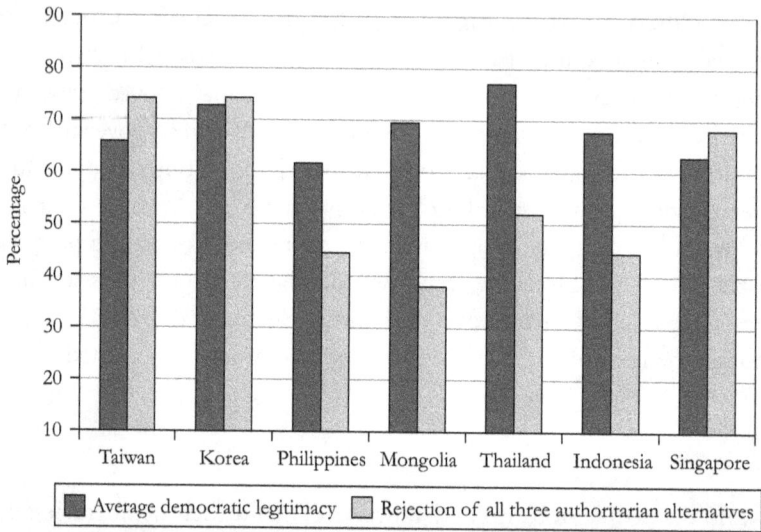

FIGURE INT.8 Democratic legitimacy in East Asia, 2010–2012

SOURCE: Asian Barometer, *Surveys—Data Release (Wave 3)*, www.asianbarometer.org/newenglish/surveys/Data Release3.htm.

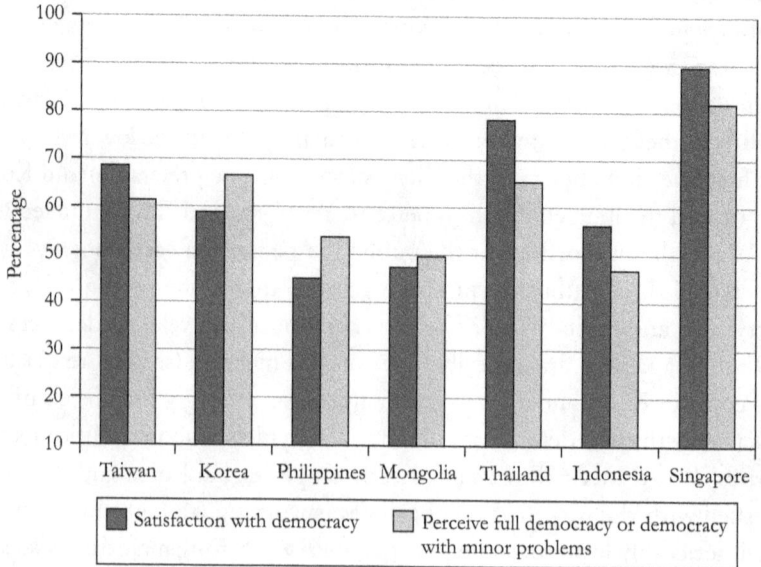

FIGURE INT.9 Democratic satisfaction in East Asia

SOURCE: Asian Barometer, *Survey—Data Release (Wave 3)*, www.asianbarometer.org/newenglish/surveys/Data Release3.htm.

the Chapter 1, satisfaction with democracy has generally been on the rise in each country.

In valuing democracy, citizens in Korea and Taiwan appear to be on par with or ahead of their peers from the more developed Latin American countries, such as Chile, Argentina, and Mexico (see Table INT.4). Their levels of support for democracy are similar, but they reject the authoritarian option of military rule much more decisively (in fact, nearly universally) compared to Latin Americans.[10] Yet here is the puzzle: Koreans and Taiwanese are significantly more distrusting of their representative institutions—their parliament and political parties—than are their peers in Latin American democracies (who are themselves fairly cynical), yet they nevertheless express significantly higher levels of satisfaction with the way democracy is working in the country. The levels of trust that Koreans and Taiwanese register for these institutions (under 20 percent) are among the lowest of any established democracies, and they have been steadily low (or, in the case of Korea, falling) over the last decade or two. Other state institutions in these two countries are only somewhat more broadly trusted: the courts (36 percent in Korea and 30 percent in Taiwan), the national government (22 and 33 percent), the civil service (35 and 48 percent), and the election commission (47 and 55 percent). These findings suggest that citizens in Korea and Taiwan are satisfied with the overall progress of democratization but feel that the

TABLE INT.4

Democratic attitudes (percentage supporting) in Korea, Taiwan, and Latin America

Item	Korea	Taiwan	Chile	Argentina	Mexico	Latin America (avg.)
Democracy is always best	66	51	63	66	49	61
Democracy may have problems but is best	83	87	85	83	67	77
Reject military rule	91	93	73	73	53	66
Satisfaction with democracy	59	69	56	49	27	44
Trust Congress	11	19	41	39	28	34
Trust political parties	12	14	23	21	19	23

SOURCE: Asian Barometer, Round 3 (2010–2012), Latin Barometer 2010 and 2011, www.latinobarometro.org.

political institutions that represent their interests, especially political parties, have not developed as well.

Perhaps the greater confidence in elections helps to sustain popular faith in democracies. When asked if "People have the power to change a government they don't like," 52 percent of Koreans and 57 percent of Taiwanese agreed. As Park and Chu note in Chapter 1, citizens of both countries are critical of many aspects of their democratic system, particularly pertaining to corruption and the rule of law. But they do perceive that their democracies are competitive systems offering voters "a real choice," and that they enjoy significant civil freedoms (though this perception is higher in Taiwan than Korea).

Geopolitics

Many of the new challenges of maturing democracy in Korea and Taiwan are not so different from the ones facing other third-wave democracies, particularly European ones like Spain, Portugal, and Greece, with some of the postcommunist states and the Latin American ones not far behind. But Korea and Taiwan face particular advantages and disadvantages as they seek to manage their transformations. Each chose a growth model that depends on international trade, and each must constantly reevaluate and deepen its trading partnerships to remain competitive, while also continuing to innovate technically and move up the ladder of production. Consequently, the geopolitical environment shaped the economy and politics of Korea and Taiwan in a way very different from the countries of Southern Europe and of Central and Eastern Europe, which saw their economic development accelerated after democratization by integration into and transfers from the European Union (EU), and which were given a strong external stimulus to rapid democratic consolidation by the political conditionality for membership in the EU (or, previously, the European Economic Community).

None of the other third-wave democracies in our data set have faced a regional security environment as potentially perilous as the ones faced by Korea and Taiwan, in the shadow of a once hostile and still very dangerous neighbor. For Korea, this means not only living with a rising China close to its shores, but also facing across the Demilitarized Zone a North Korean regime that, while largely a developmental failure, is heavily armed, deeply aggrieved, and provocative and unpredictable in its behavior. The fact that a growing number of North Koreans are fleeing the miserable circumstances of the north and settling in South Korea adds to the moral and security dilemma. As Moon discusses in Chapter 10, there are over 23,000 defectors living in South Korea today, and incorporating them into South Korean society as equal citizens, not just as fellows of the same nation, presents an important test to Korean democracy. For Taiwan, its relations with China are less contentious than inter-Korean relations, but its challenge is how to manage a much larger and more powerful neighbor that also makes territorial claims on its land. Under the presidency of Ma Ying-jeou, Taiwan has made considerable progress in defusing and relaxing cross-strait relations by promoting increased trade and investment through the Economic Cooperation Framework Agreement (ECFA) and through other diplomatic initiatives. But the great question of Taiwan's future remains unresolved, at a time when China is rapidly emerging as a major world power, with some apparently major frustrations and ambitions.

Challenges for Maturing Democracy

The chapters that follow take a creative and comparative view of the new challenges and dynamics confronting the maturing democracies of Taiwan and Korea. Numerous works deal with political change in the two societies,[11] but few of them adopt a comparative approach. When they do, these comparative studies have largely focused on the emergence of democracy or the politics of democratization processes.[12] In particular, these studies look at how the countries' successful economic development led to political liberalization and examine the ways in which democratic transition has occurred. For instance, while economic development was crucial to democratization in both countries, these studies indicate that social movements and the growth of civil society played a larger role in Korea than in Taiwan.[13] Therefore, they concentrate on the causes or earlier stages of democratization. This book, however, gives careful attention to postdemocratization phenomena and key issues that arise in maturing and consolidating democracies. We go beyond the existing studies of transition to democracy, examining the issues and challenges arising from the consolidation and maturation of democracy in the two societies with a broad, interdisciplinary approach. We intend for this study to contribute to the expanding body of literature on Korean and Taiwanese democratization by investigating the social, cultural, and international dimensions of political change in the two societies.

We begin with the question of political culture. In Chapter 1, Chong-Min Park and Yun-han Chu compare Korean and Taiwanese attitudes toward democracy and investigate how these attitudes and the social values underlying them in turn compare with those in other East Asian democracies. Analyzing three representative public opinion survey series (the Korea Democracy Barometer, the Asian Barometer Survey, and the Taiwan Election and Democracy Survey), Park and Chu offer a comprehensive account of the trends in ordinary citizens' views of democracy since the late 1990s in the two societies that may differ from experts' views as expressed in the Freedom House Index. Their findings suggest that people's desire for democracy remains strong in both societies, but their commitments may not be deep, noting that liberal norms of limited government and the importance of procedures over outcomes are not widespread and deeply rooted in either country. Satisfaction with the way democracy works in each country fluctuates with events, including economic crises, political scandals, and polarized political conflict; and trust in political institutions such as parties and the national legislature is extremely low. The result, Park and Chu argue, is that representative institutions "in both Korea and in Taiwan are in trouble," posing some concerns for the future of their democracies.

Part II addresses the development of party politics and the enduring role of social identity in each country's political arena. With democratization, both countries have developed a very competitive party system beyond the personalistic or patrimonial types of the past, but the power of nationalism continues to shape political behavior in both societies. Using a variety of data sources, Jiyoon Kim in Chapter 2 considers the influence of Korean nationalism on policy debates and voting behavior. According to Kim's analysis, while economic and social issues have emerged as crucial factors, Korean society is sharply divided between conservative and progressive forces, and sentiments toward the North and the United States remain the most vital determinant of party choice for the South Korean public. Thus, Kim concludes, identity politics not only determine one's partisan affiliation but also hamper rational policy debates. In Chapter 3, Shelley Rigger discusses how "national identity" cleavage structures partisanship and affects political mobilization in Taiwan. As in Korea, Rigger argues, feelings of national identity have made it difficult for Taiwan to address domestic problems effectively because they continually project policy debates onto cross-strait relations. Both Chapters 2 and 3 show the continuing, not diminishing, role of identity and nationalism in politics. Taming the power of nationalism in order to ensure rational policy debate remains a key challenge for both societies as democracy matures.

In Part III, we examine one of the most recent features of contemporary politics: the "new media"—such as the Internet and social media—that are radically changing social life and political campaigns. Minjeong Kim and Han Woo Park investigate in Chapter 4 the relationship between digital media and the transformation of politics in Korea. In particular, they show how digital media, as an alternative source of political information, cover issues that the traditional mainstream media ignore, and how digital media are being used by Korean parties and politicians as well as by civil society. Kim and Park caution that while the power of digital media in bringing changes to the traditional arena of politics may be considerable among the young and educated in large cities, conventional media continue to influence older voters and voters in rural, provincial areas. In Chapter 5, Chen-Dong Tso similarly reviews the role of the Internet and social media in transforming social movements and political participation in Taiwan, with an emphasis on how the dynamics of political competition have evolved over the course of the Internet era. Tso concludes that political decisions in the Internet era in Taiwan tend to have shorter time frames and are less substantive, despite the fact that many people "feel empowered with the aid of the Internet to take part in the decision-making process."

In Part IV, we turn to global economic challenges and consider how each of the two maturing democracies has sought to adapt to the demands of an evolving global economy. Yoonkyung Lee in Chapter 6 surveys the socioeconomic transformations that have occurred in post-1997 Korea (after the financial crisis) and discusses how the role of the government has changed in terms of engaging market actors and adopting strategies to create new engines for growth in the neoliberal era. Lee maintains that corporations in Korea, especially the *chaebŏl* groups, have become less and less hampered by government regulations and have successfully expanded into global markets. At the same time, the looming stratification between regular and non-regular employment and the growing unemployment among college graduates have begun to emerge as the most serious challenges to South Korea's socioeconomic stability. In Lee's view, it is this dichotomy between the global ascendance of Korean firms and the domestic fracture among ordinary working people that best captures the political economy of contemporary Korea. Likewise, in Chapter 7, Wan-Wen Chu reviews the trajectory of Taiwan's growth in the wake of its economic and political shifts in the late 1980s and explores how the developmental state has been transformed and how economic change has affected democratization. A major element in Taiwan's globalization, Chu notes, was the opening up of cross-strait relations with mainland China, which began at about the same time as its economic and political liberalization. Chu argues that the China factor has been a crucial element in Taiwan's transformation since 1990 but that increasing economic integration with China poses significant political challenges to Taiwan. Chapters 6 and 7 show that economic and social disparities have grown substantially, posing an acute challenge for both societies. Sustaining economic growth while addressing popular demands for expanded social welfare is one of the toughest policy challenges confronting these maturing democracies.

Part V more specifically addresses one of the signature challenges of societal maturation: its implications for social policy, particularly health care. Korea and Taiwan are both wrestling with the ramifications of fast-aging populations. Sangho Moon analyzes in Chapter 8 the relationship between Korean democratization and health care from both historical and empirical perspectives and argues that increasing health costs and disparities in health care accessibility are urgent issues to be dealt with in Korea. According to Moon's analysis, income-related health disparities, intensified by a widening income gap between the poorest and richest 20 percent, also raise doubts about the effectiveness of integrated health reform that sought equity and redistribution. In Chapter 9, Wan-I Lin investigates the links between political contestation and social welfare development in Taiwan. Arguing that heightened competition among parties for ruling positions in government makes it more difficult to debate social welfare policies rationally, Lin suggests that greater public pressure must be levied so as to make welfare development a less sensitive issue in the midst of political competition.

Finally, in Part VI we consider how South Korea and Taiwan can manage relations with powerful and potentially threatening neighbors while sustaining and deepening democracy. Katharine H. S. Moon discusses in Chapter 10 how a rising China and inter-Korean relations would affect the future of democracy on the peninsula. In particular, Moon argues that integration and fragmentation within South Korea's democracy, especially as new actors such as defectors from the North seek political equality and participation, are endogenous challenges that Koreans must face. If the process of reconciliation and reunification between the two Koreas ever comes to a head, Moon believes, democracy on the peninsula will confront a severe test of survival and direction. In dealing with the rise of China, Richard Bush in Chapter 11 proposes a strategy of Finlandization as applicable to Taiwan. Finland eschewed the option of external balancing but did not ignore the importance of internal balancing, seeking to foster a consensus that ruled out playing politics with foreign policy. Like Finland, Bush suggests, Taiwan can create a stable society and an effective economy by pursuing a mixed strategy to meet the challenge of a rising power.

What emerges from our study is a picture of two evolving democracies, now secure but still imperfect and at times disappointing to their citizens, who, because of higher levels of education and access to information, have also become more cynical. That is another common feature and challenge of democratic maturation. As our chapters demonstrate, it will fall to the elected political leaders of these two countries to rise above the most narrow and immediate of party interests. Instead, they will need to mobilize some consensus so as to craft policies that will guide the structural adaptation and reinvigoration of the society and economy in an era that clearly presents for both Korea and Taiwan not only steep challenges but also new opportunities.

Notes

1. Samuel P. Huntington, *The Third Wave: Global Democratization in the Late Twentieth Century* (Norman: University of Oklahoma Press, 1990); Larry Diamond, *The Spirit of Democracy: The Struggle to Build Free Societies Throughout the World* (New York: Times Books, 2008).

2. See the edited book by Gi-Wook Shin and Paul Y. Chang, *South Korean Social Movements: From Democracy to Civil Society* (New York: Routledge, 2011).

3. See Larry Diamond and Doh Chull Shin, *Institutional Reform and Democratic Consolidation in Korea* (Stanford, CA: Hoover Institution, 1999); Aurel Croissant, David Kuehn, and Philip Lorenz, "Breaking with the Past? Civil-Military Relations in the Emerging Democracies of East Asia," *Policy Studies* 63 (Honolulu, HI: East-West Center, 2012). Also see, Howard Handelman, "The Explosion of Third World Democracy," in *The Challenge of Third World Development*, 3rd ed. (Upper Saddle River, NJ: Prentice-Hall, 2002), Ch. 2.

4. Larry Diamond, *In Search of Democracy* (London: Routledge, forthcoming).

5. For an explanation of these measures, their measurement methodology, and their data sources, see the World Bank's Worldwide Governance Indicators website, http://info.worldbank.org/governance/wgi/resources.htm.

6. Human Development Report 2011, United Nations Development Programme, http://hdr.undp.org/en/media/HDR_2011_EN_Tables.pdf.

7. Ibid., "Human Development Index Trends, 1980–2011," Table 2:132, http://hdr.undp.org/en/media/HDR_2011_EN_Tables.pdf.

8. Because the UNDP does not report human development scores from Taiwan, we have had to rely on computations provided by the Taiwan government, and these contained some missing years that required us to interpolate (as well as having two different methods of calculation according to the formula used by the UNDP in a particular year; in 2005 there was a change in the UNDP's method of calculation of the HDI). Thus, while it is possible to compare Taiwan today and in certain years with other countries in those particular years, it is more difficult to establish the degree of change over time (using the current method of calculating HDI). We are nevertheless grateful to the Office of National Statistics, of the Executive Yuan, Government of the Republic of China (Taiwan), for providing us with this data.

9. To this question, respondents are given two other options: "Sometimes an authoritarian government can be preferable" or "It doesn't matter to me." The other two questions asked whether the respondent agreed or not that "Democracy is capable of solving the problems of our society" and "Democracy may have its problems, but it is still the best form of government." Citizens of Korea and Taiwan responded less democratically to the first item than to the second and third, perhaps reflecting a favorable memory of the accomplishments of their developmental authoritarian regimes.

10. Data on the other two items of rejection of authoritarianism were not available for Latin America. For the relevant Latin Barometer (Latinobarómetro) data for 2010 and 2011, see www.latinobarometro.org/latino/LATContenidos.jsp [in Spanish].

11. For studies of Taiwan, see for example Hungmao Tien, *The Great Transition: Political and Social Change in the Republic of China* (Stanford, CA: Hoover Institution, 1989); Yun-han Chu, *Crafting Democracy in Taiwan* (Taipei: Institute for National Policy Research, 1992); Ramon Myers and Linda Chao, *The First Chinese Democracy: Political Life in the Republic of China, Taiwan* (Baltimore, MD: Johns Hopkins University Press, 1997); Charles Chi-Hsiang Chang and Hung Mao Tien, eds., *Taiwan's Electoral Politics and Democratic Transition: Riding the Third Wave* (Armonk, NY: M. E. Sharpe, 1996); and Philip Paolino and James David Meernik, *Democratization in Taiwan: Challenges in Transformation*

(Hampshire, UK: Ashgate, 2008). For studies of Korea, see Samuel S. Kim, *Korea's Democratization* (Cambridge, UK: Cambridge University Press, 2003) and Tae-gyu Yun, *Law and Democracy in South Korea: Democratic Development Since 1987* (Boulder, CO: Lynne Rienners, 2010).

12. See Becky Shelley, *Democratic Development in East Asia* (New York: Routledge, 2005). Also, see Yin Wah Chu, "The Struggle for Democracy: A Comparative Study of Taiwan and South Korea," Ph.D. diss., University of California–Davis, 1995. For an early treatment of the challenges of democratic consolidation that places Taiwan in a comparative perspective, see Larry Diamond, Marc F. Plattner, Hung-mao Tien, and Yun-han Chu, *Consolidating the Third Wave Democracies* (Baltimore, MD: Johns Hopkins University Press, 1997).

13. See Shin and Chang (2011). Also see Sunhyuk Kim, *The Politics of Democratization in Korea: The Role of Civil Society* (Pittsburgh, PA: University of Pittsburgh Press, 2000). See also Charles K. Armstrong, ed., *Korean Society: Civil Society, Democracy, and the State* (New York: Routledge, 2002). Also, see John Kie-Chiang Oh, *Korean Politics: The Quest for Democratization and Economic Development* (Ithaca, NY: Cornell University Press, 1999). See Yun Fan, "Taiwan: No Civil Society, No Democracy," in *Civil Society and Political Change in Asia: Expanding the Contracting Democratic Space*, ed. Muthiah Alagappa (Stanford, CA: Stanford University Press, 2004), 164–190.

PART ONE

Political Culture

ONE

Trends in Attitudes Toward Democracy in Korea and Taiwan

Chong-Min Park and Yun-han Chu

Introduction

In East Asia, new democracies began to emerge immediately after the people's power revolution in the Philippines overthrew the long-standing dictatorship in 1986. First, South Korea (Korea hereafter) embarked on democratic transition by adopting a democratic constitution and holding a free and open election for president in 1987. Then Taiwan started its democratic transition by lifting martial law in 1987 and then successively holding its first parliamentary election in 1992 and its first popular election for president in 1996.[1] In 1990, following the collapse of the Soviet Union, Mongolia made a quick transition to democracy by abolishing its one-party Communist rule and holding its first multiparty parliamentary election in more than sixty years. With the emergence of these three new democracies, Japan was no longer the only democracy in East Asia.

Korea and Taiwan are widely recognized as the two most successful third-wave democracies in Asia.[2] For nearly two decades, these young democracies have regularly held free and competitive elections at all levels of government. Both nationally and locally, citizens choose the heads of government and the members of the parliament and councils through periodic electoral contests. More important, unlike many of their peers in the region, they have peacefully undergone two power rotations, passing "the two-turnover test" for democratic consolidation.[3] There is little doubt that the political regimes in Korea and Taiwan fully meet the minimum requirements of democracy, such as free and fair elections, universal adult suffrage, and multiparty competition.[4]

Various international assessments of democracy confirm the two Asian tigers' steady institutional progress toward liberal democracy. The Polity IV Project evaluates regime authority characteristics on a 21-point scale ranging from –10 (hereditary monarchy) to +10 (consolidated democracy). In each of the first ten years after the transition, Korea received a Polity score of +6. In each of twelve years from 1998 to 2010, it received a score of +8, two notches below the maximum score. Taiwan performs better in democratizing the authority structure. Before 1992, it received a score of –1; thereafter it was accorded a score of +7 or higher. Since 2005, Taiwan's Polity score has been raised to the maximum, +10.[5] The political regimes in both countries are rated either consolidated or nearly consolidated democracies.

The political systems in both Korea and Taiwan are judged as having progressed beyond electoral democracy. Freedom House assesses the condition of political rights and civil liberties on a 7-point scale with 1 (most free) to 7 (least free). Korea received an average combined score of 2.5 in each of the first five years after the transition (1988–1992); a score of 2.0 in each of the next eleven years (1993–2003); and a score of 1.5 in every year since 2004. Taiwan received an average combined score of 3.0 between 1992 and 1996. It received a score of 2.0 between 1996 and 2000, and after 2001 its score was upgraded to 1.5, the same as that in Korea. These young democracies now rank with long-lasting advanced democracies in the West.[6]

The World Bank reports the quality of state governance in six dimensions: voice and accountability, political stability and absence of violence, government effectiveness, regulatory quality, rule of law, and control of corruption. The values of these Worldwide Governance Indicators range from –2.5 to +2.5. In every year since 1996, Korea received positive ratings in all six dimensions.[7] Taiwan also has received positive ratings in all the dimensions since 1996. In 2011, Korea received higher percentile ranking on every dimension except for political stability and absence of violence, on which it was a middling performer. In contrast, Taiwan was a high performer on every dimension. Although the indicators lack comparability over time, the pattern of the ratings suggests that political institutions and practices in both countries have made progress toward high-quality democratic governance.

Do the people's views of democracy in Korea and Taiwan reflect such expert-based assessments of democracy? How do ordinary Koreans and Taiwanese view democracy as an idea? Do they believe in the legitimacy of democracy? How supportive are they of liberal norms and democratic institutions? Meanwhile, how do they evaluate the performance of their regime-in-practice? How do they perceive the democratic quality of their prevailing system of government? How much confidence do they have in existing political institutions? Has their support for democracy and evaluation of regime performance changed? If so, does the change reflect the influence of generational replacement or the effects of events that occurred during the period surveyed? By addressing these and other related questions, we seek to provide a comprehensive account of the trends in popular attitudes toward democracy in these most successful third-wave democracies in Asia.

For this purpose, we rely on three public opinion survey series—the Korea Democracy Barometer (hereafter KDB),[8] the Asian Barometer Survey (hereafter ABS),[9] and the Taiwan Election and Democracy Survey (hereafter TEDS).[10] For the Korean case, we use five surveys (1996, 1997, 1998, 1999, and 2001) of the KDB series and three surveys (2003, 2006, and 2011) of the ABS series.[11] For the Taiwanese case, we employ three surveys (2001, 2005, and 2010) from the ABS series and one survey (1998) from the TEDS series. It should be noted that the earliest survey data analyzed here were collected several years after the democratic transition, and the earliest and the latest survey data were more than ten years apart. When comparing the two countries, only equivalent items from the different survey series were used so as to achieve the highest level of comparability.

Structures of Citizen Views of Democracy

We take David Easton's theory of political support as a starting point for mapping citizen views of democracy.[12] Easton defines political support as an attitude by which a person orients himself to a political system positively or negatively. He distinguishes between three levels of a political system: the political community, the regime, and the authorities. The political community refers to "a group of persons bound together by a political division of labor." The regime refers to the authority structure as well as its legitimating values and operating norms. The authorities refer to the present incumbents in authority roles. Since we are concerned with attitudes toward democracy as a political regime, the focus is on types of political support at the regime level.

According to Easton, the regime has three components: values and principles, norms and rules, and the structure of authority.[13] Values and principles "serve as broad limits with regard to what can be taken for granted in the guidance of day-to-day policy." Norms and rules refer to "procedures that are expected and acceptable in the processing and implementation of demands." The structure of authority refers to "formal and informal patterns in which power is distributed and organized with regard to the authoritative making and implementing of decisions." Hence, citizen views of democracy involve attitudes toward the values of democracy, its operating norms, and its institutional arrangements.

Much of empirical research on support for democracy builds upon this conceptual distinction between different aspects of the regime.[14] For instance, Pippa Norris distinguishes between three objects of regime support:[15] principles, performance, and institutions. Specifically, support for regime principles concerns attitudes toward the core values of a political system; support for regime performance concerns attitudes toward the functioning of a political system in practice; and support for regime institutions concerns attitudes toward actual institutions of government, such as parliament, courts, the police, political parties, and the military. Similarly, Russell Dalton distinguishes between three targets of regime support: principles, norms and procedures, and institutions.[16] Furthermore, he differentiates between two modes of orientation: affective and evaluative. The former represents "adherence to a set of values" and the latter reflects "judgments about political phenomena."

Despite such conceptual clarifications and theoretical distinctions, researchers have difficulties in distinguishing empirically between different types of regime support. It is admitted that empirical measurement lags far behind the multidimensional nature of regime support. Nonetheless, the multidimensional conceptualization of regime support is helpful in mapping citizen views of democracy and unraveling their complexity. By specifying the targets of regime support, we should be better able to understand the implications of changes in attitudes toward democracy.

Following prior theory and research, we distinguish between three aspects of citizen views of democracy: values, norms and rules, and institutions. Moreover, we differentiate between two modes of orientation: affective orientations to democracy as an idea, and evaluative orientations to a democracy-in-practice. The former pertains to idealist views of democracy, whereas the latter pertains to realist views of democracy.[17]

Of *affective orientations to democracy as an idea,* the first aspect focuses on the values of democracy. Despite little consensus on the values of democracy, freedom and equality are widely viewed as its foundational values. In public opinion surveys, however, this aspect of orientation is often measured by agreement that democracy is the best form of government or the most preferred political system. In this study we use different expectations of democracy to ascertain attitudes toward the values of democracy. In addition, we employ four more indicators: preference for democracy, desire for democracy, perceived suitability of democracy, and perceived efficacy of democracy. The second aspect pertains to the operating norms and rules of democracy. In this study we select three indicators: support for checks and balances, the rule of law, and social pluralism—key liberal norms associated with the idea of limited government. The third aspect concerns democratic institutions. In this study we indirectly ascertain support for them by tapping attitudes toward major forms of authoritarian rule: strongman rule instead of elections and parliament, one-party rule instead of multiparty competition, and military rule.

Of *evaluative orientations to a democracy-in-practice,* the first aspect pertains to the perceived supply of democracy. In public opinion surveys, satisfaction with democracy is often used to measure evaluation of general democratic performance. Although its meaning is contested,[18] we use this standard measure as well. In addition, we employ two more indicators to ascertain the perceived democratic level of the ongoing political order. The second aspect concerns the democratic quality of political institutions and practices. In this study we focus on five dimensions of democratic governance: control of corruption, electoral competition, both vertical and horizontal accountability, and freedom.[19] The third aspect deals with performance of actual political institutions. In this study we select two indicators: trust in both parliament and political parties—key institutions of representative democracy.

Values of Democracy

The survey series used here included no relevant question directly measuring support for the values of democracy such as liberty and equality. Fortunately, however, the 2006 ABS included a single question with which we ascertained the values of democracy our respondents emphasized. It asked: "People often differ in their views on the characteristic that is essential to democracy. Which one would you choose as the most essential to a democracy?" Four response categories were provided: opportunity to change the government through elections, freedom to criticize those in power, a small income gap between rich and poor, and basic necessities like food, clothes, and shelter for everyone. The first two options reflect political values of democracy whereas the last two reflect socioeconomic values.

The pattern of responses in both countries shows a strong contrast. As presented in Figure 1.1, in Korea more than one-third chose social justice by replying "a small income gap between rich and poor," and a similar percentage chose popular control by replying "opportunity to change the government through elections." Less than one-fifth selected political freedom by answering "freedom to criticize those in power"; and only one-tenth selected basic welfare by answering "basic necessities like food, clothes and shelter for everyone." In Taiwan, by contrast, almost a half chose basic welfare; more than a quarter chose popular control; one-fifth chose social justice; and only a few chose political freedom.

Notable is that in Taiwan nearly a two-thirds majority conceived the essential characteristics of democracy in terms of socioeconomic values, whereas in Korea there was no single dominant value of democracy; political values and socioeconomic values competed for popular support. Another notable finding is that political freedom was least frequently chosen in

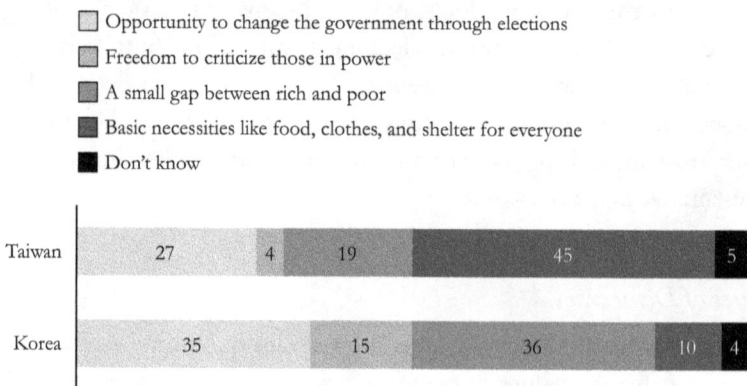

☐ Opportunity to change the government through elections
▨ Freedom to criticize those in power
▨ A small gap between rich and poor
▨ Basic necessities like food, clothes, and shelter for everyone
■ Don't know

Taiwan	27	4	19	45	5
Korea	35	15	36	10	4

FIGURE 1.1 Essential characteristics of democracy
SOURCES: Asian Barometer Survey (hereafter ABS) Korea 2006; ABS Taiwan 2006.

Taiwan, while less frequently chosen than social justice or popular control in Korea. This finding suggests that citizens in these new East Asian democracies were less supportive of liberal democracy than either social or electoral democracy.[20] That the values of democracy appeared to be more contested or even polarized in Korea than in Taiwan suggests that a potential conflict resulting from disagreement over regime values would be greater in the former than in the latter. This finding also suggests that political democratization itself did not necessarily encourage satisfaction with democracy. The expansion of political and civil rights may not matter much to those who hold the welfare-state conception of democracy. For them, social and welfare policy outcomes would be more likely to encourage approval of a democracy-in-practice. Perhaps this is why citizen evaluations of democratic performance in these countries often differed from expert-based assessments, as will be discussed later.

Support for Democracy

To ascertain support for democracy as an idea, we use four indicators: preference for democracy, desire for democracy, perceived suitability of democracy, and perceived efficacy of democracy. The former two tap largely affective orientations, whereas the latter two tap cognitive evaluations. By targeting democracy as an undifferentiated whole, these indicators reflect the most general and diffuse support for democracy.

PREFERENCE FOR DEMOCRACY

The KDB series and the ABS series included a widely used question that asked respondents to choose among three statements: "Democracy is always preferable to any other kind of government," "Under some circumstances, an authoritarian government can be preferable to a democratic one," and "For people like me, it does not matter whether we have a democratic or a non-democratic regime." The first option indicates unconditional acceptance of democracy. The second option reflects conditional rejection of democracy or conditional acceptance of authoritarian rule. The last option manifests apathy or indifference to democracy.

As shown in Figure 1.2, unconditional acceptance of democracy in Korea exhibited a considerable fluctuation during the period surveyed: Those who replied that democracy is always preferable to any other kind of government

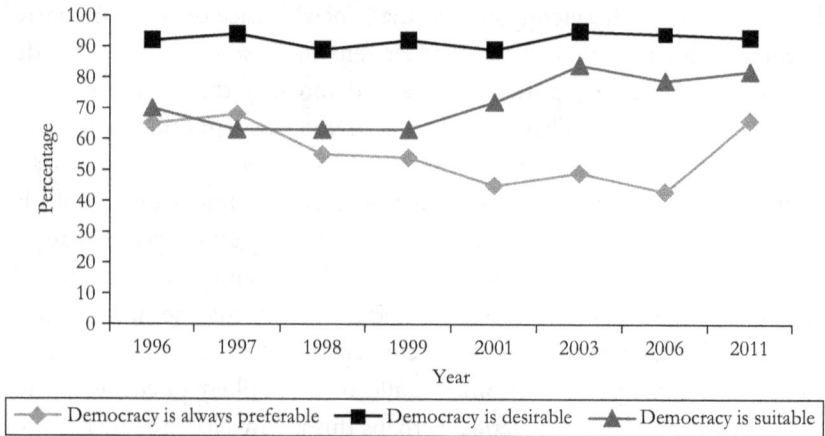

FIGURE 1.2 Support for democracy: Korea
SOURCES: Korea Democracy Barometer (hereafter KDB) 1996, 1997, 1998, 1999, and 2001; ABS Korea 2003, 2006, and 2011.

peaked at 68 percent in 1997. Then it steadily fell from 65 percent of the electorate in 1996 to 55 percent in 1998, 45 percent in 2001, and 43 percent in 2006, until it sharply rose to 66 percent in 2011. A steady decline for a decade was followed by a recent dramatic reversal, although whether the rise marks a turnaround remains to be seen. It is noteworthy that the largest drop (13 percent) in unconditional acceptance of democracy occurred in the wake of the economic crisis in 1997, indicating that a belief in the legitimacy of democracy is closely related to economic performance. However, the largest increase (23 percent) occurred after the replacement of an unpopular incumbent through free and fair elections in 2007, suggesting that the experience of electoral accountability contributed to the growth of democratic legitimacy. It is intriguing that unconditional preference for democracy steadily declined under two left-leaning governments (the Kim Dae-jung government from 1998 to 2003 and the Roh Moo-hyun government from 2003 to 2008), suggesting that democratically elected governments would not necessarily guarantee the growth of democratic legitimacy. Notable is that conditional acceptance of authoritarian rule had gradually grown until the most recent survey: Those who replied that an authoritarian government can be preferable under certain circumstances increased 17 percent in 1996 to 31 percent in 1998, 37 percent in 2001, and 36 percent in 2006, and then declined to 20 percent in 2011. More than two decades

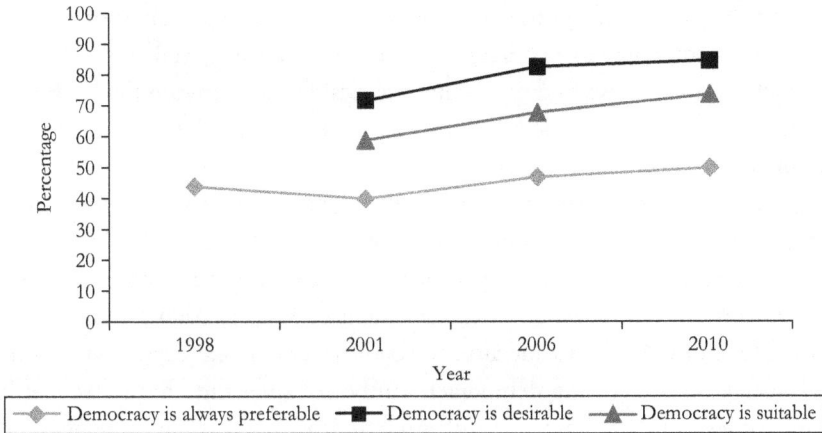

FIGURE 1.3 Support for democracy: Taiwan
SOURCES: Taiwan Election and Democracy Survey 1998; ABS Taiwan 2001, 2006, and 2010.

after the democratic transition, at least one in five Koreans still felt nostalgia for authoritarian rule.

As shown in Figure 1.3, citizens' democratic preference had traveled a somewhat different trajectory in Taiwan. Those who replied that democracy is always preferable to any other kind of government accounted for 44 percent in 1998, which dropped to 40 percent in 2001, and then climbed up to 47 percent in 2006 and 50 percent in 2010. The level of democratic preference remained 6 percent higher than what it was a decade earlier.

The only drop in democratic preference that occurred between 1998 and 2001 stemmed in part from the fumbles and travails of democratic governance on many fronts after the end of the four-decade-long Kuomintang (KMT, or Nationalist Party) rule and the historical power rotation in 2000.[21] The first shocking experience came from an unlikely quarter—the economy. First, under Democratic Progressive Party (DPP) rule, the worst recession in almost three decades hit Taiwan in 2001, bringing 2.2 percent negative growth, falling incomes, rising unemployment, a loss in value of 12 percent for the currency, and a stock market drop of more than 40 percent. The severity and magnitude of this economic downturn exceeded that of the 1997–1998 regional financial crisis. Also, many citizens became disillusioned as the government run by the DPP (long self-billed as the party of clean politics) failed to root out structural corruption in electoral politics or to end the long tradition of collusion between big business and politicians. Citizens' confidence in democracy's superiority was also shaken by the extremely nasty, endless, and paralyzing political battles between the DPP minority government and the KMT-controlled legislature. Popular confidence in democracy, however, began to grow steadily between 2001 and 2010.

It is also worth noting that much like what we have witnessed in Korea, a substantial portion (around 24 percent by 2010) of the Taiwanese population still believed that an authoritarian government can be preferable under certain circumstances. This sentiment of authoritarian nostalgia persisted for more than a decade after the country underwent democratization. This suggests that young democracies in both Korea and Taiwan were still more or less burdened by their authoritarian legacy, which, in some people's memories, was often associated with a strong record in delivering economic prosperity, social stability, and clean politics.[22]

DESIRE FOR DEMOCRACY

The KDB series and the ABS series also asked respondents to indicate where they wanted their country to be on a 10-point dictatorship–democracy scale.[23] A score of 1 means "complete dictatorship" whereas a score of 10 indicates "complete democracy." Since the midpoint of the scale lies between 5 and 6, those in the top half (6 or above) may be regarded as expressing a desire for democracy. As shown in Figure 1.2, in Korea those expressing a desire for democracy accounted for 92 percent in 1996, 94 percent in 1997, 89 percent in 1998, 92 percent in 1999, 89 percent in 2001, 95 percent in 2003, 94 percent in 2006, and 93 percent in 2011. For the period surveyed, on average, nine out of ten Koreans expressed a desire for democracy.[24] Even the economic crisis of 1997 did not dampen the Korean people's aspirations for democracy. Unlike preference for democracy, there had been little fluctuation. Noteworthy is that the median voter had a score of 9 on the scale for most years under study, only one notch below a perfect mark, "complete democracy." Taiwan's citizens' desires for democracy had been less vibrant but steadily strong. As Figure 1.3 shows, the level of democratic desirability was 72 percent in 2001, but it grew to 85 percent in 2010. This finding suggests that there was little electoral space for antidemocratic political parties or candidates. There is no doubt democracy was widely desired as the only political regime that was available.

On closer inspection, however, the desire for a full democracy was neither deep nor stable in Korea. For instance, the proportion of Korean respondents who placed their desired score at either 9 or 10 declined from 58 percent in 1996 to 50 percent in 1997, 40 percent in 1998, 42 percent in 1999, 32 percent in 2001, and 31 percent in 2003, and then climbed up to 57 percent in 2006 and 2011. The level of desire for a full democracy had steadily declined in the wake of the 1997 economic crisis until it began to turn around in 2006. In Taiwan the level of desire for a full democracy had been stable but not deep. In 2001 when popular confidence in democracy was shaken by the ensuing political turmoil and the economic downturn after the historical power rotation in 2000, only 44 percent of our respondents still embraced a full democracy. This level of desire for a full democracy had stayed about the same throughout the decade surveyed. Overall, support for a full democracy had not grown much and remained limited in both countries.

PERCEIVED SUITABILITY AND EFFICACY OF DEMOCRACY

The KDB series and the ABS series also asked respondents to indicate the level of suitability of democracy for their country on a 10-point scale. A score of 1 means "completely unsuitable," whereas a score of 10 indicates "completely suitable." As in the dictatorship–democracy 10-point scale, those in the top half (6 or above) may be seen as conveying a belief in the suitability of democracy. As presented in Figure 1.2, in Korea those judging democracy to be suitable declined from 70 percent in 1996 to 63 percent in 1998, and then rebounded to 72 percent in 2001, 84 percent in 2003, 79 percent in 2006, and 82 percent in 2011. A popular belief in the suitability of democracy weakened in the wake of the economic crisis of 1997, but it had been restored steadily since then. As shown in Figure 1.3, in Taiwan a popular belief in the suitability of democracy had steadily gained strength over the decade surveyed, rising from 59 percent in 2001 to 68 percent in 2006 and 74 percent in 2010. In both countries at all times a great majority of the citizenry had believed that democracy is suitable for their country, and by and large that belief had strengthened over time. This confirms the socializing effect of participation in democratic processes, as suggested by political institutionalists.

The ABS series also asked respondents to choose between two statements: "Democracy is capable of solving the problems of our society" and

"Democracy cannot solve our society's problems." In Korea, a popular belief in the efficacy of democracy first dropped and then bounced back during the decade surveyed: Those judging democracy to be effective accounted for 72 percent in 2003, 55 percent in 2006, and 70 percent in 2011. In Taiwan, popular confidence in the efficacy of democracy started out at a low level of 47 percent in 2001 but had visibly strengthened over the years, rising to 55 percent in 2006 and 59 percent in 2010.

Overall, the results indicate a mixed picture of support for democracy as an undifferentiated whole in the two young democracies. In both countries, nearly everyone wanted the country to be democratic and a large majority considered democracy suitable for the country. However, in Korea unconditional preference for democracy had declined until recently and still remained low. In Taiwan the trend line appeared to be promising as the young democracy weathered through political turmoil during the Chen Shui-bian administration, with more people believing in the efficacy and suitability of democracy. However, unconditional preference for democracy was still far from robust, with a substantial portion of the population registering some reservations about democracy more than a decade after the country became fully democratized.

Under authoritarian rule both Korea and Taiwan registered a remarkable economic growth. This legacy of authoritarian economic success in conjunction with the sluggish economic performance (and occasional economic crises) under democratic rule weakened a belief in the time-invariant superiority of democracy. Although democracy was desired as the only game in town, a skeptical view of democracy gained strength in the wake of its poor performance, especially during periods of economic downturn.

Support for Liberal Norms

In this section we examine support for key liberal norms associated with the idea of limited government. While the democratic aspect of liberal democracy emphasizes "rule by the people" or popular election, the liberal aspect underlines limits to the authority of government. Liberal norms legitimate institutions and mechanisms of limited government essential for protecting individual freedom and autonomy from the arbitrary use of government power. They include checks and balances, the rule of law (official law-abidingness), and social pluralism (a pluralist civil society).[25]

CHECKS AND BALANCES

The operating norm of checks and balances legitimates the authority structure that separates powers into independent branches of government and institutionalizes the mechanism of horizontal accountability. To ascertain support for checks and balances, the ABS series asked respondents whether they agreed or disagreed with the following statements: "When judges decide important cases, they should accept the view of the executive branch" and "If the government is constantly checked by the legislature, it cannot possibly accomplish great things." Negative response to the former reflects support for an independent judiciary, whereas negative response to the latter reflects support for legislative oversight.

As shown in Table 1.1, those in Korea who disagreed with the first statement accounted for 69 percent in 2003, 72 percent in 2006, and 67 percent in 2011. On average, more than two-thirds were in favor of an independent judiciary. Those who disagreed with the second statement accounted for 54 percent in 2003, 57 percent in 2006, and 62 percent in 2011. On average, nearly three-fifths were in favor of legislative oversight of the executive branch. Noteworthy is that support for an independent judiciary was greater than support for legislative oversight. In Taiwan, those who were supportive of an independent judiciary accounted for 54 percent in 2001, 57 percent in 2006, and 59 percent in 2010. This was somewhat lower than what we observed in Korea. Furthermore, far fewer people in Taiwan than in Korea were supportive of legislative oversight, accounting for only 25 percent in 2001, 34 percent in 2006, and 38 percent in 2010. This large shortfall was probably due to an extremely low level of popular trust in the legislature and the partisan gridlock between the DPP-controlled executive and the KMT-dominated Legislative Yuan during the eight years of the Chen Shui-bian presidency.

By combining responses to both questions, we seek to ascertain overall commitment to checks and balances. In Korea, those who disagreed with both statements accounted for 39 percent in 2003, 46 percent in 2006, and 47 percent in 2011. In Taiwan, they accounted for only 16 percent in 2001, 22 percent in 2006, and 26 percent in 2010. On average, a large minority in Korea and only a small minority in Taiwan endorsed the liberal norm of checks and balances. Although the trend in both countries appeared to be upward, public support for checks and balances still remained low.

TABLE 1.1
Support for liberal norms

	KOREA			TAIWAN		
	2003 (%)	2006 (%)	2011 (%)	2001 (%)	2006 (%)	2010 (%)
CHECKS AND BALANCES						
When judges decide important cases, they should accept the view of the executive branch (Disagree)	69	72	67	54	57	59
If government is constantly checked by the legislature, it cannot possibly accomplish great things (Disagree)	54	57	62	25	34	38
Both	**39**	**46**	**47**	**16**	**22**	**26**
RULE OF LAW						
When the country is facing a difficult situation, it is acceptable for the government to disregard the law in order to deal with the situation (Disagree)	77	74	71	58	68	68
The most important thing for political leaders is to accomplish their goals, even if they have to ignore the established procedures (Disagree)	77	75	—	76	83	—
Both	**63**	**59**	**—**	**50**	**60**	**—**
SOCIAL PLURALISM						
Harmony of the community will be disrupted if people organize many groups (Disagree)	65	55	59	34	37	42
If people have too many different ways of thinking, society will be chaotic (Disagree)	53	52	56	24	31	32
Both	**39**	**36**	**42**	**14**	**19**	**23**

SOURCES: ABS Korea 2003, 2006, and 2011; ABS Taiwan 2001, 2006, and 2010.

This finding suggests that the greater support for democracy found in both countries was not firmly based on support for checks and balances, one of the hallmarks of liberal democracy.

THE RULE OF LAW

The rule of law is another liberal norm justifying constraints on the exercise of government power. As Rose and his colleagues point out, the liberal conception of rule of law is more than formal legality used as a means of social control.[26] More important, it emphasizes self-restraints of government, namely that government should be bound by the rules of society. To ascertain support for the rule of law, the ABS series asked respondents whether they agreed or disagreed with the following statements: "When the country is facing a difficult situation, it is OK for the government to disregard the law in order to deal with the situation" and "The most important thing for political leaders is to accomplish their goals even if they have to ignore the established procedures." Negative responses to the questions indicate support for official law-abidingness.

As reported in Table 1.1, those who disagreed with the first statement accounted for 77 percent of the Korean electorate in 2003, 74 percent in 2006, and 71 percent in 2011. They accounted for roughly the same proportion of the population in Taiwan, with 58 percent in our 2001 survey and 68 percent in both our 2006 and 2010 surveys rejecting any deviation from the rule of law even during hard times. On average, three-quarters in Korea and two-thirds in Taiwan rejected the arbitrary use of government power even if it was intended to overcome a crisis. Next, those who disagreed with the second statement accounted for 77 percent of the Korean electorate in 2003 and 75 percent in 2006. Similarly, among the Taiwanese electorate, a great majority rejected the idea of ends justifying the means, with 76 percent registering disapproval in 2001 and 83 percent in 2006. In both countries, on average, more than three-quarters rejected the notion that political leaders could be allowed to circumvent the established procedures to achieve their goals.

By combining responses to both questions, we seek to ascertain overall commitment to the rule of law. Those who disagreed with both statements accounted for 50 percent of the Taiwanese electorate in 2001 and 60 percent in 2006. They accounted for 63 percent of the Korean electorate in 2003 and 59 percent in 2006. In both countries, on average, three out of every five citizens displayed support for official law-abidingness, which was higher than support for checks and balances, suggesting that the rule of law was more valued than horizontal accountability as an operating norm of democracy.

SOCIAL PLURALISM

Social pluralism essential for creating a pluralist civil society is not directly related to the norms and rules justifying the authority structure. However, since civil society serves as a safeguard for civil liberties and a venue for societal accountability, social pluralism is considered one of the liberal norms associated with the idea of limited government. To ascertain support for social pluralism, the ABS series asked respondents whether they agreed or disagreed with the following statements: "Harmony in the community will be disrupted if people organize lots of groups" and "If people have too many different ways of thinking, society will be chaotic."

As presented in Table 1.1, in Korea those who disagreed with the first statement accounted for 65 percent in 2003, 55 percent in 2006, and 59 percent in 2011. On average, three-fifths rejected the notion that associational diversity and vibrancy undermined social harmony. In Taiwan the ratio was significantly lower but had steadily gained strength, with 34 percent in 2001, 37 percent in 2006, and 42 percent in 2010 indicating that at most only two out of every five Taiwanese embraced the idea of a vibrant and diverse associational life. Next, those in Korea who disagreed with the second statement accounted for 53 percent in 2003, 52 percent in 2006, and 56 percent in 2011. On average, more than half endorsed the notion of a "marketplace of ideas," a rationale for freedom of expression. Among the Taiwanese electorate the ratio was consistently lower, with only 24 percent in 2001, 31 percent in 2006, and 32 percent in 2010.

By combining responses to both questions, we seek to ascertain overall commitment to social pluralism. In Korea those who disagreed with both statements accounted for 39 percent in 2003, 36 percent in 2006, and 42 percent in 2011. On average, only two-fifths were tolerant of social pluralism. In Taiwan even fewer embraced a pluralist civil society, with only 14 percent in 2001, 19 percent in 2006, and 23 percent in 2010 disagreeing with both statements. On average, fewer than one in five approved of social pluralism.

The patterns that we observed in Korea and Taiwan appeared strikingly similar. In both countries, only the rule-of-law norm was widely embraced by a great majority of the citizenry. It is noteworthy that a large majority of citizens did not find the idea of a horizontally accountable government and a pluralist civil society as appealing as a law-abiding government. This finding indicates the legacy of Confucian political culture and tradition in both countries, which emphasizes social harmony and anti-adversarial politics.[27] Another noteworthy finding is that citizens' reservations about liberal norms were so persistent that they changed very little for nearly a decade surveyed.

Support for Democratic Institutions

As indirect evidence of support for democratic institutions, we examine public attitudes toward three forms of authoritarian rule—strongman rule, single-party rule, and military rule. These non-democratic alternatives occupy different places in the memories of Taiwanese and Koreans. In Taiwan there was a legacy of single-party rule, whereas in Korea there was no such legacy. During the KMT's four-decade-long reign, a hegemonic party was at least partially institutionalized.[28] The strongman rule under Chiang Kai-shek and Chiang Ching-kuo was always embedded in the hegemonic presence of the KMT. By contrast, in Korea a single-party system had never been institutionalized, although party politics was limited under authoritarian rule. Even though the military played a key role in establishing and maintaining authoritarian rule, military rule (meaning direct rule by a military junta) was an exception. The type of regime remaining most vividly in the memories of most Korean people is strongman rule, or civilian dictatorship backed by the military.[29] Bearing such political historical differences between the two countries in mind, we present the results of our analysis.

To ascertain rejection of authoritarian rule, the KDB series and the ABS series asked respondents whether they agreed or disagreed with the following statements: "We should get rid of parliament and elections and have a strong leader decide things" and "The army (military) should come in to govern the country." The ABS series also asked whether the respondents agreed or disagreed with the following statement "Only one political party is allowed to stand for election and hold office."

As shown in Figure 1.4, in Korea there was wide rejection of strongman rule: Those who rejected strongman rule accounted for 85 percent in 1996, 80 percent in 1997, 76 percent in 1998, 81 percent in 1999, 76 percent in 2001, 85 percent in 2003, 83 percent in 2006, and 80 percent in 2011. Public disapproval of strongman rule fluctuated, declining after the economic crisis of 1997, bouncing back after the presidential election in 2002, and then slightly declining in the midst of growing problems of democratic governability. Nonetheless, on average, four-fifths of Koreans remained opposed to replacing the National Assembly and elections with a civilian dictatorship, suggesting that support for popular control, the hallmark of electoral democracy, was prevalent. The legacy of authoritarian economic success no longer induced ordinary people to entertain strongman rule as

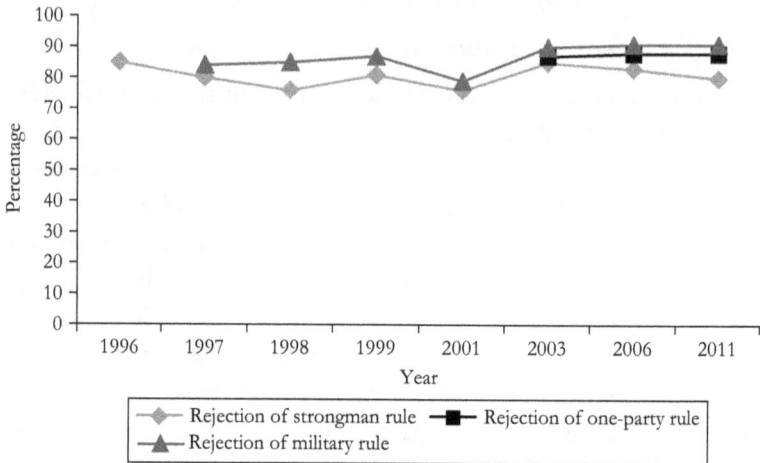

FIGURE 1.4 Rejection of non-democratic alternatives: Korea
SOURCES: KDB 1996, 1997, 1998, 1999, and 2001; ABS Korea 2003, 2006, and 2011.

an alternative to representative democracy. Yet, it should be noted that an-tipathy to strongman rule had not deepened. Those who *strongly* rejected civilian dictatorship accounted for 51 percent in 1996, 47 percent in 2001, 34 percent in 2006, and 47 percent in 2011, suggesting that outright rejec-tion of strongman rule remained relatively shallow.

In Taiwan, a great majority rejected strongman rule even during the most turbulent years of Chen Shui-bian's administration (see Figure 1.5). In 2001, 68 percent of the respondents rejected strongman rule; this detachment had slightly gained strength during the decade surveyed, rising to 77 percent in 2006 and 79 percent in 2010. However, the intensity of outright rejection of strongman rule was less than what we saw in Korea, with only 22 percent of our respondents "strongly" rejecting civilian dictatorship in 2010.

Second, public antipathy to military rule turned out to be wider in both countries (see Figure 1.4). In Korea, even in the wake of the worst economic crisis in its history, public disapproval of military rule steadily increased from 84 percent in 1997 to 85 percent in 1998 and 87 percent in 1999. Yet it suddenly dropped to 79 percent in 2001 and then climbed to 90 percent in 2003 and 91 percent in 2006 and 2011. Perhaps the sudden decline in 2001 was related to uneasiness about national security among large conservative segments of the population created by the left-leaning president's surprise visit to North Korea in 2000. Nonetheless, on average, nearly nine-tenths of Koreans remain opposed to military rule. Yet, on closer examination, the strength of antipathy toward military rule had not grown. Those who rejected military rule *strongly* accounted for 65 percent in 1996, 53 percent in 2000, 51 percent in 2006, and 67 percent in 2011. Although public disapproval of military rule remained wide, outright rejection had not grown much.

In Taiwan where there was no legacy of military rule, popular detachment from this non-democratic alternative was strong all the time. In 2001, 82 percent of Taiwan's electorate rejected the statement that the military should come in to govern the country. This figure increased to 88 percent in 2006 and 92 percent in 2010. The intensity of popular aversion to military rule grew much stronger, with almost half of the population strongly disapproving in 2010. This suggests that military rule was never a viable form of governance in Taiwan under any historical circumstance.

Last, in both countries public antipathy to single-party rule was also evident, albeit with some notable differences. In Taiwan, those who disapproved of single-party rule accounted for 70 percent in 2001, substantially fewer than those who disapproved of military rule (see Figure 1.5). As the country gradually pulled itself out of political turmoil and the economic downturn, popular resistance to the restoration of single-party rule gained strength, rising over the decade surveyed to 83 percent in 2006 and 86 percent

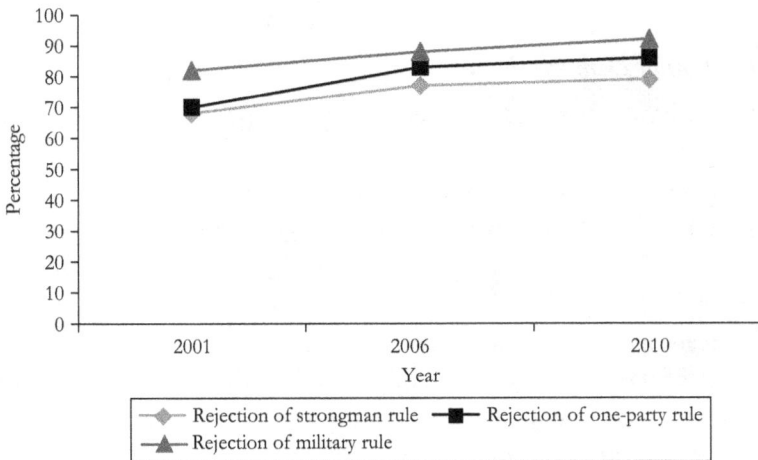

FIGURE 1.5 Rejection of non-democratic alternatives: Taiwan
SOURCES: ABS Taiwan 2001, 2006, and 2010.

in 2010. However, outright rejection was still not very strong, with only 28 percent of the electorate strongly disapproving of this non-democratic alternative in 2010. In Korea, by contrast, those who disapproved of single-party rule accounted for 87 percent in 2003, and 88 percent in 2006 and in 2011, significantly higher than what we found in Taiwan. On average, nearly four out of five Koreans remained opposed to party dictatorship, suggesting that multiparty competition, one of the minimum requirements of democracy, was overwhelmingly accepted. Unlike strongman rule or military rule, moreover, antipathy to party dictatorship grew even stronger over the decade surveyed. Those who strongly rejected single-party rule accounted for 41 percent in 2003, 43 percent in 2006, and 55 percent in 2011. Public antipathy to party dictatorship was substantially deeper in Korea than in Taiwan, reflecting their differences in the party system under authoritarian rule.

In sum, despite some fluctuations, popular detachment from authoritarian rule had become more entrenched in both countries. All the findings indicate that major forms of authoritarian rule had little appeal as alternative systems of governance for either Koreans or Taiwanese. Moreover, they suggest that core representative institutions of democracy such as parliament, elections, and political parties, the hallmarks of electoral democracy, remained overwhelmingly accepted in both countries. Yet the strength of antipathy to major forms of authoritarian rule differed in both countries, reflecting their respective political legacies.

Evaluation of Democratic Supply

So far we have attempted to ascertain how supportive Koreans and Taiwanese were of different aspects of democracy as an idea. We now turn to evaluation of their regime-in-practice. In this section, we first examine how Koreans and Taiwanese view the general supply of democracy.

PERCEIVED EXTENT OF DEMOCRACY

The perceived extent of democracy pertains to evaluation of the democratic character of the prevailing system of government. The KDB series and the ABS series asked respondents to indicate where their country was at the time of survey on a 10-point dictatorship–democracy scale. A score of 1 means "complete dictatorship" whereas a score of 10 indicates "complete democracy."[30] Since the midpoint of the scale lies between 5 and 6, those in

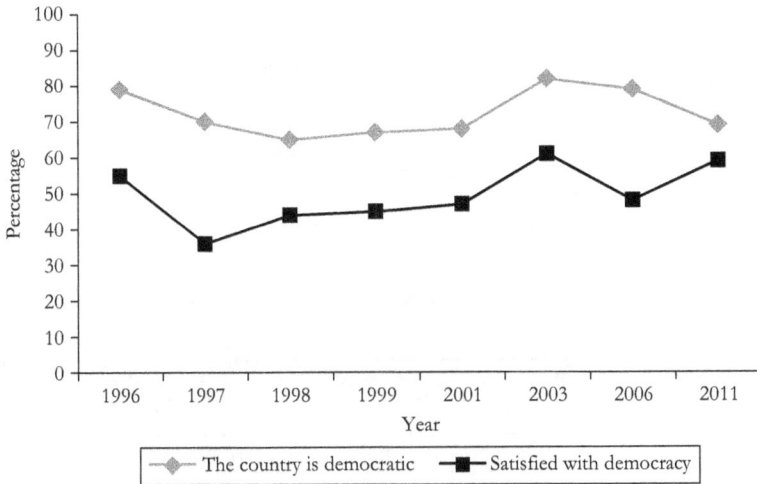

FIGURE 1.6 Evaluation of democratic supply: Korea
SOURCES: KDB 1996, 1997, 1998, 1999, and 2001; ABS Korea 2003, 2006, and 2011.

the top half (6 or above) may be seen as locating their country in a democratic territory. As shown in Figure 1.6, in Korea those who consider the
current system democratic accounted for 79 percent in 1996, 70 percent in
1997, 65 percent in 1998, 67 percent in 1999, 68 percent in 2001, 82 percent
in 2003, 79 percent in 2006, and 69 percent in 2011. The perceived extent of
democracy steadily declined under the Kim Dae-jung administration, temporarily surged after the 2002 presidential election, and then declined again
during the Roh Moo-hyun and Lee Myung-bak administrations. Much
of the fluctuation seemed related to growing ideological polarization and
winner-loser political conflict. Among Taiwan's electorate the perceived extent of democracy was at a comparable level. The ABS survey registered
73 percent of the respondents rating the present system above 6 on the
10-point scale in 2001, 74 percent in 2006, and 68 percent in 2010 (see
Figure 1.7). It is also notable that after Taiwan's second power rotation in
2008, the perceived extent of democracy visibly declined. This had a lot to
do with the polarization of the society over national identity and cross-strait
relations. If we take a closer look at the Taiwan ABS 2010 data, we find that
there was a 20 percent gap between the so-called Pan-Blue camp and the
Pan-Green camp, with 83 percent of Pan-Blue voters and only 64 percent of
Pan-Green voters rating the system at 6 or above.

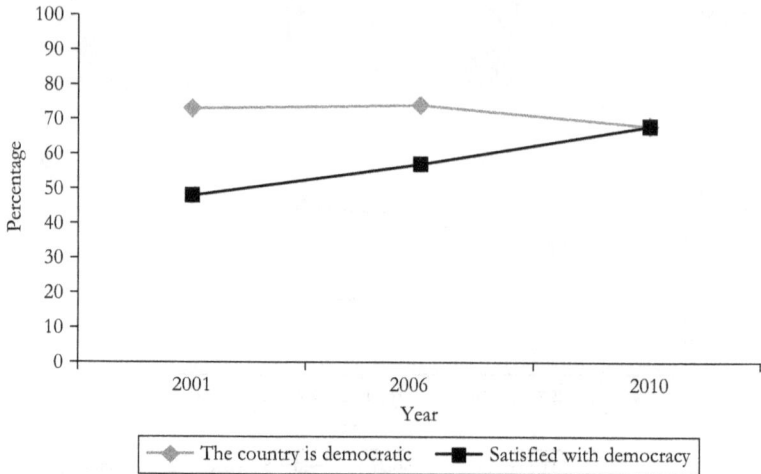

FIGURE 1.7 Evaluation of democratic supply: Taiwan
SOURCES: ABS Taiwan 2001, 2006, and 2010.

In both Korea and Taiwan, three out of four respondents, on average, considered the current system more or less democratic. Yet only a few considered their system a full democracy. For instance, in Korea those placing their country at either 9 or 10 accounted for only 9 percent in 1996, 3 percent in 1997, 4 percent in 1998, 3 percent in 1999, 5 percent in 2001, 5 percent in 2003, 10 percent in 2006, and 7 percent in 2011. In Taiwan, only 12 percent of the respondents placed the island in the category of a full democracy (9 or 10) in 2010, a decline from 20 percent in 2001. It is notable that despite expert-based assessments that Korea and Taiwan ranked with advanced democracies in the West, only a few ordinary people in either country considered their current system to be a full democracy. It is interesting that in both countries those who expressed a desire for a full democracy outnumbered those who considered the current system a full democracy, indicating a wide gap between expectations and perceived realities.

The ABS also used a verbal scale to ascertain perceptions of the democratic level of the prevailing system of government. It asked respondents to rate how democratic their country was at the time of survey. A list of four responses was offered: a full democracy, a democracy with minor problems, a democracy with major problems, and not a democracy. In Korea, those replying "a full democracy" accounted for only 5 percent in 2006 and

4 percent in 2011, whereas 56 percent in 2006 and 63 percent in 2011 chose "a democracy with minor problems." By contrast, those selecting "a democracy with major problems" accounted for 34 percent in 2006 and 28 percent in 2011, whereas only 2 percent in 2006 and 3 percent in 2011 answered "not a democracy." On average, two-thirds of Koreans considered their system either a full democracy or a slightly flawed democracy. In Taiwan only 6 percent in 2006 and 9 percent in 2010 considered their country "a full democracy"; 44 percent in 2006 and 53 percent in 2010, "a democracy with minor problems"; 37 percent in 2006 and 30 percent in 2010, "a democracy with major problems"; and 7 percent in 2006 and 6 percent in 2010, "not a democracy." On average, more than half of Taiwanese, lower than that in Korea, considered their system either a full, or a slightly flawed, democracy. It is not clear whether the perceived level of democracy reflected poor democratic performance or high standards of evaluation or both. Nonetheless, the findings suggest that in the eyes of ordinary people, their regime-in-practice fell short of their ideals of democracy.

SATISFACTION WITH DEMOCRACY

Satisfaction with democracy is widely used as an indicator of overall evaluation of democratic performance, although its meaning is still contested. The KDB series used a 10-point numeric scale to tap satisfaction or dissatisfaction with the workings of democracy. A score of 1 indicates "completely dissatisfied" whereas a score of 10 means "completely satisfied." In contrast, the ABS series used a 4-point verbal scale, the value of which ranges from 1 ("very satisfied") to 4 ("not at all satisfied"). In order to make both scales comparable, the bottom five (1–5) and top five (6–10) numeric ratings on the 10-point scale were collapsed into two categories: satisfied or dissatisfied. Likewise, the four values on the verbal scale were also collapsed into the two categories.

As presented in Figure 1.6, in Korea those expressing satisfaction by placing themselves at 6 or above declined sharply from 55 percent in 1996 to 36 percent in 1997, perhaps partially resulting from high-level political corruption and poor economic management toward the end of Kim Young-sam's presidency. During the following decade, satisfaction with democracy displayed a dramatic turnaround, after the power rotation in 2002. Yet it dropped sharply to 48 percent in 2006, perhaps due to an unpopular incumbent, but then climbed to 59 percent in 2011 after "the rascals" were thrown out through elections. The level of democratic satisfaction in Taiwan was higher than that in Korea and exhibited a clear-cut upward trend with 48 percent in 2001, 57 percent in 2006, and 68 percent in 2010 (see Figure 1.7). In Taiwan the gap between the extent of democracy and satisfaction with democracy had steadily narrowed over the decade surveyed, whereas in Korea it remained wide only until 2011, when the perceived extent of democracy declined and satisfaction with democracy rose. This suggests that the size of a democratic deficit was greater in Korea than in Taiwan and that there were more critical citizens in the former than in the latter.

Evaluation of Democratic Quality

In this section we examine the extent to which Koreans and Taiwanese consider their prevailing system of government to reflect the norms and mechanisms of democracy. Since democratic performance is a multidimensional phenomenon, we distinguish between key performance dimensions and separately ascertain their evaluation of performance on each dimension. Considering data availability and cross-time comparability, we focus on five dimensions—control of corruption, electoral competition, vertical and horizontal accountability, and freedom (see Table 1.2).[31]

First, to ascertain the evaluation of corruption control, we chose two questions: One asked about the incidence of official corruption at the local level and the other about corruption at the national level. The former largely reflects low-level bureaucratic corruption while the latter reflects high-level political corruption. For the period surveyed, in Korea, on average, about one-half considered hardly anyone or not many officials in the local government corrupt, whereas in Taiwan three-tenths did. Taiwanese citizens also gave disparaging evaluations with regard to the extent of corruption at the national level. Only three-tenths in Taiwan and slightly less than half in Korea considered hardly any or not many officials in the national government corrupt. Combining responses to both questions shows that a large minority in Korea and a small minority in Taiwan made a favorable evaluation of corruption control, suggesting that government corruption was still perceived as rampant for the period surveyed. This disparaging assessment should be taken seriously, because corruption is empirically shown to be one of the important factors that erode people's confidence in institutions of democracy.[32]

TABLE I.2
Evaluation of democratic quality

	KOREA		TAIWAN	
	2006 (%)	2011 (%)	2006 (%)	2010 (%)
CONTROL OF CORRUPTION				
Hardly anyone/not many local officials are corrupt	55	45	30	31
Hardly anyone/not many national officials are corrupt	50	42	29	32
Both	**44**	**36**	**19**	**23**
ELECTORAL COMPETITION				
Political parties or candidates have equal access to the mass media during elections (Agree)	66	65	63	71
Elections always/most of the time offer the voters a real choice between parties or candidates	47	51	52	57
Both	**33**	**34**	**36**	**43**
VERTICAL ACCOUNTABILITY				
People have the power to change government (Agree)	44	51	60	56
Between elections, people have no way of holding the government responsible for its actions (Disagree)	36	35	34	39
Both	**16**	**18**	**22**	**20**
HORIZONTAL ACCOUNTABILITY				
When the government breaks the law, there is nothing the legal system can do (Disagree)	43	40	38	48
The legislature is very capable/capable of keeping the government in check	53	50	52	47
Both	**25**	**22**	**25**	**31**
FREEDOM				
People are free to speak what they think without fear (Agree)	57	52	73	74
People can join any organization they like without fear (Agree)	64	66	78	78
Both	**51**	**47**	**67**	**68**

SOURCES: ABS Korea 2006 and 2011; ABS Taiwan 2006 and 2010.

Second, to ascertain the evaluation of electoral competition, we chose two questions: One asked respondents whether they agreed or disagreed with the statement "Political parties or candidates in our country have equal access to the mass media during the election period." The other asked how often elections offered the voters "a real choice" between different parties or candidates. For the first question, in both countries, on average, two-thirds answered affirmatively. For the second question, on average, only one-half in Korea and two-thirds in Taiwan replied either "always" or "most of the time." In both countries there existed ambivalent citizens who held mixed views: They considered elections as fair and competitive but remained skeptical of their significance. Combining responses to both questions shows that only a minority in both countries considered elections both fair and meaningful. Despite the fact that both countries experienced two transfers of power through elections, the quality of elections still remained short of public expectations.

Third, to ascertain the evaluation of vertical accountability, we asked respondents whether they agreed or disagreed with the following statements: "People have the power to change a government they don't like" and "Between elections, people have no way of holding the government responsible for its actions." For the first question, in Korea those who replied affirmatively, on average, accounted for slightly less than half of the electorate, whereas in Taiwan, they accounted for more than half. For the second question, in Korea and Taiwan those who answered negatively, on average, accounted for only one-third of their respective electorates. Public evaluations of vertical accountability were somewhat mixed in Taiwan, whereas they were considerably lower in Korea. Combining responses to both questions reveals that, on average, only a small minority in both countries made a favorable evaluation of overall performance on vertical accountability, which runs from citizens to the state.

Fourth, to ascertain the evaluation of horizontal accountability, we chose two questions: One asked respondents whether they agreed or disagreed with the statement "When the government breaks the law, there is nothing the legal system can do."[33] The other asked to what extent the legislature was capable of keeping the government (or government leaders) in check. For the first question, on average, more than two-fifths in both countries replied negatively. For the second question, on average, about one-half in both countries replied either "very capable" or "capable." Noteworthy is that in these countries legislative oversight was evaluated more favorably than judicial review. Combining responses to both questions shows that only a small minority in both countries made a favorable evaluation of overall performance on checks and balances among state institutions.

Finally, to ascertain the evaluation of freedom, we asked respondents whether they agreed or disagreed with the following statements: "People are free to speak what they think without fear" and "People can join any organization they like without fear." For the first question, on average, more than one-half in Korea and about three-quarters in Taiwan replied affirmatively. For the second question, on average, about two-thirds in Korea and three-quarters in Taiwan answered affirmatively. Combining responses to both questions indicates that a bare majority in Korea and a two-thirds large majority in Taiwan made a favorable evaluation of overall performance on freedom. This shows that Taiwanese citizens felt freer than Korean counterparts.

Overall, citizens in Korea and Taiwan found their current system lacking in the rule of law and political accountability. Taiwan's democracy was particularly faulted for its inability to control official corruption. In contrast, both democracies were viewed as performing better in the protection of civil and political rights. Yet the electoral process was judged as competitive but not always meaningful. Contrary to expert-based assessments, the democracies in Korea and Taiwan were not of high quality or flawless in the eyes of their citizens.

Trust in Institutions

Trust in political institutions has been widely used when assessing support for the prevailing system of government, namely, regime affect, which is distinguishable from incumbent affect.[34] Public institutions as the objects of trust often include the armed forces, the legal system, the police, the parliament, political parties, and the civil service. The KDB series and the ABS series asked respondents how much trust they had in these public institutions. In this study we focus on two pivotal institutions of representative democracy: parliament and political parties. As a comparison, we include the military and the police, which had served the needs of the respective authoritarian regimes.

As shown in Figure 1.8, in Korea public trust in the representative institutions had dramatically declined over the period surveyed. Those who displayed trust in the National Assembly fell from 49 percent in 1996 to 15 percent in 2003, to 7 percent in 2006, and then increased slightly to

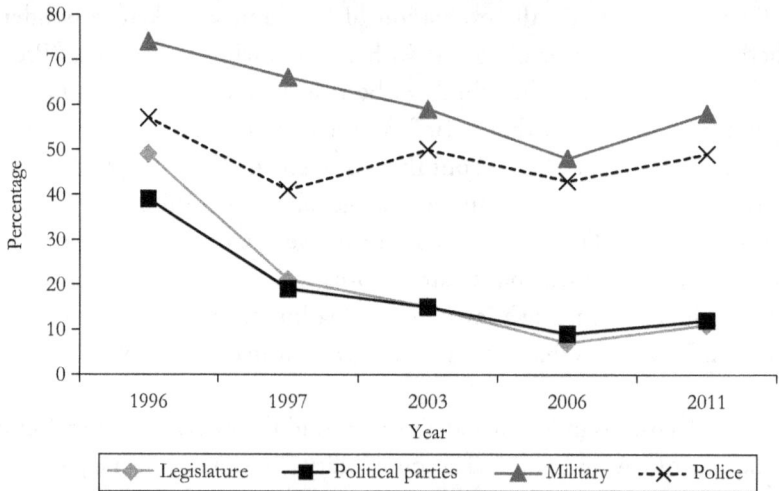

FIGURE 1.8 Trust in public institutions: Korea
SOURCES: KDB 1996 and 1997; ABS Korea 2003, 2006, and 2011.

11 percent in 2011. Those who expressed trust in political parties dropped from 39 percent in 1996 to 15 percent in 2003, to 9 percent in 2006, and then rose slightly to 12 percent in 2011. Taiwan displayed an equally bleak picture, although there was no downward trend. Those who expressed trust in the legislature constituted a small minority (20 percent) in 2001 and this figure did not change throughout the decade (see Figure 1.9). The level of trust in political parties remained low without any notable change: from 16 percent in 2001 and 2006 to 14 percent in 2010. This finding indicates the prevalence of political cynicism in our most successful third-wave democracies in East Asia.

In contrast, the military and the police enjoyed much greater public trust than parliament and political parties. Nevertheless, public trust in the military had declined over the years as well. In Korea, those who expressed trust in the military fell from 74 percent in 1996 to 59 percent in 2003, to 48 percent in 2006, and then climbed to 58 percent in 2011. In Taiwan the number fell from 58 percent in 2001 to 53 percent in 2006 and then to 43 percent in 2010. Yet both countries exhibited a different trend in trust in the other coercive state institution. In Taiwan, trust in the police was lower to begin with and had stagnated over the years. Those who had trust in the police constituted about 46 percent of the population throughout the decade sur-

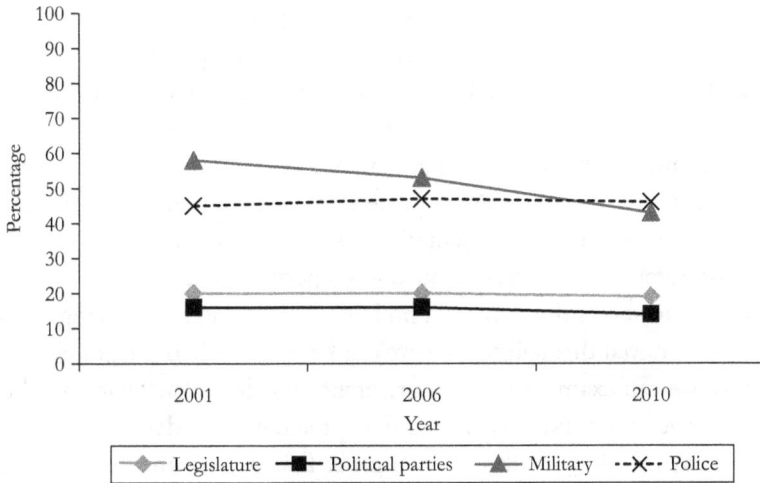

FIGURE I.9 Trust in public institutions: Taiwan
SOURCES: ABS Taiwan 2001, 2006, and 2010.

veyed. In Korea, by contrast, trust in the police fluctuated considerably: It fell from 57 percent in 1996 to 50 percent in 2003, to 43 percent in 2006, and then rose to 49 percent in 2011.

It is noteworthy that the trust gap between both types of institutions had widened. For instance, in Korea the trust gap between the police and the National Assembly was 8 percentage points in 1996, whereas it was 36 percentage points in 2006. The trust gap between the military and the National Assembly was 25 percentage points in 1996, whereas it was 41 percentage points in 2006. The legislature and political parties constitute key institutions of representative democracy. The marked drop in public confidence in these institutions in Korea and the persistent low public confidence in them in Taiwan may indicate a crisis of representative institutions, if not democracy, in these most consolidated third-wave democracies in Asia.

Sources of Change: Generational or Period Effects

So far we have documented how the citizens of Korea and Taiwan viewed democracy as an idea and how they evaluated the performance of their democracy-in-practice. We found some dramatic changes, particularly in Korea. Change may be due to certain unprecedented events, resulting in nearly all segments of the population changing their views in the same direction. Change may also result from generational replacement even if individuals retain their original views. In order to understand the nature of shifting citizen views of democracy in Korea and Taiwan, we examine how attitudes toward democracy changed within age cohorts over time. Among citizen attitudes toward democracy, we selected two, that is, preference for democracy and trust in representative institutions, because they displayed the most notable rise or decline during the period examined.

Figure 1.10 shows the change in preference for democracy among cohorts as Koreans moved through the life cycle. The year-of-birth categories remain fixed, so we can examine the way preference for democracy within cohorts changed over time. Noteworthy is that preference for democracy sharply declined across all age cohorts during the first decade and then bounced back across all the cohorts during the next five years. More specifically, the preference level within the cohort born between 1967 and 1976 declined from 63 percent in 1996 to 50 percent in 2001 and 43 percent in 2006 and then rose to 67 percent in 2011. The cohort born between 1957 and 1966, the so-called the 386 generation, was known to play a pivotal role in the democratic transition. The preference level within this cohort also dropped from 69 percent in 1996 to 44 percent in 2001 and 42 percent in 2006 and then climbed to 65 percent in 2011. The preference level within the cohort

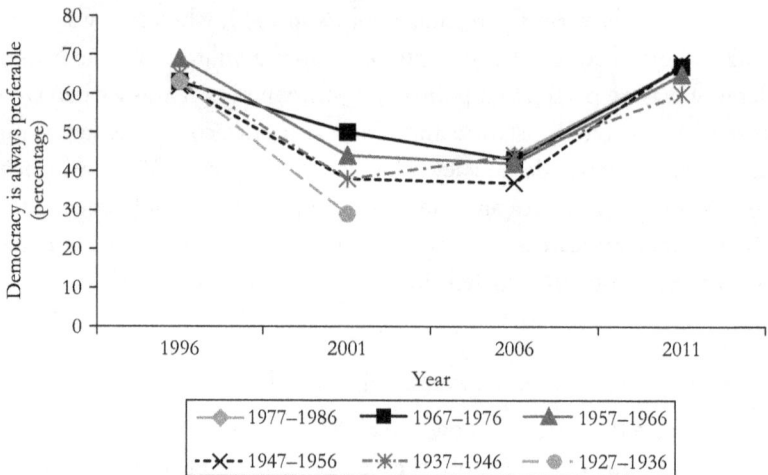

FIGURE 1.10 Preference for democracy by age cohort: Korea
SOURCES: KDB 1996 and 2001; ABS Korea 2006 and 2011.

born between 1947 and 1956 fell from 62 percent in 1996 to 38 percent in 2001 and 37 percent in 2006 and then jumped to 68 percent in 2011. Last, the preference level within the cohort born between 1937 and 1946 declined from 65 percent in 1996 to 38 percent in 2001 and 44 percent in 2006 and then climbed to 60 percent in 2011. The results suggest that both the decline and the rise in preference for democracy were largely reflective of period rather than generational effects. It must have been dramatic events that took place between 1996 and 2001 that were responsible for the shifting views of democracy among the Korean electorate. One such event, causing nearly all segments of the population to lose confidence in democratic legitimacy, was the 1997 economic crisis, the worst one since Korean War. Another event might be the surprise visit of the left-leaning president to North Korea in 2000 for the first South–North Korean summit. In contrast, the replacement of an unpopular government through elections in 2008 seemed to be responsible for the recent rebound in public confidence in democracy across all age cohorts. However, it is noteworthy that the effects of these events were not the same across all age cohorts, as indicated by notable differences in the drops between 1996 and 2001. The largest drop (34 percentage points) was found in the oldest age cohort (born between 1927 and 1936), whereas the smallest drop (13 percentage points) was found in the youngest age cohort (born between 1967 and 1976) for the period surveyed. This indicates the varying effects of events on different age cohorts that had their respective formative experiences. The finding suggests that the belief in democratic legitimacy held by the old was more shallow or superficial than that held by the young.

Figure 1.11 shows the changes in preference for democracy among four age cohorts in Taiwan. Unlike Korea, Taiwan displayed an upward trend across all the cohorts. More specifically, the preference level within the age cohort born between 1967 and 1976 increased from 43 percent in 2001 to 49 percent in 2006 and 48 percent in 2010. The cohort born between 1957 and 1966 were in their twenties when the island embarked on the path of democratization. The preference level within this cohort also increased from 40 percent in 2001 to 47 percent in 2006 and 53 percent in 2010. This is one of the two cohorts that displayed the largest increase (13 percent) during the period surveyed. They were the people who had little experience with the harsh repression during the early years of KMT rule but became accustomed to the high growth, full employment, and ever-rising living standards

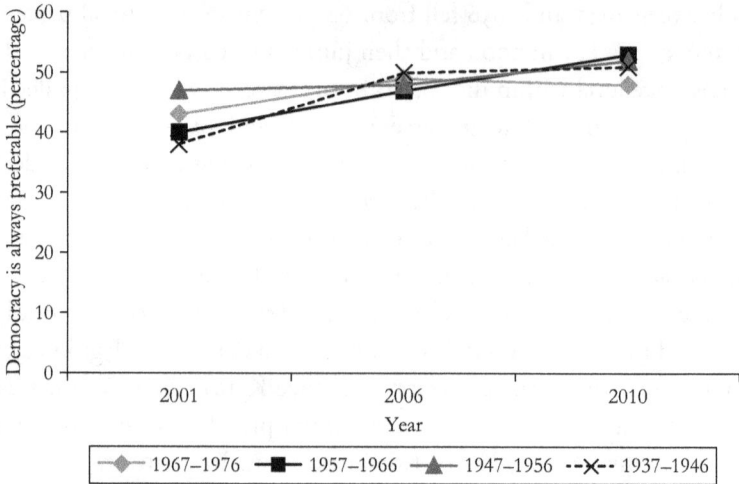

FIGURE I.II Preference for democracy by age cohort: Taiwan
SOURCES: ABS Taiwan 2001, 2006, and 2010.

of the 1970s and 1980s. The preference level within the cohort born between 1937 and 1946 also increased from 38 percent in 2001 to 50 percent in 2006 and 51 percent in 2010. They were born during the Civil War and fully exposed to the KMT's four-decade-long rule and were in their forties when the country was at the juncture of democratic opening. It is the second of the two cohorts that displayed the largest increase (13 percent). The preference level within the other two cohorts also increased between 2001 and 2010, but the increase was modest (5 percent).

The results suggest that the rise in preference for democracy in Taiwan reflected both generational and period effects. Yet the generation effect was still overwhelmed by the period effect (i.e., the effect of political learning acquired during different stages of regime evolution and historical junctures). Across all age cohorts, the level of support for democracy peaked in 1998, or at the closing stage of KMT rule. The political turmoil and economic contraction followed by the 2000 power rotation triggered the biggest drop in the level of democratic preference across all age cohorts. From 2001 on, the level of democratic preference rose slowly across all age cohorts, but never reached its previous peak.

Trust in representative institutions was another political phenomenon that displayed a dramatic change for the period examined. Figure I.12 shows

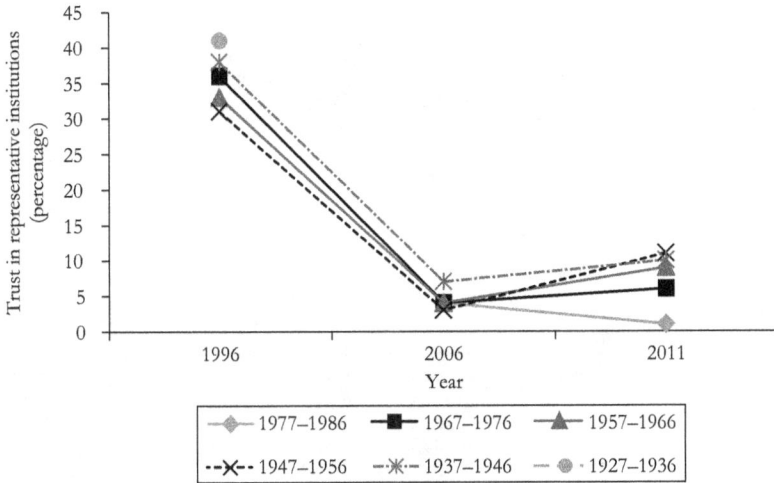

FIGURE 1.12 Trust in representative institutions by age group: Korea
SOURCES: KDB 1996; ABS Korea 2006 and 2011.

the change in the percentage of Korean citizens expressing trust in both parliament and political parties within various age cohorts. It is noteworthy that political trust plummeted across all age cohorts. The level of trust among those born between 1967 and 1976 declined from 36 percent in 1996 to 4 percent in 2006 and 6 percent in 2011. The level of trust among those born between 1957 and 1966 also dropped, from 33 percent in 1996 to 4 percent in 2006 and 9 percent in 2011. Similarly, the level of trust among those born between 1947 and 1956 fell from 31 percent in 1996 to 3 percent in 2006 and 11 percent in 2011. Last, the level of trust among those born between 1937 and 1946 declined from 38 percent in 1996 to 7 percent in 2006 and 10 percent in 2011. The results suggest that the decline in political trust reflected period rather than generational effects. As in preference for democracy, poor economic performance, political corruption, and excessive party strife may be responsible for the sharp decline in political trust across the board.

Figure 1.13 shows the change in the percentage of Taiwanese who had trust in the representative institutions of democracy within four age cohorts. Unlike Korea, political trust remained more or less the same during the period examined. More specifically, the trust level among those born between 1967 and 1976 declined from 20 percent in 2001 to 16 percent in

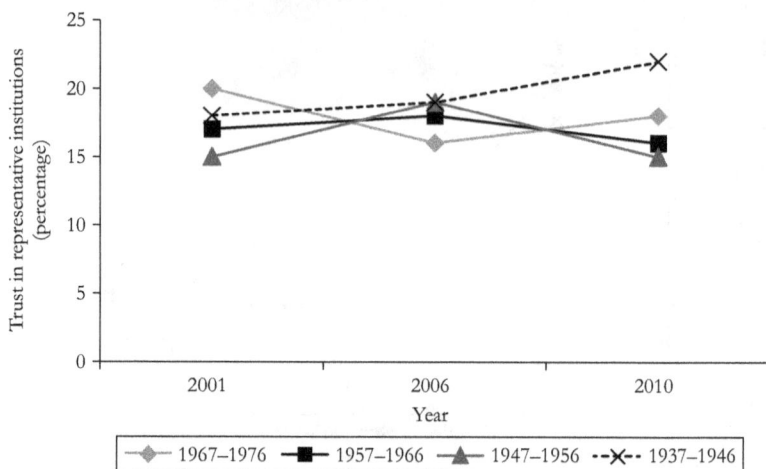

FIGURE 1.13 Trust in representative institutions by age group: Taiwan
SOURCES: ABS Taiwan 2001, 2006, and 2010.

2006 and 18 percent in 2010. The trust level among those born between 1957 and 1966 changed little: from 17 percent in 2001 to 18 percent in 2006 and 16 percent in 2010. The trust level among those born between 1947 and 1956 increased from 15 percent in 2001 to 19 percent in 2006 and then fell back to 15 percent in 2010. The trust level among those born between 1937 and 1946 increased from 18 percent in 2001 to 19 percent in 2006, and 22 percent in 2010. This is the only age cohort that displayed an upward trend. The findings show that the patterns of change were different in Korea and Taiwan. The drop in the trust level in Korea was so sharp that the period effects overwhelmed any generational differences. In contrast, although the pattern of change in Taiwan appeared to be complex, we found that both generational and period effects were at play in Taiwan. The level of trust did not decline for every age cohort. At the same time, those born between 1947 and 1956 registered the same lowest level of trust in 2001 and 2010. Noteworthy is that the oldest cohort born between 1937 and 1946 displayed an upward trend. All these findings suggest that the influence of formative experiences persisted over time, despite any external events. The four age cohorts retained their relative positions to their older and younger cohorts between 2001 and 2010. This indicates that in Taiwan the period effect over the decade surveyed was not overwhelming, at least not enough to wipe out generational differences.

There is another clue indicating some influence of formative experiences. The 2001 ABS survey shows that the relationship between age and trust in political parties was linear and no longer curvilinear. The trust level increased with age. This is most likely because partisanship rises with age and the youngest generation is least committed to any political party. However, between 2001 and 2010 the level of trust in political parties shifted lower for every age cohort (except for the youngest cohort that just turned twenty years old in the 2010 survey). At the same time, those who were in their twenties in the 2001 survey and in their thirties in the 2010 survey registered the same lowest level of trust in political parties. Again, this suggests that in Taiwan the period effect over the decade surveyed was not overwhelming, at least not enough to remove the generational effect completely.

Overall, events in Korea during the decade between 1997 and 2006 caused every category of the population to become less supportive of democracy and more cynical about representative institutions of democracy. Poor economic performance, high-level political scandals, and increasing ideological polarization perhaps caused every segment of the Korean electorate to become more disillusioned with democracy and more dissatisfied with the functioning of representative institutions. It is noteworthy that in the wake of the recent power rotation, support for democracy bounced back to its previous level while political trust remained low, suggesting different sources of attitudes toward various aspects of democracy. In Taiwan, the most shocking political experiences took place around the year 2000 power rotation. Over the decade surveyed, the country had gradually pulled itself out of its worst political crisis and economic downturn. Popular confidence in the superiority of democracy had gradually been restored but cynicism about democratic institutions continued to slip, albeit at a slower pace.

Summary and Conclusion

In this chapter we document how citizens in Korea and Taiwan viewed various aspects of democracy and examine how their views changed over time. Following prior theory and research, we consider citizen attitudes toward democracy as a multidimensional phenomenon. Hence, we distinguish between three aspects of democracy—values, norms and rules, and institutions. Furthermore, we distinguish between two modes of orientation—affective orientations to democracy as an idea and evaluative orientations to a democracy-in-practice. Lacking longer series of public opinion data, we relied on the KDB series (five surveys), the ABS series (three surveys), and the TEDS series (one survey). With these we were able to describe trends in public attitudes toward different aspects of democracy in both countries over a decade or so.

Although the data series are thin, our analysis reveals some notable findings. First, people's preference for democracy as a universal value had eroded or stagnated. In Korea it steadily declined until a recent resurgence. In Taiwan it suffered from a drop after the first power rotation in 2000. But the timing of the decline always coincided with an economic crisis or political turmoil, or a combination of the two. Nonetheless, the people's desire for democracy remained robust in both countries. The political difficulties and economic crises did not destroy their strong aspirations for democracy. The median voter's desire for democracy indicates that at least rhetorically democracy remained the only game in town. Although the perceived suitability of democracy fluctuated somewhat in response to transient events, Korea's and Taiwan's respective electorates continued to be more or less supportive of full democratization. Moreover, non-democratic alternatives proved to have little appeal to the absolute majority in both countries, although in Korea the strength of outright opposition to strongman rule had somewhat abated.

Second, the political values of democracy were not widely accepted in either country. In Korea both the political and social conceptions of democracy competed for popular loyalty. In Taiwan the social conception, especially the welfare-state conception of democracy, was far more prevalent. The vision of liberal democracy was not widely accepted. The expectations of democracy are likely to determine criteria of evaluation, which shape perceived performance of the prevailing system of government. Hence, such less-political conceptions of democracy might be responsible for popular evaluations of democratic performance that were less favorable than expert-based assessments, which largely emphasized the ideal of liberal democracy.

Third, in both countries people's apparent aspirations for democracy were not firmly rooted in the liberal idea of limited government. Support for checks and balances and tolerance of social pluralism remained low, whereas support for the rule of law was relatively high. Nonetheless, there existed wide consensus about the legitimacy of basic democratic institutions such as parliament, elections, and multiparty competition.

Fourth, in both countries the people had mixed views of democratic performance. They unmistakably viewed the current political system as a democracy, if not a full democracy. Yet their satisfaction with the functioning of democracy had fluctuated in response to transient events, including economic crises, political scandals, and polarized political conflict. Their evaluations of the provision of basic freedoms were largely favorable. Yet people remained largely critical of other aspects of democratic governance. In particular, the rule of law and accountability were regarded as most lacking. In Taiwan people were particularly appalled by high-level government corruption.

Fifth, there existed a sharp decrease in, or low levels of, public confidence in representative institutions of democracy. Particularly in Korea, trust in the legislature as well as in political parties all plummeted. Moreover, over time these representative institutions had been outshone by coercive state institutions, such as the military and the police, which by and large had managed to retain public trust.

Finally, cohort analysis shows that the decline in preference for democracy and political trust among the Korean electorate reflected period rather than generational effects. It was due to an economic disaster that nearly all segments of the Korean population lost their confidence in democracy and faith in representative institutions. The most dramatic drop in popular preference for democracy coincided with Taiwan's worst economic recession in decades. This is consistent with a recent finding that "objective economic performance is the most important system-level factor for system support."[35]

Overall, the findings suggest that representative institutions, if not democracy itself, in both Korea and Taiwan were in trouble. The recent political malaise in both of these new democracies appeared to be largely related to dissatisfying performance of representative institutions. The legislative branch and political parties were the most salient targets of public cynicism. Fortunately, a lack of confidence in institutions of democracy did not encourage approval of strongman or military rule. However, in view of the low levels of support for some liberal norms, it should not be overlooked that the apparent greater desire for democracy in both countries might lack "deep-rooted orientations or strong motivations."[36]

The young democracies in Korea and Taiwan faced more complicated political challenges than long-standing Western democracies did.[37] As in trilateral democracies, they faced loyal "critical citizens" who were supportive of democracy but cynical about political institutions.[38] In addition, the young democracies in Korea and Taiwan also encountered disloyal, critical citizens who were skeptical of democracy as well as cynical about political institutions. As citizens have more experience with the working of electoral accountability, their faith in democracy would grow rather than shrink, as evidence from Korea suggests. However, a prolonged lack of confidence in representative institutions would undermine the legitimacy of democracy and threaten the viability of the ongoing political order. Establishing public confidence in representative institutions of democracy appears to be one of the most critical challenges for maturing democracies in Korea and Taiwan.

Notes

1. Before 1992, the KMT regime introduced supplementary elections that allowed only a partial reelection of the national legislative body.

2. Yun-han Chu, Larry Diamond, Andrew J. Nathan, and Doh Chull Shin, eds., *How East Asians View Democracy* (New York: Columbia University Press, 2008); Larry Diamond and Marc F. Plattner, *Democracy in East Asia* (Baltimore, MD: Johns Hopkins University Press, 1998); Doha Chill Shin and Jaechul Lee, "The Korea Democracy Barometer Surveys: Unraveling the Cultural and Institutional Dynamics of Democratization, 1997–2004," *Korea Observer* 37, no. 2 (2006): 237–275.

3. Samuel P. Huntington, *The Third Wave: Democratization in the Late Twentieth Century* (Norman: University of Oklahoma Press, 1991), 266.

4. Yu-tzung Chang and Yun-han Chu, "How Citizens View Taiwan's New Democracy," in *How East Asians View Democracy*, eds. Chu et al., 83–113; Doh Chull Shin and Chong-Min Park, "The Mass Public and Democratic Politics in South Korea: Exploring the Subjective World of Democratization in Flux," in *How East Asians View Democracy*, 39–60.

5. "Polity IV Project," www.systemicpeace.org/polity/polity4.htm.

6. "Freedom in the World," at www.freedomhouse.org/report/freedom-world/freedom-world-2012.

7. World Bank Worldwide Governance Indicators, http://info.worldbank.org/governance/wgi/index.asp.

8. Doh Chull Shin, *Mass Politics and Culture in Democratizing Korea* (Cambridge, UK: Cambridge University Press, 1999); Shin and Lee, "The Korea Democracy Barometer Surveys."

9. For the background and methodology of the ABS, see www.asianbarometer.org/newenglish/introduction/default.htm.

10. For the background and methodology of the TEDS, see www.tedsnet.org/ cubekm2/front/bin/home.phtml.

11. The five surveys of the KDB series were conducted in January 1996 (N=1,000), May 1997 (N=1,117), October 1998 (N=1,010), November 1999 (N=1,007), and March/April 2001 (N=1,007). The three Korea surveys of the ABS series were conducted in February 2003 (N=1,500), September 2006 (N=1,212), and May 2011 (N=1,207).

12. David Easton, *A Systems Analysis of Political Life* (New York: Wiley, 1965), 171–219; David Easton, "Theoretical Approaches to Political Support," *Canadian Journal of Political Science* 9 (1975): 431–448.

13. Easton, *A Systems Analysis of Political Life*, 171–219.

14. Pippa Norris, "Introduction: The Growth of Critical Citizens?" in *Critical Citizens: Global Support for Democratic Government*, ed. Pippa Norris (Oxford, UK: Oxford University Press, 1999), 9–13; Russell J. Dalton, "Political Support in Advanced Industrial Democracies," in *Critical Citizens*, ed. Norris, 58–59; Hans-Dieter Klingemann, "Mapping Political Support in the 1990s: A Global Analysis," in *Critical Citizens*, ed. Norris, 33–38; Richard P. Gunther and José Ramón Montero, "The Multidimensionality of Political Support for New Democracies: Conceptual Redefinition and Empirical Refinement," in *Political Disaffection in Contemporary Democracies: Social Capital, Institutions, and Politics*, eds. Mariano Torcal and José Ramón Montero (London: Routledge, 2006), 46–78; John A. Booth and Mitchell A. Seligson, *The Legitimacy Puzzle in Latin America: Political Support and Democracy in Eight Nations* (New York: Cambridge University Press, 2009).

15. Norris, "Introduction: The Growth of Critical Citizens?"

16. Russell J. Dalton, *Democratic Challenges, Democratic Choices: The Erosion of Political Support in Advanced Industrial Democracies* (Oxford, UK: Oxford University Press, 2004), 24.

17. Richard Rose, Doh C. Shin, and Neil Munro, "Tensions Between the Democratic Ideal and Reality: South Korea," in *Critical Citizens*, ed. Norris, 146–165; Doh Chull Shin, "Democratization: Perspective from Global Citizenries," in *The Oxford Handbook of Political Behavior*, eds. Russell J. Dalton and Hans-Dieter Klingemann (Oxford, UK: Oxford University Press, 2007), 259–282.

18. Damarys Canache, Jeffery J. Mondak, and Mitchell A. Seligson, "Meaning and Measurement in Cross-National Research on Satisfaction with Democracy," *Public Opinion Quarterly* 65, no. 4 (Winter 2001): 506–528.

19. Since freedom is generally seen as one of the foundational values of democracy, evaluation of the provision of freedom can be regarded as reflecting practical democratic support at the level of regime values.

20. The same survey in Korea further asked respondents the second-most essential characteristic; the analysis showed that 28 percent chose political freedom;

25 percent chose basic welfare; 22 percent chose social justice; and 16 percent chose popular control. By combining the first- and second-most essential characteristics, we constructed three types of democratic conceptions: political, mixed (liberal-social), and social. Those who held the political conception of democracy accounted for 28 percent of the electorate, whereas those who held the social conception of democracy accounted for 27 percent. By contrast, those who held both political and social conceptions accounted for 46 percent. This finding indicates low levels of support for political democracy.

21. Yun-han Chu, "Taiwan's Year of Stress," *Journal of Democracy* 16, no. 2 (April 2005): 43–57.

22. Yu-tzung Chang, Yun-han Chu, and Chong-Min Park, "Authoritarian Nostalgia in Asia," *Journal of Democracy* 18, no. 3 (July 2007): 66–80.

23. The ABS 2010–2011 asked respondents to indicate where they want their country to be in the future on a 10-point democracy scale. A score of 1 indicates "completely undemocratic," whereas a score of 10 indicates "completely democratic."

24. Although preference for democracy steadily declined in Korea, desire for democracy remained high. To understand this discrepancy, we should note that whereas the preference question reflects universal acceptance of democracy, the desire question reflects context-dependent aspirations for democracy. Even skeptics of democracy could express a desire for democracy because they believe that the country is not under those "certain circumstances" justifying authoritarian rule.

25. Nancy L. Rosenblum, "Liberalism," in *The Encyclopedia of Democracy*, ed. Seymour Martin Lipset (London: Routledge, 1995), 3,756–3,761; Joe Foweraker and Roman Krznaric, "Measuring Liberal Democratic Performance: An Empirical and Conceptual Critique," *Political Studies* 48, no. 4 (September 2000): 759–787.

26. Richard Rose, William Mishler, and Christian Haerpfer, *Democracy and Its Alternatives: Understanding Post-Communist Societies* (Baltimore, MD: Johns Hopkins University Press, 1998).

27. Chong-Min Park and Doh Chull Shin, "Do Asian Values Deter Popular Support for Democracy in South Korea?" *Asian Survey* 46, no. 3 (May/June 2006): 341–361.

28. Yun-han Chu, "A Born-Again Dominant Party? The Transformation of the Kuomintang and Taiwan's Regime Transition," in *The Awkward Embrace: One-Party Domination and Democracy*, eds. Hermann Giliomee and Charles Simkins (Capetown, South Africa: Tafelberg, 1999), 61–96.

29. In this sense, strongman rule, not military rule, was associated in the minds of many Koreans with not only political repression but also economic development.

30. The ABS 2010–2011 uses a 10-point democracy scale where a score of 1 indicates "completely undemocratic" and a score of 10 indicates "completely democratic."

31. Larry Diamond and Leonardo Morlino, "The Quality of Democracy: An Overview," *Journal of Democracy* 15, no. 4 (October 2004): 20–31.

32. Chang and Chu, "How Citizens View Taiwan's New Democracy."

33. Instead of this question, the third wave of the ABS asked the following: "When government leaders break the law, there is nothing the courts can do."

34. Ola Listhaug and Matti Wiberg, "Confidence in Political and Private Institutions," in *Citizens and the State*, eds. Hans-Dieter Klingemann and Dieter Fuchs (Oxford, UK: Oxford University Press, 1995), 298–322; Arthur Miller and Ola Listhaug, "Political Performance and Institutional Trust," in *Critical Citizens*, ed. Norris, 204–216.

35. Peter Kotzian, "Public Support for Liberal Democracy," *International Political Science Review* 32, no. 1 (January 2011): 23–41; Seymour Martin Lipset, "Some Social Requisites of Democracy: Economic Development and Political Legitimacy," *American Political Science Review* 53, no. 1 (March 1959): 69–105.

36. Christian Welzel and Ronald Inglehart, "The Role of Ordinary People in Democratization," *Journal of Democracy* 19, no. 1 (January 2008): 126–140.

37. Chong-Min Park, "Political Discontent in South Korea," *International Review of Sociology* 21, no. 2 (July 2011): 391–412.

38. Susan J. Pharr and Robert D. Putnam, eds., *Disaffected Democracies: What's Troubling the Trilateral Countries* (Princeton, NJ: Princeton University Press, 2000); Mariano Torcal and Jose Ramon Montero, "Political Disaffection in Comparative Perspective," in *Political Disaffection in Contemporary Democracies*, eds. Torcal and Montero, 3–19; Dieter Fuchs, Giovanna Guidorossi, and Palle Svensson, "Support for the Democratic System," in *Citizens and the State*, eds. Hans-Dieter Klingemann and Dieter Fuchs (New York: Oxford University Press, 1995).

PART TWO

Political Parties and Identity Politics

TWO

The Party System in Korea and Identity Politics

Jiyoon Kim

Introduction

Although South Korea is considered one of the most successfully consolidated new democracies in the world, its political parties and party system developed differently from those in other advanced democracies. The claim that political conflicts, and the party systems formed thereof, are based on social cleavages such as class or religion has been a traditional theory in the literature on Western democracies.[1] Yet, even after the democratization in 1987, a comparable competitive party system arguably did not emerge in South Korea for many years. Instead, party competition in South Korean politics has long been based on perceived regional animosities and the power of a leading political figure in each region. Some scholars have even claimed that due to the unclear and distorted relations between the ruling and opposition parties in Korea, it was unforeseeable that a competitive political party system would emerge.[2]

South Korean politics after 1987 was indeed plagued by regionalism. However, after the initial dominance of regionalism, the "Sunshine Policy" during the Kim Dae-jung administration came to the fore as the first major and vital political agenda. It drew dividing lines between parties and identity politics by presenting two subjects: North Korea and America. Those who supported the "Sunshine Policy" tended to stand behind the New Millennium Democratic Party (MDP) and to have a relatively pro-North attitude. In contrast, supporters of the Grand National Party (GNP) followed their party's hard-line policy, perceiving that North Korea posed a constant threat to the security of South Korea.

Identity politics played a significant role during the 2002 presidential elections. During this dramatic election, Roh Moo-hyun's upset victory over Lee Hoi-chang was largely due to the strong nationalism present at the time, fostered in particular by South Korean youth. In addition to the accommodating sentiment toward North Korea, anti-American sentiment, reaching its peak during this period, created intense partisan cleavages. Followers of the GNP harbored strong animosity toward North Korea and also supported the alliance with the United States for national security reasons. From that time on, the national security agenda and attitudes toward the United States have also been critical in distinguishing the conservatives from the progressives in South Korean politics.

Some political pundits and scholars assert that the wave of national identity politics subsided after the 2007 presidential elections. The victory of Lee Myung-bak, and the 2012 election of Park Geun-hye, was not attributable to nationalism, inter-Korean relations, or the alliance with the United States.[3] In these two elections, the economy was the most salient issue. Does this mean that identity politics and national security ceased to play a part in the formation of the party system in South Korea? In this chapter, I first explore the historical development of party system of Korea after the democratization. Then, I attempt to answer this question.

Personalization, Regionalism, and Politics of Presidential Elections

Few can deny that democracy cannot function effectively without legitimate political parties and a party system. This premise has been emphasized by numerous scholars, such as Duverger, Huntington, Lijphart, Lipset, and Sartori, among others.[4] Dahl recognized that one of the most important institutional criteria for evaluating the level of democratic consolidation in a country is the existing party system.[5] Lipset, arguing that a stable party system is prerequisite for a democracy, emphasized the role of political parties in a democratic system to accommodate and provide a platform for the constituents' political options and demands.[6]

Political parties not only represent the constituents but also play a primary role in consolidating democracy. A healthy and strong political party system fosters legislative approval of government policies. In doing so, it reinforces the legitimacy of the democratic government and as a consequence increases the capacity of the government to govern responsibly and effectively. How well political parties respond to and interact with constituents determines the level of consolidation of democracy in a society.[7]

The debate on formation of party systems can be divided into two mainstream arguments. First, institutionalists argue that a country's party system is largely determined by the electoral system of the country.[8] One of the most thoroughly explored theories in electoral politics is Duverger's law. Maurice Duverger stated that the single-member-district system tends to generate the two-party system.[9] Indeed, we find more parties constitute the party system in a country with the proportional-representation system than with the single-member-district system.

South Korea currently employs a mixed-member electoral system for the National Assembly. A number of electoral reforms took place over the years, but the current mixed-member system has been used since 2004. As an unlinked mixed-member system, about three-quarters of the assembly seats are filled by elected members via a single-member-district system. The remaining—approximately one-quarter—seats are filled by members elected through a party list. Partly because of the mixed-member system, which allows minor parties to enter the legislative institution, and partly because of long-time regionalism, which is the bedrock for small regional parties, South Korean modern history reveals that a robust two-party system was never fully formed in the country. The party system in South Korea is actually a "two-major-party-plus" system.[10] That is, in addition to two major competing parties, there have always been minor third parties that have often played a critical role in the decision-making process (see Table 2.1).

The other stream of thought argues that the cleavage structure defines the party system. Proposed by sociologists Lipset and Rokkan, societal cleavages present for decades are key in forming party blocks. The cleavages Lipset and Rokkan suggested include regional cleavages between center and periphery, the class cleavage between owners and laborers, a sectoral cleavage of primary economy–secondary economy, and the division between the traditional church and a secular national government.[11]

There have been attempts to bridge these two streams by suggesting the intertwined effects between electoral rules and social cleavage structures.[12] Other scholarship has challenged this claim by arguing that the importance of conventional class cleavages has eroded, and class cleavage issues are being replaced by postmaterial ideological cleavages.[13]

TABLE 2.1

National Assembly election results since 1987, by seat shares

	13th (1988)	14th (1992)	15th (1996)	16th (2000)	17th (2004)	18th (2008)	19th (2012)
DJP-DLP-NKP-GNP-Saenuri	42%	50%	46%	40%	40%	51%	51%
PDP-PPC-MDP-URI-UNDP-DUP	23%	32%	29%	42%	51%	27%	43%
NDRP-ULD-LFP	12%	—	17%	6%	1%	6%	2%
RDP	20%	—	—	—	—	—	—
DLP-UPP	—	—	—	—	3%	2%	4%

SOURCE: National Election Commission.

DJP: Democratic Justice Party
DLP: Democratic Liberal Party
NKP: New Korea Party
GNP: Grand National Party
Saenuri: Saenuri Party

PDP: Peace Democratic Party
PPC: New People's Politics Confederation
MDP: New Millennium Democratic Party
URI: Open Uri Party
UNDP: United New Democratic Party
DUP: Democratic United Party

NDRP: New Democratic Republican Party
ULD: United Liberal Democratic Party
LFP: Liberty Forward Party

RDP: Reunification Democratic Party
DLP: Democratic Labor Party
UPP: United Progressive Party

Despite South Korea's exemplary development of democracy, the major political parties should not be placed on a conventional left–right spectrum, similar to that of the parties in Western democracies. In fact, scholars often assert that few Asian countries follow the cleavage patterns of Western Europe. Dalton attributes the absence of social cleavage structures in emerging democracies to the rapid transition toward democracy.[14] He also asserts that constituents in new democracies tend to make their electoral choices based on short-term factors, such as the candidates' image and their positions on certain issues.

South Korea's political parties and its party system are largely recognized as legitimate by political scientists. However, many experts point out that

South Korea, a so-called successful consolidated democracy, lacks a stable and institutionalized political party system. The South Korean party system traditionally has been viewed as weak because there are no clear ideological differences between the parties' platforms, institutional autonomy, and solid party identification by electorates.[15] The weakness of the party system in South Korea can be traced back to two sources: the personalization of the political parties and the notorious regionalism that emerged and was most strongly sustained after the democratization movement in 1987.[16]

The personalization of parties by Korean political leaders began with its first president. Syngman Rhee was against the idea of political parties even prior to becoming president. He argued that political parties promote factionalism which, in turn, impedes national unity and development. Nonetheless, once he faced opposition in the National Assembly, he organized his own party to deal with the opposition.[17]

As Steinberg and Shin accurately denote, Korean parties were based on personal loyalty to a party boss. The authority of the party emanated from the party boss and the party existed to serve the boss's political ambitions. For example, if the party boss were unable to secure the nomination for president, or if he or she thought that the party should be refurbished to attract new constituents, the boss would break up the existing party and create a new one.[18] Thus, South Korean political parties have experienced continuous mergers, splits, and name changes. Using a lineage of party lines, Figure 2.1 shows the history of the party system in South Korea since 1987.[19]

The period from 1987 to 2002 is called the "Three Kims Era," because at the time these three well-known politicians—Kim Young-sam, Kim Dae-jung, and Kim Jong-pil—and their parties dominated legislative and presidential politics in South Korea. Each had his own political party that in essence was formed to support his political aspirations and the presidential bidding process. Hence, political parties in South Korea were densely comprised of a party leader's networks. Once a bid failed, parties were easily dissolved, split, or merged with other parties to prepare for the next round of elections.[20]

Kang points out that the authority political leaders wield over parties had several fundamental sources. South Korean political leaders used their names to raise funds and assist the election campaigns of party members. The decision-making process was top-down. The long military dictatorship created unequal relations between the executive and legislative branches, which

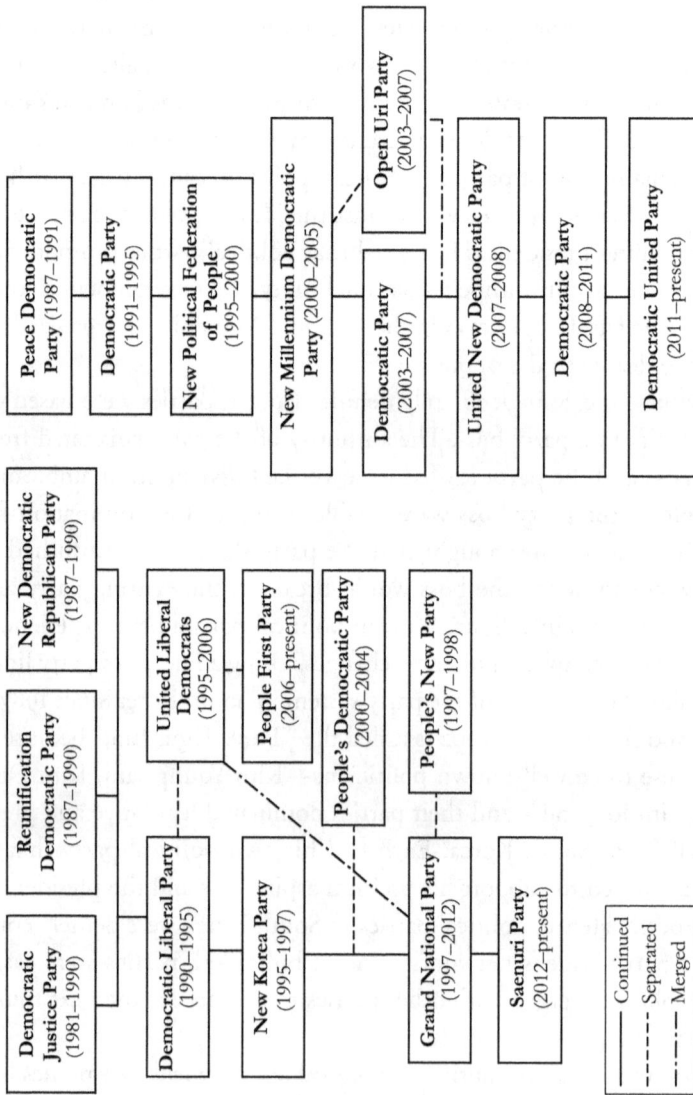

FIGURE 2.1 Political parties of South Korea since 1987

crippled the parties as an organization. Moreover, the nomination process to field candidates running for an office was under the supervision of a party leader. Given the fact that one's political career is virtually at the mercy of a party leader who holds nomination power, strong party discipline was inevitable.[21] Parties were not yet an institution, but party bosses were.

For this reason, South Korean political parties have not enjoyed long lives but have experienced frequent ruptures and fragmentation. Since 1987 the average life span of a Korean political party has been five years.[22] The GNP, which renamed itself the *Saenuri* Party (translated as New Frontier Party) in February 2012, holds the record for the longest existence—fourteen years—whereas the People's New Party (1997–1998) only survived eleven months. Without a reasonably long and stable life span for political parties, it is not surprising that a strong party system did not develop in South Korea (see Figure 2.1).

Despite this, the Korean party system has been a competition between two robust pillars since democratization. On one end, early party mergers generated the conservative Democratic Liberal Party led by Roh Tae-woo, Kim Young-sam, and Kim Jong-pil. At the opposite end, Kim Dae-jung and his dissident followers formed the Peace Democratic Party (PDP), which represented progressive voters. The aforementioned "two-major-party-plus" system is less apparent in presidential elections than in general elections, but by and large there have been competitions between two major parties under different names (see Table 2.2 and Figures 2.2 and 2.3).

Along with personalization, regionalism is a significant factor that undermined the establishment of a strong party system in South Korea. The regional voting behavior of South Koreans is widely known for creating a unique partisan divide. This trend intensified when regionalism was an unpredicted and unintended by-product of the democratization process in 1987. In general, those living in Kyŏngsang, the southeastern region of the Korean Peninsula that produced three presidents during the period of military rule, were traditional supporters of the authoritarian and conservative party. Those living in the southwestern region of Chŏlla supported progressive leaders such as Kim Dae-jung, a proud son of the region and a prominent dissident who led the democratization movement. The midwestern region, Ch'ungch'ŏng, had a political link with Kim Jong-pil and his parties, the New Democratic Republican Party and the United Liberal Democrats.[23]

TABLE 2.2
Presidential election results since 1987

	13th (1987)	14th (1992)	15th (1997)	16th (2002)	17th (2007)	18th (2012)
DJP-DLP-NKP-GNP- Saenuri	37%	42%	39%	47%	49%	51%
PDP-DP-PPC-MDP- UNDP-DUP	27%	34%	40%	49%	26%	48%
RDP (Kim Young-sam)	28%	—	—	—	—	—
NDRP (Kim Jong-pil)	8%	—	—	—	—	—
PNP (Lee In-je)	—	—	19%	—	—	—

SOURCE: National Election Commission.

DJP: Democratic Justice Party
DLP: Democratic Liberal Party
NKP: New Korea Party
GNP: Grand National Party
Saenuri: Saenuri Party

PDP: Peace Democratic Party
DP: Democratic Party
PPC: New People's Politics Confederation
MDP: New Millennium Democratic Party
UNDP: United New Democratic Party
DUP: Democratic United Party

RDP: Reunification Democratic Party
NDRP: New Democratic Republican Party
PNP: People's New Party

Deeply divided by the birthplaces of political leaders, Korean voters used the regional base of a political leader as a critical voting cue. When they went into a voting booth, there was no party platform, no party ideology, nor even any pork-barrel projects promised by the local politician. The most important consideration, especially for Kyŏngsang, Chŏlla, and Ch'ungch'ŏng voters, was which candidate the region's party had nominated. The voting disparities across regions were so huge that parties later did not even field candidates in opposition regions. And even if they attempted to do so, the candidate was likely unqualified or incompetent. (See Figures 2.4 and 2.5 for the regional disparities in the National Assembly elections since 1988.)

Of course, a regionally based political party is not unique in South Korea. Around the world, numerous regional parties exist, even in the advanced Western democracies. South Korean regionalism, however, is distinct from

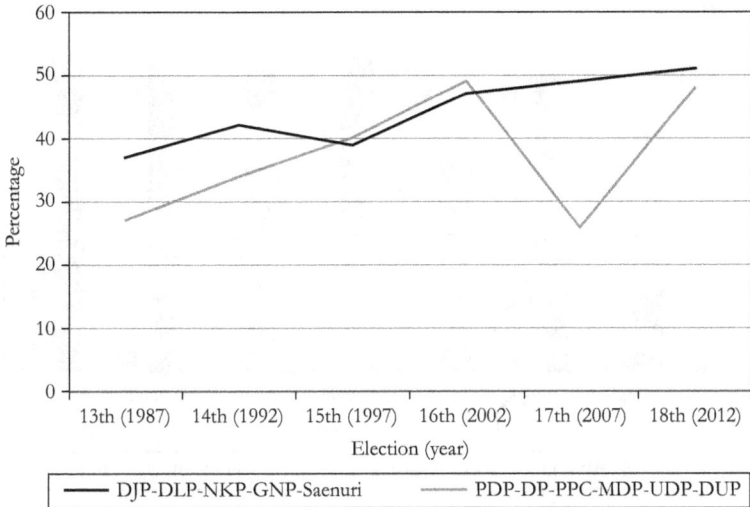

FIGURE 2.2 Presidential election results for the two major parties
SOURCE: National Election Commission, www.nec.go.kr/engvote_2013/05_resourcecenter/07_01.jsp.

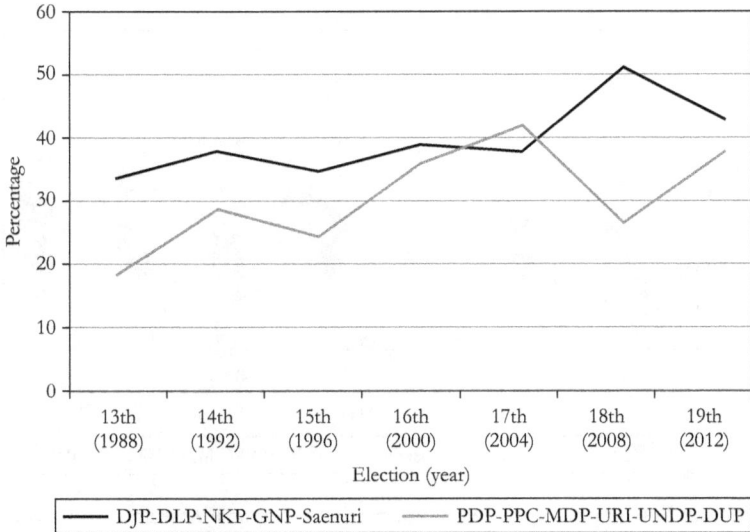

FIGURE 2.3 Vote shares for the two major parties in National Assembly elections
SOURCE: National Election Commission, www.nec.go.kr/engvote_2013/05_resourcecenter/07_01.jsp.

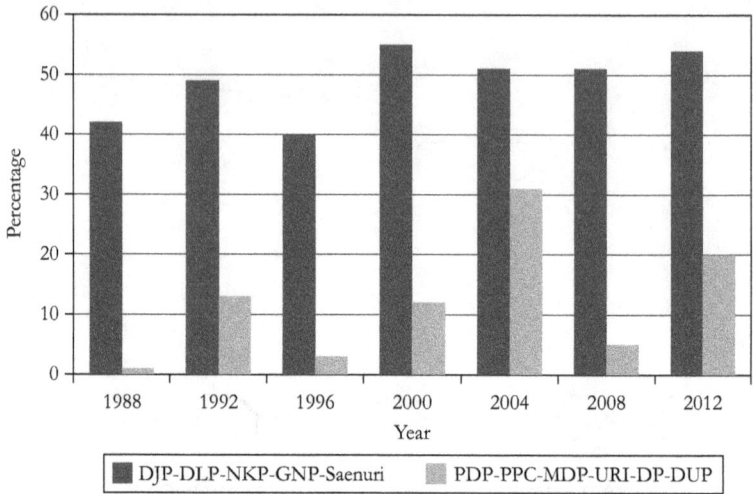

FIGURE 2.4 Vote shares for the two major parties in National Assembly elections in the Kyŏngsang region

SOURCE: National Election Commission, www.nec.go.kr/engvote_2013/05_resourcecenter/07_01.jsp.

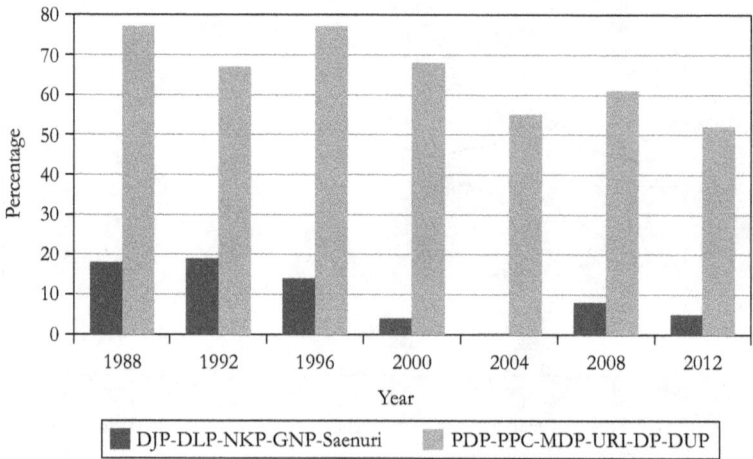

FIGURE 2.5 Vote shares for the two major parties in National Assembly elections in the Chŏlla region

SOURCE: National Election Commission, www.nec.go.kr/engvote_2013/05_resourcecenter/07_01.jsp.

the types of regionalism observed elsewhere. It is not founded on the belief that the regions should secede or that a region has faced economic discrimination and should be compensated. The place of origin of a political leader, that is, kinship ties, constitutes the foundation of South Korean regionalism. The political agenda, such as secession or economic discrimination, has never been introduced in a platform by the parties and has not been followed by South Korean voters. And to make matters worse, the regional divides in South Korea have been used intensively by politicians to guarantee votes and seats in the National Assembly. The fact that appealing to the voters' regional ties can almost automatically produce a certain number of safe seats in the National Assembly understandably discourages politicians from developing distinct party platforms.

The Presidential Election in 1987: Divided We Stand

In 1987, President Chun Doo-hwan declared that South Korea would retain its representative electoral system in its upcoming presidential election. The plan was to maintain his political connections through this showcase election even after his retirement by providing his friend, Roh Tae-woo, the Democratic Justice Party (DJP) candidate, an easy path to the presidency. Furious with this declaration, South Koreans demanded a change in the electoral system. This was the first nationwide step to end the authoritarian government's military rule, which eventually led to a huge national democratization movement and finally a direct election for president (the thirteenth).

Even though it was not perfect, the direct election of the president in 1987 not only let South Koreans enjoy the right to vote in a democratic environment, but also it led to the emergence of unprecedented political and electoral phenomena that South Koreans did not expect. The result of the 1987 presidential elections surprised Koreans and proved just how acute the regional divide was. In due course this would create one of the most robust partisan divides, lasting for the next twenty years.

All of Korea's military rulers—Park Chung-hee, Chun Doo-hwan, and Roh Tae-woo—hailed from Kyŏngbuk province, the northern part of the Kyŏngsang region. It was widely known that the Kyŏngbuk province benefited from the largesse of these rulers as well as high official appointments of people from the region. Therefore, the area was loyal to these past presidents, becoming a political bastion for the conservative and authoritarian parties. Being supportive of the Chun government, the voters of Kyŏngbuk solidly voted for Roh in 1987. Roh's share of the vote in Kyŏngbuk was almost 70 percent, far exceeding the 37 percent he received nationwide.

However, the province of Kyŏngnam, located in the southern part of the Kyŏngsang region, took a different stance. Instead of Roh, who came from a military background, residents of Kyŏngnam province—and those in the city of Pusan in particular—voted for Kim Young-sam, the once-renowned dissident. Kim Young-sam was originally from Pusan, the largest city in the Kyŏngsang area, and his share of the vote in Kyŏngnam was over 50 percent, much higher than his nationwide share of 28 percent.

Likewise, the Chŏlla region showed unanimous support for its favorite political son, Kim Dae-jung. Since he did not have to divide the vote in the Chŏlla area, as Roh Tae-woo and Kim Young-sam did in Kyŏngsang, the percentage of the vote Kim Dae-jung received in Chŏlla was phenomenal. He received more than 90 percent of the votes from the Chŏlla province including Kwangju, whereas his national vote share was 27 percent (see Figures 2.6 and 2.7).

The "hometown boy" effect enjoyed by prominent political leaders also influenced the outcome of other elections. In the 1988 National Assembly

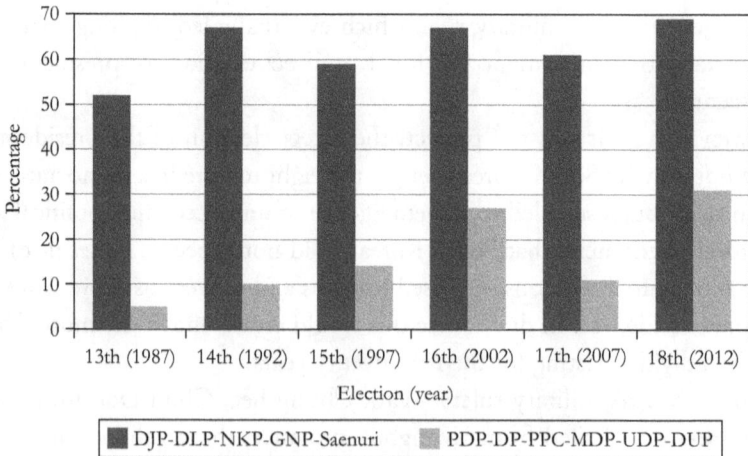

FIGURE 2.6 Vote shares for the two major parties in presidential elections in the Kyŏngsang region

SOURCE: National Election Commission, www.nec.go.kr/engvote_2013/05_resourcecenter/07_01.jsp.

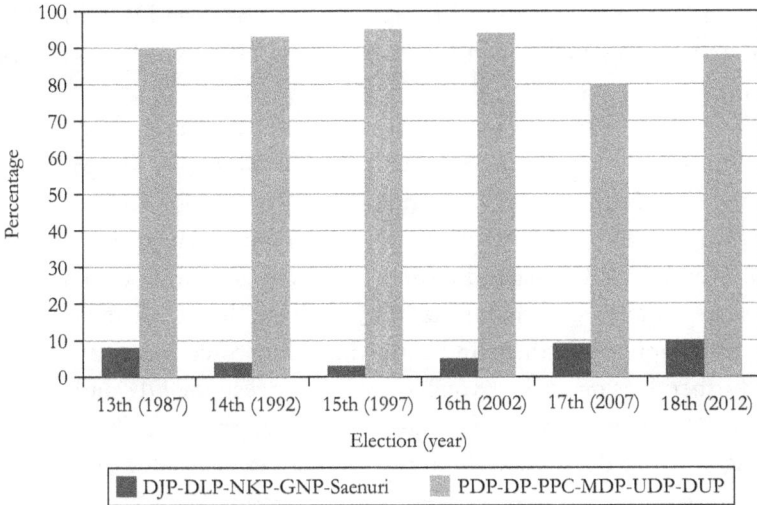

FIGURE 2.7 Vote shares for the two major parties in presidential elections in the Chŏlla region

SOURCE: National Election Commission, www.nec.go.kr/engvote_2013/05_resourcecenter/07_01.jsp.

elections, regionally divided party vote shares were noticeable, as well. For instance, the ruling DJP, and the Reunification Democratic Party (RDP) led by Kim Young-sam, both of whose political bases were in the Kyŏngsang region, together garnered around 80 percent of the votes in the region. Less than 2 percent of the total votes went to the PDP led by Kim Dae-jung. Instead, the PDP obtained around 75 percent in the Chŏlla region, far exceeding its national share of 19 percent.

Aware that they were unable to win the majority if the division of votes in the Kyŏngsang region between the DJP and the RDP continued, in 1990 the DJP and RDP decided to merge. The merger also included Ch'ungch'ŏng's leading party, the New Democratic Republican Party led by Kim Jong-pil. Not only did the merger give birth to a new mega-ruling party, the Democratic Liberal Party (DLP), it also practically isolated the Chŏlla electorates from the rest of the country. In addition, the merger placed the new mega-party in a politically different position; until then, the DJP had been beholden to the anti-democratic and authoritarian regime. After the merger, particularly by adding Kim Young-sam and his RDP that represented the opposition under the military rule, the new party was able to rid itself of the image of having served the former authoritarian military governments to a certain extent. Last but not least, the DLP was able to hold a two-thirds majority in the National Assembly, which was sufficient to amend the Constitution.[24]

The merger is another typical case of a South Korean party existing for the purpose of achieving the political aims of a party boss. The parties were formed, dissolved, split, or merged at the will of the political boss, in this case, Kim Young-sam and Kim Jong-pil.[25] The regional voting blocs were reinforced by the Chŏlla and Kyŏngsang electorates, after all. The Chŏlla voters began to vote solely for the PDP, believing that it was the only party that truly represented them and with which they could identify.[26] Without any further division of the Kyŏngsang votes between the DJP and the RDP, the DLP began to dominate Kyŏngsang. The merger eventually helped Kim Young-sam win the presidency in 1992. But, in exchange for this, the DLP and its successors, such as the New Korea Party, the Grand National Party and the current Saenuri Party, have not been able to obtain any substantial number of votes or seats in the Chŏlla region. Similarly, the PDP, and its successors the MDP, the Uri Party, and the current Democratic United Party (DUP), have experienced extreme difficulty in garnering votes and obtaining seats in the Kyŏngsang region.[27]

The party line starting with the establishment of the DJP and connecting down through the Saenuri Party has received very strong support in the Kyŏngsang region, including Pusan, Taegu, and Ulsan. But their shares of the vote in the Chŏlla region have not exceeded double-digit numbers, except in 1987. Conversely, the party line extending from the PDP, built by Kim Dae-jung, down through the Democratic United Party in 2012 has not been able to garner any significant number of votes from the Kyŏngsang region, even though it has dominated the Chŏlla region. The best performance of a presidential candidate in the Kyŏngsang region was by Moon Jae-in as the DUP candidate when he garnered roughly 31 percent of the vote during the presidential election of 2012. The sudden rise in vote share can be attributed to the fact that Moon Jae-in was a son of the Kyŏngsang region. In the previous presidential elections of 2007, the shares in the same region for the Democratic Party candidate, Jung Dong-young, was 10 percent, implying persistent regional voting behavior in these two regions.[28]

With severe regional divisions and the dominance of the party bosses over the parties, the political parties of South Korea were far from what one would expect in a well-functioning democratic system. Discernible differences in platforms, policies, and ideological positions were not observed, and it appeared that this would continue to be the case for the foreseeable future.

The Presidential Election in 1997 and the Sunshine Policy

The Korean presidential election of 1997 deserves attention because a new party system had arrived. After three disappointing failed attempts for the presidency, Kim Dae-jung realized that he would not be able to win the presidency based only on his long-lasting political bastion in Chŏlla and some additional votes from Seoul and the Kyŏnggi region. The population of Chŏlla province was simply insufficient to win the presidency. Furthermore, his supporters in the Seoul and Kyŏnggi metropolitan areas were always ready to swing. Knowing that the 1997 presidential election was going to be his last chance, Kim made a politically controversial decision: He aligned with Kim Jong-pil in order to draw in votes from the Ch'ungch'ŏng region.[29] The formation of this coalition represented a sacrifice of principles on the part of Kim Dae-jung because Kim Jong-pil had been the right-hand man of his political nemesis Park Chung-hee and the founding director of the Korean Central Intelligence Agency—the exact agency that had abducted Kim Dae-jung in 1971.

The year 1997 was also a critical year for the South Korean economy. The outgoing Kim Young-sam government had faced one of the worst economic crises in South Korean history and had to accept a bailout from the International Monetary Fund, leaving a tremendous electoral burden for the GNP's presidential candidate, Lee Hoi-chang. Furthermore, Lee In-je, who had vied for the GNP nomination, refused to accept a primary defeat. He therefore left the GNP to build his own People's New Party to run for president. Lee In-je's departure, with his supporters, from the GNP basically cost Lee Hoi-chang the presidency, since it effectively divided GNP supporters. Lee In-je won almost five million votes, a 19 percent share. Considering that the vote shares margin between Kim Dae-jung and Lee Hoi-chang was only 1.5 percent, Lee In-je's share was far more than critical. Due to the split of GNP supporters and his newly formed coalition with Kim Jong-pil and Ch'ungch'ŏng voters, Kim Dae-jung's bid for the presidency was successful.

At this time regionalism was still the most significant issue dividing voters along partisan lines. Lee Hoi-chang won strong support from the

Kyŏngsang region, whereas Kim Dae-jung received even stronger support from the Chŏlla region. As seen in Figure 2.6, Kim Dae-jung took more than 90 percent of the Chŏlla votes, whereas Lee Hoi-chang garnered almost 60 percent of the Kyŏngsang votes (see Figure 2.7). Neither party could win any sizable number of votes from the opposition region.

A turning point toward a party system based on policy-driven differences emerged during the Kim Dae-jung administration through the introduction of the Sunshine Policy.[30] The Sunshine Policy of the Kim Dae-jung government was a bilateral engagement policy with North Korea, aimed at enticing North Korea to open up. The policy became the hallmark of Kim's administration. The GNP, representing mainstream conservatives, had to oppose it, thus predictably creating conflict between the MDP and the GNP.[31] Although most Koreans agreed with the engagement policy, they did so to varying degrees. Whereas the progressives supported giving almost unconditional humanitarian aid and open engagement with the North, the conservatives insisted on abiding by a strong reciprocity rule based on the precondition that the freezing of the North Korean nuclear program could be verified. Therefore, attitudes and policies toward North Korea surfaced as crucial issues dividing the conservatives and the progressives generated a rift between the GNP and the MDP.

In June 2000, the first inter-Korean summit was held in Pyongyang. President Kim Dae-jung's visit to Pyongyang and his meeting with Kim Jong-il were televised nationwide. This historic summit between the leaders of the two Koreas certainly sent a signal to the South Korean public that the North and the South could coexist peacefully. Thereafter, people's perceptions of both North Korea and General Secretary Kim Jong-il became much more positive. South Koreans began to recognize North Koreans as brothers who shared a similar identity and to believe that the South and the North should be unified. This so-called Sunshine Policy received an approval rating as high as 87 percent in August 2000.[32] Yet, support for the Sunshine Policy was particularly solid among the progressives. The conservatives, still harboring doubts about the North's hidden motives for engagement, were less convinced of the effectiveness of the policy.

As domestic politics began to experience fissures between progressives and conservatives with respect to the North, there was also a critical change outside of the Korean peninsula. After the controversial count and re-count in the state of Florida, George W. Bush was inaugurated as president of the United States in 2001. His presidency created a seemingly noncoopera-tive relationship with President Kim Dae-jung, especially with regard to the "Sunshine Policy" and the Kim administration's aggressive efforts to engage the North. Unlike his predecessor, Bill Clinton, Bush essentially ignored North Korea and did not initiate any diplomatic negotiations. Most criti-cal, in his 2002 State of the Union address, Bush labeled the North Korean regime part of the "axis of evil."[33]

The "axis of evil" remark had a polarizing impact on the positions of the South Korean political parties toward North Korea, resonating even further with the South Korean public. The progressives stood behind the MDP and opposed the Bush administration's hard-line policy. Sympathizing with North Korea, the South Korean progressives condemned the United States as being an obstacle to engagement with North Korea. In contrast, oppo-nents of the "Sunshine Policy" lined up with the GNP, setting off a barrage of criticism against President Kim Dae-jung's engagement policy and call-ing for a strong alliance with the United States. The most dramatic clash, however, was yet to come.

The Presidential Election in 2002 and Anti-Americanism

When Gi-Wook Shin warned American officials in his 1996 article of their naive view of anti-Americanism in South Korea, concluding that it was the political rhetoric by only a particular segment of the Korean public, he must have surmised what would happen six years later.[34] In June 2002, two South Korean junior high school girls were accidentally killed by a U.S. armored vehicle. The soldiers who were driving the vehicle were tried in a South Ko-rean court but acquitted because of the Status of Forces Agreement. The in-cident enraged the South Korean public. Large groups of civil organizations and Korean citizens organized massive candlelight vigils in protest. South Koreans became increasingly polarized over the incident, provoking heated disputes over nationalism and the presence of U.S. troops on the Korean peninsula and widening the gap between conservatives and progressives.

The 2002 elections were dominated by anti-Americanism, supported by the progressives but reverberating among the youth, the educated, and white-collar workers.[35] The MDP's candidate Roh Moo-hyun, a former at-torney, human rights advocate for student activists, and a former member of the National Assembly, had unconventional views about the United States

that differed significantly from those of previous presidents and his opponent Lee Hoi-chang. Roh spoke firmly and openly about the incident, and
during the campaign he supported taking an anti-American position for the
sake of national interest. He argued that *panmi* (anti-American) sentiment
is not necessarily bad and could be understood under certain circumstances.

In contrast, candidate Lee Hoi-chang, because he was supported by the
conservative segment of the population, did not react as vociferously as
Roh to the incident, nor did he criticize the presence of U.S. troops on the
Korean peninsula. This lukewarm reaction cost Lee many votes, especially
among the youth. After his disappointing loss Lee Hoi-chang was forced to
retire from South Korean politics.

The upset victory by Roh Moo-hyun in 2002 was precipitated by the
rise in anti-Americanism that achieved unprecedented prominence due
to the tragic death of the two junior high school girls. According to Pew
Research Center's Global Attitudes Project, in 2002 the favorability rating
of the United States in South Korea was 52 percent. This was the lowest
among all Asian countries and higher only than the ratings in Turkey, Jor-
dan, Lebanon, Pakistan, and Argentina.[36] The election and campaign created yet another crucial ideological schism between the conservative and the
progressive factions. The polarized view of the United States created a corol-
lary ideological position for the political parties in South Korea. The MDP,
and later the Uri Party of President Roh, sided with the progressives' rising
voice of anti-Americanism, whereas the GNP fell in line with the conservatives defending strong alliance between South Korea and the United States.

Identity Politics: Unification, North Korea, and the United States

Adding to pro–North Korean sentiment that had been rising under the
Kim Dae-jung government, anti-Americanism was becoming a decisive factor that fostered fissures between conservatives and progressives in Korean
domestic politics. These divisions and the contentious politics they bred in
turn became more institutionalized within the South Korean party system.

Identity politics relating to North Korea and the United States should
not be taken at its face value to generate animosity between conservatives
and progressives in South Korea. How identity politics is translated into
the policy sphere has been the source of strife between the two ideological
groups and the political parties. Shin notes that although South Koreans

share a strong ethnic national identity regardless of their ideological positions, they differ dramatically when it comes to policy toward the North.[37] In particular, sharp divisions over the unification process and attitudes toward North Korea and the United States have been established along partisan lines as well as between ideological factions. In addition, as Suh aptly illustrates, South Korea has been torn between two identities at odds: the identity that sees the United States as an ally, and the Korean nationalist identity that posits against the United States. The first coincides with the ideological perspectives of the conservatives and the Saenuri Party. The national identity shared by the conservatives reflects a Cold War anti-Communist perspective; a cautious approach to engagement with the North; and deeply embedded trust in the U.S. alliance. The latter exists in conjunction with the sense of shared ethnicity and sympathy with the North and feelings of anti-Americanism, as reflected in the position of the progressives.[38]

The gap in attitudes toward North Korea and the United States among voters is remarkable. Using 2005 survey data from the East Asia Institute, Table 2.3 presents a comparison between a person's party affiliation and his/her perspectives on unification, policy toward North Korea, and attitude toward the United States.

TABLE 2.3
Public opinion on North Korea, unification, and the United States (2005), by partisan affiliation

Question 1: How much do you support unification?

| | PARTISAN AFFILIATION | | | | |
	Uri Party	GNP	DLP	Non-partisan	Total
Unification as soon as possible	21%	19%	27%	14%	17% (181)
Should take into account all circumstances	57%	46%	55%	58%	54% (564)
No need to hurry	17%	25%	12%	19%	20% (205)
No need to unify at all	6%	10%	7%	8%	8% (83)
Total	16% (170)	25% (261)	8% (86)	44% (458)	100% (1,038)

SOURCE: *Identity of the Korean Public* (East Asian Institute and Joong Ang Daily, 2005). Data at Korea Social Science Data Archive, www.kossda.or.kr/eng/index_kossda.asp.

(continued)

TABLE 2.3 (continued)

Question 2: Opinion on economic aid to North Korea (2005)

	PARTISAN AFFILIATION				
	Uri Party	GNP	DLP	Non-partisan	Total
Should increase the amount of aid	20%	6%	40%	14%	15% (159)
Maintain the current level	49%	44%	41%	44%	44% (459)
Should decrease the amount of aid	19%	33%	14%	28%	27% (282)
Should not provide any aid at all	8%	13%	4%	6%	8% (82)
Don't know/refused	4%	3.8%	2.3%	7%	5% (56)
Total	16% (170)	25% (261)	8% (86)	44% (458)	100% (1,038)

SOURCE: *Identity of the Korean Public* (East Asian Institute and Joong Ang Daily, 2005).

Question 3: Level of trust in the United States (2005)

	PARTISAN AFFILIATION				
	Uri Party	GNP	DLP	Non-partisan	Total
Trust very much	1%	2%	0%	1%	1% (12)
Trust on the whole	19%	29%	8%	14%	19% (193)
Do not particularly trust or distrust	33%	33%	34%	37%	34% (356)
Do not trust very much	33%	28%	40%	34%	33% (337)
Do not trust at all	12%	8%	19%	13%	12% (124)
Total	16% (170)	25% (261)	8% (86)	44% (458)	100% (1,038)

SOURCE: *Identity of the Korean Public* (East Asian Institute and Joong Ang Daily, 2005).

NOTES: Totals may not equal the sum of the cells. Other minor party supporters and "Don't know" answers are not included.

Progressives were more likely than conservatives to express an unreserved attitude toward unification. Whereas the GNP supporters had some reservations about imminent unification (35 percent) and answered that there was no reason to hurry, or to unify at all, only 23 percent of the Uri Party supporters took a similar position.[39] The Democratic Labor Party supporters, those reported to be most left-leaning, demonstrated a pattern of responses similar to those of the Democratic Party supporters.

With respect to economic aid to North Korea, the difference across voters becomes even more evident—20 percent of those identifying with the Uri Party were in favor of increasing the amount of aid to North Korea. In contrast, only 6 percent of GNP supporters approved an increase. Instead, almost 46 percent of GNP supporters asserted that the government should decrease or even suspend economic aid to North Korea, far exceeding the 27 percent of supporters of the Uri Party. The differences of opinion are even more apparent with respect to DLP supporters. About 40 percent of DLP supporters were in favor of increasing the amount of aid to North Korea, thereby taking the most accommodating view of the North.

The discrepancy in attitudes toward the United States is also related to partisan affiliation, though the relationship is not as apparent as it is with respect to views on economic aid to North Korea. Grand National Party supporters were one and a half times more likely than Uri Party supporters to trust the United States (31 percent vs. 20 percent). Uri Party supporters distrusted the United States more than GNP supporters by a similar gap of 9 percentage points. The most anti-American and pro-unification views, however, were held by supporters of the smaller DLP, which was to the left of Uri on the political spectrum.

The 2002 election marked important progress in the development of South Korea's party system. Before 2002, the political parties of South Korea had been barely discernible and their platforms rarely, if at all, went beyond banalities. It was the national identity issues promoted by the prolonged Sunshine Policy and anti-Americanism that facilitated the emergence of policy-driven differences among South Korean political parties.

As a result, the National Assembly election in 2004 was one of the most politicized. President Roh was impeached by the GNP and his former party, the MDP, for unlawfully intervening in the election as a public official. The progressives and Uri Party members were furious about the questionable accusations and organized a massive candlelight vigil. Indeed, the impeachment catalyzed more support among voters for President Roh and his Uri Party. Inadvertently, the entire event propagated extreme hostility and aggravated the divisions between the progressives and the conservatives. As Hahm Chai-bong describes, it became truly "a house divided."[40]

The Presidential Election in 2007 and 2012: Demise of Identity Politics?

Identity politics, pro–North Korean sentiment, and anti-Americanism played prominent roles in 2002, but they seemingly dissipated by the 2007 presidential election. The GNP's Lee Myung-bak defeated his most formidable political rival, Park Geun-hye, in the party's primary by a razor-thin margin to win the candidacy. The candidate for the incumbent ruling party was Jung Dong-young, the former minister of unification under the Roh administration. Aided by the low approval rating of the outgoing Roh Moo-hyun government, Lee won the presidency without much difficulty. The gap between the winner and the runner-up was by far the largest in South Korean history. Lee won 49 percent of the votes, whereas Jung received only 26 percent.

The most salient issue in the 2007 presidential election was the economy. Unification, policy toward North Korea, and anti-Americanism were all marginalized. In fact, the issue of anti-Americanism that had once carved great differences between the parties ostensibly retreated from the political scene.[41]

A similar phenomenon was observed in the 2012 presidential election in which the conservative Saenuri Party's Park Geun-hye defeated the DUP's Moon Jae-in. Creating jobs, economic democratization, and social welfare were the most important issues perceived by South Koreans. Neither North Korea nor the United States emerged as determinant during the election. For instance, North Korea launched a satellite into space on a long-range rocket on December 12, only a week before the election. It had long been believed that a provocation by North Korea was an electoral advantage for the conservative party and its candidates. Nonetheless, the election polls indicated that Park, the front-runner throughout the race, reaped little or no benefit. As a matter of fact, regardless of the North's provocation, the race between Park and Moon tightened even further as Moon caught up near the end. From the beginning of the race, domestic issues prevailed.

Does this mean that identity politics ceased to have an impact on South Korean politics? To search for any indication of the demise of identity politics in Korea, I use the Asan Annual Public Opinion Survey conducted in 2012.

Table 2.4 displays public opinion of South Koreans on unification, how to deal with North Korea's nuclear program, and attitudes toward the

TABLE 2.4
Public opinion on North Korea, unification, and the United States (2012), by partisan affiliation

Question 1: How much do you support unification?

| | PARTISAN AFFILIATION | | | | |
	Saenuri	DUP	UPP	Non-partisan	Total
Unification as soon as possible	12%	18%	18%	15%	15% (225)
Should take into account all circumstances	58%	65%	61%	63%	62% (922)
No need to hurry	24%	15%	17%	18%	19% (288)
No need to unify at all	6%	2%	4%	4%	4% (64)
Total	32% (476)	24% (362)	3% (46)	40% (602)	100% (1,500)

SOURCE: *Asan Annual Public Opinion Survey 2012* (Seoul, Korea: Asian Institute for Policy Studies, 2012). Data available upon request.
NOTE: Chi-square score = 25.861, df = 9, p = .002.

Question 2: Opinion on economic aid to North Korea (2012)

| | PARTISAN AFFILIATION | | | | |
	Saenuri	DUP	UPP	Non-partisan	Total
No economic aid without North's apology	89%	50%	46%	66%	69% (1,035)
Unconditional economic aid	11%	50%	54%	34%	31% (465)
Total	32% (476)	24% (362)	3% (46)	40% (602)	100% (1,500)

SOURCE: *Asan Annual Public Opinion Survey 2012* (Asan Institute for Policy Studies, 2012).
NOTE: Chi-square score = 163.835, df = 3, p = .000.

(*continued*)

TABLE 2.4 (continued)

Question 3: How do you think that we should deal with North Korea's nuclear program?

| | PARTISAN AFFILIATION | | | | |
	Saenuri	DUP	UPP	Non-partisan	Total
Economic and military pressures	41%	19%	26%	27%	29% (435)
Diplomatic and economic persuasion	59%	81%	74%	73%	71% (1,065)
Total	32% (476)	24% (362)	3% (46)	40% (602)	100% (1,500)

SOURCE: *Asian Annual Public Opinion Survey 2010* (Asian Institute for Policy Studies, 2010).
NOTE: Chi-square score = 76.834, df = 9, p = .000.

Question 4: Favorability rating of the United States and North Korea

| | PARTISAN AFFILIATION | | | | |
	Saenuri	DUP	UPP	Non-partisan	Total
Favorability rating of the U.S.	7.0	5.4	4.2	5.6	6.0
Favorability rating of North Korea	2.5	4.0	4.9	3.4	3.3

SOURCE: *Asan Annual Public Opinion Survey 2012* (Asian Institute for Policy Studies, 2012).
NOTES: T-score for the United States = 10.325, df = 836, p = .000. T-score for North Korea = −9.220, df = 836, p = .000. Totals may not equal the sum of the cells. Other minor party supporters and "Don't know" answers are not included. For Question 4, 0 is the least favorable and 10 is the most favorable.

United States and North Korea in 2012. Regarding unification, the results are dubious. Supporters of DUP and United Progressive Party (UPP) were more inclined to support unification than their Saenuri counterparts. It is also noteworthy that since 2005 overall reservations about imminent unification increased across party lines. Yet the gap is much more discernible than earlier when it came to the demand for immediate unification. Only 12 percent of Saenuri supporters supported immediate unification, whereas 18 percent of DUP and UPP supporters stated the same. There was a 7 percentage point drop from the East Asia Institute's 2005 survey among GNP supporters, and they appear to have moved to a more cautious position of "taking into account all circumstances."

There are substantial partisan differences on the issue of how to deal with economic aid to North Korea and the North's nuclear weapons program.

Since the second nuclear test by North Korea in 2009 and two military provocations in 2010, the Lee Myung-bak government took a hard-line policy toward North Korea by stopping the provision of economic aid. As to resuming economic aid to North Korea, the partisan division is striking. Almost 90 percent of Saenuri supporters objected to any economic aid without North Korea's official apology for previous provocations in 2010, asking the administration to abide by the reciprocity rule. On the contrary, DUP supporters were evenly split in this regard. As many as 50 percent responded that economic aid should be unconditional. A similar contrast is observed when it comes to how to deal with a nuclear North. Whereas roughly 41 percent of Saenuri supporters preferred economic and military pressures to coerce North Korea to end its nuclear program, 81 percent of DUP voters preferred resolving the issue through diplomacy and economic cooperation. The positions of UPP voters were largely consistent with those of DUP voters.

Next, I examine the favorability ratings of the United States and North Korea in 2012. Respondents were asked to rate the country on a scale from 0 to 10, with 10 being the most favorable. As the numbers in the table indicate, Saenuri supporters gave the United States the highest favorability rating (7.0), 1.6 more than the 5.4 rating given by supporters of the DUP. The favorability rating for North Korea among Saenuri supporters was 2.5 and 4.0 among those who support the DUP, indicating that DUP voters were more sympathetic to North Korea.

Besides North Korea, sentiment toward the United States is an important measure for identity politics in Korea. Four questions measured the overall attitude toward the United States by party line. These included whether or not the respondent agreed with the following statements: 1) the United States is responsible for the division of Korea; 2) in the past the United States was an obstacle to South Korean democratization; 3) the United States is an obstacle to reconciliation and cooperation between the North and the South; 4) the long-term military presence of the United States on the Korean Peninsula is necessary.

Overall, cross-tabulations show the persistent disparities between party members in the two major political parties of South Korea with regard to the United States (see Table 2.5). The United States was blamed for the division of Korea not only by the progressives but also by the conservatives. Slightly more than a majority of Saenuri supporters agreed with the

TABLE 2.5
Perception of the United States (2012), by partisan affiliation

Statement 1: The United States is responsible for the division of Korea between the North and the South.

	PARTISAN AFFILIATION				Total
	Saenuri	DUP	UPP	Nonpartisan	
Agree	53%	73%	76%	64%	63% (945)
Do not agree	47%	27%	24%	36%	37% (555)
Total	32% (476)	24% (362)	3% (46)	40% (602)	100% (1,500)

SOURCE: *Asan Annual Public Opinion Survey 2012* (Asian Institute for Policy Studies, 2012).
NOTE: Chi-square score = 51.876, df = 9, *p* = .000.

Statement 2: The United States was an obstacle to South Korean democratization in the past.

	PARTISAN AFFILIATION				Total
	Saenuri	DUP	UPP	Nonpartisan	
Agree	28%	51%	72%	40%	40% (600)
Do not agree	72%	49%	28%	60%	60% (900)
Total	32% (476)	24% (362)	3% (46)	40% (602)	100% (1,500)

SOURCE: *Asan Annual Public Opinion Survey 2012* (Asian Institute for Policy Studies, 2012).
NOTE: Chi-square score = 100.339, df = 9, *p* = .000.

Statement 3: The United States is an obstacle to reconciliation and cooperation between the North and the South.

	PARTISAN AFFILIATION				Total
	Saenuri	DUP	UPP	Nonpartisan	
Agree	25%	53%	73%	48%	43% (645)
Do not agree	75%	47%	27%	52%	57% (855)
Total	32% (476)	24% (362)	3% (46)	40% (602)	100% (1,500)

SOURCE: *Asan Annual Public Opinion Survey 2012* (Asian Institute for Policy Studies, 2012).
NOTE: Chi-square score = 152.998, df = 9, *p* = .000.

(*continued*)

TABLE 2.5 (continued)

Statement 4: The long-term military presence of the United States in the Korean peninsula is necessary.

| | PARTISAN AFFILIATION | | | | |
	Saenuri	DUP	UPP	Nonpartisan	Total
Agree	89%	55%	31%	62%	68% (1,020)
Do not agree	11%	45%	69%	38%	32% (480)
Total	32% (476)	24% (362)	3% (46)	40% (602)	100% (1,500)

SOURCE: *Asan Annual Public Opinion Survey 2012* (Asian Institute for Policy Studies, 2012).

NOTES: Chi-square score= 162.410, df = 3, *p* = .000. Totals may not equal the sum of the cells. Other minor party supporters and "Don't know" answers are not included.

first statement, and a disproportionately large number of DUP supporters agreed with it. With the second statement, America's hindrance to South Korean democratization, partisan division is more noticeable. Whereas 72 percent of Saenuri voters disagreed with the statement, a slim majority of DUP voters pointed the finger at the United States. The third statement even further severs supporters of the Saenuri voters from those of the DUP. When asked about the United States being a liability in dysfunctional North and South relations, 75 percent of Saenuri partisans disagreed, in contrast to 53 percent of DUP partisans saying that the United States was a stumbling block. Last but not least, the supporters of the two major parties displayed a very different opinion with respect to the U.S. military presence.

From the results, we can confirm that identity politics remains powerful in Korean party politics. There exist not only considerable discrepancies across partisans on various sets of security issues, but also they are statistically significant.[42] How, then, can we interpret the salience of economic issues that reportedly decided two previous presidential elections?

While the economy was the main driving factor in the 2007 election of Lee Myung-bak, at that time economic issues did not create a fissure between conservatives and progressives as they do now. Then, the consensus of economic growth was shared by a large majority. It is safe to say that the issue of choice between economic growth and redistribution of wealth came to the fore over the free-lunch debate. Then-mayor Oh Se-hoon, who had been recognized as a GNP presidential hopeful along with Park Geun-hye, called for a city referendum on the free-lunch program, a program he had fiercely opposed. It was proposed and passed by the progressive-filled City Council of Seoul, but ex-mayor Oh staked his political career on killing it. The progressive opposition coalition pleaded with voters not to vote so that turnout would be lower than 33.3 percent. If the referendum turnout did not surpass this threshold, the referendum would be dismissed without even opening the ballot box. Mr. Oh intensified the battle by promising that he would resign from his position if turnout did not meet the threshold. The final turnout was 25.7 percent, and Oh kept his promise, which led the city to a by-election for a new mayor on October 26, 2011. This led to the election of Park Won-soon, a unified opposition candidate.

The 2012 presidential election was the continuation of the similar debate. Social welfare and resolving economic inequality emerged as top economic issues during the campaign. It should be noted, however, that the issues were not entirely owned by the progressives. In fact, it was the conservative Park Geun-hye who brought so-called economic democratization to the fore, which in essence requested reform of Korea's big businesses, known as *chaebŏl*. Apparently, her position on this came out of the calculation that it was a way to garner votes from moderates. Nevertheless, it should be also noted that there was a difference in matter of degree between Park Geun-hye and Moon Jae-in, and people became aware of the Saenuri Party as being growth-driven and the DUP as being redistributive. In sum, partisan division on economic issues began to emerge.

To investigate the presence of partisan divide on economic issues, I select three questions that are closely related to a person's ideological position on economic issues. They are: Should the government 1) increase regulations over big corporations; 2) raise the personal tax; 3) emphasize economic growth over social welfare?

As seen in Table 2.6, Saenuri supporters and DUP supporters demonstrate significant differences over economic issues. Saenuri supporters are more likely than DUP supporters to oppose increasing government regulation on big business. When asked about the preference between economic growth and social welfare, a disproportionately large number of Saenuri supporters chose economic growth (69 percent). On the contrary, DUP supporters tended to respond that social welfare is more important (66 percent). With respect to taxation policy, a slight difference between Saenuri and DUP supporters is found, but it is not statistically significant.

There is much to be gleaned from these results. In general, nationalism is still actively creating the fabric of party politics in South Korea. Voters'

TABLE 2.6

Public opinion on economic issues (2012), by partisan affiliation

Question 1: Do you think the government should increase, stay the same, or should decrease regulations over big corporations?

| | PARTISAN AFFILIATION | | | | |
	Saenuri	DUP	UPP	Nonpartisan	Total
Increase	24%	46%	51%	41%	37% (555)
Stay the same	28%	19%	16%	19%	22% (330)
Decrease	48%	35%	33%	39%	41% (615)
Total	32% (476)	24% (362)	3% (46)	40% (602)	100% (1,500)

SOURCE: *Asan Annual Public Opinion Survey 2012* (Asian Institute for Policy Studies, 2012).
NOTE: Chi-square score = 57.597, df = 6, p = .000.

Question 2: Do you think the government should increase, stay the same, or should decrease the personal tax?

| | PARTISAN AFFILIATION | | | | |
	Saenuri	DUP	UPP	Nonpartisan	Total
Increase	14%	19%	21%	17%	17% (255)
Stay the same	46%	39%	38%	44%	43% (645)
Decrease	40%	42%	41%	39%	40% (600)
Total	32% (476)	24% (362)	3% (46)	40% (602)	100% (1,500)

SOURCE: *Asan Annual Public Opinion Survey 2012* (Asian Institute for Policy Studies, 2012).
NOTE: Chi-square score = 6.794, df = 6, not significant.

Question 3: Do you think the government should emphasize economic growth or social welfare?

| | PARTISAN AFFILIATION | | | | |
	Saenuri	DUP	UPP	Nonpartisan	Total
Economic growth	69%	34%	25%	42%	48% (720)
Social welfare	31%	66%	75%	58%	52% (780)
Total	32% (476)	24% (362)	3% (46)	40% (602)	100% (1,500)

SOURCE: *Asan Annual Public Opinion Survey 2012* (Asian Institute for Policy Studies, 2012).
NOTES: Chi-square score = 130.917, df = 3, p = .000. Totals may not equal the sum of the cells. Other minor party supporters and "Don't know" answers are not included.

views on policy toward North Korea and perception of the United States by and large are still connected to their party affiliation. However, it is undeniable that discourse on redistribution of wealth or economic growth is gradually being integrated in the party system, too. Therefore, an interim answer should be that Korean party politics is in the phase of preparing to write another chapter. Having expended much of political disputes on North Korea, the United States, and party-boss politics, the parties and their supporters are beginning to move into new dimensions.

Conclusion

In this chapter, I have explored the development of the party system in South Korea. These parties were used as political vehicles by the political leaders, and thus South Korea failed to develop a full-scale institutionalized party system right after the democratization.

Formerly dominated by regionalism, at the beginning of the 2000s the party system in South Korea gradually became competitive because of differences over the issue of rapprochement with North Korea. The most salient partisan divisions emerged during the Kim Dae-jung administration when the government introduced its Sunshine Policy. The progressives supported the engagement policies to North Korea and the MDP and later the Uri Party. The opposition party, the GNP, was skeptical, and other conservatives with hard-line views toward North Korea gathered under the GNP umbrella.

The 2002 presidential election produced an addendum that caused a rift between the conservatives and the progressives. The unfortunate death of two junior high school girls engendered strikingly different attitudes toward the United States. The progressives asserted a Korea more autonomous from the United States, while the conservatives emphasized the importance of the South Korea–United States alliance coming from patriotism to protect the country from North Korean threat. The distinct party line was formed accordingly.

In this homogenous country, one that has a unique political situation and a history of sixty years of armistice, nationalism plays a distinct role. Once viewed as a negative influence on democratic consolidation, nationalism in South Korea has been a prominent player in building a modern party system.[43] Nationalism and identity politics have created new political and electoral cleavages between parties whose former role had been confined to assisting a leading political figure to fulfill his political ambitions and to maintain his political networks.[44]

More recently, North Korea, unification, and the United States seem to have faded as important issues, whereas other concerns, such as economic and social issues, have become more prominent. However, according to the analysis in this chapter, identity politics still determines one's partisan affiliation.

It is premature to conclude that economic issues prevail in the political scene. Nor should the significance of them be downplayed. According to the Asan Monthly Public Opinion Surveys from January to November 2011, the South Korean public was most focused on economic issues and job creation. The redistribution of wealth was second most important, whereas North–South relations were the second least important. This was a harbinger that economic issues would be crucial factor in South Korean politics. Partisan disparities based on economic cleavages are likely to come to the fore in the foreseeable future. Meanwhile, sentiment toward the North and attitudes toward the United States continue to be vital determinants of party affiliation among the South Korean public.

On that front, political parties in South Korea are now facing new challenges. Issue dimensions are becoming more complex than before. Combining security with economic issues to create distinguishable party platforms and party lines is imminent. As well, the party base is weakening and the number of nonpartisans who do not support any of the conventional parties is increasing. The Ahn Cheol-soo syndrome in the 2012 presidential election revealed the shaky status of political parties in South Korea. A former CEO of a computer antivirus program company, and without any political experience, Dr. Ahn was a formidable candidate in the race. He garnered most of his supporters from those who do not support any party as well as young voters, which confirms that parties are not successfully adapting to the electorates' needs. Presidential elections tend to breed new political environments. How to design and manage this new environment is what Park Geun-hye and the South Korean parties need to confront.

Notes

1. Seymour M. Lipset and Stein Rokkan, "Cleavage Structures, Party Systems, and Voter Alignments: An Introduction," in *Party Systems and Voter Alignments,* eds. Seymour M. Lipset and Stein Rokkan (New York: The Free Press, 1967), 1–64.

2. Chi-Young Park, *Political Opposition in Korea, 1945–1960* (Seoul: Seoul National University Press, 1980).

3. This does not imply that Lee did not express his views on inter-Korean relations, the alliance with the United States, or policy toward the North. It is more accurate to say that the South Korean public and mass media were much less attentive to these issues.

4. Maurice Duverger, *Parties: Their Organization and Activity in the Modern State* (New York: Wiley, 1954); Samuel P. Huntington, *Political Order in Changing Societies* (New Haven, CT: Yale University Press, 1968); Arend Lijphart, *Democracies: Patterns of Majoritarian and Consensus Government in Twenty-One Countries* (New Haven, CT: Yale University Press, 1984); Seymour M. Lipset, *Political Man: The Social Bases of Politics*, exp. ed. (Baltimore, MD: Johns Hopkins University Press, 1981); and Giovanni Sartori, *The Theory of Democracy Revisited* (Chatham, NJ: Chatham House, 1987).

5. Robert A. Dahl, "The Evaluation of Political Systems," in *Contemporary Political Science: Toward Empirical Theory*, ed. Ithiel de Sola Pool (New York: McGraw-Hill, 1967), 166–181.

6. Seymour M. Lipset, "The Social Requisites of Democracy Revisited: 1993 Presidential Address," *American Political Science Review* 59, no. 1 (February 1994): 1–22.

7. Larry Diamond, "Introduction: In Search of Consolidation," in *Consolidating the Third Wave Democracies: Themes and Perspectives*, eds. Larry Diamond et al. (Baltimore, MD: Johns Hopkins University Press, 1997), xiii–xlix.

8. Pippa Norris, *Electoral Engineering: Voting Rules and Political Behavior* (New York: Cambridge University Press, 2004).

9. Duverger, *Political Parties: Their Organization and Activity in the Modern State*.

10. The term "two-party-plus" system was introduced by Epstein to describe the Canadian party system. Leon D. Epstein, "A Comparative Study of Canadian Parties," *American Political Science Review* 58, no. 1 (March 1964): 46–59.

11. Lipset and Rokkan, "Cleavage Structures, Party Systems, and Voter Alignments."

12. Gary Cox, *Making Votes Count: Strategic Coordination in the World's Electoral Systems* (Cambridge, UK: Cambridge University Press, 1997).

13. Ronald Inglehart, *Culture Shift in Advanced Industrial Society* (Princeton, NJ: Princeton University Press, 1990); Mark N. Franklin, "The Decline of Cleavage Politics," in *Electoral Change: Responses to Evolving Social and Attitudinal Structures in Western Countries*, eds. Mark N. Franklin, Tom Mackie, and Henry Valen (Cambridge, UK: Cambridge University Press, 1991), 383–405; Oddbjørn Knutsen and Elinor Scarbrough, "Cleavage Politics," in *The Impact of Values*, eds. Jan W.

van Deth and Elinor Scarbrough (Oxford, UK: Oxford University Press, 1995), 492–523.

14. Russell J. Dalton, *Citizen Politics: Public Opinion and Political Parties in Advanced Industrial Democracies*, 2nd ed. (Chatham, NJ: Chatham House, 1996).

15. The number of electorates who identify themselves with a party is limited in South Korea. Public opinion polls indicate that as many as 40 percent of South Koreans do not affiliate themselves with any of the existing political parties. See Asan Annual Public Opinion Survey, 2010. An indirect reason for the weak Korean party system is the strong president, often called the "imperial" president. As Linz indicates, parliamentarism is more conducive to democratic norms than presidentialism, as presidentialism places enormous power in the hands of the winner. Juan J. Linz, "The Perils of Presidentialism," *Journal of Democracy* 1, no. 1 (Winter 1990): 51–69; Juan J. Linz, "The Virtues of Parliamentarism," *Journal of Democracy* 1, no. 4 (Fall 1990): 84–91.

16. Teh-fu Huang, "Party Systems in Taiwan and South Korea," in *Consolidating the Third Wave Democracies*, eds. Diamond et al., 135–159; David I. Steinberg and Myung Shin, "Tensions in South Korean Political Parties in Transition," *Asian Survey* 46, no. 4 (July–August 2006): 517–537; Jung Bock Lee, "The Political Process in Korea," in *Understanding Korean Politics: An Introduction*, eds. Soong Hoom Kil and Chung-in Moon (Albany: State University of New York Press, 2001), 141–174. David Kang and others also suggest that the way democracy and the party system were introduced to Korea explains the weak party system. Unlike Western democracies where political parties mobilized people and underwent the process of establishing a party system for more than two hundred years, democracy and the party system were introduced to the Korean people after liberation from Japanese colonial rule. David C. Kang, "The Institutional Foundations of Korean Politics," in *Understanding Korean Politics*, eds. Kil and Moon, 71–106.

17. Lee, "The Political Process in Korea," 141–174.

18. Steinberg and Shin, "Tensions in South Korean Political Parties in Transition," 517–537.

19. Although the political parties in South Korea have been institutionally weak, the party system has consisted of two major factions throughout its history. Before the Sunshine Policy was introduced, in the 1970s and 1980s party lines were divided between the democratic faction and the authoritarian faction.

20. Steinberg and Shin, "Tensions in South Korean Political Parties in Transition," 525.

21. Kang, "The Institutional Foundations of Korean Politics."

22. Average years are calculated only for the major parties presented in Figure 2.1.

23. Kim Jong-pil was Park Chung-hee's right-hand man and a native of the Ch'ungch'ŏng region.

24. This political deal was made under the condition that the constitution would be amended to transform the presidential system into a parliamentary system so that the two other party leaders, Kim Young-sam and Kim Jong-pil, would be able to become prime ministers sometime in the future.

25. John Kie-Chiang Oh, *Korean Politics: The Quest for Democratization and Economic Development* (Ithaca, NY: Cornell University Press, 1999).

26. If we look at the 1988 National Assembly election results, the DJP received 26 percent of the votes in Chŏlla province, even though it failed to obtain a seat.

27. Two National Assembly seats were obtained by the Uri Party and the Democratic Party (the successor of the Uri Party, established in 2007) in the Kyŏngnam region in the 2004 and 2008 National Assembly elections. The success of the Uri Party in winning seats in Kyŏngnam was due to the fact that Roh Moo-hyun was from Kyŏngnam and Kimhae was his birthplace.

28. The second best performance was by Roh Moo-hyun, who received 28 percent of the vote in 2002. Roh was also from Kyŏngnam region, Kimhae.

29. In return, Kim Jong-pil was appointed the first prime minister in the Kim Dae-jung government.

30. Norman D. Levin and Yong-Sup Han, *Sunshine in Korea* (Santa Monica, CA: Rand Corporation, 2003).

31. By this time, the name of the New Political Federation of People had changed to the New Millennium Democratic Party.

32. Choong Nam Kim, "The Sunshine Policy and Its Impact on South Korea's Relations with Major Powers," *Korean Observer* 35, no. 4 (Winter 2004): 589.

33. George W. Bush, "State of the Union Address," January 29, 2002, www .mtholyoke.edu/acad/intrel/bush/stateoftheunion.htm.

34. Gi-Wook Shin, "South Korean Anti-Americanism: A Comparative Perspective," *Asian Survey* 36, no. 8 (August 1996): 787–803.

35. As Shin notes, the recently elevated nationalism explained the abrupt rise of anti-Americanism. The Sunshine Policy and the June 2000 summit between Kim Dae-jung and Kim Jong-il cultivated favorable sentiment toward the North, which reduced the level of perceived threat among South Koreans. This was particularly the case among youth who had not been exposed to the anti-Communist education system under the authoritarian regimes. Gi-Wook Shin and Paul Y. Chang, "The Politics of Nationalism in U.S.–Korean Relations," *Asian Perspective* 28, no. 4 (2004):119–145.

36. The favorability rating of the United States in Korea declined further in the following year, 2003, to 46 percent. Pew Global Attitudes Project, "Obama More Popular Abroad Than at Home, Global Image of U.S. Continues to Benefit," Pew Research Center (2010). However, it should be noted that even progressives and MDP supporters would later consider the South Korea–United States

alliance important and necessary. According to Chae, the conservatives consider the United States to be their most important ally, and even a friend. The liberals and the MDP supporters agree about the importance of the alliance, but for pragmatic reasons. Haesook Chae, "South Korean Attitudes Toward the ROK–U.S. Alliance: Group Analysis," *PS: Political Science & Politics* 43, no. 3 (2010): 493–501.

37. Gi-Wook Shin, *One Alliance, Two Lenses: U.S.–Korea Relations in a New Era* (Stanford, CA: Stanford University Press, 2010).

38. J. J. Suh, "Bound to Last? The U.S.–Korea Alliance and Analytical Eclecticism," in *Rethinking Security in East Asia: Identity, Power, and Efficiency*, eds. J. J. Suh, Peter J. Katzenstein, and Allen Carlson (Stanford, CA: Stanford University Press, 2004), 169.

Also see Gi-Wook Shin and Kristin C. Burke, "North Korea and Identity Politics in South Korea," *Brown Journal of World Affairs* 15, no. 1 (Fall–Winter 2008): 287–303.

39. The numbers represent the combined percentage of two active unification answers and two passive answers.

40. Chaibong Hahm, "The Two South Koreas: A House Divided," *The Washington Quarterly* 28, no. 3 (Summer 2005): 57–72.

41. According to Pew Research Center's Pew Global Attitudes Project, the U.S. favorability ratings by the South Korean public in 2008, 2009, and 2010 were 70, 78, and 79 percent, respectively.

42. The Chi-square statistics reveal that all measures are statistically significant at $p = .05$.

43. In fact, South Korean regionalism resembles the nationalism described by Jack Snyder. Snyder explains that nationalism is a convenient tool for political elites to further their own political ambitions when democratic consolidation is not yet complete. Regionalism was frequently used by the political elites in South Korea, particularly during election campaigns.

44. Moon correctly shows how nationalism, anti-Americanism in particular, worked toward democratic consolidation in South Korea by engendering and promoting civic movements to advance human and labor rights, the rule of law, and environmental protection. Katharine H. S. Moon, "Nationalism, Anti-Americanism, and Democratic Consolidation," in *Korea's Democratization*, ed. Samuel S. Kim (New York: Cambridge University Press, 2003), 135–158.

THREE

Political Parties and Identity Politics in Taiwan

Shelley Rigger

Introduction

Since Taiwan's ban on new political parties was lifted in 1987, almost 150 political parties have registered and more than 30 have offered candidates in legislative elections, but barely a handful have competed more than once and only two have demonstrated the staying power to survive and thrive in Taiwan's rough-and-tumble democracy. Those two are the original pair with which Taiwan entered its democratic era: the old ruling party, the Kuomintang (KMT) and the opposition party that formed a year before the new-party ban was lifted, the Democratic Progressive Party (DPP). Taiwan's electoral rules could have accommodated a multiparty system, but the trajectory toward two-party politics was set even before democratic reforms had fully taken hold, and the new electoral system adopted in 2005 almost certainly will lock in the KMT and DPP as Taiwan's dominant parties.

For decades, political scientists argued over whether electoral rules or social cleavages best explained the development of particular party systems.[1] Some research focuses on the interaction between the two, as well as politicians' strategic decisions. Taiwan's steady march toward a two-party system exemplifies a line of argument Jakub Zielinski summarized in a 2002 article: "In new democracies the early rounds of electoral competition determine not only who wins or loses a particular election but also, and perhaps more importantly, which social cleavages will be depoliticized and which will be established as permanent bases of political conflict . . . [P]arty systems in new democracies should be seen as critical founding moments when political elites forge long-term political identities that define the party system for years to come."[2] In Taiwan, those first few national elections established Taiwan's relationship to China as the primary issue dividing party loyalties. The precise content of the issue has changed over time, but its centrality defines Taiwan politics and structures its party system to this day.

Taiwan's Parties by the Numbers

Party competition came to Taiwan in the mid-1980s after four decades in which electoral competition was confined within the KMT. The first real partisan competition at the national level occurred in 1986, when candidates recommended by the DPP joined supplementary legislative elections (see Table 3.1).[3] In that year, KMT- and DPP-backed candidates captured 92 percent of the vote. In 1989 the DPP's nominees were identified on the ballot for the first time, and again the KMT and DPP dominated the balloting. The 1992 legislative election was especially important because it was Taiwan's first comprehensive legislative election. Until that year, legislators elected in mainland China in the 1940s were retained in office to preserve the fiction that the Republic of China (ROC) government represented Chinese on the mainland. By the late 1980s, this pretext was no longer persuasive, and Taiwan's Council of Grand Justices ruled that the "senior legislators" must step down, setting up the 1992 race.

In 1995 a third party joined the KMT and DPP. The New Party (NP) was a conservative, pro-unification party fronted by a handful of popular politicians who enjoyed substantial support in Taipei City. The party's 13 percent vote share in the 1995 election came entirely at the KMT's expense, and it seemed it might become a strong contender for third-party status. Instead of growing into a significant third party, though, the NP's vote share peaked in 1995 and declined steadily until 2008 when it effectively folded its electoral wing into the KMT (see Table 3.2).

An even more potent competitor emerged in 2001. The People First Party (PFP) was founded in the wake of the KMT's disastrous defeat in the 2000 presidential election. Its founder and head was James Soong (Song Chu-yu), a KMT dropout whose independent candidacy in the 2000 race split the KMT and helped hand the presidency to the DPP's Chen Shui-bian. Soong's party picked up 20 percent of the vote in the 2001 legislative elections and cost the KMT its status as the majority party. But like the NP, the PFP peaked in its

TABLE 3.1
Vote share, seat share, and seat bonus, by party, 1986–2008

	Vote share (%)	Seat share (%)	Seat bonus (%)
KMT '86	67	79	12
DPP '86	25	12	−13
KMT '89	60	72	12
DPP '89	30	16	−14
KMT '92	53	59	6
DPP '92	31	32	1
KMT '95	46	52	6
DPP '95	33	33	0
NP '95	13	13	0
KMT '98	46	55	8
DPP '98	30	31	2
NP '98	7	5	−2
TAIP '98	2	0	−1
KMT '01	31	30	−1
DPP '01	37	39	2
PFP '01	20	20	0
TSU '01	9	6	−3
NP '01	3	0	−2
KMT '04	35	35	0
DPP '04	38	40	2
PFP '04	15	15	0
TSU '04	8	5	−3
NP '04	0	0	0
KMT '08[a]	54	72	18
DPP '08[a]	38	24	−14
TSU '08[a]	1	0	−1

SOURCE: Central Election Commission data, archived at the Election Studies Center, National Chengchi University, Taipei, www.esc.nccu.edu.tw/english/.

[a]Includes constituency, aboriginal, and at-large seats.

TABLE 3.2
Party performance in the 2008 presidential and legislative elections

	PRESIDENTIAL	LEGISLATIVE: DISTRICT AND ABORIGINAL SEATS						LEGISLATIVE: PARTY LIST			
	Vote share (%)	Candidates	Seats	Success rate (%)	Seat share (%)	Vote share (%)	Seat bonus (%)	Seats	Vote share (%)	Seat share (%)	Seat bonus (%)
KMT	58.45	74	61	82.43	77.21	53.50	23.71	20	51.20	58.82	7.62
DPP	41.33	71	13	18.31	16.46	38.60	−22.14	14	36.90	41.18	4.28
TSU		13	0	0.00	0.00	0.90	−0.90	0	3.50	0.00	−3.50
NP		0						0	4.0		
PFP		3	1	33.33	0.01	0.30	−0.29				
Other		134	4	0.00	0.00	0.60	−0.60	0	3.70	0.00	−3.70

SOURCE: Central Election Commission data, archived at the Election Studies Center, National Chengchi University, Taipei, www.esc.nccu.edu.tw/english/.

first election; its vote share declined to 15 percent in 2004, and in 2008 it, too, chose to list nearly all of its candidates under the KMT banner.

The Taiwan Solidarity Union (TSU) also formed in the wake of the 2000 presidential election. The TSU adopted former president Lee Teng-hui as its spiritual leader. Lee quit the KMT to take responsibility for the debacle in 2000, but his new party was a far cry from the one he had headed until a few months earlier. The TSU took a strong pro-independence line, and it steadfastly refused to be absorbed into Taiwan's other independence-leaning party, the DPP. In 2004 it captured 8 percent of the legislative vote; but, like the NP and PFP, the TSU's star soon faded. In 2008 it ran an ambitious slate of thirteen candidates, all of whom were defeated. In party-list voting introduced that year, the TSU won 3.5 percent—well below the 5 percent threshold for representation in the legislature.

As Table 3.1 illustrates, none of the minor parties that have contested Taiwan's legislative elections has developed a durable following. The electoral formula applied from 1986 to 2004 was single, nontransferable voting, or SNTV, in multimember districts. The relatively proportional SNTV system should have allowed—even encouraged—parties to proliferate, but the cleavage that emerged to dominate the early rounds of partisan elections privileges the competition between two parties, the KMT and DPP, leaving little room for others.[4]

In 2005, Taiwan's election laws were revised and a new electoral system was adopted. The new rules cut the size of the legislature in half, from 225 to 113, and it created a two-ballot system that includes seventy-three single-member, first-past-the-post district seats and thirty-four at-large seats elected under party-list proportional-representation rules. Parties that receive more than 5 percent of the proportional-representation vote assign those seats according to a published list. An additional six seats are reserved for Taiwan's aboriginal minority.

The new electoral system radically altered the institutional environment for political parties. If the 2008 results are any indication, the new rules strongly favor large parties—a predictable result. As Table 3.1 shows, the largest party (the KMT) captured an outsized share of seats relative to its share of the vote. In the district elections, the KMT won 77 percent of the seats with less than 54 percent of the popular vote. The high threshold for representation at the proportional-representation stage reinforced the large parties' dominance by squeezing out all the other parties.

The Origins of Taiwan's Party System

The ROC assumed control of Taiwan when the Japanese empire surrendered the island along with its other colonies at the end of World War II. For the next four decades, it confined electoral competition within a single party, the KMT. That is not to say, however, that competitive elections did not exist. The ROC constitution called for local autonomy, and beginning in 1947, Taiwanese participated in elections at many levels: village, township, town, city, county, and province. The most important of these elections were for members of the Taiwan Provincial Assembly and mayors and city councilors in Taipei and Kaohsiung (although after a string of embarrassing defeats, the KMT converted the mayorships in Taipei and Kaohsiung to appointive positions).

In addition to local self-government, the ROC constitution also established two national-level elected bodies: the Legislative Yuan and the National Assembly.[5] Elections to those institutions were suspended when the ROC government lost control of mainland China to the Chinese Communist Party in 1949. Under the theory that representation for the ROC's mainland provinces required elections in territory "occupied" by the Communists, the Legislative Yuan and National Assembly members elected in 1947 remained in office until the early 1990s. Inevitably, the passage of time created vacancies in both bodies. At first, runners-up from 1947 were appointed to fill the empty seats, but in 1969 the ROC government began holding supplementary elections aimed at maintaining a quorum in the rapidly aging parliaments. While the number of supplementary seats was limited, elections were competitive, and non-KMT candidates gained a foothold in the legislature and the assembly.

Even during the so-called White Terror of the 1950s and '60s, when civil liberties were not respected and unsanctioned political groups faced severe repression, Taiwan's elections were remarkably competitive. The KMT not only permitted nonparty candidates to compete, it actually encouraged their participation as a way to strengthen grassroots support for the regime. Local democracy made it easier for the Mainlander (*waishengren*) minority—the 15 percent of Taiwan residents who had arrived on the island after World War II and who dominated the central government—to manage a society made up primarily of people whose ancestors had arrived centuries earlier. The latter group—known in English as "Taiwanese" and in

Chinese as *benshengren*—spoke a dialect of Chinese few Mainlanders could understand and practiced traditions that were unfamiliar to the Mainlander ruling class. Mainlander leaders, and even Taiwanese appointed by a Mainlander-dominated central state, would have been hard-pressed to govern local communities as effectively as officials elected by their peers. Moreover, once a local politician had proven himself at the ballot box, the KMT could target him for recruitment. In this way, competitive local elections became a tool the KMT used to build a broad and deep network of grassroots support throughout Taiwan.

Decades of local electoral competition prepared Taiwanese voters well for national elections. The opportunity to elect all-new legislators in 1992 was a huge breakthrough, but the actual conduct of the elections was routine: Its rules and procedures were familiar to Taiwanese from four decades of local and supplementary national elections. Likewise, the first direct presidential election in 1996 represented a big step forward for Taiwan's democracy, but it was familiar ground for Taiwanese who had been electing various *shouzhang*—executive officials—since the 1950s.

Democratization may not have changed the electoral rules, but it did bring at least one wholly new element to the political landscape: party competition. The right to form new political parties was one of many guaranteed by the ROC constitution that the KMT-led ROC government suspended when it fled mainland China. For thirty-eight years, Taiwan was ruled as a single-party authoritarian state. To create a democratic facade, the KMT tolerated two small parties, the China Youth Party and the China Democratic Socialist Party, but neither ever challenged the KMT's dominant position.

When the regime repealed the martial law provisions under which new parties had been forbidden, *The New York Times* reported, "Lifting of martial law means opposition political parties can be formed legally for the first time, giving Taiwan's fragmented but increasingly vocal opposition a new chance to organize."[6] At the time, Taiwan's opposition did seem weak and fragmented, and the expectation that many parties would form was understandable. In fact, thirty-five new parties registered with the authorities between 1987 and 1989. But one party had the jump on the rest. In September 1986—almost a year before martial law ended—a group of activists flouted martial law and founded the DPP. Although technically illegal, the party operated openly in the months between its founding and the end of martial law.

As Jiyoon Kim makes clear in her discussion of Korean party development in Chapter 2, simply being first does not guarantee a party's success
in a new democracy; so while the DPP's early entry into the political fray
undoubtedly gave it an advantage over competitors that entered later, its
success cannot be explained by timing alone. A more important reason for
the DPP's success is that the KMT and the DPP have jointly managed the
cleavages dividing Taiwan's society in ways that enable the two parties to
monopolize the available political space. In 2005 they cemented their dominance in the electoral reform, which is almost certain to give large parties an
insurmountable advantage.

The roots of Taiwan's two-party system lie in the pre-reform one-party
system. Beginning in the early 1950s, the KMT constructed a wide social
base. In 1952 it inserted a plank in its platform that promised to establish organizations for farmers and workers. The party's goals for those groups were
to raise living standards, promote democracy, and encourage cooperative
relationships between labor and capital.[7] Over time, the regime incorpo-
rated nearly every social sector into the party-state through one or another
corporatist institution. It set up groups for farmers, workers, business owners, women, aboriginal people, and professionals—not to mention the large
number of Taiwanese who worked directly for the state, including military
and school personnel, police, and government officials.

Semiofficial corporatist organizations connected Taiwanese to the KMT-
controlled state while local elections drew them into the KMT itself. Meanwhile, the regime pursued policies aimed at bringing balanced development
and prosperity to all economic sectors. It enacted a thoroughgoing land
reform that sparked sharp increases in agricultural productivity and rural incomes. It guided Taiwan's economy through decades of rapid development;
millions of Taiwanese moved into the industrial economy, many of them
as owners of small and medium-sized enterprises that powered the island's
growth. By the 1970s the KMT enjoyed broad popularity among rural voters, urban voters, working-class voters, white-collar voters, and the business
class. It also had the firm support of its so-called iron ballots (*tiepiao*)—the
public employees, military officers, and retired servicemen who made up
the core of the Mainlander minority.

The KMT redoubled its efforts to incorporate Taiwanese in the 1970s. In
1972 it adopted reforms aimed at relaxing the state's authoritarian tendencies and increasing the number and influence of Taiwanese party members.

The percentage of KMT members of Taiwanese (not Mainlander) back-ground grew from 39 percent in 1969 to 53 percent in 1977.[8] The increase was significant enough to prompt resistance from Mainlanders who "are now beginning to complain that the government's policy of increasing the appointment of Taiwanese is reducing their job prospects."[9] "Taiwaniza-tion" allowed even people who resented the central government's authori-tarian and elitist tendencies to build friendly working relationships with grassroots KMT politicians. The 1972 reforms also raised standards for KMT politicians, improved central supervision over local party branches, and explicitly recognized local elections as an "institutionalized feedback mechanism" between the party and society.[10]

In sum, by the time opposition parties came on the scene, the KMT had reinvented itself as a broad-based party that enjoyed wide support through-out Taiwanese society. From labor unions and farmers' associations to the chamber of commerce, every significant associational grouping was tied to the KMT in one way or another, leaving little room for an opposition party to mobilize particular economic sectors or geographic areas against the ruling party. Instead of dividing along socioeconomic or regional lines, therefore, Taiwan's society lined up along a cleavage that was fundamentally political.

In the 1970s there were two kinds of people in Taiwan: the kind who be-lieved the KMT's virtues outweighed its vices and the kind who believed its vices outweighed its virtues. Opposition to the KMT came from the second group, and the name they chose for their movement perfectly captured their raison d'être. They called themselves the *Dangwai*, or Non-party. The KMT was The Party, so anyone who did not identify with the KMT was welcome to identify with the *Dangwai*. Different groups adopted the term *Dangwai* at different moments—from Mainlander intellectuals in the early 1960s to independent local Taiwanese politicians in the '70s—but the meaning of the term was clear: The *Dangwai* was defined by what it was not, and what it was not was the KMT.

Resentment of the KMT mirrored an underlying cleavage in society that was itself a political by-product. The regime's most fervent detractors were individuals who had suffered under its authoritarian grip, including victims of an island-wide crackdown in 1947 that killed thousands of Taiwanese, including many students and local elites. The so-called February 28 (or 228) Incident, named after the date on which it began, was an open wound in

Taiwan society, but one that could not be mentioned for fear of White Terror–era repression. In the 1950s and '60s, thousands of Taiwanese and Mainlanders were jailed—and sometimes tortured or killed—on often-dubious charges of consorting with communists or conspiring against the regime. Those conditions left Taiwanese living overseas to be the KMT's most active antagonists. Taiwan's exile community pushed agendas far more radical than anything openly discussed on the island, including the idea of Taiwan independence.

In addition to those directly affected by KMT repression, the opposition attracted support from several quarters. At the core of the *Dangwai* were individuals who had felt the sting of KMT repression only indirectly, but who could not accept a government they saw as undemocratic and unjust. Authoritarianism was part of the problem: Even for many Mainlanders, the regime's failure to live up to the democratic promise of the ROC constitution was a grave disappointment. For Taiwanese, meanwhile, the desire for a more fully representative government dovetailed with a second, equally important, grievance.

Many Taiwanese viewed the KMT-led ROC government as an outsider regime (*wailai zhengquan*) imposed on Taiwan by the international community without regard for the preferences of the Taiwanese people. At first, most Taiwanese regarded that outcome as inevitable—not unlike the Qing dynasty's decision to turn Taiwan over to Japan in 1895—but the killings in 1947 and the subsequent White Terror turned resignation into resentment. Beneath the specific complaints lay a more fundamental grievance: The KMT regarded Taiwan as a means to an end (the survival of the ROC), not as an end in itself. Kuomintang officials were bitterly disappointed at having "lost" mainland China, and they viewed their retreat to Taiwan as a profound failure.

Taiwanese lived in the shadow of that failure and of their assumed "complicity" with a Japanese colonial regime whose masters in Tokyo had invaded and devastated China. Kuomintang leaders viewed Taiwan as a temporary refuge from which they would recover their rightful position as the rulers of all of China; they expected Taiwanese to dedicate their lives and their land to that same goal. The KMT's Mainlander leadership understood that not all Taiwanese shared their understanding of Chinese nationalism; they considered it part of their sacred duty to inculcate those feelings in the local population. Nationalistic propaganda was ubiquitous and the regime brooked no challenge to the KMT's Sino-centric vision of Taiwan's history and destiny. The KMT's authoritarian edifice was built on the idea that Taiwan's needs and interests must take a backseat to those of the ROC. Authoritarian politics, military preparation, cultural discrimination, ethnic favoritism—all were justified on the grounds that they were necessary to achieve the ROC's historic mission of recovering the mainland.

Taiwanese who resented the KMT's heavy-handed ruling style and Sino-centric ideology found a voice for their views in *Dangwai*-affiliated publications such as *The Intellectual, Apollo, The Eighties, The Journalist,* and *Formosa Magazine.* The magazines—few of which published more than a few issues before being shut down—were backed by independent-minded entrepreneurs and staffed by reformist intellectuals. They encouraged their readers to support yet another set of *Dangwai* activists: local politicians. Some of these had competed in elections as independents and jumped at the opportunity to team up with like-minded activists. Others started out in politics as KMT members but found the party insufficiently supportive of their careers. A good example of the latter group was Hsu Hsin-liang. Hsu was an up-and-coming KMT politician in Taoyuan County, but he found himself unable to advance as quickly as he had hoped and began contesting elections as an independent. Hsu saw the advantages of collective action and readily joined forces with other independents under the *Dangwai* banner.

The split between pro-KMT and anti-KMT Taiwanese is often assumed to follow the ethnic cleavage between Mainlanders and Taiwanese, but that analysis is incomplete. The activists who founded the *Dangwai* and the DPP believed that the regime's insistence on treating Taiwan as a means to its own ends violated the Taiwan people's humanity and outweighed the KMT's successes in other realms, but for most ethnic Taiwanese the benefits of living in an orderly, economically vibrant state outweighed the petty humiliations associated with single-party authoritarianism.

The deep roots the KMT had put down in Taiwanese communities over forty years of local elections enabled most voters to distinguish their local KMT politicians from the national party. As a result, the cleavage that split the KMT and DPP has never perfectly mirrored ethnic or regional divisions. The DPP's membership and leadership are overwhelmingly Taiwanese, but the KMT has always enjoyed strong support from both Mainlanders and conservative Taiwanese. Table 3.3 shows the support (defined

TABLE 3.3
Ethnicity and partisanship

Party	FATHER'S ETHNICITY		
	Hakka	Minnan	Mainlander
KMT	72	286	78
% of row	16.40%	65.15%	17.77%
% of column	72.00%	50.89%	96.30%
DPP	24	261	3
% of row	8.33%	90.63%	1.04%
% of column	24.00%	46.44%	3.70%

SOURCE: Taiwan Elections and Democratization Survey, 2008.

as "leaning toward") for parties in 2008 across different ethnic categories. Until the early 1990s, ethnicity, defined as one's father's "provincial origin," was a formal demographic category. Today, Taiwanese may choose to self-identify with a particular ethnic group, but the pattern of ethnicity and partisanship can still be measured.

Table 3.3 uses the conventional definition to measure "ethnicity": It records the respondent's father's ethnic designation as Taiwanese (in Chinese *benshengren,* or "this province") Hakka, Taiwanese Minnan, Mainlander (*waishengren,* or "other province"), or Aboriginal (the number of Aboriginal respondents in the survey was too small to be useful, so they are excluded).[11] The table, using data from 2008, reveals an interesting contrast between the two parties. Mainlanders overwhelmingly lean toward the KMT (96 percent), but they constitute fewer than 20 percent of KMT partisans. The DPP, meanwhile, relies almost entirely on Taiwanese Minnan people for its support (90 percent), but fewer than half of Taiwanese Minnan lean toward the DPP (46 percent). In fact, Taiwanese Minnan constitute majorities in *both* parties. Taiwanese Hakka, meanwhile, incline strongly toward the KMT, although not as strongly as Mainlanders. In other words, the KMT is an ethnically diverse party, while the DPP is not, and Taiwanese (both Minnan and Hakka) are diverse in their partisan leanings, while Mainlanders are not.

The split that defined Taiwan's party system in the late 1980s was not simply an ethnic cleavage.[12] Instead, the parties were divided between the KMT and its supporters, both Mainlander and Taiwanese, and those ROC citizens—nearly all ethnic Taiwanese—who could not make peace with the KMT's authoritarianism and its inability to authentically represent the Taiwanese people. In both cases, economic interests played at most a limited role; both parties counted on farmers, workers, professionals, and entrepreneurs for votes, and the DPP, in particular, survived on financial contributions from anti-KMT businessmen.

Another way to understand the division between the KMT and the DPP at the inception of Taiwan's democracy is to consider their respective goals. By the mid-1980s KMT leaders had shifted their rhetorical focus from "recovering the mainland" to "peaceful unification." Their hope was that the People's Republic of China (PRC) and the ROC would craft a political settlement that united both sides of the Taiwan Strait while preserving some vestige of the ROC state. The plan was light on detail, but unification remained the goal. At the same time, however, the KMT was genuinely committed to developing Taiwan; almost no one still believed that Taiwan's own welfare should or could be sacrificed to the unificationist project. In short, the KMT was holding on to competing goals: one ideological and rhetorical, the other practical and utilitarian. A third objective bridged those contradictory desires: the party's determination to remain in power. In fact, political survival was the imperative that drove President Chiang Ching-kuo and his successor, Lee Teng-hui, to open the political market to new parties and actors.

The DPP's founders had two fundamental goals: democratization and ethnic justice. As a practical matter, these goals overlapped: The Democratic Progressives believed that Taiwan should be governed by and for Taiwanese people, and making that happen meant removing the KMT from power. In their view, the KMT's insistence on unification predetermined Taiwan's future and denied Taiwan people the opportunity to decide their own fate. True democracy, understood as full self-determination, meant inviting the Taiwanese electorate to decide for itself whether to pursue unification. In addition, the KMT remained a disproportionately Mainlander party, especially in its leadership, and the DPP's founders were convinced that the Taiwanese people could never be truly represented by a Mainlander party. Their deepest fear was that the Mainlander leadership would sidestep the Taiwanese people altogether to cut a unification deal with the PRC.

Each party sought political power in order to implement its own vision for Taiwan. For the KMT, that meant stabilizing the political system through incremental reforms. For the DPP, it meant achieving full democracy and self-determination. Almost immediately, though, those visions began to converge. When Chiang Ching-kuo died and conservatives within the KMT challenged Taiwan-born Lee Teng-hui's bona fides as their leader, Lee doubled down on political reform.

To avoid being captured and controlled by a small but powerful Mainlander elite, Lee unleashed Taiwan's electorate. In the first five years of his presidency he rolled out one democratic reform after another. In 1990 he hosted a National Affairs Conference that brought together political parties, civil society, economic groups, and intellectuals to demonstrate the broad social consensus behind the reform process. Every year of his presidency brought new firsts—first comprehensive election of the National Assembly, first comprehensive legislative election, first direct election of the provincial governor, and then, in 1996, the first direct presidential election in ROC history.

Lee Teng-hui's presidency handed the DPP a string of policy victories, but, ironically, his "generosity" to the Democratic Progressives undermined their political appeal. As the successor to the *Dangwai*, the DPP expected to own the issue of democratization, but Lee—who had the authority to make reforms happen—usurped their signature issue. Political scientists distinguish between positional issues—issues on which there is real disagreement—and valence issues—those about which nearly all voters agree. By expanding political competition beyond KMT insiders, thereby marginalizing the anti-reform conservatives, Lee transformed democratization from a positional issue to a valence issue. That forced the DPP to come up with a new positional issue to differentiate itself from the KMT.

The new issue emerged organically out of the DPP's earlier agenda, but it represented a real and consequential shift. Democracy and ethnic justice had been the party's founding demands, so President Lee's speedy implementation of democratic reforms left identity politics as the DPP's obvious choice for a new positional issue. Identity politics had much to recommend it—it was an emotional issue for many Taiwanese, one that charismatic DPP politicians were good at mobilizing—but it carried risks, too. For one thing, identity politics could easily shade into ethnic politics, and in particular a form of ethnic chauvinism that excluded and offended not only Mainlanders, but also Taiwan's long-standing minorities—the aboriginal and Hakka peoples, too. Also, identity politics activated a line of argument that ended in a dangerous place: support for Taiwan independence.

Advocates of formal, juridical independence viewed democratization and independence as two sides of a single coin. In their view, because the majority of voters in Taiwan did not share the conservative Mainlanders' devotion to unification, a democratic Taiwan inevitably would vote the KMT out of office. With the KMT out of office and Taiwanese in command, unification would have no support, and Taiwan naturally would become independent. The inverse logic was also widely embraced in DPP circles: Because the KMT used the imperative for unification—the need to preserve the ROC state as a government for all China—to justify its restrictions on Taiwan's democracy, abandoning unification—making Taiwan independent—would remove the last obstacle to democracy. In short, one way or another, democracy would bring down the KMT, and the fall of the KMT would end Taiwan's commitment to unification, opening the door for an independent Taiwan.

When the DPP was founded in 1986, Chiang Ching-kuo implied that he could tolerate the party so long as it eschewed two taboos: Taiwan independence and communism. For several years the Democratic Progressives complied with that demand. After martial law was lifted, the marketplace for ideas expanded rapidly, and by 1990, even the independence taboo was gone. In 1991 the government stopped enforcing the blacklist that had kept Taiwan Independence Movement activists out of the country, prompting an influx of pro-independence figures. These independence activists had spent decades overseas developing the case for independence; they did not share the homegrown activists' timidity about the issue, and they pressed the DPP to embrace independence.

Independence was not an easy sell, even in the DPP. Many Democratic Progressives were gun-shy after years of repression. Others were not convinced that independence would be a winning issue politically. But the passion of the independence activists, both returned-from-exile and homegrown, and the need to find an issue on which to differentiate the DPP from Lee Teng-hui's reformist KMT won the day. In 1991 the Democratic Progressives inserted in their party platform a plank supporting juridical independence for Taiwan.

The decision to endorse independence had far-reaching and costly consequences for the DPP. The party campaigned on a strong pro-independence platform only twice, in 1991 and in the 1996 presidential election, and in both cases the results were dismal. Making Taiwan the subject of its own story—as opposed to an object in Chinese history—was a popular cause, but declaring independence was not. Not only was it anathema to the KMT, but also it was a casus belli for the PRC as well. Most Taiwanese voters were unwilling to take that risk. For almost two decades the DPP has struggled to rebrand itself as a party that puts Taiwan first, but not to the point of choosing independence at all costs. It has not yet fully succeeded.

The DPP's endorsement of independence eased the KMT's burden, at least temporarily, because it allowed Lee to move his own party away from unification. In the early 1990s, Lee balanced pro-unification gestures with diplomatic tactics aimed at securing international support for Taiwan's autonomy. At the same time, Lee was redefining Taiwanese identity to accommodate all the island's ethnic communities. Lee developed his "New Taiwanese" concept to naturalize Mainlanders as people of Taiwan, and he declared that everyone living on the island shared a common fate. These ideas narrowed the distance between the DPP and the KMT, but the DPP's association with formal independence and the KMT's continued image as a pro-unification party prevented the parties' images from collapsing into one another entirely. In Dafydd Fell's words, the parties followed a path of "moderate differentiation."[13]

After 1996, the unification/independence issue itself became a valence issue, in the sense that both the political parties and the electorate preferred a centrist position—preserving the status quo—to either independence or unification. After the PRC's hostile reaction to Taiwan's first direct presidential election, Lee Teng-hui talked more about Taiwan's community of shared fate and less about unification. In 1999 he infuriated Beijing by describing the relationship between Taiwan and the PRC as a "special state-to-state relationship." At the same time, the DPP was putting distance between itself and the pro-independence camp. In 1999 it adopted a resolution that stated, "Taiwan is a sovereign and independent country. . . . Taiwan, although named the Republic of China under its current constitution, is not subject to the jurisdiction of the People's Republic of China."[14] The resolution showed the DPP's willingness to accept the status quo: autonomy under the ROC label. For die-hard independence activists, surrendering the idea of a Republic of Taiwan was a significant concession.

The parties' retreat from strong positions made sense in light of public opinion. As Figure 3.1 shows, few Taiwanese then or now favor immediate independence or immediate unification; most prefer some variant of the status quo (see also Table 3.4). What they want, in other words, is for

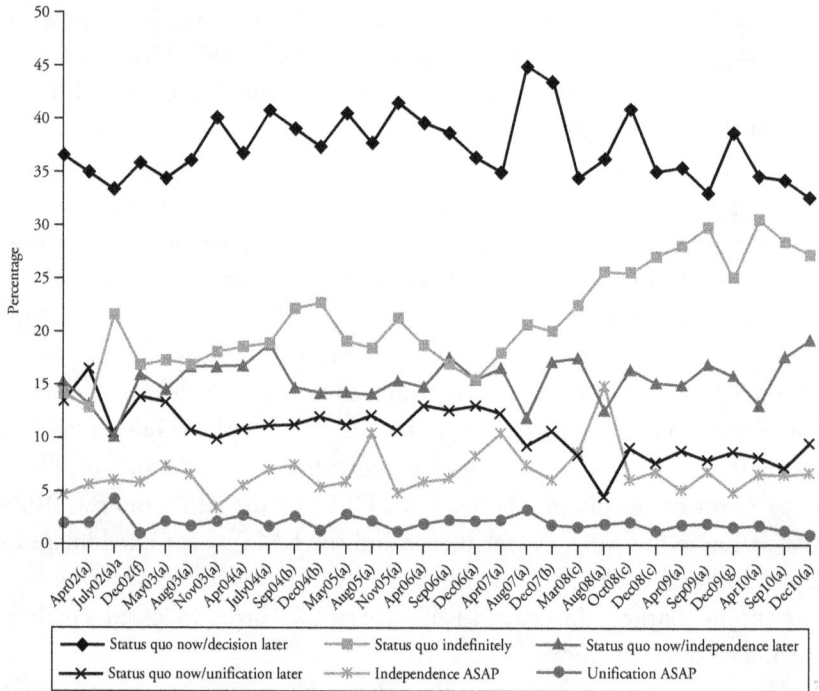

FIGURE 3.1 Support for independence or unification

SOURCES: (a) Election Study Center, National Chengchi University; (b) Burke Marketing Research, Ltd.; (c) China Credit Information Service, Ltd.; (d) Center for Public Opinion and Election Studies, National Sun Yat-Sen University; (e) Survey and Opinion Research Group, Dept. of Political Science, National Chung-cheng University; (f) e-Society Research Group, Taipei; and (g) Center for Public Opinion and Public Policy, Taipei Municipal University of Education.

NOTE: Survey respondents were Taiwanese adults aged 20–69 who were accessible to telephone interviewers.

Taiwan to remain as it is: autonomous and separate, but free of conflict with the PRC. For the KMT, unification was an electoral liability it could shed once the conservatives had been marginalized and the PRC had demonstrated its hostility. For the DPP, the association with independence was harder to shake, in part because many Democratic Progressives continued (and continue today) to hope that an opportunity for full independence may yet arise.

With Taiwanese in broad agreement on the desirability of the status quo, the positional issue differentiating the parties narrowed even further. Since 2000, party competition in Taiwan has been driven largely by a disagreement over how best to manage relations with the mainland so as to preserve the status quo. The KMT tends to stress the economic opportunities offered

TABLE 3.4

Two measures of national identity

	INDEPENDENCE VERSUS UNIFICATION					
Self-identification	Immediate unification	Status quo, unification later	Status quo, decide later	Status quo forever	Status quo, independence later	Immediate independence
Taiwanese	6	34	172	119	124	70
% of row	1.14	6.48	32.76	22.67	23.62	13.33
% of column	20.69	24.11	40.95	45.95	80	89.74
Both	17	87	242	124	29	7
% of row	3.36	17.19	47.83	24.51	5.73	1.38
% of column	58.62	61.7	57.62	47.88	18.71	8.97
Chinese	6	20	6	16	2	1
% of row	11.76	39.22	11.76	31.37	3.92	1.96
% of column	20.69	14.18	1.43	6.18	1.29	1.28

SOURCE: Taiwan Elections and Democratization Survey, 2008.

NOTE: Chi-square score = 213.5119, p = .000.

by engagement with the mainland and downplay the possibility that the PRC might use economic and political leverage to coerce Taiwan. The DPP, for its part, acknowledges the benefits of engagement but emphasizes the economic and political risks of relying too heavily on the PRC.

The two parties' concrete policy proposals are similar but not identical. The KMT insists that engaging the PRC reduces political and military tensions and improves Taiwan's economic situation. The KMT politicians also argue that only the PRC can ease Taiwan's international isolation. They acknowledge that too much intertwinement with the PRC could reduce the island's freedom of action, but they believe that wise leaders in Taiwan can manage that vulnerability. The policies they propose, therefore, favor increasingly open interactions with the mainland. They emphasize economic cooperation, but they do not rule out the possibility of talking with the PRC about political topics. For example, in 2005 the KMT and Chinese Communist Party agreed that it was in both sides' interest to negotiate a peace agreement, although the KMT has dragged its feet on that initiative. The DPP, for its part, understands that Taiwan's economy is far too deeply entangled with the PRC's to be separated. At the same time, however, DPP politicians and supporters believe that Beijing's determination to absorb

Taiwan is still strong, so they prefer policies that diversify Taiwan's economic and political relationships and minimize its dependence on the mainland.

National Identity and Partisanship

While specific policy differences between the KMT and the DPP have changed over time, the dividing lines between the parties in the twenty-first century are direct lineal descendants of the original points of differentiation. In other words, the conflicting worldviews that undergird the parties have evolved, but not ruptured, since the onset of democratic elections in the mid-1980s. Political scientists have put considerable effort into defining, naming, and measuring the difference in those worldviews, but the cleavage is hard to specify. There is an ethnic component to it, but it is not merely an ethnic cleavage. Education matters (KMT supporters tend to have more of it), but it is far from determinative. It has a regional element (the DPP does much better in the south than in the north), but parties are not regionally based (political geography reflects the regional distribution of other preferences, not regional interests). It also has a policy element—unification supporters vote for the KMT, independence supporters vote for the DPP—but policy alone cannot capture it, because most Taiwanese do not prefer independence *or* unification, and those voters (typically identified as supporters of the status quo) can be found in *both* parties.

Researchers have labeled the cleavage "national identity," but this solution raises new problems of definition and measurement. According to Anthony Smith, national identity is "the continuous reproduction and reinterpretation by the members of a national community of the pattern of symbols, values, myths, memories and traditions that compose the distinctive heritage of nations, and the variable identification of individual members of that community with that heritage and its cultural elements."[15] By this definition, national identity is an *action*, not a state of being, but Smith's subsequent descriptive statement that national identity "sums up the members' perceptions of difference and distinctiveness vis-à-vis other national communities and their members" at least suggests the possibility of measurement, although it hardly makes the task look easy.[16]

Smith's definition rests on another problematic concept: the nation. He defines the nation as "a named human community residing in a perceived homeland, and having common myths and a shared history, a distinct public culture, and common laws and customs for all members" and "a felt and lived community whose members share a homeland and a culture."[17] To differentiate a nation from an ethnic community Smith further stipulates that a human community "must reside in a perceived homeland of its own, at least for a long period of time, in order to constitute itself as a nation; and to aspire to nationhood and be recognized as a nation, it also needs to evolve a public culture and desire some degree of self-determination."[18]

Smith's definitions are appropriate to the study of Taiwan because they differentiate between the nation, which may merely *aspire* to recognition, and the national state, which must possess recognized sovereignty. Taiwan's status as a national state is a matter of contention, and those who would claim that it is a national state are probably in the minority, even among scholars. But there is strong momentum behind the idea that Taiwan is a nation as Smith defines it, and, therefore, that Taiwan's national identity is a meaningful object of study.

The study of Taiwan's national identity did not emerge from scholars' decisions to apply and explore a particular conceptual framework in a particular case. Instead, studies of national identity in Taiwan are motivated by an empirical reality: There is a difference of opinion among Taiwan residents about their island's relationship to mainland China. As a policy matter, the debate is over whether Taiwan should be separate from or unified with mainland China. At a more philosophical level, the debate is over whether Taiwan is obligated in any meaningful way to a Chinese national entity, be it in the past, present, or future. It is this objective, observable difference of opinion about Taiwan's status relative to China that has led scholars to seek an explanation for Taiwan politics through the concept of "national identity."

In approaching this problem, scholars have been particularly keen to quantify national identity. They are motivated by their desire to observe, measure, and track national identity trends over time and to use those trends to anticipate future developments. They also want to quantify national identity so they can use it as an independent and dependent variable in explanatory arguments. In their effort to measure the phenomenon, political scientists have gravitated toward two measures of national identity:

- A subjective feeling of membership/identification with Taiwan as a "nation"; and
- A preference regarding Taiwan's relationship with and status relative to the Chinese nation.

The first measure, which comes closest to Smith's definitions, is typically operationalized using a deceptively simple question: "Are you (or do you think of yourself as) Taiwanese, Chinese, or both?" As a scheme for measuring national identity, this procedure rests on a problematic assumption: When respondents say they think of themselves as Taiwanese, they understand Taiwan to be a nation. The possibility that "Taiwanese" might carry a different meaning—one closer to Smith's ethnic community—is not taken into account. For that reason, the descriptive inferences taken from such a survey (e.g., 48.5 percent of respondents in the 2008 Taiwan Election and Democracy Survey [TEDS] possess a Taiwanese *national* identity) might not be valid. The emotional identification with Taiwan that is conveyed when a respondent chooses "Taiwanese only" often does not align with a preference for an independent Taiwanese state, as Table 3.4 illustrates.

That is not a contradictory finding; after all, many nations lack states, and the decision to seek national state status is often fraught and contingent. If it *is* a nation, Taiwan is hardly the first to shy away from seeking formal independence because the costs of doing so are high. The problem is not inconsistent or irrational respondents, it is the inability of the survey to differentiate between respondents for whom the gap between survey designer and survey taker is conceptual (the respondent is not thinking of Taiwan as a nation but identifies as Taiwanese nonetheless) and those who understand the question as it was intended but give pragmatic responses (the respondent sees Taiwan as a nation but is unwilling to incur the costs of pursuing national state status).

The second approach to measuring national identity is to focus not on respondents' feeling of membership in a particular group, but on their preference for a particular outcome in cross-strait relations. In this measurement scheme, respondents are asked some variation of this question: Do you prefer independence or unification? By directly measuring the respondents' enthusiasm for establishing a national state in Taiwan, this approach separates national identity from ethnic identity. But support for independence is a problematic way to define national identity, because there are many people who "feel Taiwanese"—and may even believe Taiwan is a nation—who nonetheless shrink from supporting formal independence. The assumption of a binary choice may make sense to political scientists socialized to believe that sovereignty is an all-or-nothing proposition, but simply dismissing respondents who reject this binary as incoherent or confused is not informative.

A less-dogged community of political scientists might have given up on the idea of measuring Taiwan national identity altogether, but for those who are interested in this question, surrender is not an option. To begin with, the fact that something is hard to measure does not mean it does not exist, and it is abundantly obvious to all that whether you call it Taiwan consciousness or identity or subjectivity or something else, a phenomenon exists, and it is important. And as Tables 3.5 and 3.6 show, by either measure, "national identity" is related closely, although not perfectly, to partisanship.

The most persistent and creative students of Taiwan national identity have developed more-sophisticated survey techniques designed to separate respondents' guts from their heads. One technique, pioneered by Wu Nai-teh, uses conditional statements to get at respondents' "true preferences" between unification and independence. This conditional approach asks, in essence, "If independence could be achieved peacefully, would you support it" and "If Taiwan and the mainland had the same political, social, and economic systems, would you support unification?" This is certainly a better approach than demanding that respondents choose between independence and unification, but it yields a surprising number of respondents whose answers—yes to both questions, or no to both questions—leave the underlying issue of national identity ambiguous. In the 2008 TEDS survey, for example, 62 percent of respondents either agreed or strongly agreed with

TABLE 3.5
Self-identification and party preference

	SELF-IDENTIFICATION		
	Taiwanese	Both	Chinese
KMT	111	293	34
	25.34%	66.89%	7.76%
DPP	224	56	6
	78.32%	19.58%	2.10%
NP	4	11	1
	25.00%	68.75%	6.25%
TSU	9	2	0
	81.82%	18.18%	0.00%

SOURCE: Taiwan Elections and Democratization Survey, 2008.
NOTE: Chi-square score = 205.0871, p = .000.

TABLE 3.6
Unification–independence preference and party preference

	Immediate unification	Status quo, unification later	Status quo, decide later	Status quo forever	Status quo, independence later	Immediate independence
KMT	17	86	190	117	19	4
	3.93%	19.86%	43.88%	27.02%	4.39%	0.92%
DPP	4	18	78	43	87	44
	1.46%	6.57%	28.47%	15.69%	31.75%	16.06%
NP	1	3	7	4	1	0
	6.25%	18.75%	43.75%	25.00%	6.25%	0.00%
PFP	0	0	1	0	0	0
	0.00%	0.00%	100.00%	0.00%	0.00%	0.00%
TSU	0	1	2	1	5	2
	0.00%	9.09%	18.18%	9.09%	45.45%	18.18%

SOURCE: Taiwan Elections and Democratization Survey, 2008.
NOTE: Chi-square score = 205.0871, p = .000.

the pro-independence statement, while 38 percent agreed or strongly agreed with the pro-unification statement. Twenty-four percent agreed or strongly agreed with *both* statements, and 20 percent (the die-hard status quo extremists?) disagreed with both statements (see Table 3.7).

None of these measurement schemes perfectly captures the dividing line between the DPP and the KMT, but studies show that national identity measured by any of these methods consistently outperforms other variables in explaining individuals' preferences between the two parties. The fact that a voter's preference for independence versus unification explains his or her preference between a pro-independence and a pro-unification party may seem too circular to be helpful, but the persistence of this association even after the parties retreated from strong positions on unification and independence suggests that national identity is an enduring cleavage, and the unification/independence question "gets at" that cleavage. In short, while supporters of both political parties prefer to maintain the status quo in cross-strait relations, DPP supporters today share their predecessors' preference for treating Taiwan as distinctive and central, while KMT supporters are more inclined to emphasize the ways in which Taiwan is connected to China (even if they are not interested in making it part of the PRC).

TABLE 3.7
Conditional preferences for unification versus independence

"If, after declaring independence, Taiwan could maintain peaceful relations with the PRC, then Taiwan should establish a new, independent country."	"If the economic, social, and political conditions were about the same in both the mainland and Taiwan, then the two sides should unify."				
	Strongly agree	Agree	Disagree	Strongly disagree	**Row total**
Strongly agree	1.25%	3.61%	5.96%	3.45%	**14.26%**
	(8)	(23)	(38)	(22)	**(91)**
Agree	0.78%	18.18%	26.33%	2.04%	**47.34%**
	(5)	(116)	(168)	(13)	**(302)**
Disagree	0.94%	12.70%	15.52%	0.94%	**30.09%**
	(6)	(81)	(99)	(6)	**(192)**
Strongly disagree	0.94%	3.76%	2.19%	1.41%	**8.31%**
	(6)	(24)	(14)	(9)	**(53)**
Column total	**3.92%**	**38.24%**	**50.00%**	**7.84%**	
	(25)	**(244)**	**(319)**	**(50)**	**(638)**

SOURCE: Taiwan Elections and Democratization Survey (TEDS), 2008.

NOTE: Numbers in parentheses indicate the amount of respondents falling into each cell of the table. Percentages represent the proportion of the entire sample falling into each cell.

Summary and Implications

In the late 1980s, Taiwanese were offered the choice between an authoritarian-leaning, Mainlander-dominated KMT and a pro-democracy, Taiwanese-dominated DPP. The KMT did surprisingly well in those early elections, but its leaders—especially Lee Teng-hui—recognized that those qualities would not serve it well in the long run. Before long, the KMT morphed into a democratic, Taiwan-identified—albeit conservative—party. In the process, it took one of the founding issues of the party system— democratization—off the agenda. To maintain its distinctiveness, the DPP stressed another, closely related issue: "Taiwan for the Taiwanese." Those early interactions established the two parties' identities and divided the electorate. The KMT attracted the many Taiwanese who valued stability above other goals, while the DPP appealed to those who were willing to shake things up in order to build what they viewed as a more just society and polity.

Both the KMT and DPP have tried at various times to introduce other issues—including economic, social welfare, and foreign policy initiatives—

but positioning Taiwan relative to the PRC remains the dominant issue and point of differentiation between the two parties. In the 1990s the issue was couched in terms of independence and unification; two decades later it is expressed as a debate between advocates and skeptics of engagement and integration with mainland China. But while the specific policy questions under debate have changed, the underlying cleavage they activate has not: Taiwanese who believe the island would be better off without KMT leadership and all that it represents—including, fundamentally, a Chinese identity for Taiwan—support the DPP. Taiwanese who believe that the KMT's record of bringing political stability and economic prosperity is ultimately more important than identity politics tend to vote for the KMT. The Taiwan case supports Zielinski's argument: A cleavage that was activated and politicized at the onset of democratization ended up defining the political competition that ensued.

There is little space in this cleavage structure for minor parties. The New Party appealed to conservative Mainlanders (*waishengren*), but their numbers were too few to sustain a political party, and even at the height of the NP's popularity, most Mainlanders continued to support the KMT. The Taiwan Independence Party (TAIP) and TSU both hoped to mobilize the hard-core pro-independence supporters, but this group, too, proved too small to constitute a significant presence in politics. For most independence enthusiasts, an imperfect DPP is still preferable to an impotent TAIP or TSU. As for Taiwan's most successful minor party, the PFP, it formed around a personality, not a social cleavage. It is hardly surprising that it folded back into the KMT when the political potency of its leader, James Soong, dwindled. After Taiwan adopted a majoritarian electoral system for its national legislature, the opportunities for small parties were more limited than ever.

The way the "national identity" cleavage structures partisanship in Taiwan has important policy consequences. Above all, it has made it difficult for Taiwan to address domestic problems effectively because it continually projects policy debates onto cross-strait relations. For example, Taiwan occupies an extremely important position in the global economy; it plays a critical role in some of the world's most profitable supply chains. But its domestic market is relatively small, so its continued economic relevance rests on constant upgrading. Maintaining its position at the cutting edge of technical innovation and manufacturing competitiveness thus is a huge challenge for Taiwan's policy makers. Nonetheless, most debates about economic policy in Taiwan's political arena focus on the PRC and cross-strait economic relations. It is exceedingly difficult to get Taiwanese to see beyond the Strait, to recognize the global nature of their economic predicament. Nor is economic policy the only realm in which the national identity cleavage refracts the policy process in unhelpful ways. Displacing policy debates onto the cross-strait issue constructs pragmatic policy decisions as ideological battles for the heart and soul of Taiwan and further pressurizes Taipei's relationship with Beijing. Unfortunately, however, the consolidation of the island's two-party system means these trends are likely to persist well into the future.

Notes

1. The seminal work in this literature is by Maurice Duverger. See Maurice Duverger, *Political Parties: Their Organization and Activity in the Modern State* (New York: Wiley, 1963) [Translated by Barbara and Robert North].

2. Jakub Zielinski, "Translating Social Cleavages into Party Systems: The Significance of New Democracies." *World Politics* 54:2 (2002), 201.

3. Because the DPP was not formally registered until 1987, the 1986 legislative ballot did not list a party affiliation for the DPP's nominees. A predecessor organization, the *Dangwai*, or "Non-Party," had organized candidate slates in previous elections, but they were not formally acknowledged either.

4. Gary W. Cox, "SNTV and 'd'Hondt' Are Equivalent." *Electoral Studies* 10:2 (1991).

5. The National Assembly existed to amend the constitution and elect the president. After Taiwan instituted direct presidential elections in 1996, most Taiwanese began to see the Assembly as anachronistic and wasteful, and it was effectively disbanded in 2005.

6. "Taiwan Ends 4 Decades of Martial Law," *New York Times*, July 15, 1987, www.nytimes.com/1987/07/15/world/taiwan-ends-4-decades-of-martial-law.html.

7. *The Kuomintang Manifesto and Platform Adopted by the Seventh National Convention, October 1952* (Taipei: China Cultural Service, 1954), 33.

8. Teh-fu Huang, "Elections and the Evolution of the Kuomintang," in *Taiwan's Electoral Politics and Democratic Transition*, ed. Hung-mao Tien (Armonk, NY: M. E. Sharpe, Inc., 1996), 115.

9. Ralph Clough, *Island China* (Cambridge, MA: Harvard University Press, 1978), 63.

10. Bruce Dickson, "The Kuomintang before Democratization: Organizational Change and the Role of Elections," in *Taiwan's Electoral Politics and Democratic Transition*, ed. Hung-mao Tien (Armonk, NY: M. E. Sharpe, Inc., 1996), 58.

11. The table also excludes respondents leaning toward the NP, PFP, and TSU; all had too few supporters to yield meaningful results. Interestingly, the number of nonresponses to the ethnicity question was very small; virtually every respondent reported an ethnic category for his/her father.

12. Taiwanese Minnan support for the KMT was even stronger in the early years of Taiwan's democracy than it is today, as overall preference for the DPP has risen from less than 15 percent of survey respondents in the early to mid-1990s, to over 25 percent in the most recent surveys.

13. Dafydd Fell, *Party Politics in Taiwan: Party Change and the Democratic Evolution of Taiwan, 1991–2004* (New York: Routledge, 2005).

14. "Resolution of the Democratic Progressive Party," National Congress, May 8, 1999.

15. Anthony Smith, *Nationalism: Theory, Ideology, History*, 2nd ed. (Cambridge, UK: Polity Press, 2010), 20.

16. Ibid.

17. Ibid., 12–13.

18. Ibid., 13.

PART THREE

New Media and the Transformation of Politics

FOUR

Digital Media and the Transformation of Politics in Korea

Minjeong Kim and Han Woo Park

Introduction

New communication technologies have long been considered transformational to politics by reshaping political communication. The advent of television, for one, begot the optimistic view that television would inform and stimulate the political interests of the public. The late and former CBS president Frank Stanton, who organized the 1960 Kennedy-Nixon televised presidential debates that signaled the arrival of television as "a dominant force in presidential politics,"[1] once said: "Television, with its penetration, its wide geographic distribution and impact, provides a new, direct and sensitive link between Washington and the people."[2]

Digital technology is no exception. Numerous commentators and scholars have praised and documented the potential and power of digital media—ranging from websites through blogs to social networking sites/ services (SNSs)—to bring changes to political deliberation and participation. Specifically, as well summarized by Nisbelt and Scheufele, scholars enthusiastic about the Internet's ability to promote civic engagement argue: "the Internet will lead to new forms of campaign participation and to direct democracy, with a vast potential to reach young, isolated, and minority citizens; reduce communication or transaction costs; provide direct links to policy makers; and reduce barriers to campaign participation by leveling financial hurdles and expanding opportunities for political deliberation and debate."[3] Conversely, both "cyber-skeptics" and "reinforcement theorists" contend that the Internet either will not change much or will strengthen the status quo of political communication.[4]

However, now it seems almost pointless to ask if digital media have transformed or are transforming politics. In one of the earlier books examining online politics, Cornfield wrote that if forecasters—who predicted that the Internet [would spur] great changes at a dizzying pace—made a mistake in the 1990s, it was "one of proportion, not direction."[5] Similarly, Chadwick started his book, a comprehensive overview of Internet politics, by setting the tone as follows: "The issue is no longer whether politics is online, but *in what form and with what consequences?*"[6]

South Korea (Korea, hereinafter), one of the most well-connected countries in the world, provides leading cases showing the transformation of politics in the digital age. In addition, Korea has fully embraced the Internet in the realm of politics,[7] similar to Taiwan that has been undergoing rapid informatization in a wide range of public services. Both Korea and Taiwan have a relatively short journey in democracy—so that the openness of political regime and broad participation in procedural terms may not necessarily bring about sound outcomes in the two countries.

This chapter gives an overview of recent Korean examples and past Korean research to delineate the changes digital media bring to how Koreans engage in and think about politics. Before documenting the impact of digital media on the transformation of Korean politics, the next section reviews the literature on digital media and political communication. Next, we review Internet penetration and usage in Korea. Against the backdrop of this knowledge, we examine the relationship between digital media and the transformation of politics in Korea in the following three parts: (1) digital media as an alternative source of political information, covering issues ignored by the traditional mainstream media; (2) e-campaigning by Korean parties and politicians; and (3) e-mobilization by Korean civil society. The chapter concludes with some final thoughts.

Theoretical Framework: Media and Political Communication

Digital technology has caused various changes throughout society including politics. Specifically, digital media have brought changes to publicity patterns of election campaigning among politicians; have innovated how politicians communicate with the public; and have encouraged the public to participate in politics. Numerous political talks have been produced in real time through SNSs. To tackle the relationship between digital media and the transformation of politics, this section briefly examines major concepts and past research in the following three areas of political communication: (1) digital media as a source of political information, (2) digital media and political deliberation, and (3) digital media and political participation.

DIGITAL MEDIA AS A SOURCE OF POLITICAL INFORMATION

Communication researchers contend that news media including the Internet have positive impacts on political participation. For instance, McLeod, Scheufele, and Moy found that newspaper readership plays a strong role in conventional acts of local political participation.[8] Norris found that viewing televised news and public affairs programming is positively related to various forms of participatory behaviors.[9] Dhavan et al. found empirical support that both online information seeking and interactive civic messaging strongly influence civic engagement, often more so than do traditional print and broadcast media.[10]

However, news media use is considered to have a mediating effect, in that the impacts of news media consumption on civic engagement are indirect, influencing political participation through their effects on political knowledge and political efficacy. Moreover, media use alone may not be enough to increase civil engagement. In other words, the impact of media use on a person's understanding of politics and participation in politics is considered highest when the person gets relevant political information from mass media and also talks about it with other people.[11] This interplay between news media consumption, interpersonal discussion, and political empowerment is closely related to the concept of social capital.

Although the term "social capital" has been used in multiple disciplines since its first occurrence in 1916,[12] in recent times Robert Putnam's work[13] has been most influential. Putnam defines social capital as "the features of social organization such as networks, norms, and trust that facilitate coordination and co-operation for mutual benefit."[14] In *Bowling Alone*, Putnam noted the decline in civic participation in the United States and attributed this decline to new individualized ways of spending leisure time, such as television viewing. Putnam contended that an aggregate decline in membership in traditional social organizations is detrimental to democracy. For example, bowling alone, as opposed to bowling in leagues, does not enhance political awareness and efficacy because people do not engage in social interaction and civic discussion.

If watching television at home—consuming mainly soft news and entertainment—lowers civic participation, it can be argued that using interactive online media, especially SNSs that allow people to share their political opinions and concerns with others, is positively related to the increase of social capital and civic participation. Indeed, many scholars have noted the potential of digital media to contribute to deliberate democracy.

DIGITAL MEDIA AND POLITICAL DELIBERATION:
THE NETWORKED PUBLIC SPHERE

The role of communication in deliberative democracy is emphasized through the concept of the public sphere. The ideals of rational self-government and democratic participation are based on the principle that citizens gather together and discuss societal issues. A public sphere can be understood as a communicative space in society that permits the circulation of information, ideas, debates, and public opinion.[15]

Yochai Benkler, among others, noted the emergence of a networked public sphere, consisting of "universal intake and the potential for bottom-up agenda setting, filtering for potential political relevance (issue salience) and accreditation (credibility), synthesis of public opinion, and independence from governmental control."[16] Such a networked public sphere, Benkler asserts, is more democratic than a public sphere mediated by the mass media.[17] Similarly, Gimmler expressed optimistic views on the potential of the Internet to enable the uncoerced communication of equal participants with equal access and equal rights to intervene or propose themes.[18]

However, the downside of the networked public sphere has also been observed. For instance, while online anonymity can be liberating to enable citizens to express their dissenting opinions or unpopular ideas without the fear of reprisal,[19] false rumors and unverified facts can proliferate under the cloak of online anonymity, due to the lack of accountability. Cass Sunstein pointed out that online discourses are fragmented and polarized.[20] He argued that online users—instead of being exposed to a wide range of opinions, some of which might differ from their own—are increasingly consuming information that fits their viewpoints and interests, and are interacting largely with like-minded people. As a result, Sunstein contended that the Internet could be detrimental to the possibility of common discourse in a public sphere.

DIGITAL MEDIA AND POLITICAL PARTICIPATION

Questioning Putnam's conclusion about the decline of civic participation in the United States, scholars like Dalton argued that the nature of political participation is changing in advanced industrial societies[21]: While traditional forms of political participation in elections and campaigns are declining, alternative forms, such as protests, citizen action groups, and policy-oriented forms, are increasing.[22]

In a similar vein, Bennett, Wells, and Rank identified changes in youth civil orientation across the postindustrial democracies. In the digital age, younger citizens are becoming "actualizing citizens" who have a weak sense of duty to participate in politics in conventional ways and are more inclined to embrace issues that connect to lifestyle values, ranging from moral concerns to environmental quality.[23]

Internet Penetration and Usage in Korea

Korea's Internet originates from the System Development Network (SDN) established in 1982.[24] The SDN was a network between the Seoul National University and the Korea Institute of Electronic Technology. In 1994, commercial Internet service providers such as Korea Telecom and LG Dacom started their services; and in 1998, a commercial broadband Internet service called Korea Thrunet emerged in the market. In 1999, the number of Internet users in Korea exceeded ten million, more than 20 percent of the population at the time.

Korea is one of the most well-connected countries in the world. In 2001, Korea ranked first in the world in broadband networks, and Korean Internet users exceeded twenty million, doubling in two years from 1999. In 2002, Korea ranked first in the world in terms of broadband Internet penetration, with more than ten million households subscribing. In 2009, Korea was the second highest-ranked country by the ICT Development Index developed by the International Telecommunication Union; and in 2010, Korea ranked first on the U.N. E-Government Development Index and E-Participation Index. In addition, smartphone subscribers exceeded seven million in 2010. According to the 2010 world Internet statistics, as Figure 4.1 shows, Korea ranked fifth among Organisation for Economic Co-operation and Development countries in percentage of broadband subscribers, with 34 subscribers per 100 inhabitants.

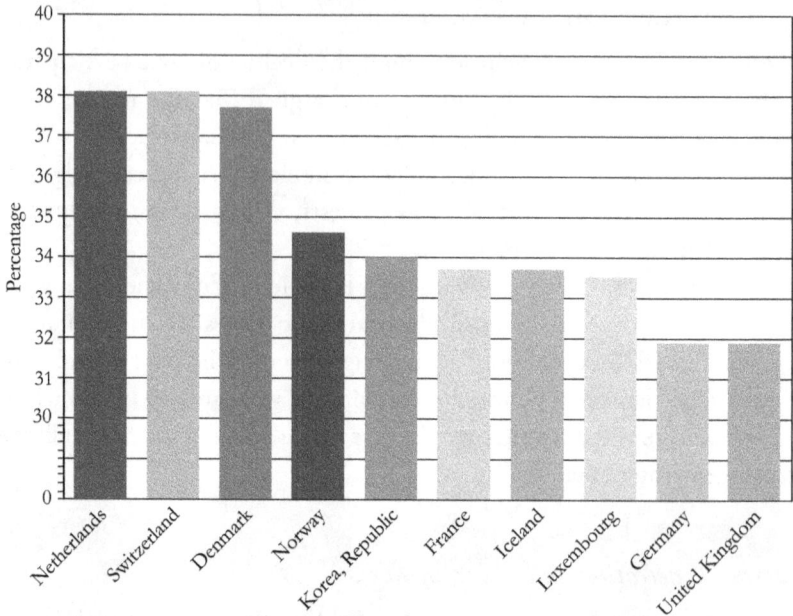

FIGURE 4.1 Top ten countries with the highest percentage of broadband subscribers
SOURCE: Korea Internet Security Agency (hereafter, KISA), *World Internet Statistics*, www.kisa.or.kr/eng/internet information/wis.jsp.

According to a 2011 survey, the number of Internet users who had used the Internet at least once in the last month was estimated at 78 percent of the total population aged three and over.[25] Figure 4.2 shows the changes in Internet usage over time including the year 2011. Among Internet users, males account for slightly over a half (53.7 percent) of users. By age group, almost 100 percent of teens and those in their twenties and thirties use the Internet (Figure 4.3).

By occupation, the Internet usage rates are highest for students (99.9 percent), office workers (99.8 percent), and professionals/managers (99.7 percent). In contrast, only 56.4 percent of production workers and 66.3 percent of stay-at-home housewives use the Internet.

The Korea Internet and Security Agency 2011 survey also found: (1) Koreans spend an average of 15.4 hours a week on the Internet; (2) about half (51.8 percent) of Internet users access the Internet "anywhere" with their wireless devices such as smartphones, which was more than a 10 percent

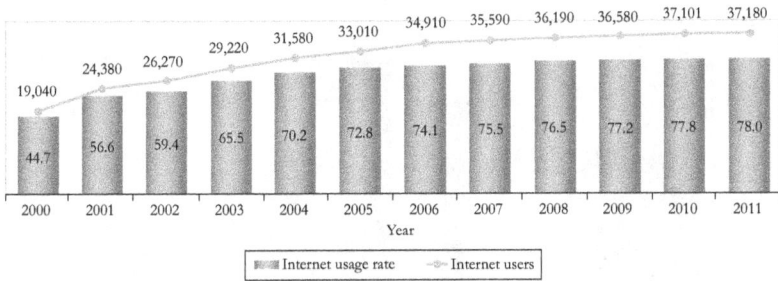

FIGURE 4.2 Trends in Internet usage rate (%) and Internet users (in thousands)
SOURCE: KISA, *2011 Survey on the Internet Usage*, http://isis.kisa.or.kr/eng/board/index.jsp?pageId=040100&bbs
Id=10&itemId=317&pageIndex=1.

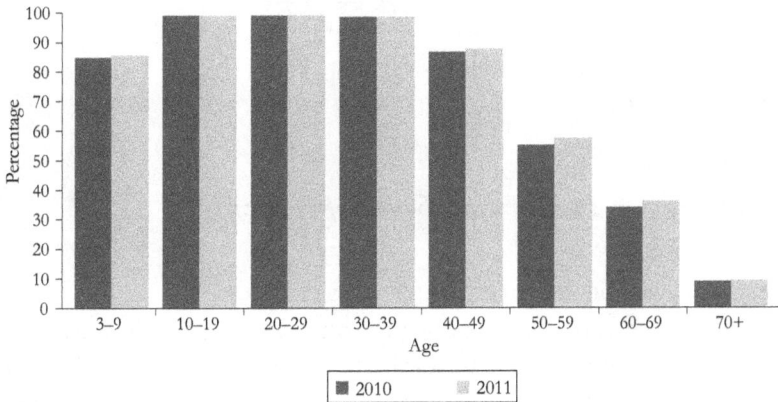

FIGURE 4.3 Internet usage rate by age
SOURCE: KISA, *2011 Survey on the Internet Usage*, http://isis.kisa.or.kr/eng/board/index.jsp?pageId=040100&bbs
Id=10&itemId=317&pageIndex=1.

increase from the year 2010; and (3) the main purposes of using the Internet
are "getting information or data" (92 percent), "communicating via email or
messenger" (87.9 percent), and "leisure activities such as music and game"
(87.9 percent).

In addition, SNS usage is on rise in Korea. Out of the Internet users aged
six and over, 66.5 percent of them have used an SNS in the last year. Close
to 90.0 percent of Internet users in their twenties are SNS users (Figure 4.4).
Among the SNS users, about 18.4 percent of them use profile-based SNS
such as Facebook, and another 12.8 percent of them use microblog services
such as me2day and Twitter.

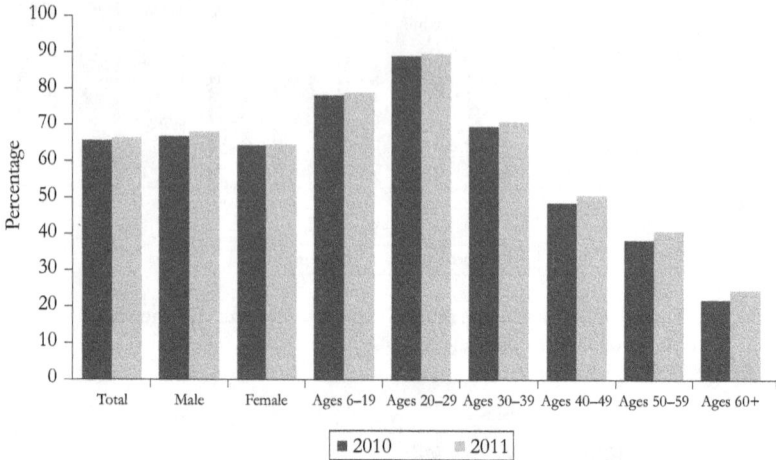

FIGURE 4.4 SNS usage rate among Internet users age 6 and over
SOURCE: KISA, *2011 Survey on the Internet Usage*, http://isis.kisa.or.kr/eng/board/index.jsp?pageId=040100&bbs Id=10&itemId=317&pageIndex=1.

Digital Media as an Alternative Source of Political Information in Korea

Political information delivered through news media can have a critical impact on activities such as voting and persuasion often associated with conventional politics. This section touches on Korean digital media that deliver alternative political news and viewpoints by examining the two most prominent examples: the online newspaper *OhmyNews* and podcast *Nanŭn Kkomsuta*.

OHMYNEWS

Long before Howard Dean embraced the Internet for U.S. presidential election campaigning, the underdog politician Roh Moo-hyun won the 2002 Korean presidential election, and his victory was ascribed to his supporters' use of the Internet and mobile messaging.[26] However, another critical contribution to the victory of Roh Moo-hyun may have come from an online newspaper named *OhmyNews*.

The role of *OhmyNews*, though hard to assess precisely,[27] may have been crucial in Roh's victory in the 2002 election, especially because of the closed and conservative Korean media environment where three conservative daily newspapers—*Chosun Ilbo, Dong-A Ilbo,* and *Joong Ang Ilbo*—monopolized 80 percent of daily circulation[28] and provided biased coverage against liberal and minority politicians.[29] Indeed, the founder of *OhmyNews*, Oh Yeon-ho, said he launched the first online newspaper in 2000 because he was concerned with the traditional Korean media environment—eight conservative media outlets versus only two progressive media outlets—and hoped to make the Korean media environment more progressive.[30]

During Roh's presidential campaign, *OhmyNews* became a prominent alternative source of news for the younger and net-savvy generation. *OhmyNews'* coverage of the presidential election hit twenty million page views per day in a country with forty-eight million people.[31] While other major newspapers focused more on the other presidential candidates, *OhmyNews* covered the underdog candidate Roh. *OhmyNews* also reported the issues that the traditional news media largely ignored.[32] One of those issues was the death of two middle-school girls hit by a U.S. military vehicle on training in June 2002. The grief over the loss of two young lives turned to anger in a growing wave of anti-U.S. sentiment. When a U.S. military court acquitted the two soldiers of negligent homicide on November 19, 2002, massive protests broke out against the U.S. military presence in Korea. During this time, *OhmyNews* provided information that was not being provided by the Korean traditional media, and an *OhmyNews* citizen reporter, Angma, organized the first candlelight vigil, which ten thousand people attended. Similar vigils followed in other Korean cities, and the vigils made anti-Americanism a key campaign issue in the presidential election.[33]

On the 2002 Election Day, *OhmyNews* provided continuous video and text coverage of the events, and its readers—who were monitoring exit polls and realized that Roh was behind his conservative challenger by a small margin—mobilized last-minute support for Roh by sending e-mail and SMS text messages that urged young voters to come out to vote for Roh.[34] In the late afternoon of Election Day, Roh was in the lead according to exit polls and eventually won the day with 48.9 percent of the vote compared to his opponent's 46.8 percent.[35] Polls showed that Roh's victory came from huge support from twenty- and thirty-somethings.[36] Shortly after taking office in February 2003, President Roh granted his first interview to *OhmyNews*.[37]

NANŬN KKOMSUTA

In April 2011, a weekly podcast dedicated to making fun of South Korean President Lee Myung-bak started. The podcast, *Nanŭn Kkomsuta*,[38] is a talk show in which four men sitting around in a rented studio, with loud laughs and occasional expletives, raise allegations against President Lee. The podcast is the most popular podcast in Korea, with two million weekly downloads[39] and has become one of the world's most downloaded political podcasts from the Apple iTunes store.[40] The podcast, which hosts some of the most vociferous critics of President Lee, rose to national fame and gained rock-star status among its fans.

The podcast, with its phenomenal popularity, has emerged as an influential force in Korean politics. Political commentators say the satirical podcast helped sway Seoul's mayoral election in October 2011.[41] The podcast also seemed to have had great sway over younger voters during the Korean National Assembly elections in April 2012 and the Korean presidential election in December 2012. However, the podcast's sway over younger voters did not result in the victory of the opposition party in both elections.

The popularity of *Nanŭn Kkomsuta* also reflects "a widespread belief that mainstream media are 'not delivering the truth, for the sake of partisan or company interests.'"[42] A Korean journalism professor interviewed by the *New York Times* seconds this view by pointing out there is "a growing disenchantment with the country's three most powerful newspapers, all of them conservative and accused of favoring Mr. Lee [President Lee Myung-bak], as well as with the country's two leading television networks, whose heads are effectively appointed by the government."[43] Conversely, some commentators urge *Nanŭn Kkomsuta* to be more responsible and unbiased.[44] Also, as its popularity grows, there is a danger of digital populism.

Whatever the reason for *Nanŭn Kkomsuta*'s popularity, it seems clear that the hosts of the satirical podcast have been successfully using "digital media to rally disenfranchised youths in a challenge to the status quo."[45] When the podcast hosts organized a live street performance opposing the ratification of the Korea–United States free trade agreement in November 2011, fifty to a hundred thousand citizens gathered at a park in Seoul.

E-Campaigning

Politicians use online networks for efficient political communication. The 2002 presidential election was considered the first Korean cyber-election, with six out of the seven candidates posting their platforms as well as detailed stumping schedules online.[46] The website of Roh's New Millennium Democratic Party reported they had a daily average of four hundred thousand page views.[47] Also, supporters of politicians voluntarily use online networks for fund-raising[48] and other supporting activities for their candidates. During the 2002 presidential election campaign, a group called *Rohsamo*[49] actively used the Internet to build support for the presidential candidate Roh Moo-hyun. However, this section focuses on how Korean politicians and political parties use online media to stay connected with other politicians and parties, and with their constituents to build support during election campaigning.

HYPERLINK NETWORKS OF KOREAN POLITICIANS' HOMEPAGES AND BLOGS

One way to analyze Internet communication networks among Korean politicians and political parties is to examine the hyperlink data in their Internet homepages. Hyperlinks enable readily moving to a specific web page or website. The hyperlink between individual websites interconnects users who manage websites and can be used as a mechanism for social relationships and information sharing. Network analysis is a study method to examine the relational structure of a specific system, rather than to focus on the characteristics of individual members in a certain social system.[50]

Hyperlinks in the Web 1.0 era among Korean politicians provided connections between websites, and such connections were mostly between members of the same political party. In both 2000 and 2001, Park, Kim, and Barnett found that the number of hyperlink connections between the politicians in the same political party was larger than the number of hyperlink connections between the politicians in different political parties.[51] Also, such connections failed to develop as an interactive communication network. This may be also attributable to the characteristics of homepages as a medium that puts more emphasis on one-way information delivery, rather than on interactive communication.

In the years between 2005 and 2008, both Korea and Taiwan saw the emergence of blogs as new campaign tools. Blogs provide people with an opportunity to recognize the Internet as a social medium, with completely different characteristics from those of conventional media. Generally, blogs provide an online venue where individuals are allowed to post their writings freely on the matters of their various interests. In addition, blogs may form a community by establishing relationships between users with common interests and helping users actively exchange information. This may result in continuous expansion of social relations and information sharing.[52]

Park examined the network structure of the 17th National Assembly members' blogs to investigate how they established a relationship with other political actors in the blogspace.[53] The study results showed that the network structure was significantly influenced by party affiliation, gender, and the region of political actor, with party affiliation having the biggest influence. Thus, it seems that political communication in the blogosphere tends to produce a homogeneous political community. Moreover, the network structure of politicians in the Web 2.0 era, which is based on reciprocity, did not look significantly different from the hyperlink structure of homepages in the Web 1.0 era.

WEB VISIBILITY OF KOREAN POLITICIANS

To investigate the relationship between the level of web visibility of Korean politicians and the actual election results, Lim and Park analyzed changes in domestic blogspace during the campaign period leading up to the October 28, 2009, Korean National Assembly elections, as measured by the total number of blog resources that mentioned the elections.[54] They found that the level of web visibility of candidates closely correlated with the number of votes obtained. This suggests that Internet election campaigns are effective in Korea, and that the level of online information exchanged about politicians helps predict actual election results.

A more in-depth study analyzed the web visibility of the 18th Korean National Assembly members by examining various forms of online information including blogs, news, images, and websites.[55] The study demonstrated that the probability of being reelected, and of winning a direct constituency election (as opposed to being elected as the party list), had significant and positive correlations with the level of web visibility. Consequently, lawmakers who had secured a colorful political career and popularity offline showed a high level of web visibility, while lawmakers who were elected by party-list proportional representation, newly elected, or elected in a constituency with low population density had low web visibility. The results again suggest that politicians have a mutually exclusive political structure that is based on homogeneous solidarity among them.

TWITTER NETWORK OF KOREAN POLITICIANS

Twitter, which has seen the number of its users in Korea increase rapidly since 2009, has played the role of a networked public sphere since the local elections held in June 2010. When compared to existing digital media, Twitter is a remarkable political communication tool in that, while Twitter allows a politician to campaign digitally and garner support, the politician is simply one of the many Twitter users who participate in the electronic political discourse. Thus, the politician has to listen and respond to diverse voices, not only supporters but also people with different political views. In this sense, Twitter is expected to become a field for deliberative politics, linking not only fellow politicians but also random members of the general public. Moreover, Twitter has a structure that shows how active its users are in real time, so that users cannot help facing social pressure to respond to their followers.

However, in the Twitter sphere as in other digital networks, politicians still mainly connect with their fellow party members. Analyzing the Twitter network of 189 Korean politicians, a 2011 study found that more politicians were connected with other politicians of the same political orientation than those of the opposing political parties. The percentage of following–follower interconnectivity between the members of the ruling party was 48.6 percent, while the percentage of following–follower interconnectivity between a member of the ruling party and a member of minority parties was 25.4 percent. Also, following–follower interconnectivity (counterfollowing) was significantly higher among politicians, which confirms that the network relationship on Twitter shows social and ritual characteristics. The results of network analysis demonstrated that there were many mentions of prominent politicians, suggesting that politicians express their political support by sending mentions to other prominent politicians with high visibility or popularity on Twitter. Moreover, the greater the number of followers politicians have on Twitter and the higher the number of messages they post on Twitter, the higher the chance they will be mentioned in tweets from their colleagues in the same political party, underscoring that this is a tool to express support for prominent politicians or show connectivity with them.

Two other studies examined Korean politicians' Twitter use. The first was an exploratory study that conducted an in-depth analysis of five prominent Korean politicians' Twitter usage from data collected in June 2010. The study found that non-mainstream, resource-deficient politicians were likely to maximize Twitter's potential as an alternative means of political communication. Roh Hoe-chan, a New Progressive Party (a labor party) member, exemplified this trend. Roh's Twitter reciprocity was 61 percent, which indicates that Roh followed more than half of his followers and that his followers used Twitter as a direct communication channel to connect with Roh. In addition, Roh sent tweets in response to tweets he received, demonstrating that he sought a conversational and interactive relationship with his followers. In contrast, two conservative politicians showed only 2.9 percent and 1.0 percent Twitter reciprocity, respectively. The study also found some evidence of polarization among Twitter followers. Approximately 34 percent of Twitterians who followed a progressive (left-wing) politician also followed another progressive politician, but only 5 percent of them followed a conservative politician.

The other study of Korean National Assembly members' Twitter profiles found that (as of April 2010) seventy-two National Assembly members (about 25 percent of the total) were using Twitter. Liberal or progressive politicians were more likely to use Twitter than conservative politicians, and the majority of links were within the same party, although the Twitter network showed a higher level of inter-party communication than the homepage and blog networks.

E-Mobilization

E-mobilization refers to "uses of the Internet by interest groups and social movements for political recruitment, organization, and campaigning."[56] This section does not draw a distinction between interest groups and social movements, because interest groups and social movements are said to be converging in terms of their goals, constituencies of support, tactics, and policy impact. Interest groups that used to deliberately work within established political institutions have been making appeals for mobilization that reach far beyond their membership base. Meanwhile, social movements that once mobilized for collective action away from policy elites are now increasingly institutionalized in conventional policy making. The Internet accelerated these trends toward convergence.[57]

The first case of e-mobilization in Korea began in the Defeat Movement of 2000.[58] Before the National Assembly General Election held in April 2002, more than 450 civic organizations united to form the Citizens Alliance for the General Election (CAGE). This group aimed to prevent incompetent and corrupt politicians from being elected. Based on the deliberation of a Committee of One Hundred Voters appointed by CAGE,

CAGE created and released three blacklists of 135 corrupt candidates who were deemed unfit for office.[59]

In 2002, as noted earlier, massive offline protests against the U.S. military presence in Korea was initiated by an online posting by a netizen under the pseudonym Angma who was also a citizen journalist for *OhmyNews*. In 2008, Korean netizens launched a campaign for the revision of a provision in the Korean election law that, starting from six months ahead of elections, restricted online and offline activities to support or undermine a particular candidate or a party. Arguing that the provision infringes upon the right of netizens to freely voice political opinions, a coalition of thirty-one civic groups sent letters to legislators.[60]

Probably the most prominent example of online mobilization in Korea is the mad cow disease protests that took the form of candlelight vigils in 2008. In May of that year, news broke that President Lee Myung-bak would open the Korean market to U.S. beef. United States beef imports had been banned in Korea since 2003, because several sources of U.S. beef had been revealed to be contaminated with mad cow disease. But, in 2008, as a part of a free trade agreement between Korea and the United States, the two governments negotiated a reopening of the Korean market to U.S. beef. The Korean government's decision to import U.S. beef upset many of its citizens who wanted to be consulted but had not been.[61] Also, the issue of food safety was something to which everyone—regardless of their political orientation and their age—could relate.

The mad cow disease protests were a grassroots movement that had several distinctive features.[62] First, the mad cow disease protests lasted for a long time, spanning three months. Second, they started small and grew to massive scale: More than 3.5 million people came out to the streets and stayed overnight in the parks. By early June 2008, the mad cow disease protests were the largest in Korea since the 1987 protests that had led to the first free direct presidential election held in Korea. Third, the mad cow disease protests were unique in that over half the protesters were teenagers, especially teenage girls, most of whom had not participated in public political action before. Also, women in their twenties and thirties were major participants in the protests.

Most relevant to the topic of this section, the mad cow disease protesters coordinated their action through digital media. To disseminate information and share opinions, the protesters used online forums and chat rooms offered by the large portal sites Daum and Naver, the social media site Cyworld, and other websites. By contrast, the Korean government disseminated information about the safety of U.S. beef mainly through ana-log media, a unilateral and vertical channel toward citizens.[63] The protest-ers also sent images and text via their mobile phones, through which they sometimes changed the venue and route of the protests to avoid colliding with police. The sustained mad cow disease protests finally led President Lee to issue an official apology for lifting the ban without adequately con-sulting the Korean people.[64]

Analyzing 2,504 messages that were posted in two online communities and one political discussion portal site, Park and Myung found that online discussion about the import of U.S. beef became more active after the dis-cussion took place offline through the mad cow disease protests. In addi-tion, they found that the protests were the result of voluntary participation by the general public, not policy elites' mobilization.[65]

Twitter also started playing an important role in e-mobilization in Korea. What is particularly interesting is the popularity of Twitaddons that is an additional service on Twitter. Twitaddons works as a community space for Korean Twitter users. Just as online communities have been formed based on a specific subject, users with a common interest have formed their com-munities on Twitaddons.[66] A community established on Twitaddons on topic X is called "Twit X party."

A recent study examined what activities Twit parties had engaged in and what influences they had on social participation.[67] Users who established Twit parties were information disseminators more than information con-sumers. In addition, the founders of Twit parties on social and consumer is-sues had a higher number of replies and mentions than general participants. This finding demonstrates that the founders of Twit parties on social and consumer issues had taken the lead in conversation (interactive commu-nication) on Twitter. By contrast, all members of Twit parties on political issues actively participated in exchange of opinions regardless of their role within the Twit parties. However, the founders of the political Twit parties had played a more conspicuous role as information disseminators than did the founders of Twit parties on other topics.

Conclusion

With the focus on political communication, this chapter reviewed how dig-ital media have been transforming Korean politics. The first part dealt with the role of digital media in providing alternative political information. This role has been critical in Korea because the traditional, mainstream Korean media have been largely skewed toward conservative and pro-establishment viewpoints. The success of the online newspaper *OhmyNews* and podcast *Nanŭn Kkomsuta* provided political balance from a new direction. The second part of the chapter explored e-campaigning by summarizing past research on the characteristics of online networks among Korean politicians. The third part focused on political mobilization that is mediated or coordinated through digital media. A few prominent cases including the mad cow disease protests illustrated the rise of alternative forms of political participation in Korea.

What implications do these Korean developments hold for the evolution of democracy in Korea, as well as in other democratic countries? First, the changes in media characteristics have led to changes in political communication. The relatively low cost of entering the digital media market helped level the media playing field, enabling the emergence of alternative political news and opinions. The online newspaper *OhmyNews* covered the underdog candidate Roh, who had not been covered much by major newspapers. Also, *OhmyNews* reported the issues—such as the death of two middle-school girls hit by a U.S. military vehicle—that traditional news media outlets largely ignored; and it made anti-Americanism a key campaign issue. The role of *OhmyNews*, at least in part, was crucial in Roh's victory in the 2002 presidential election.

Similar things continue to happen in Korea. The weekly podcast *Nanŭn Kkomsuta* that started in April 2011 has been shaping the political agenda of the nation by bringing allegations against the incumbent President Lee and his aides that are largely unreported by the country's most powerful newspapers and leading television networks. The phenomenal popularity of the podcast may be a testimony to the public's eagerness to receive alternative political news and opinions, at a time when the majority of the citizens believe the mainstream media have failed to be a watchdog of the government.

The power of digital media in bringing changes to the traditional arena of politics may be largely true among young, educated people in large cities. Although online media outlets such as *Nanŭn Kkomsuta* mostly criticized the incumbent president and his political party, the ruling party managed to win majority seats in the general election held in April 2012 as well as to win the 2012 presidential election. The victory of the ruling party seems to suggest that conventional media continue to influence older voters and voters in rural, provincial areas.

Another change in political communication came from the feature of online media that enables the communication of equal participants with equal access and equal rights to intervene or propose themes. This means that political input is no longer limited to the issues determined by politicians, policy elites, or institutionalized channels. In fact, individual politicians may not have any more power to shape political issues and conversations than individual members of the general public. Especially with the rise of social media, a powerful social media user (e.g., a Twitter user with a large number of followers) can be as influential as, if not more influential than, a prominent politician in spreading and magnifying political issues online. Moreover, politicians are now expected to use various online media tools to interact with random members of the public in real time.

Second, these changes in political communication have been accompanied by changes in the nature of citizens who engage in political deliberation and political participation. A new kind of citizenship has appeared. The so-called actualizing or engaged citizen may no longer feel obligated to take part in conventional political activities, such as voting and party or political campaigning activities. Instead, digitally engaged citizens tend to deliver their voices directly to policy makers via alternative forms of political participation including protesting, petitioning, boycotting, and occupying. The mad cow disease protests in 2008 that drew more than 3.5 million people over a three-month period would have not been possible without coordination efforts via online and mobile media.

In addition, that many of the mad cow disease protesters were teenage girls and younger women signaled the rise of a new kind of politics. This new generation of political actors has been tearing down the boundary between political and nonpolitical issues. Communication patterns observed in online political communities of women in their twenties and thirties were similar to communication patterns in online communities that deal with entertainment and lifestyle issues in that many postings were playful, including parodies and fun images, and personal talk of daily life among the members was rampant and encouraged.[68] Also, there were fandoms of their favorite politicians in those political communities, which indicated this new generation of political actors broke down the seriousness, formality, and authority of traditional politics.[69]

These trends may suggest the development of "dialogic" democracy as an alternative to liberal democracy. Anthony Giddens defined dialogic democracy as "a situation where there is developed autonomy of communication, and where such communication forms a dialogue by means of which policies and activities are shaped."[70] While liberal democracy is a system of representation that forms government by regular elections under the principle of pluralism, dialogic democracy focuses on social interchanges that are based upon mutual tolerance and that contribute to the reconstruction of social solidarity.[71]

Similar trends have been observed in Taiwan. As Chen-Dong Tso notes in Chapter 5, the Internet transformed election campaigns in Taiwan into a "daily-life campaign" that resulted in weakening the traditional role of political parties and policies. There is more focus on lifestyles, sports, and personal stories of politicians; and a new group of professionals—such as film producers, music composers, cartoonists, and online auction experts—plays an important role in Taiwanese election campaigns online.

Third, although reaching a consensus through public deliberation is no longer an ideal goal under the paradigm of dialogic democracy, it may still prove meaningful to look at the nature of public deliberation mediated in the networked public sphere. Past studies of online networks among Korean politicians found that Korean politicians essentially formed a homogenous network with regard to their political affiliation and their traditional background. In addition, the pattern of political power structure, already established offline, was indirectly reflected in online networks in terms of web visibility and centrality of prominent politicians. These trends are consistent with the criticisms of the networked public sphere, which may create strong divides in our perception of political reality, polarize political deliberation, and reinforce political imbalance. Moreover, the rise of "a politics of negation"—further explained by Chen-Dong Tso in Chapter 5—seems to hurt the quality of public deliberation online.

Last, a troubling thing has developed in Korea: There has been an increase in online censorship by the government. In January 2009 an anonymous blogger named Minerva, who had successfully predicted the collapse of Lehman Brothers and the sharp decline in Korea's currency, was arrested by the government for spreading false rumors damaging to the economic stability of the country. Although Minerva was later acquitted, the prosecution against him had a great chilling effect among Korean net users. Then, the government expanded the real-name system that requires net users to register their real name and national identification card number when they post to the Internet. The online real-name law was held unconstitutional in August 2012 by the country's constitutional court. In December 2011 one of the podcast *Nanŭn Kkomsuta* co-hosts, Chung Bong-ju, was sent to prison for one year after he was convicted of spreading unconfirmed rumors connecting President Lee to allegations of stock fraud. Chung Bong-ju was a national lawmaker when he made the statements during the 2007 presidential election campaign. His supporters claim that the verdict was politically motivated and designed to stifle the podcast *Nanŭn Kkomsuta*. Under President Lee, the Korean authorities have been accused of filing criminal defamation suits for statements that are true and are in the public interest to suppress political dissent.[72]

Korea, a country that witnessed the victory of iconoclast politician Roh in the 2002 presidential election with his supporters' use of the online and mobile media, is now seeing digital media platforms fall victim to governmental regulations to limit free speech online. Thus, the power of digital media to transform politics seems inevitably related to the swing of the political pendulum.

Notes

1. Holcomb B. Noble, "Frank Stanton, Broadcasting Pioneer, Dies at 98," *New York Times,* December 25, 2006, www.nytimes.com/2006/12/25/business/media/25cnd-stanton.html?pagewanted=all.

2. Angus Campbell, "Has Television Reshaped Politics?" www.museum.tv/debateweb/html/equalizer/essay_campbell.htm.

3. Matthew C. Nisbelt and Dietram A. Scheufele, "Political Talk as a Catalyst for Online Citizenship," *Journalism & Mass Communication Quarterly* 81, no. 4 (2004): 877–896, 877, accessed March 10, 2012, doi: 10.1177/107769900408100410.

4. Nisbelt and Scheufele, "Political Talk," 877–896.

5. Michael Cornfield, *Politics Moves Online: Campaigning and the Internet* (New York: Century Foundation Press, 2004), 5.

6. Andrew Chadwick, *Internet Politics: States, Citizens, and New Communication Technologies* (London: Oxford University Press, 2006), 1. (Italics in original).

7. Yeon-Ok Lee and Han Woo Park, "The Reconfiguration of E-Campaign Practices in Korea: A Case Study of the Presidential Primaries of 2007," *International Sociology* 25, no. 1 (2010): 29–53.

8. Jack M. McLeod, Dietram A. Scheufele, and Patricia Moy, "Community, Communication, and Participation: The Role of Mass Media and Interpersonal

Discussion in Local Political Participation," *Political Communication* 16 (1999): 315–336.

9. Pippa Norris, "Does Television Erode Social Capital? A Reply to Putnam," *PS: Political Science and Politics* 29 (1996): 474–480.

10. Dhavan V. Shah et al., "Information and Expression in a Digital Age: Modeling Internet Effects on Civic Participation," *Communication Research* 30, no. 5 (2005): 531–565, doi: 10.1177/0093650205279209.

11. Nisbet and Scheufele, "Political Talk," 877–896.

12. Lyda J. Hanifan, "The Rural School Community Center," *Annals of the American Academy of Political and Social Science* 67 (1916): 130–138.

13. Robert D. Putnam, "Bowling Alone: America's Declining Social Capital," *Journal of Democracy* 6:1 (1995): 65–78; Robert D. Putnam, *Bowling Alone: The Collapse and Revival of American Community* (New York: Simon & Schuster, 2000).

14. Robert D. Putnam, "Bowling Alone," 66.

15. Peter Dahlgren, "The Internet, Public Spheres, and Political Communication: Dispersion and Deliberation," *Political Communication* 22 (2005): 147–162.

16. Karina Alexanyan et al., "Exploring Russian Cyberspace: Digitally-Mediated Collective Action and the Networked Public Sphere," *Berkman Center Research Publication No. 2012–2*, (March 2, 2012): 5.

17. Yochai Benkler, *The Wealth of Networks: How Social Production Transforms Markets and Freedom* (New Haven, CT: Yale University Press, 2006).

18. Antje Gimmler, "Deliberative Democracy, the Public Sphere, and the Internet," *Philosophy & Social Criticism* 27, no. 4 (2001): 21–39.

19. Minjeong Kim, "The Right to Anonymous Association in Cyberspace: US Legal Protection for Anonymity in Name, in Face, and in Action," *SCRIPTed* 7, no. 1 (2010): 51, www.law.ed.ac.uk/ahrc/script-ed/vol7-1/kim.asp.

20. Cass R. Sunstein, *Republic.com 2.0* (Princeton, NJ: Princeton University Press, 2007).

21. Russell J. Dalton, *Citizen Politics: Public Opinion and Political Parties in Advanced Industrial Democracies* (Washington, D.C.: CQ Press, 2006), 73.

22. Dalton, *Citizen Politics,* 73.

23. W. Lance Bennett, Chris Wells, and Allison Rank, "Young Citizens and Civic Learning: Two Paradigms of Citizenship in the Digital Age," *Citizenship Studies* 13, no. 2 (2009): 105–120.

24. "2011 Korea Internet White Paper," Korea Internet and Security Agency (KISA), http://isis.nida.or.kr/ebook/ebook.html [in Korean]. The subsequent information also comes from the White Paper.

25. "2011 Survey on the Internet Usage Executive Summary," Korea Internet and Security Agency (KISA), http://isis.kisa.or.kr/eng/board/index.jsp?pageId=040100&bbsId=10&itemId=317&pageIndex=1.

26. "Korean Move May Pave Way for Global Online Clampdown," *The Irish Times*, August 21, 2009, 6.

27. Political pundits point out that another important reason for Roh's victory was a unified candidacy with Chung Mong-joon. Chung, a conservative politician, formed a coalition with Roh in the 2002 presidential election to swing conservative voters away from the opposing candidate Lee Hoi-chang. But Chung controversially withdrew his endorsement of Roh in the last hour, which might also have ignited the support for Roh in liberal voters.

28. Dan Gillmor, *We the Media: Grassroots Journalism by the People, for the People* (Sebastopol, CA: O'Reilly Media, 2004), 93.

29. In-Young Rhee, "The Korean Election Shows a Shift in Media Power," *Nieman Reports* 57, no. 1 (2003): 95.

30. Ronda Hauben, "Advancing 'News Guerrillas': OhmyNews and 21st Century Journalism," *Telepolis*, August 9, 2005, www.ais.org/~ronda/new.papers/articles/ohmynews.txt.

31. Tee Jong Lee, "Korea: Online Paper Helped Get Roh Elected; Paper with 50,000 Citizen Reporters Was Credited with President's Poll Win," *The Straits Times*, June 9, 2007.

32. Daniel Jisuk Kang and Laurel Evelyn Dyson, "Internet Politics in South Korea" (paper presented at the 18th Australasian Conference on Information Systems, Toowomba, Australia, December 5–7, 2007).

33. Mary Joyce, "The Citizen Journalism Web Site 'OhmyNews' and the 2002 South Korean Presidential Election," *The Berkman Center for Internet & Society Research Publication Series, Research Publication No. 2007–15*, December 2007, 23.

34. Kang and Dyson, "Internet Politics in South Korea."

35. Joyce, "The Citizen Journalism Web Site 'OhmyNews,'" 28.

36. Jonathan Watts, "World's First Internet President Logs On: Web Already Shaping Policy of New South Korean Leader," *The Guardian*, February 24, 2003, 16.

37. Lee, "Korea: Online Paper."

38. The title of the podcast, "*Nanŭn Kkomsuta*," is roughly translated into "I'm a petty-minded creep" or "I'm a cheat who uses dirty tricks." The petty-minded creep/cheat refers to President Lee in this context.

39. Sang-Hun Choe, "South Korean Anger, Downloaded by Millions, Carries a Satirical Bite," *The International Herald Tribune*, November 2, 2011, 1.

40. Sang-Hun Choe, "Comic Critic of President Sent to Jail in South Korea; One-Year Prison Term for Host of Satirical Podcast Upheld by Court," *The International Herald Tribune*, December 27, 2011, 4.

41. Chan-Kyong Park, "Satirical Talk Show Becomes Phenomenon in S. Korea," *AFP*, December 5, 2011, www.google.com/hostednews/afp/article/ALeqM5i20p62cPKidBTXi_vsYUPrQ_ZKTA?docId=CNG.598626a4b87e150b6b89473d89e5a47e.3d1.

42. Park, "Satirical Talk Show."

43. Choe, "South Korean Anger."

44. Whan-woo Yi, "Nakkomsu urged to be more responsible," *The Korea Times*, February 3, 2012, www.koreatimes.co.kr/www/news/nation/2012/02/113_104115.html.

45. John M. Glionna, "South Korea's 'Weasel' Ferrets out the Funny," *Los Angeles Times*, November 18, 2011, http://articles.latimes.com/2011/nov/18/world/la-fg-korea-weasel-20111119.

46. "Net Campaigning the Norm in U.S., S. Korea," *The Nikkei Weekly*, April 23, 2007.

47. "Net Campaigning the Norm."

48. In Taiwan, online donations were first accepted in the 2002 Taipei mayoral election.

49. *Rohsamo* means "people who love Roh, Moo-hyun."

50. Peter R. Monge and Noshir Contractor, *Theories of Communication Networks* (New York: Oxford University Press, 2003).

51. Han Woo Park, Chun-Sik Kim, and George A. Barnett, "Socio-Communicational Structure among Political Actors on the Web in South Korea: The Dynamics of Digital Presence in Cyberspace," *New Media & Society* 6, no. 3 (2004): 403–423.

52. Myeong-hee Yoon, "Blog-ŭi Sahoechŏk Yuhyŏng Punsŏk: 1-in community-ŭi Tach'ŭnghwa [An Analysis of Social Characteristics of Blogs: Diversified One-person Community]," *Han'guk Sahoehak* [Korean Journal of Sociology] 41, no. 1 (2007): 156–193. (The article is written in Korean and published in a Korean journal.)

53. Han Woo Park and Mike Thelwall, "Developing Network Indicators for Ideological Landscapes from the Political Blogosphere in South Korea," *Journal of Computer-Mediated Communication* 13:4 (2008), doi: 10.1111/j.1083-6101.2008.00422.x.

54. Steven Sams, Yon Soo Lim, and Han Woo Park, "e-Research Applications for Tracking Online Socio-Political Capital in the Asia-Pacific Region," *Asian Journal of Communication* 21, no. 5 (2011): 450–466. The web visibility visualizes the relation with actors, incidents, or issues that Internet users (i.e., the general public) pay attention to in online space. It helps visually confirm the responses by the general public that can be observed on the Internet in regard to politicians or political issues.

55. Yon Soo Lim and Han Woo Park, "How Do Congressional Members Appear on the Web?: Tracking the Web Visibility of South Korean Politicians," *Government Information Quarterly* 28, no. 4 (2011): 514–521.

56. Chadwick, *Internet Politics*, 114.

57. Ibid., 116.

58. Sung Yi Yoon and Woo Young Jang, "Han'gugŭi ollain Chŏngch'ich'amyŏ t'ŭksŏng: suyongja chungsim moterŭl chungsimŭro [The Special Characteristics of Online Political Participation in Korea: Focusing on the User-Centered Model]," *Chŏngbohwa Chŏngch'aek* [Information Policies] 14, no. 4 (2007): 82–101. (The article is written in Korean and published in a Korean journal.)

59. Joyce, "The Citizen Journalism Web Site 'OhmyNews,'" 19–20.

60. "S Korean Netizens Launch Attack on Election Law," *Korea Times*, February 18, 2008.

61. Clay Shirky, *Cognitive Surplus: Creativity and Generosity in a Connected Age* (New York: Penguin, 2010), 35.

62. Ibid., 32.

63. Woo-young Chang and Han Woo Park, "The Network Structure of the Korean Blogosphere," *Journal of Computer-Mediated Communication* 17 (2012): 216–230.

64. Shirky, *Cognitive Surplus*, 36.

65. Chi Sung Park and Sung Jun Myung, "Chŏngch'aegoeche sŏlchŏng gwachŏnge issŏ int'ŏnesŭi yŏkhare kwanhan tamsaekchŏk yŏn'gu [An Exploratory Study on the Role of the Internet in Policy Agenda Setting]," *Han'gukchŏng ch'aekhoepo* [The Gazette of the Korean Association for Policy Studies] 18, no. 3 (2009): 41–69. (The article is written in Korean and published in a Korean journal.)

66. Twitaddons grants the concept of group to individual networks on Twitter. The growing popularity of Twitaddons reflects one of the traditional characteristics of Korean culture that prefers group over an individual.

67. Soo Jin Choi and Han Woo Park, "Shared Identity and Collective Actions of a Twitter-based Community for a Political Goal in South Korea" (paper presented at the International Communication Association's Preconference titled "New Media and Citizenship in Asia: Social Media, Politics, and Community-Building," Phoenix, Arizona, May 24, 2012).

68. Chang Sik Park and Il Kwon Chung, "Chŏngch'ichŏk sotongŭi saeroun Chŏnmang: 20–30dae yŏsŏngdŭrŭi ollain Chŏngch'i k'ŏmyunit'irŭl ch'ungsimŭro [New Directions in Political Communication: Online Political Communities of Women in Their Twenties and Thirties]," *Han'gugŏllonhakpo* [The Gazette of Korean Society for Journalism & Communication Studies] 55, no. 1 (2011): 220–244. (The article is written in Korean and published in a Korean journal.)

69. Ibid.

70. Anthony Giddens, *Beyond Left and Right: the Future of Radical Politics* (Stanford, CA: Stanford University Press, 1994), 115.

71. Ibid., 112–115.

72. Choe, "Comic Critic of President Sent to Jail."

FIVE

Digital Media and the Transformation of Politics in Taiwan

Chen-Dong Tso

Introduction

One of the features that define modern public life is usage of digital media, which contain digitized content to be transmitted over the Internet and other computer networks. Media as such include websites, blogs, microblogs, video-sharing websites, and other social networking services like Facebook. The Internet serves as the key platform to carry most of the applications.

Scholars have long debated whether the advent of the Internet might create opportunities for democracy.[1] Optimists believe that the Internet can continue interpersonal and social relations and thus strengthen real-life social bonds and transform geography-based local communities into interest-based selective communities.[2] In addition, the Internet's decentralizing tendencies facilitate formation of intimate political communities and strengthen democracy and participatory localism.[3] Furthermore, information technology may increase government transparency.[4] In turn, discussion forums on the Internet can foster rational deliberations on public policy issues, thereby creating a distinctive public sphere.[5] The anonymity of online communications gives every posting equal footing and encourages free, diverse, and sincere discussion. Most of all, the Internet has a magical power to encourage the politically apathetic to become involved by overcoming time and space constraints, thereby improving the quality of participation.[6]

In contrast, pessimists see online information as leading to extreme disorder. Although the Internet transforms the preexisting interest groups into issue-oriented communities, these new communities are fluid and poorly organized. The Internet does not necessarily empower the emerging communities. Instead, it can make resourceful multinational corporations even more powerful due to a growing need for advertisement.[7] In addition, the Internet may prevent community-building efforts by encouraging atomic individualism.[8] Finally, online forums may not necessarily attract qualified participants because most people are preoccupied with their daily lives and have no time to become involved. The anonymity, in turn, may be a counterincentive since it can also produce insincere discussions, thus deepening social cleavages and exacerbating group confrontations.[9] Although the Internet's decentralizing trends do not necessarily render mediation useless in terms of interest aggregation,[10] its role in promoting government transparency can be counterproductive by allowing the government to consolidate its control.[11]

This optimism–pessimism dichotomy forms the basis for subsequent scholarship on Internet politics. In a deeper sense, the dichotomy implies that certain presumed values should be held above others. These include a number of values, such as egalitarianism, as well as transparency and participation, which are mostly procedural issues. What is usually forgotten is that the implied value change and procedural adventure of electronic democracy would not move forward without sufficient supply of new information, in which digital media make tremendous differences. Earlier research has found that the Internet serves as an important source of political information.[12] Recent research further differentiates between traditional and emerging sources of information online and finds that both are important predictors of political engagement.[13] So the source of political information matters; and as an important source of political information, the Internet undoubtedly matters. That the Internet matters as a source of political information can be factored into the optimism–pessimism dichotomy in two ways. One is that having in place the Internet with robust infrastructure and abundant political information is a precondition for any optimism–pessimism debate to become meaningful. The other is that the quality and orientation of the information supplied through the Internet could affect civic engagement. While some consider the Internet as a savior of democracy in terms of its ability to activate youth participation in public affairs in general and in voting in particular,[14] there are possibilities that online activism and offline indifference may substitute each other to the extent of singling out the democratic potential of the Internet. This could add a new element within the old and unresolved dichotomous debate.

What is similarly downplayed is the critical importance of issues of outcome and the quality of democracy. The outcomes of the political processes and the quality of democracy are well covered in the notion of good governance. According to a widely accepted definition provided by World Bank experts, good governance consists of the following features: voice and accountability, political stability and absence of violence, government effectiveness, regulatory quality, rule of law, and control of corruption.[15] Among these six indicators, government effectiveness, regulatory quality, and control of corruption represent outcomes. Conventional wisdom contends that a participatory policy-making procedure that prevents the abuse of power should come hand in hand with good governance. Nonetheless, recognizing that direct participation is both complex and resource-consuming, it is obvious that the relationship between procedure and outcome is much more complicated. In many ways, the relationship reflects orientations and directions of competition between key players within the broader institutional setup. Hence, how Internet-enabled procedural change impacts governance outcomes can be understood by exploring the manner in which key players compete with other changes.[16] Competition for power is crucial to solving the optimism–pessimism stalemate. Thus we need to ask not only whether the less-privileged become empowered over the more-privileged, but also if so, how does this come about and what are the consequences in terms of outcomes and quality issues?

In this respect, Taiwan represents a good case study. Taiwan is a young democracy undergoing rapid informatization in a wide range of public services. The infrastructural condition is met by and large, and the political regime is basically open and able to accommodate broad participation in procedural terms. Nevertheless, this does not bring about good performance in terms of outcomes. On the one hand, since 2000 there has been a continuous reshuffling of political forces and short-lived power configurations. On the other hand, it is questionable whether either the Democratic Progressive Party (DPP) government or the incumbent Kuomintang (KMT) government is capable of delivering sound governance outcomes in terms of government effectiveness and regulatory quality. This is most obvious in the area of economic policies where the government is torn between pursuing pro-growth, pro-business policies and pursuing pro-distribution, environment-friendly policies. The seesaw struggle between these two forces has resulted in government ineffectiveness and inconsistent regulation. There is a clear discrepancy between procedural openness and the soundness of outcomes during Taiwan's short march toward democracy. Given its complexity, this issue will not be examined here. Instead, in order to provide some insightful clues about the role of the Internet in democratization, this chapter is limited to looking at how the dynamics of political competition have changed during the Internet era. As mentioned earlier, there must be a robust infrastructure of the Internet in place; and, accordingly, this chapter supplies a snapshot of the status of Internet diffusion in Taiwan as a precondition for such dynamics to come into play. Before presenting these two sections, the next section introduces the conventional conceptions of political competition and the roles the Internet might play in political competition.

Political Competition and the Role of the Internet

It is difficult to arrive at a generally accepted conception of political competition, even though for many it is too obvious to warrant specific definition. But a proper model of political competition has long been debated. Anthony Downs places political competition at the center of a democratic system where "two or more political parties compete in periodic elections for control of the governing apparatus." Political parties, in turn, are teamed up by people who "seek office solely in order to enjoy the income, prestige, and power that go with running the government apparatus." By this definition, political parties do not regard seeking office as a means to carry out certain policies; rather, the reverse it the case.[17] Economist Donald Wittman has challenged Downs's model by arguing that political parties are utility maximizers and as such they are solely interested in certain policies. This leads to two conclusions: 1) political parties regard winning elections as a means to implement certain policies, and 2) political parties may collude against voters to carry out certain policies.[18] The critical point to be drawn from the Downs-Wittman debate is that political competition may focus either on vote getting or on policy making.[19] Although the desire for vote maximization is only apparent among political parties, the desire for policy making is also shared by many other social groups.

Accordingly, an accurate definition of political competition should include competition between government and social groups regarding whether to take or implement certain policy stands. Furthermore, political parties will compete over policy issues not only during periods of elections, but also by persuasion through the mass media, negotiations within the legislature, and coercion on the streets. Competition between political parties over public policy issues through coercion on the streets, or quasi-social movements, most vividly illustrates inter-party competition and the impact of the new technologies. Accordingly, this chapter divides political competition into three types. The first is competition between political parties to win votes during election campaigns. The second is competition between government and social groups over certain policy stances through social movements. The third is competition between political parties over certain policy stances through quasi-social movements (see Table 5.1).

Among these three types of political competition, the impact of the Internet is most visible during election campaigns and in social movements. In his seminal book published in 2006, Andrew Chadwick presents a comprehensive literature review on Internet campaigns and online social movements.[20] His main message bolsters those of the optimism school, arguing that the Internet empowers the less powerful in traditional political structures at the expense of the more powerful during election campaigns and social movements. On the one hand, the Internet intensifies inter-party competition by facilitating organizing into political parties those who are less resourceful and by strengthening the influence of grassroots organizations over the central party apparatus.[21] On the other hand, the Internet increases the chance for cooperation by creating permanent campaign networks, and it accelerates movement formation by improving organizational flexibility. Both are critical factors to the success of social movements.[22] However, parallel with many other works in the field, Chadwick also notes the possible setbacks, such as insufficient transparency and democracy in campaign sites, the continuity of central leader dominance based on patronage

TABLE 5.1
Typology of political competition

		TARGET OF COMPETITION	
		Position	Policy
Competing entities	**Party to party**	Election campaign	Quasi-social movement
	Social groups to government		Social movement

NOTE: In a mature democracy, it is unlikely that any social group can compete with the government in determining government positions through non-election means. As a result, the lower-left column is left blank.

networks, and the coexistence of movement success and on-site physical harm that becomes more difficult when participation goes online.[23] This inevitably discredits the persuasiveness of the optimist message. Moreover, the thesis does not consider the outcome issue nor does it pay sufficient attention to the experiences of other countries, thereby further limiting its contribution.

Several scholars have attempted to bring the experience of Internet-aided election campaigns and social movements in Taiwan into this theoretical debate. Gary Rawnsley, for example, contends that the constraints of formal and informal institutions can hinder the efficiency of campaign structures, thus causing candidates to take up opportunities offered by professional political-marketing techniques. On the one hand, for both the KMT and the DPP, a formal institutional design like a presidential election through direct popular vote places the image of the candidates rather than the parties' policies at the center of the competition. In addition, the different sizes of the constituency can also explain the high Internet use during the presidential election of 2000 and the mayoral election of 2002 when the constituency was large, and the low Internet use during the Legislative Yuan election in 2001 when the constituency was small.[24] On the other hand, reliance upon informal institutions like the patron–client network and the necessity of keeping a distance from traditional campaign management explain the KMT's slowness in turning to professional consultancies and the DPP's adoption of modern market techniques, including online campaigns.[25]

With respect to the impact of candidate websites during Taiwan's elections, Rawnsley pessimistically argues that they only serve voters who actively search for related information, thus they only "preach to the converted."[26] Research on subsequent elections, however, displays a mixed picture. During the 2006 mayoral election, voters' use of traditional media had a stronger effect than the new media on perceptions of the candidates' images.[27] But another study of the same election finds that those who viewed the candidates' websites more frequently were less cynical and more willing to explore detailed information about the individual candidates.[28] A study of the 2004 Legislative Yuan election finds that the intensity of the voters' viewing of online election news was positively correlated with their participation in election-related activities.[29]

Similarly, strategies to use the Internet varied among the social movements during the early days when social movements first began appearing online in

Taiwan. By tracing all the social movements at the time, Holin Lin and Lu-Lin Cheng find that the degree of Internet adoption across different social movements was determined by three factors: the marginalization of the individual social movement by the traditional mass media, the socioeconomic status of the target audience, as measured by Internet access, and the effect of spatial agglomeration on movement mobilization. By this set of factors, it was found that the gay rights movement had the greatest Internet usage and the labor movement the lowest.[30] Following this typology, the advantage of using the Internet is discounted when a rampant digital divide across regions exists to cut off part of the target audience from the movement's network because of their lack of Internet access. By the same token, a substantial difference in computer literacy could expand the gap between different generations within the same social movement community. Both of these situations existed in Taiwan in the early 2000s.[31] Furthermore, as the gay rights movement in Taiwan illustrates, although the Internet helped expand the movement when it was still socially unacceptable, support online substituted for on-site action, thereby restricting media visibility and dramatizing conflicts upon which the building of any movement legitimacy depends.[32]

Although the above research provides a good starting point, it also has obvious shortcomings. With respect to Internet campaigns, the constraints of formal and informal institutions on the campaign strategies of the political parties are obvious. However, after its defeat in the 2000 presidential election, the KMT made great efforts to transform its election machine into one as effective as that of its rival, the DPP. Internet campaigns, of course, were part of this transformation. With the rapid spread of Internet use across the island, the Internet had already become a major battlefield that no presidential candidate dared to underestimate. But the candidates' "must" does not equal the voters' "must." Positive research on the Internet indicates that it can either change undecided voters' perceptions or reinforce the thinking of decided voters. But these findings contradict mainstream research in the field. Similarly, Internet mobilization is also a "must" for social movements in Taiwan. However, it does not substitute for on-site action. Regardless, Internet-aided social movements have become a reality. However, neither the research on the influence of the Internet on election campaigns nor the research on the influence of the Internet on social movements considers the outcomes. Moreover, inter-party competition over public policies, a hybrid type of political competition, has yet to be explored. In order to fill this gap and to provide a more positive account of Internet politics based on a case study, this chapter analyzes Internet-aided election campaigns, inter-party policy competition, and social movements in Taiwan to determine how the Internet has changed the relationship between democratic procedures and democratic outcomes. In the next section we will introduce the status of Internet diffusion in Taiwan as background for the subsequent analysis.

Internet Diffusion in Taiwan

Taiwan was a pioneer in the spread of Internet use. In 1994 three Internet service providers (Silkera, HiNet, and SeedNet, the latter two being state-owned) emerged in the market to provide dial-up Internet connection services. With three portal companies—Yam, Kimo, PCHome—Internet usage increased rapidly. By the end of 1997, there were already one million Internet users, and by the end of 2000 there were about six million. With the introduction of asymmetric digital subscriber line, or ADSL, in 1999, the number of Internet users took off. The user population made three consecutive jumps between 2003 and 2005, gaining at least one million new users per year. The growth rates thereafter slowed down, but still by the beginning of 2011 there were 16.9 million users.

The distribution of users displays a modest gender divide but strong age and location divides. In 2004, male users accounted for 62 percent of the total male population and female users accounted for 59 percent of the total female population. By January 2011 these figures had expanded modestly to 77 percent and 73 percent, respectively. In absolute terms, male users outnumbered female users by less than two hundred thousand.[33] However, among the different age groups, the differences were significant. In 2011, the age group with the highest user ratio was 12–24-year-olds, with ratios at almost 100 percent. Among the 25–34-year-old age group, users constituted 96 percent of the total population. Among the 35–44-year-old age group the figure was 90 percent, and among the 45–54-year-old age group the figure was 71 percent. Among those 55 years old or older, Internet users constituted only 33 percent.[34] The location divide was even more obvious. The two largest cities, Taipei and Kaohsiung, had the highest rate of Internet users, both reaching over 80 percent in a 2011 survey. In the northern and central regions, the figures were 78 percent and 74 percent, respectively; whereas in the southern and eastern regions; the figures were 68 percent and 64 percent, respectively.[35] This is in line with the distribution of wealth across different regions of the island (see Figures 5.1 through 5.5).

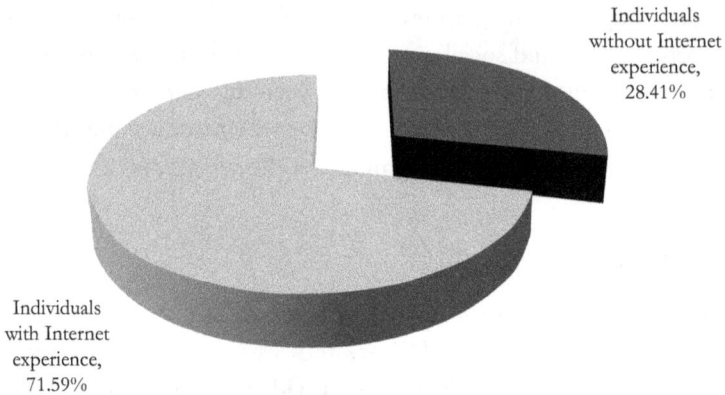

Individuals
without Internet
experience,
28.41%

Individuals
with Internet
experience,
71.59%

FIGURE 5.1 Internet users in Taiwan, 2011

SOURCE: Taiwan Network Information Center (hereafter, TWNIC), www.twnic.net.tw/english/statistics/stats_01
.htm [in Chinese].

NOTE: Sampling Error: ±1.60% (95% confidence level).

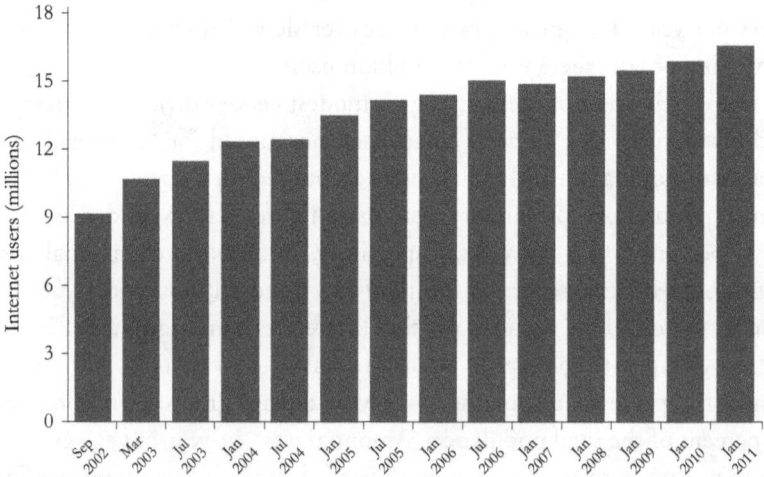

FIGURE 5.2 Growth of Internet users in Taiwan, 2002–2011 (in millions)

SOURCE: TWNIC, various years, www.twnic.net.tw/english/statistics/stats_01.htm [in Chinese].

NOTES: The data from the Taiwan Network Information Center (TWNIC) for September 2002 and Ministry of
Transportation and Communications (MOTC) for March 2003 are based on data collected from Taiwan residents
aged 15 and above. Other data are from the TWNIC and collected from or about Taiwan residents aged 0–100.

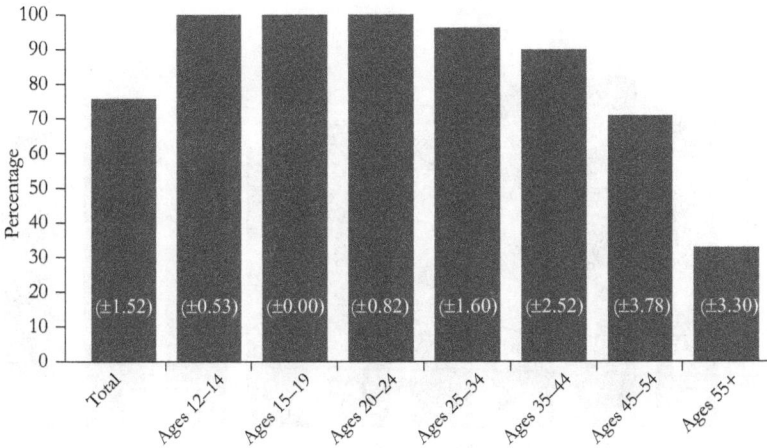

FIGURE 5.3 Digital divide by age in Taiwan, 2011
SOURCE: TWNIC, www.twnic.net.tw/english/statistics/stats_01.htm [in Chinese].
NOTE: Digits inside the parentheses are the percentage of sampling errors.

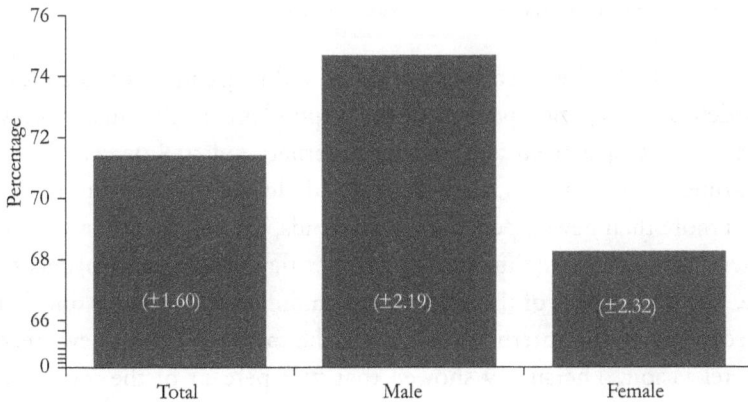

FIGURE 5.4 Digital divide by gender in Taiwan, 2011
SOURCE: TWNIC, www.twnic.net.tw/english/statistics/stats_01.htm [in Chinese].
NOTE: Digits inside the parentheses are the percentage of sampling errors.

The widespread use of the Internet also prompts a change in news-reading behavior. Before the Internet diffused widely in the society, television and newspaper were the two media most frequently accessed. As early as 2004, the Internet had already taken over magazines and broadcasting as third most-accessed media after television and newspaper. In addition, the gap between newspaper readers and Internet surfers continues to

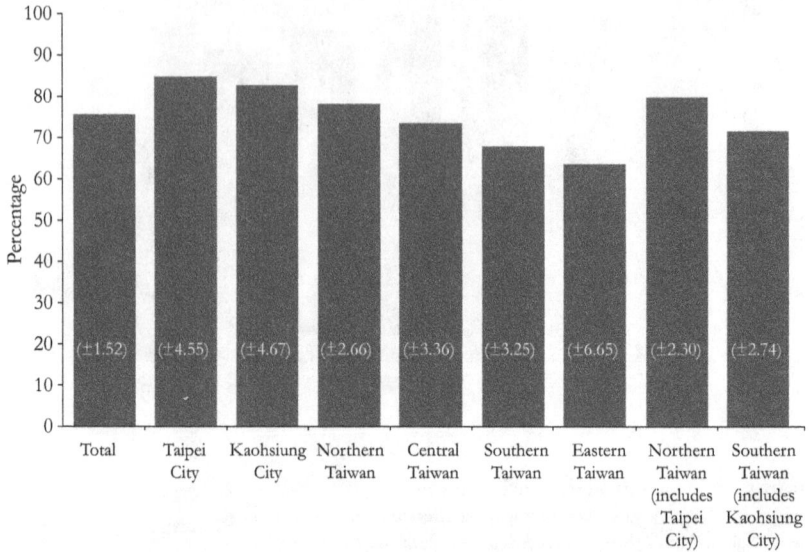

FIGURE 5.5 Digital divide by location in Taiwan, 2011
SOURCE: TWNIC, www.twnic.net.tw/english/statistics/stats_01.htm [in Chinese].

narrow, while that between Internet surfer and magazine readers continues to widen. In 2004, 74.8 percent of the respondents in the survey accessed newspapers, 53.4 percent accessed the Internet, and 50.8 percent accessed magazines. In 2010 a local survey had already found that the Internet is accessed more than newspapers during weekends. Those who access the Internet tend to spend more time surfing websites than reading newspapers every time. For the purpose of this chapter, it is more critical to point out that in the 2010 survey the Internet was already the major source of news second after television. The survey showed that 71.4 percent of the respondents chose television as their primary source of news, whereas 14.7 percent chose the Internet and 10.1 percent chose newspapers.[36] In 2012 access to the Internet further increased as the Internet took over newspapers as the second most-accessed medium only after television. In the 2012 survey, those who accessed television took the percentage of 97.4 percent, while those who accessed the Internet took 74.9 percent, and those accessing newspapers 73.4 percent. In addition, 64.8 percent of the respondents chose television as their primary source of news, whereas 18.5 percent chose the Internet and 12.5 percent chose newspapers.[37] The survey makes it clear that the Internet has changed the information-receiving behavior of the general public and become a major source of news. Though still not on a parity with television, its importance continues to increase.

The Internet and Election Campaigns

The application of Internet-related devices to election campaigns in Taiwan evolved over three distinct periods. The first began with the 1994 Taipei City mayoral election, the first election in which candidates used the Internet in their campaigns. In that election, DPP candidate Chen Shui-bian took the lead in setting up a bulletin board station (BBS)-based municipal information portal with ten dedicated telephone lines to reach out to young voters. The other candidates soon followed suit, producing even larger and more fantastic campaign devices.[38] After this groundbreaking mayoral election, the three major political parties—the KMT, the DPP, and the New Party—went online and set up official websites. After a short break during the 1995 parliamentary elections, the Internet appeared again during the 1996 presidential election when all four candidates built intricate campaign websites to display information and to convey messages that had already appeared through other channels.[39] During this period all major candidates in single-seat elections used the Internet, though with different degrees of sophistication.

The second period of Internet use, between 1998 and 2004, saw expansion in both scope and depth to include a wide range of multimedia instruments. In the 1998 Taipei City mayoral election, the two leading candidates, Chen Shui-bian and Ma Ying-jeou, both used eye-catching and cartoonlike multimedia tools on their campaign websites. This presaged a new stage of Internet use that peaked during the 2000 presidential election when DPP candidate Chen Shui-bian took the lead in developing a more sophisticated website, which was an extension of his website in the previous mayoral election. Chen's web campaign distinguished itself from the others by two features. It was the only site in this election that was built by a professional public relations firm, Fantasy. The other two candidates, Soong Chu-yu (James Soong) and Lian Chan, each had more than one website, and each had a patron with a personal connection to the candidate. The latter reflects a lower level of professionalization and less coordination in their Internet campaign strategies, which may account for the fewer visitors to their sites.

In the 2002 Taipei mayoral election, the DPP challenger Lee Ying-yuan intended to copy Chen in pioneering a new web campaign that included accepting online donations for the first time. Because of the substantial difference in popularity between Lee and the incumbent Ma Ying-jeou, however, there was little confrontation on either the online or the offline battlefields. Nevertheless, the DPP's aggressiveness and flexibility in embracing the new technology paid off in the 2004 presidential election. Although both camps, the incumbent Chen Shui-bian (DPP) and the challenger Lian Chan (KMT), used motion pictures and online games to deliver political messages on their campaign sites, the KMT candidate had numerous websites competing with each other as in the 2000 presidential election. The DPP remained focused on one platform and continued to be innovative. One example is its production of a twenty-four-episode serial, titled *Hydrant Legend (Shuilongtouchuanqi)*, which became extremely popular before the campaign season and was integrated into DPP's campaign website iParty.[40] In addition, online donations continued to be a distinctive feature of the DPP campaign website.[41] Although the differences in innovation between Chen's camp and Lian's camp in 2004 were less remarkable, the effectiveness and attractiveness to youth remained standing markers that differentiated the two.

The following period, between 2005 and 2008, saw the emergence of personalized social media (i.e., blogs) as new campaign tools. In the 2005 magistrate elections, blogs were still on the sidelines. Had it not been for the lawsuit against one blogger by Chou Hsi-wei, the KMT candidate for Taipei magistrate, the general public might not have been aware that blogs had already become an election battlefield.[42] By the 2006 mayoral election, however, all candidates had their own blogs for sharing their personal reflections on daily life or making policy statements.[43] In particular, candidates began to compete in terms of who was more familiar with different Internet functionalities and how much was actually written by the candidate. Some of the candidates even built video blogs (v-logging) to present campaign videos, though v-logging remained much less popular than blogging. Nevertheless, neither blogs nor v-logs replaced the websites, as the latter could accommodate applications requiring more memory and could integrate content from diverse sources. Well into the 2008 presidential election, the way to conduct an Internet campaign did not change very much. It should be noted, however, that a latent demand gradually became dominant in the following years, both in terms of content in diverse formats and platforms capable of integration.[44]

The latest period is marked by wide-ranging social media with multimedia programs. This period began in the aftermath of the 2008 presidential election when DPP politicians shifted their focus to the virtual world in an effort to seek political rejuvenation. The endeavor paid off: A number of DPP politicians, with their mastery of new social media like Plurk and Facebook, soon regained popularity among the young generation. Plurk and Facebook become flagship platforms for carrying out the majority of online political communication during the 2009 magistrate elections. What changed was not only the venue of communications, but also the content and format. Replacing the reflective writing on blogs, Plurk and Facebook feature reckless exchanges of simple and clever words on an hourly, or even a minute-by-minute, basis. In line with this format, funny and gibberish content in short films or motion pictures dominate. The Internet campaign evolved even further during the 2010 mayoral election as people from the entertainment industry, such as producers, composers, and singers, took a more central stage in the campaigns through online videos over YouTube and spread by Plurk and Facebook. More radical moves were taken by the DPP candidate for Taipei mayor, Su Tseng-chang, whose camp showed films and held park concerts as campaign events to replace traditional rallies. His "Open Taipei" concert was so successful that before long his competitor KMT Hau Long-bin followed suit.

From the above, it can be argued that the main driver in the evolution of Internet campaigns was the emergence of new technology and the continuing electoral competition. It should be noted that geography also accounted for the variation in web campaigns. Although utilization of web tools did not really vary among candidates during presidential elections, it has varied substantially during mayoral elections. In the 2010 election, for example, candidates in the northern urban region (Taipei City and New Taipei City) paid much more attention to campaign websites and other web tools than did people in the central and southern regions (Taichung City, Tainan City, and Kaohsiung City). The two candidates in Taipei City took the lead in web campaigns over candidates in other cities. Furthermore, the evolution from blogs to YouTube videos strengthened the candidate-centered, image-focused orientation of the election campaigns at the expense of inter-party competition and serious policy debates. How these trends impact policy outcomes and the quality of democracy are covered in the remaining section of this chapter.

The Internet and Social Movements

Similar to election campaigns, social movements began appearing online in the late 1990s. The earliest such undertakings occurred among environmental movements in remote communities, such as advocacy to conserve the Beinan aboriginal heritage site and for natural resource conservation in the Rukai aboriginal communities, both in mid-1997. By the end of 1999, there were more than thirty activist groups using the Internet for issue-specific advocacy. In these undertakings, the Internet is used for event promotion, petition signing, and fund-raising.[45] A distinctive feature of online social movements in Taiwan is the steady growth of alternative media, whose existence relies solely on Internet. Some of the alternative media are issue-specific but others, like Coolloud and the South Community and Culture Interactive Database, cover a wide range of social movements,[46] which not only have attracted media attention and public sympathy but also have become a different type of social movement in their own right.[47] By the late 2000s, the two converged effectively and became formidable forces in promoting the re-emergence of social movements. The three notable examples are three advocacies: one against the relocation of Lesheng Sanatorium, another against the building of the Suao-Hualien Highway, and the third against the Kuokuang petrochemical complex project. The dispute over whether to preserve the Lesheng Sanatorium complex as a historic site was brought to public attention when, in March 2007, the Mass Rapid Transit (MRT) Bureau of Taipei City planned to build a train depot in the area as part of a new MRT project. With the help of mobile-phone text messaging, the leading advocacy group—the Lesheng Youth Alliance—successfully mobilized hundreds of students and other supporters within a very short time to block the meeting that was to decide whether or not to remove the complex. Later, the alliance launched a demonstration in a march to the prime minister's residence and performed a "kneel and obeisance" session.[48] With a simple blog as its platform, the Lesheng Youth Alliance continued to network concerned students to keep them posted of the latest developments and mobilize supporters for important events. However, despite the mobilization, more than half of the classical buildings in the complex were dismantled by force.

The project to construct a new superhighway linking Taipei and Hualien—the Suao-Hualien Highway—had been planned in the early 1990s but was not placed on the government agenda until the end of the decade. After the DPP assumed office in 2000, the government hastened the process. Beginning in 2001, local activists began gathering clout to oppose the project. As a result, prolonged negotiations among the central government, the Hualien County government, and the environmental and community activist groups ensued. In March 2007 a few heavyweight public figures[49] voiced their dissenting opinions, bringing the issue to the fore. Amid the escalating confrontation, one of the dissenting leaders, Yan Chang-shou, called for support from the business sector to build an Internet platform (called the Volunteer Organization for Creating a Purified Hualien and Taitung [*Jianshechunjinghuadongyigongzuzhi*]) where information on the pros and cons of the project could be fully disclosed. Thereafter, a workshop titled "Workshop for Suao-Hualien Experts" (*Suhuagaoshougongzuofang*) was held to organize study on the project. A student-run platform, the "Suao-Hualien Cake Shop" (*Suhuagaobinpu*) was also set up to spread knowledge about the project through the use of motion pictures and folk songs that were disseminated via electronic newsletters.[50] Because of these pressures, neither of the two candidates in the 2008 presidential election took a clear position on the project. Nevertheless, the KMT reopened the case, renaming it "Suao-Hualien Highway upgrade." The project was given a conditional pass in its environmental impact assessment in November 2010.

After the KMT returned to power, social movements witnessed explosive growth. Most noteworthy are the Wild Strawberry Movement, the Penghu anti-casino referendum, the lawsuit against expansion of the Central Taiwan Science Park, the protest against compulsory acquisition of Dapu Township in Miaoli County, an anti–nuclear plant demonstration, the anti–Kuokuang Petrochemical Complex Movement, and the White Rose Campaign against incompetent judges. Among them, the anti-Kuokuang Petrochemical Complex Movement was the most shocking and dramatic. There had been lobbying and counter-lobbying regarding the request by an alliance of oil refinery companies, the Kuokuang Petrochemical Company, to locate a new plant for upstream petrochemicals in the central part of Taiwan. In January 2008 the leading investor, the state-owned CPC Corporation, Taiwan, decided to locate the plant at the mouth of the Jhuoshuei River in Changhua County. The complex would include refineries, naphtha crackers, and plants producing petrochemicals such as ethylene and aromatic hydrocarbon. It was expected to create some 6,800 new jobs and produce almost US$10.5 billion in annual output. After a series of public hearings, in January 2010 a local environmental activist group, the Changhua Environmental Protection Union, initiated an online petition calling for listing the proposed site as a national wetland and ending the petrochemical complex project. In April 2010 a group of environmental activists initiated an online petition to place the proposed site in the hands of concerned citizens through an environmental trust. In another series of public hearings that followed, groups of college students joined the movement and utilized new approaches to express their opposition and used Facebook and Plurk to mobilize the opposition to disseminate reports about their activities. In addition, a number of eminent figures from the arts and cultural communities as well as hundreds of physicians and professors, including leading scholars from the Academia Sinica, called for an end to the project. Within three months, the petition to establish an environmental trust had obtained thirty thousand signatures. In November 2010 a loose alliance of several student groups also initiated a petition to oppose the project, and one month later all the various groups launched a demonstration that attracted about eight thousand participants. By early 2011 even local high school students had joined the movement by sending postcards to the president and joining in rounds of sit-in demonstrations and candlelight vigils.[51] Pressure became so strong that in late April 2011, after attending an anti-Kuokuang luncheon held at the site of the complex, President Ma decided to drop the project.

As illustrated above, the Internet has played a pivotal role in the burgeoning social movements. First, websites serve as a platform to present facts and analyses, in most cases to oppose a target, be it a new MRT depot, a new superhighway, or a new industrial complex. Some of the websites also rely on crowdsourcing to build databases. Second, the new communication tools, such as e-mails, text messaging, electronic BBS, and social media like Facebook and Plurk, have become effective means of mobilization. Third, the Internet proves to have a seemingly magical power to stir up a movement from scratch by mobilizing a huge number of unrelated people within a short time. Internet power is threefold: It mobilizes and disseminates information to win sympathy and support from the general public. It allows for movements to emerge literally overnight, but they can also disappear overnight as well. The White Rose Campaign is a good case in point. Finally, students are important players in all such movements. On the one hand, their familiarity with the latest information and communications technology tools allow for the rapid growth of movements. On the other hand, with their image of purity and vulnerability, devoted students are able to win sympathy and support. It should be noted that such social movements are not part of the opposition movement, as the opposition party tends to focus on cross-strait issues and does not offer overt involvement or resources to emerging social movements.[52] Instead, these social movements should be considered apolitical. The quasi-social movements that have the explicit backing of the political parties will be discussed in the following section.

The Internet and Quasi-Social Movements

As noted above, political competition is not limited to inter-party electoral competition or government–society policy competition. There is also inter-party competition over public policy. In a broader sense, this should include all inter-party competition during non-electoral periods. It can be best illustrated in the movement-like campaigns by either of the two parties over certain policy or non-policy issues. These campaigns can be considered to be quasi-social movement in the sense that they enlisted citizens to join the fight against the government in order to promote certain policy stances. Two of the most notable examples are the anti-corruption movement in 2006[53] and the anti–Economic Cooperation Framework Agreement (ECFA) movement in 2010.

The anti-corruption movement was a product of a succession of strong reactions to the numerous financial scandals among the first family and President Chen's close aides that were disclosed beginning in late 2005. On July 15, 2006, fifteen DPP-leaning scholars promulgated a joint public statement signed by another sixty-five scholars and a great many online supporters calling for Chen Shui-bian's resignation. In addition, the Democratic Action Alliance initiated a demonstration calling for Chen to step down. Later, Shih Ming-teh—a veteran political activist and former DPP chairman—called for one million people to show their support to unseat Chen by each donating US$3. Within six days, more than one million people had signed up to donate more than US$3 million. On September 9 about three hundred thousand people in red shirts joined a rally in front of the Presidential Hall calling for Chen's resignation. This was called the "Depose

Chen Shui-bian" or "Red Shirt" army. During one month, a number of activists appealed to anonymous netizens for support by joining the protest or by delivering soft drinks or snacks to the protesters. Some even used the Internet to organize young girls to encourage the protesters by visiting the demonstration site in attractive clothing. They also used blog connections and MSN display pictures. Even though this unprecedented large-scale movement received huge media attention and won wide social support, President Chen refused to budge. An undercurrent countering the movement's overwhelming influence among the youth emerged. Some amusing films that mocked the movement as well as leading KMT figures, especially Ma Ying-jeou, were released over YouTube at the height of the Depose Chen Shui-bian Movement. But its real effect did not become apparent until the KMT returned to power in May 2008.

The anti-ECFA movement is another example of a quasi-social movement. If such a movement actually exists, it is the result of a succession of endeavors by the opposition camp to challenge President Ma Ying-jeou's China policy. After Ma came to office 2008, there were three major demonstrations claiming to protest his pro-China policies. A number of pro-independence civic groups led by Taiwan social groups played a critical role in promoting these demonstrations. The catalysts for the demonstrations included President Ma's remark on the legal definition of cross-strait relations, the tainted food imported from China, and the visit to Taiwan of Chen Yunlin, chairman of the Association for Relations Across the Taiwan Straits. During these events, the Internet served as a mobilizing tool to promote and report on events. Instead of having dedicated websites, these demonstrations relied on blogs and personal news stations of cyber-activists for information sharing and promotion of ideas. Although they were relatively short-lived, these demonstrations accumulated substantial momentum that rejuvenated the opposition to form a strong check against a future trade deal with China.

In February 2009 Ma announced that his government would begin ECFA negotiations. The government commissioned a local think tank, the Chunghwa Institute for Economic Research, to study the economic impact of the ECFA. In the meantime, the two opposition parties, the DPP and the Taiwan Solidarity Union (TSU), voiced concern about the political implications of the ECFA and launched the first round of a popular petition calling for a June 2009 referendum on the ECFA. The study revealed issues of alleged economic payoffs and non-transparency in the decision-making process. In August 2009, the referendum review committee turned down the DPP's request for a referendum. Three months later, the two governments (ROC and PRC) commissioned joint research on the economic impact of the ECFA. After completion of the research, the two sides entered into formal negotiations in January 2010. Over the course of the formal negotiations and throughout the year, the TSU alone initiated three rounds of popular petitions but none were successful. On the sidelines, Frank Hsieh, the DPP's 2008 presidential candidate, launched an ECFA referendum coalition in April 2010 and organized a large-scale demonstration in May 2010. After the ECFA was signed on June 29, 2010, the civic group, Cross-Strait Agreement Watch, was formed as a new force to check the ECFA. However, these efforts did not prevent passage of the ECFA legislation in August.

The Internet played a visible role in the campaign against the ECFA as most of the alliances sought broad support online. The ECFA referendum coalition and the Cross-Strait Agreement Watch each established websites connected with the numerous activist blogs. On the party's official website, the TSU hosted pages for the white-collar anti-ECFA alliance and follow-ups on lawsuits filed by the party against the referendum review committee. However, this time the government was well organized online. In early 2009, it established a cross-agency portal to integrate updated information from related agencies and to respond to questions and criticisms with one voice. The government was also much more aggressive in the traditional media and inter-personal communications. After informal consultations kicked off, the government provided updates on the consultations and the negotiation process through weekly press releases as well as workshops and road shows throughout the country. Most importantly, the government reached agreement with the DPP to hold a televised debate on the ECFA issue between President Ma Ying-jeou and DPP chairwoman Tsai Ying-wen on April 25, 2010. This debate was historic in that it was the first time that a debate was held between the ruling and the opposition party during a non-electoral period on one single policy issue. The government's intensive media campaign paid off as polls showed steadily increasing support for the ECFA from February 2009 through May 2010. The change in public opinion is recorded in the following table (see Table 5.2). Parallel to the change in public opinion, the opposition party also initiated a quiet shift

TABLE 5.2

Opinion poll on the Economic Cooperation Framework Agreement (ECFA)

	Approval (%)	Disapproval (%)
February 25, 2009	29	32
March 11, 2009	35	44
October 27, 2009	46	33
March 30, 2010	35	32
April 26, 2010	41	33
May 31, 2010	41	34

SOURCE: Television Broadcasts Satellite (hereafter, TVBS) Poll Center.

on the ECFA. During the 2009 magistrate elections, eight DPP candidates had joined forces to attack the ECFA as part of their strategy to delegitimize the KMT. In contrast, during the 2010 mayoral elections, DPP mayoral candidates refrained from making remarks on the ECFA during the campaign. This is indicative of the relative success of the government's media campaign in support of the ECFA.

The quasi-social movements with either implicit or explicit support of either of the two major political parties are different from the apolitical social movements in four respects. First, although there may not be a significant difference in terms of the scope of their online campaigns, apolitical social movements may attract a broader range of sympathizers, for instance, poets, producers, and composers, allowing for their more innovative online campaigns. With respect to on-site protests, however, quasi-social movements with strong political backing can mobilize demonstrations that have much broader scopes than the demonstrations launched by apolitical social movements. Second, student and youth groups are a main force in apolitical social movements, but they seldom participate in quasi-social movements for politically driven purposes. The anti-corruption movement is a case in point. High school students who supported the protest were accused of sullying student purity. Third, the effectiveness of quasi-social movements is questionable in terms of enforcing certain policy stances. As noted above, neither the anti-corruption movement that claimed over a million supporters nor the anti-ECFA movement that had support from both the DPP and the TSU were successful in blocking the ECFA or in seeking Chen Shui-bian's resignation. Fourth, these social movements are not effective in delivering sound election performance. Although the anti-corruption movement de-legitimatized the DPP regime, the DPP was still successful in maintaining the status quo in the following mayoral election when it was expected that the KMT would replace the DPP in Kaohsiung. In a similar vein, the anti-ECFA movement failed to bring the DPP an election victory in the following mayoral election, even though many had predicted that the DPP would make a breakthrough in taking at least one of the three seats held by the KMT.

Conclusion

On the basis of the above analysis, the following will provide some general observations with regard to trends in Internet politics that have gradually taken shape over the last decade and how they affect the outcome and quality of democracy in Taiwan. The trends and implications for democracy are apparent in three areas of change. First, the Internet has brought about a redefinition of election campaigns. There is much more of a focus among politicians on lifestyles, sports, and personal stories rather than on ideology or policy. On the one hand, this is due in part to the basically amusing nature of the Internet. On the other hand, politicians have taken advantage of the loss of privacy during the Internet era by including every part of his or her personal life in the campaign. I call this a "daily-life campaign." Nonetheless, the attraction of a daily-life campaign lies in the distance between the candidate and the masses. As a result, a daily-life campaign is likely to face decreasing return. This partly explains why the popularity of many top politicians declines rapidly. This was obvious in the drop in popularity of both Chen Shui-bian and Ma Ying-jeou. While enjoying a larger share of power in terms of votes and legislative support, Ma Ying-jeou's job approval rating dropped much more rapidly than that of Chen Shui-bian during the first three months of his term. A comparison is provided in the following table (see Table 5.3). It coincides with the prolonged time horizon for campaigns. Potential candidates may establish blogs or Facebook accounts long ahead of the official campaign. In the meantime, the dominant trend of criticizing the government in online chat rooms and BBS provides abundant and handy material for the opposition parties to voice their dissent and requires that the government respond. In this back-and-forth process,

TABLE 5.3
Presidential approval rate: Comparison between Chen and Ma

	Polling date (Year.Month)	2000.8	2000.11	2001.5	2002.5	2003.5	2004.5	2005.5	2006.5	2007.5
Chen Shui-bian	Approval	59%	44%	41%	51%	33%	43%	33%	16%	17%
	Disapproval	28%	48%	46%	38%	50%	42%	51%	70%	57%
	Polling date (Year.Month)	2008.8	2008.11	2009.5	2010.5	2011.5	2012.5	2013.5		
Ma Ying-jeou	Approval	41%	34%	38%	33%	36%	20%	14%		
	Disapproval	40%	52%	41%	47%	49%	64%	70%		

SOURCE: TVBS Poll Center.

NOTE: August 2000 is the time when the term of President Chen reaches its first 100 days and November 2000 is the time when the term of President Chen passes its first half year. By the same token, August 2008 is the time when the term of President Ma reaches its first 100 days and November 2008 is the time when the term of President Ma passes its first half year.

the campaign becomes a permanent battlefield in cyberspace. A direct result of such a permanent campaign is a shortened time horizon for public policies and politicized decision making.[54] This has been the case not only in American politics, but in Taiwanese politics as well during the Internet era.

The second change introduced by the Internet is the professionalization of campaigns and the weakening of political parties. As noted in the literature review, Gary Rawnsley has observed a trend of professionalization in Taiwan campaigns since the late 1990s, as evidenced by the modern organization, the careful demographic studies, the nuanced skills to communicate with voters, and the constant monitoring of change in public polls.[55] Recent elections campaigns have revealed that those who formerly did not take part in politics have now become key players on campaign teams. These players come from a wide array of disparate fields, including film producers, music composers, cartoonists, and online auction experts. These new players are able to portray the candidates in ways that are most attractive to the various constituencies whose votes are needed. However, the Internet also fosters a different type of professionalization by distancing the campaign team from the traditional party machines. This is because the online campaign platform, be it a website, Plurk, or Facebook, requires personalized messages and content. Accordingly, those who have special relationships with the candidates are well placed to supervise the online campaigns. This is especially useful in alienating voters from their own parties in neck and neck campaigns. Indeed, the Internet strengthens this trend, weakening the political parties and further decreasing the importance of substance.

The third change in the Internet era is the imbalanced empowerment and the rise of a politics of negation. Although the younger generations who are more capable of mastering online operations can play a larger role in politics, either during elections or in social movements, it should be noted that beneath the surface such empowerment may be imbalanced as many of those who spend tens of hours online and participate in verbal online battles are so-called "indoor men" (*otaku* or *zhainan*), who have limited life and social experiences. Of course, this does not mean that all the activists or people who create postings online fall within this category. But this does apply to a substantial proportion of those who function as mediators in cyberspace. Their views and preferences that are amplified in online discussions possibly become even more dominant in election campaigns and social movements due to the power of the online discussions. Furthermore, it is much easier to negate and delegitimize someone in cyberspace than it is to support and legitimize him/her. With the spread of opinions and criticisms in different blogs, chat rooms, and BBS, negative messages become dominant and leading political figures and mainstream political ideologies can be delegitimized and sidelined in public opinion.

In sum, the three changes described above indicate that in the Internet era political decisions in Taiwan tend to have shorter time frames and less substance. The irony in this transition is that as many feel empowered with the aid of the Internet to take part in the decision-making process, it is impossible to strike an authoritative balance between competing forces. An unfortunate result is an inability to make important decisions, with a further result that government indecisiveness on many critical policy fronts tends to be prolonged. Nevertheless, the above argument is based on at most superficial observations and its validation will require additional empirical studies in future follow-up research.

Notes

1. Pippa Norris, *Digital Divide: Civic Engagement, Information Poverty, and the Internet Worldwide* (Cambridge, UK: Cambridge University Press, 2001); Philip E. Agre, "Real-Time Politics: The Internet and the Political Process," *Information Society* 18:5 (2002): 311–331; Davy Janssen and Raphaël Kies, "Online Forums and

Deliberative Democracy: Hypotheses, Variables and Methodologies," *ActaPolitica* 40 (2005): 317–335; Benjamin R. Barber, *Strong Democracy: Participatory Politics for a New Age* (Berkeley: University of California Press, 1984); and Richard E. Sclove, *Democracy and Technology* (New York: Guilford Press, 1995).

2. RozaTasgrousianou, Damian Tambini, and Cathy Bryan, eds., *Cyberdemocracy: Technology, Cities and Civic Networks* (New York: Routledge, 1998).

3. William A. Galston, "(How) Does the Internet Affect Community? Some Speculation in Search of Evidence," in *Democracy.com? Governance in a Networked World,* eds. Elaine Ciulla Kamarck and J. S. Nye (Hollis, NH: Hollis Publishing, 1999); Sinikka Sassi, "The Controversies of the Internet and the Revitalization of Local Political Life," in *Digital Democracy: Issues of Theory and Practice,* eds. Kenneth L. Hacker and Jan A.G.M. van Dijk (New York: Routledge, 2001), 90–104.

4. Frances Cairncross, *The Death of Distance: How the Communications Revolution Will Change Our Lives* (Boston: Harvard Business School Press, 1997).

5. Stephen Coleman, "Cutting Out the Middle Man: From Virtual Representation to Direct Democracy," in *Digital Democracy: Discourse and Decision Making in the Information Age,* eds. Barry N. Hague and Brian D. Loader (London: Routledge, 1999); Agneta Ranerup, "Online Forums as a Tool for People-Centered Governance," in *Community Informatics: Shaping Computer-Mediated Social Networks,* eds. Leah Keeble and Brian Loader (London: Routledge, 2001), 205–219; Kees Brants, Martine Huizenga, and Reinekevan Meerten, "The New Canals of Amsterdam: An Exercise in Local Electronic Democracy," *Media, Culture and Society* 18, no. 2 (1996): 233–248; Clive Walker and Yaman Akdeniz, "Virtual Democracy," *Public Law* (Autumn 1998): 489–506; Jodi Dean, "Cybersalons and Civil Society: Rethinking the Public Sphere in Transnational Technoculture," *Public Culture* 13:2 (2001): 243–266.

6. Lawrence K. Grossman, *The Electronic Republic: Reshaping Democracy in the Information Age* (New York: Viking, 1995).

7. Jeffrey M. Ayres, "From the Streets to the Internet: The Cyber-Diffusion of Contention," *Annals of the American Academy of Political and Social Science* 566 (November 1999): 132–143; Bruce Bimber, "The Internet and Political Transformation: Populism, Community and Accelerated Pluralism," *Polity* 31:1 (Autumn 1998): 133–160.

8. Christopher May, *Information Society: A Skeptical View* (London: Polity, 2002).

9. Richard Davis, *The Web of Politics: The Internet's Impact on the American Political System* (Oxford, UK: Oxford University Press, 1999); Anthony G. Wilhelm, "Virtual Sounding Boards: How Deliberative Is Online Political Discussion?" in *Digital Democracy: Discourse and Decision Making in the Information Age,* eds.

Hague and Loader, 153–178; Hubertus Buchstein, "Bytes that Bite: The Internet and Deliberative Democracy," *Constellations* 4:2 (October 1997): 248–263; Cass R. Sunstein, *Republic.com.* (Princeton, NJ: Princeton University Press, 2001).

10. Sheryl J. Brown and Margarita S. Studemeister, "Virtual Diplomacy: Rethinking Foreign Policy Practice in the Information Age," *Information and Security* 7 (2001): 28–44; Mitra Barun Sarkar, Brian Butler, and Charles Steinfield, "Intermediaries and Cybermediaries: A Continuing Role for Mediating Players in the Electronic Marketplace," *Journal of Computer-Mediated Communication* 1:3 (December 1995): 1–14.

11. Buchstein, "Bytes that Bite"; James R. Beniger, *The Control Revolution: Technological and Economic Origins of the Information Society* (Cambridge, MA: Harvard University Press, 1986); James C. Scott, *Seeing Like a State: How Certain Schemes to Improve the Human Condition Have Failed* (New Haven, CT: Yale University Press, 1998).

12. Barbara K. Kaye and Thomas J. Johnson, "Online and in the Know: Uses and Gratifications of the Web for Political Information," *Journal of Broadcasting and Electronic Media* 46:1 (March 2002): 54–71.

13. Homero Gil De Zúñiga, Eulàlia Puig-I-Abril, and Hernando Rojas, "Weblogs, Traditional Sources Online and Political Participation: An Assessment of How the Internet Is Changing the Political Environment," *New Media & Society* 11:4 (June 2009): 553–574.

14. Ann Macintosh et al., "Electronic Democracy and Young People," *Social Science Computer Review* 21:1 (February 2003): 143–154.

15. World Bank, *World Bank Worldwide Governance Indicators*, http://info.worldbank.org/governance/wgi/index.asp.

16. This paragraph is enlightened by Philip E. Agre, who argues that it is people within institutional constraints who utilize information technology to achieve the goals set by the institution. Agre, "Real-Time Politics."

17. Anthony Downs, "An Economic Theory of Political Action in a Democracy," *Journal of Political Economy* 65:2 (April 1957): 137.

18. Donald A. Wittman, "Parties as Utility Maximizers," *American Political Science Review* 67:2 (June 1973): 495–498.

19. The author is informed by the work of John Roemer on the Downs-Wittman debate. See John Roemer, *Political Competition: Theory and Applications* (Cambridge, MA: Harvard University Press, 2001), 1.

20. Andrew Chadwick, *Internet Politics: States, Citizens, and New Communication Technologies* (Oxford, UK: Oxford University Press, 2006).

21. Ibid., 168–173.

22. Ibid., 134–137.

23. Ibid., 168–173, 140–141.

24. Gary Rawnsley, "Democratisation and Election Campaigning in Taiwan: Professionalizing the Professionals," in *Political Communication, the Mass Media and Transitions to Democracy,* eds. Katrin Voltmer and Slavko Splicahl (London: Routledge, 2006), 133–151.

25. Gary Rawnsley, "An Institutional Approach to Election Campaigning in Taiwan," *Journal of Contemporary China* 12:37 (November 2003): 767, 771–772, 775–776.

26. Rawnsley, "Democratization and Election Campaigning in Taiwan."

27. Song-In Wang, "Influence and Evaluation of Traditional and Non-traditional News Media on Candidates' Images," *Communication and Management Research* 1:1 (July 2010): 24–25.

28. Yah-Huei Hong, "Big Difference Between Taipei and Kaohsiung? A Study of Media Use Frequency and Perceived Media Importance in Relation to Political Cynicism and Voting Behavior," *Soochow Journal of Political Science* 29:2 (June 2009): 32–33.

29. Song-In Wang, "The Influence of the Internet on Political Attitudes and Campaign Participation in the 2004 Legislative Election," *Taiwan Democracy Quarterly* 3, no. 4: 95–96.

30. Lu-Lin Cheng and Holin Lin, "Social Movements in the Internet World: A Hyperlink Analysis of Social Movement Webs," *Taiwanese Sociology* 2 (December 2001): 74–77.

31. Holin Lin and Lu-Lin Cheng, "Social Movement Goes Online: An Exploratory Analysis of the Internet Experience of Taiwan's Social Movements," *Taiwanese Journal of Sociology* 25 (June 2001): 147–148.

32. Yin-Kun Chang, "The Gay Rights Movement on the Internet: Is It Possible or Not?" *Journal of Cyber Culture and Information Society* 4 (January 2003).

33. "Survey on Broadband Internet Usage: Executive Summary" (Taipei: Taiwan Network Information Service [TWNIC], January 2004), 4; "Survey on Broadband Internet Usage in Taiwan: Executive Summary" (Taipei: TWNIC, January 2011), 3.

34. Ibid., 4.

35. Ibid., 5.

36. Shih-Hsin Database for Communications Studies, "2010 Shih-Hsin List of Top Media," College of Journalism and Communications, Shih-Hsin University, November 2, 2010, http://cc.shu.edu.tw/~cjc/pages/main.html [in Chinese].

37. Shih-Hsin Database for Communications Studies, "2012 Shih-Hsin List of Top Media," College of Journalism and Communications, Shih-Hsin University, July 6, 2010, http://cc.shu.edu.tw/~cjc/pages/main.html [in Chinese].

38. Such as simple games used by the KMT candidates.

39. Po-Chung Chuang, *Internet Campaigns in Taiwan* (Taipei: Miro Books, 2007), 39–41.

40. This too is a notable example of resorting to professionals. The producer was a famous motion picture producer of Springhouse Entertainment Technology.

41. Po-Chung Chuang, *Internet Campaigns in Taiwan*, 42–47.

42. A blogger was found systematically producing defamatory postings against the KMT candidate (Chou Hsi-wei) while mocking the candidate's name on the blog's designated title tag (Brother Wei's Blog).

43. It was initially due to the introduction by United News Online (www.udn .com), the online branch of *United Daily*, that all the candidates began to write blogs.

44. Yah-Hui Hong, "Toward a New Application of Integrated Marketing Communications in Political Campaigns," *Communications and Management Research* 7:2 (January 2008).

45. Lin and Cheng, "Social Movement Goes Online: An Exploratory Analysis of the Internet Experience of Taiwan's Social Movements," 151–152.

46. The Coolloud and the South Community and Culture Interactive Database (later becoming South E-Newsletter) are the two most notable examples.

47. Shun-Hsiao Chen, "Online Civic Journalism in Taiwan: Development and Challenge," in *Revisiting Media in Taiwan*, ed. Excellence in Journalism Award Foundation (Taipei: Chuliu, 2009).

48. Cityghost, "Defending Losheng Against State Violence on March 11, 15 and 16," Cityghost Blog, *Interlocals.net*, March 17, 2007, http://interlocals.net/?q= zh-hant/node/147.

49. They appeared at a press conference to express opposition to the project. The figures included Landies Hotel CEO Chang-shou Yan, famous movie director Hsiao-hsien Hou, and several members of the Sustainable Development Commission of the Executive Yuan. Other public figures who expressed dissenting opinions on other occasions included Huai-min Lin, founder of Cloud Gate Dancing Group, and De-fu Hu, a famous singer.

50. Shujuan Zhu, "Suao-Hualian Cake Shop Website: Making it Easy to Deconstruct the Suao-Hualian Highway," *United Daily News*, January 21, 2008, A10.

51. Anti-Kuokuang Petrochemical Complex database, https://sites.google.com/ site/noguoguang/home [in Chinese].

52. Ming-sho Ho, "Understanding the Trajectory of Social Movements in Taiwan (1980–2010)," *Journal of Current Chinese Affairs* 39:3 (2010): 17.

53. Although some of the leaders of the anti-corruption movement had long histories of being in the Pan-Green camp, the movement mostly consisted of

Pan-Blue supporters. Most of the public figures in the Pan-Blue camp joined the movement and those from the People First Party were among the core leadership team.

54. Joe Klein, "The Perils of the Permanent Campaign," *TIME*, October 30, 2005.

55. Rawnsley, "An Institutional Approach to Election Campaigning in Taiwan."

PART FOUR

Economic Adaptation to the Global Economy

SIX

Global Ascendance, Domestic Fracture
Korea's Economic Transformation Since 1997

Yoonkyung Lee

Introduction

If the year 1987 marked a new period in South Korea's political develop-ment, the year 1997 signified a turning point in the transformation of its socioeconomic landscape. The neoliberal economic policies that were intro-duced in the early 1990s were implemented in the aftermath of the Asian financial crisis that severely hit the Korean economy in 1997–1998. This pro-cess accompanied a significant withdrawal of government intervention into the market, which had been a central trademark to define the developmen-tal state in South Korea during its rapid economic growth era. Economic actors, both capital and labor, became freer agents than previously to stand on their own. Capital was "freed" from the shackles of government regula-tions while labor was "freed" from the shield of government protection.

The Korean economy was swift to leave behind the shocks and humili-ations of the financial crisis and to recover its resilience by growing into the world's twelfth-largest economy.[1] Korean *chaebŏls* (large conglomerate groups), such as Samsung, Hyundai, and LG, continue to form the back-bone of this economic dynamism. These firms have become increasingly globalized and indisputably recognized as global brand-name producers. Cell phones, LCD screens, automobiles, and computer chips made by Korean conglomerates account for a significant market share in the global economy.

However, as much as there were young workers forced to work like machines during the economic miracle of the 1960s and 1970s, there are increasingly frustrated working people behind Korea's global spectacle of the 2000s. Outside of the chaebŏls, decent jobs are hard to come by. Under the euphemism of a "flexible" labor market, a rising number of workers face precarious working conditions and lack minimum social protections. Korean schoolchildren compete literally sometimes to death to be admitted into the best colleges, but what awaits them after they graduate is passage into a growing reservoir of the unemployed.

This chapter, by examining the socioeconomic transformations that occurred in post-1997 Korea, demonstrates that the Korean economy has made successful adaptations to the global market by subscribing to neoliberal reforms. But this process also created serious insecurities among the working population. This dichotomy between the global ascendance of Korean firms and the domestic fractures among the working people best captures the political economy of contemporary Korea. Furthermore, these economic disparities are not without political consequences. Growing inequalities have galvanized socioeconomic cleavages in political competition, as evidenced by the recent elections.

To fully explore Korea's economic transformation and its political implications, this chapter proceeds as follows. I first provide an overview of the changes that occurred in the Korean economy and discuss how the role of the government has shifted in this process. Then, by examining exemplary cases of successful global brand-name products in the high-tech industries, I investigate how large corporations have altered their business strategies to globalize their operations and products. In the subsequent section, I discuss the other side of the Korean economy's global ascendance: the looming stratification between regular and non-regular employees and the growing unemployment among college graduates, the most serious plagues that undermine the sustainability of South Korea's socioeconomic cohesion. Lastly, I examine how these economic changes have influenced Korean democracy, especially focusing on the emergence of a new political cleavage around the issue of social protection (*pokchi*) and economic democracy in recent electoral contests among the contending political parties.

Global Ascendance: Globalization and Economic Transformation

The Korean economy continued to grow after the nation's democratic transition in 1987, despite the two major global economic shocks that occurred in 1997 and 2008. Over the last twenty-five years, the gross domestic product (GDP) increased almost tenfold, from US$143.4 billion to US$1,014.3 billion, and per capita income rose from US$3,402 to US$20,759 (see Table 6.1).

Average growth rates were 6.68 percent in the 1990s and 4.43 percent in the 2000s. The volume of exports expanded from 38 percent of GDP in 1987 to 50 percent of GDP in 2009. According to the World Bank, Korea ranks as

TABLE 6.1
Major economic indicators, 1987–2010

Year	GDP (in billion US$)	GDP/capita (in US$)	Real GDP growth rates	Exports as % of GDP
1987	143.4	3,402	12.3	38
1988	192.3	4,548	11.7	36
1989	236.3	5,556	6.8	31
1990	270.3	6,306	9.3	28
1991	315.5	7,276	9.7	26
1992	338.1	7,714	5.8	27
1993	372.2	8,402	6.3	27
1994	435.5	9,727	8.8	29
1995	531.3	11,735	8.9	29
1996	572.8	12,518	7.2	28
1997	532.3	11,505	5.8	32
1998	358.5	7,607	–5.7	46
1999	461.6	9,778	10.7	39
2000	533.5	11,292	8.8	39
2001	504.6	10,631	4.0	36
2002	575.9	12,100	7.2	33
2003	643.6	13,460	2.8	35
2004	722.4	15,082	4.6	41
2005	844.7	17,531	4.0	39
2006	951.1	19,722	5.2	40
2007	1049.3	21,695	5.1	42
2008	930.9	19,296	2.3	53
2009	834.4	17,193	0.3	50
2010	1,014.3	20,759	6.2	51

SOURCE: Korea Statistical Information Service, http://kostat.go.kr/portal/english/index.action.

TABLE 6.2
GDP and employment by sectors

Year	Total labor force (in thousands)	AGRICULTURE		INDUSTRY		SERVICES	
		% of GDP	% of employment	% of GDP	% of employment	% of GDP	% of employment
1987	16,354	10.5	21.9	30.6	28.1	49.5	50.0
1990	19,009	8.7	14.0	27.4	26.5	64.1	59.5
1995	20,414	6.2	11.8	27.2	23.7	66.7	64.5
2000	21,156	4.6	10.6	28.6	20.4	67.0	69.0
2005	22,856	3.3	7.9	27.8	18.1	68.9	73.9
2010	23,829	2.6	6.6	30.8	17.0	66.7	76.4

SOURCE: Korea Statistical Information Service, http://kostat.go.kr/portal/english/index.action.

the world's twelfth-largest economy in the global market (based on nominal GDP) and the twenty-sixth wealthiest nation in terms of per capita income (nominal GDP per capita). While the growth rates slowed in the early 2000s, the Korean economy, with its volume and competitiveness, managed to remain a vital player in the global economy.

The economic structure was also altered during this period. The agricultural sector underwent rapid shrinkage, both in terms of its contribution to GDP (from 10.5 to 2.6 percent) and employment (from 21.9 to 6.6 percent). In contrast, industrial production remained a significant sector, generating about 30 percent of national wealth but with a much smaller labor force (from 28.1 to 17.0 percent of the total labor force). Notably, the service sector rose to the center of the Korean economy, producing about two-thirds of GDP and employing about three-quarters of the labor force (see Table 6.2). The composition of the Korean economy obviously shows its maturity as an advanced capitalist country.

GOVERNMENT AND CORPORATIONS IN POST-1997 KOREA

The Asian financial crisis of 1997–1998 marked a crucial turning point for the Korean economy by opening the door to unfettered market forces. Policy recommendations from the neoliberal economic camp in the aftermath of the crisis were twofold. One was to revive the economy's macroeconomic stability through deregulation (of the exchange rates and the financial market), and the other was to remove the inefficiencies in corporate

operations and the rigidities in the labor market.[2] The Kim Dae-jung government (1998–2002) that was sworn in amid the economic disaster was faith-
ful in following these policy recommendations. The exchange rate became
relatively free from government intervention, and the capital market that had
once been heavily protected moved into increased deregulation. After 1998
the Bank of Korea (Korea's central bank) gained greater independence, and
in 1999 the Financial Supervisory Commission was established to oversee the
operations of financial institutions and to enforce fair practices.[3]

The deregulation of the capital market resulted in an inflow of foreign
investment as well as an outflow of overseas investment by Korean capital.[4]
Barriers to mergers and acquisitions were removed, and the rules governing
foreign direct investment (FDI) were liberalized. The deregulation allowed
100 percent foreign ownership of publicly traded companies, including
complete ownership through hostile takeovers.[5] Reflecting this opening-
up of the capital market, capital inflows rose from US$17.9 billion in 1997
to US$84.7 billion in 2007.[6] Similarly, capital outflows increased from
US$16.0 billion to US$76.1 billion in the same period.[7] Among capital outflows, portfolio investments have accounted for the largest share (56 percent), in the form of equities rather than bonds. Korean chaebŏls became
active in FDI, with the annual sum of US$2.9 billion in 1997 peaking to
US$32.5 billion in 2010.[8] In terms of regional distribution, 39.9 percent
of Korean FDI goes to Asia, 23.8 percent to Europe, and 18.1 percent to
North America.[9] The United States is the top destination (US$5.0 billion,
or 15.3 percent of total FDI in 2010), followed by China (US$3.8 billion, or
11.6 percent) and Britain (US$3.7 billion, or 11.3 percent).

To remove the economic inefficiencies in the Korean economy, chaebŏl
reform was a central part of the policy recommendations. The unlimited
expansion of chaebŏl corporations had been the result of the national champion strategy adopted by the previous developmental state. However, because of the state's unconditional support, chaebŏls engaged in economically
inefficient behavior, eventually dragging the Korean economy into the 1997
financial crisis. Critics raised the issues of chaebŏl problems such as over-
investment, excessive borrowing of foreign capital, poor management of debt,
weak corporate-governance structure, and the pursuit of dominant market
shares and diversification instead of competitiveness and specialization.[10]

In terms of corporate restructuring, the Kim Dae-jung government
focused on enhancing transparency and accountability in corporate

accounting and management, improving the financial structure, and streamlining business activities among the chaebŏl groups. The goal was to turn the large corporations to specializing in core areas of industrial competence. The government pushed for the so-called big deals, in which the big five chaebŏls (Samsung, Daewoo, Hyundai, LG, and SK) swapped major lines of business among themselves to consolidate excessive and duplicative investments while achieving greater economies of scale.[11] As a consequence of the restructuring, sixteen out of the thirty largest conglomerates were sold, merged, or liquidated, including Daewoo, the second-largest chaebŏl in terms of asset size at the time.[12]

The government took a dominant and decisive role in introducing and implementing these reform policies during the post–financial crisis period. The irony of the reform outcome was that it eventually weakened state capacity to intervene in the market by enabling Korean conglomerates to become increasingly independent and to amass unchecked economic wealth as well as political influence. The introduction of deregulatory measures meant that the Korean government lost its power to control the flow of capital and to allocate credit to domestic corporations, one of its key disciplining measures in the past as a developmental state. Chaebŏls globalized their finance and operations while becoming concentrated in their capacity and wealth. By 2010, 539 corporations affiliated with the top ten chaebŏls (based on asset size and excluding affiliates in the financial sector) produced 41.1 percent of GDP, representing a significant increase from the 34.4 percent in 2005.[13]

With the unprecedented economic magnitude of large conglomerates within the Korean economy, the chaebŏls grew to command huge political power and influence. The relationship between government and business that had once been led by the state became dominated by business interests. Presidents Kim Dae-jung, Roh Moo-hyun, and Lee Myung-bak all were pressured to hold meetings with the chairpersons of the chaebŏl groups to solicit their cooperation in investment and employment.[14] This reversed power relationship between government and business was most aptly summed up when former President Roh Moo-hyun remarked in 2005 that power had already been turned over to the corporations and the global market. In this sense, the achievements of the chaebŏl reform under the Kim Dae-jung presidency remain dubious. Some aspects of chaebŏl operations were reformed to meet global standards (such as corporate accounting and financial management), but the chaebŏls amassed overwhelming private economic power within Korean society, to the extent that there was no countervailing force to harness their hubris.

Although the government position vis-à-vis the chaebŏls was significantly weakened in the post-1997 era, there was one noteworthy developmental initiative undertaken by the government. The Powerful Internet Nation (*int'ŏnet kangguk*) project signified an accelerated shift in the nation's development strategy from manufacturing to a knowledge-based economy. Economic growth would be based on information communications technology and the information technology (IT) industry. Government plans included the Korea Information Infrastructure Initiative (1995–2000), the National Framework Plan for Informatization Promotion (1996–2000), Cyber Korea 21 (1999–2002), and e-Korea Vision 2006 (2002–2006).[15] These projects were intended to guide heavy investment in building an information infrastructure to lay out a foundation for the knowledge-intensive sector and high-tech manufacturing. Government spending on research and development (R&D), for instance, increased from 4.2 percent of the 2000 national budget to 13.7 percent in 2010.[16] The government also sponsored the establishment of a number of institutions to provide infrastructural support to the IT industry. Four ministries (the Ministry of Information and Communication, the Ministry of Science and Technology, the Ministry of Culture and Tourism, and the Ministry of Trade, Industry, and Energy) and eleven public agencies and institutes were placed in charge of policy coordination for the advancement of the IT industry.[17]

As an outcome of these government initiatives, Korea has indeed risen to be a powerful Internet nation with remarkable infrastructure facilities and a globally competitive IT industry. Recent international surveys indicate that the rate of Korea's expansion in Internet use is one of the highest in the world. With 34.8 percent of households having fixed broadband subscriptions in 2009, Korea closely follows the top-ranking countries such as Denmark (37.9 percent), the Netherlands (35.6 percent), and Sweden (35.5 percent), while standing significantly ahead of the United States (25.8 percent) and Japan (24.9 percent).[18] As one of the leading nations in high-speed broadband access, South Korean Internet users dominate the entire gamut of Internet activities, from online games to digital multimedia broadcasting to Twitter and Facebook activities. As will be discussed in the following sections, these government-initiated foundations have significantly contributed to the global competitiveness of made-in-Korea high-tech products. Based on the advanced IT infrastructure, Korean firms are able to test the quality of their products with the most sophisticated IT consumers in Korea before they enter the global consumer market.

Amid government policies to liberalize the Korean economy, the chaebŏls also introduced new management strategies to make their operations more competitive, both internally and internationally. One of the initiatives for greater competitiveness can be traced back to 1993 when Lee Geon-hee, chairman of the Samsung Group, announced the "New Management Strategy" (*sin kyŏngyŏng chŏllyak*). This new strategy was eventually adopted, with variations in specific application, by other firms as well.

Korea's large corporations commonly targeted two objectives through this new approach to management. First, as in the catchphrases of "Global Management" (*segye kyŏngyŏng*) by Daewoo or "Global Super Corporation" (*ch'o illyu kiŏp*) by Samsung, the chaebŏls sought to globalize their R&D, production, marketing, and sales. Automobile industries, too, introduced strategic campaigns to become more global. For instance, Hyundai Motors initiated the "Global Top Ten Movement," with the goal of becoming among the top ten auto makers by 2000, and Kia Motors launched the "Prime 10 Strategy" with similar goals.

As discussed above, outward FDI by Korean corporations peaked in the 1990s. The destination of overseas investments was divided between developing economies and developed economies in accordance with corporations' new management strategies.[19] To avoid the rising production costs in the domestic market, Korean firms engaged in FDI in the developing economies. As such, capital went to labor-intensive sectors, such as parts assembly, textiles, apparel, toys, and footwear. Foreign direct investment to advanced capitalist economies was more aimed at obtaining technological exchanges (via R&D) and strategic access to the consumer market. Therefore, investments were concentrated in high-tech and capital-intensive manufacturing, including consumer electronic goods, semiconductors, computers, and automobiles.[20] Also, compared to their operations in Asia, Korean firms' overseas operations in North America and Europe involved more R&D labs and affiliated companies than branch offices.[21]

While globalizing their operations externally, chaebŏls had another objective in introducing the New Management Strategy, that is, to rationalize their intercorporate networks and employment management. This process involved rearranging their relationships with subsidiaries and subcontractors into a tighter vertical chain. Chaebŏls were able to gain more-efficient and streamlined production networks than before, but small firms in sub-contractor relations with chaebŏl groups were squeezed into higher levels of competition. Another component of the new strategy was to increase the chaebŏls' managerial control over labor processes against organized labor that was exercising its newly gained, rising influence on the shop floor. In the name of "rationalization," corporations introduced various methods for tighter management of labor, such as automatization, greater flexibility in employment (making hiring and dismissal easier and employing more temporary workers), performance-based remunerations and promotions (instead of based on seniority), and cultivation of a company culture and loyalty.[22]

Furthermore, employers and their associations (the Korean Employers' Federation and the Federation of Korean Industries) vigorously lobbied and pressured the government to revise the existing labor laws and to introduce stipulations for a flexible labor market. Amendments to the labor law since 1996 reflect this crucial component in the New Management Strategy.[23]

The initiatives by Korean conglomerates to globalize operations and to rationalize domestic functions since the 1990s have been instrumental in their transformation into successful global corporations. However, these strategic moves have also placed immense strains on the labor side. The exit of capital to cheaper labor markets and the tighter control of labor processes have undermined the newly invigorated labor movements by threatening the stability and security of workers.

GLOBAL CHAEBŎLS AND GLOBAL PRODUCTS

The adoption and execution of global strategies by Korean firms have con-tributed to elevating their products into global brand names. The top three chaebŏls—Samsung, Hyundai, and LG—have grown into global corpora-tions with remarkable product popularity and market shares in the global economy. The Samsung Group is indisputably the most successful Korean global firm, with twenty-seven intra-group corporations (including elec-tronics and heavy industry) and five intra-group financial institutions. Total sales have almost doubled, from US$120 billion in 2001 to US$200 billion in 2010. According to Interbrand, an international brand-assessment firm, in 2010 Samsung ranked nineteenth among the one hundred most well-established global brand names.[24] Samsung Electronics, the Samsung

Group's flagship corporation, sells more products abroad (about 20 percent in North America, 20 percent in Europe, and 10 percent in China) than to domestic consumers (accounting for only 20 percent of all of its sales).[25] Samsung is the world's largest producer in television manufacturing, especially in LCD and LED displays in addition to its computer chips. In 2012, Samsung rose to become the world's largest mobile phone maker (29 percent of the world market share), beating out its long-time competitor, Nokia (24 percent of the world market share), according to an American market research firm, IHS iSuppli.[26] Samsung smartphones Galaxy S (introduced in June 2010 and sold 22 million units by the second quarter of 2012) and Galaxy S2 (released in April 2011 and sold 20 million units by the second quarter of 2012) represent stellar examples of their global hit products by competing with Apple's iPhone.[27]

Hyundai Motors, Korea's largest automaker, has also risen to a global producer. The firm sells more cars abroad than it does domestically by exporting about 60 percent of its total sales of over 3 million vehicles.[28] Along with Kia Motors, it formed the Hyundai Motor Group and expanded its sales to 3.6 million vehicles to 193 countries in 2010.[29] According to the Organisation Internationale des Constructeurs d'Automobiles, Hyundai Motor Group ranked as the world's fourth-largest automobile manufacturer in 2010, following General Motors, Volkswagen, and Toyota.[30] LG Electronics is another Korea-born global corporation. The firm exports 97 percent of its home entertainment products, 96 percent of its mobile devices, and 85 percent of its home appliances.[31] Following Samsung Electronics, LG is the world's second-largest television manufacturer and the fifth-largest mobile phone producer.[32]

This brief survey on Korean economy's transformation since the 1990s shows that both the government and large corporations have successfully adapted to a globalizing world economy. The government was quick to introduce deregulatory measures, whereas chaebŏls aggressively pursued global strategies. On the surface, the Korean economy's overall record seems to demonstrate remarkable achievements.

Domestic Fractures: Polarization and Insecurity of Workers

Yet there is the other side of the Korean economy's global success, characterized by growing socioeconomic inequalities and insecurities among the working people. Critics have blamed the unlimited deregulation of market interests in the post-1997 era for the increasing polarization (*yanggŭkhwa*: widening economic disparities) within Korean society. The neoliberal reforms have freed corporations from government control, allowing corporations to exercise unchecked economic and political power. The economic structure has become concentrated in a small number of chaebŏls, and the labor market has undergone rapid fragmentation and stratification. At the same time, the development of the welfare state has lagged behind overall GDP levels, leaving workers without an appropriate level of state protection.

POLARIZATION WITHIN THE LABOR FORCE

Korean workers enjoyed a brief heyday before the financial crisis. Between the late 1980s and the early 1990s, they experienced both rising political influence (with increasing unionization rates and labor law reforms guaranteeing basic labor rights) and increasing economic remuneration (with collective agreements granting rising wages and benefits and more employment security). However, the political ascendance and economic gains in the aftermath of the political democratization in 1987 were short-lived, and labor unions were soon facing a tough uphill battle. On the political front, labor unions were under assault because labor was not accepted as a legitimate player in South Korea's conservative political landscape. As such, socioeconomic and distributional issues had no political representation in the formal political process, at least until the formation of the Democratic Labor Party (DLP) in 2000.[33] Furthermore, employers were becoming increasingly assertive with respect to reorganizing the labor market, producing greater flexibility and insecurity.

The onset of the Asian financial crisis and the following neoliberal reforms represented a major blow to workers and labor unions. During the crisis alone, more than 220,000 workers (including 63,000 workers in the top five chaebŏls, 45,000 in the financial sector, and 53,000 in public enterprises) were laid off, and few were able to find similar jobs even after the economy bounced back.[34] Although the Korean economy soon recovered, most firms drastically decreased or halted new recruitments of full-time employees with secure labor contracts. This was part of the New Management Strategy discussed earlier to reduce labor costs and increase employment flexibility. Even in the existing regular jobs, firms often substituted regular workers with contingent workers contracted under precarious labor conditions. With employers' insistence on greater flexibility in allocating and deploying labor, the government introduced or changed labor policies to make the labor market more flexible but highly insecure for working people.[35] A statement by non-regular workers at Hyundai Motors who went on strike in November 2010 reveals the extent of the labor market stratification, even within the same workshop: "A regular worker puts on the right wheel and I [a non-regular worker] put on the left wheel. But my paycheck is 60 percent of his."[36]

The number of non-regular workers (*pi chŏnggyujik*), including contingent, temporary, part-time, and dispatch workers, has dramatically increased in the post-1997 period. Figure 6.1 shows the share of non-regular workers as well as the share of non-regular employment within male and female workers, respectively. The ratio of non-regular workers to all paid employees that was 43.2 percent in 1996 (before the crisis) soared to 55.7 percent five years later in 2001. It reached the peak of 58.4 percent in 2000 and has since been in a gradual decline to 49.4 percent as of 2011. With the grave social consequences associated with the rising number of non-regular workers, the government introduced some protective measures in 2007. The gradual drop of non regular workers can be explained by measures that stipulate the conversion of the non-regular worker with more than a two-year contract to regular employment.

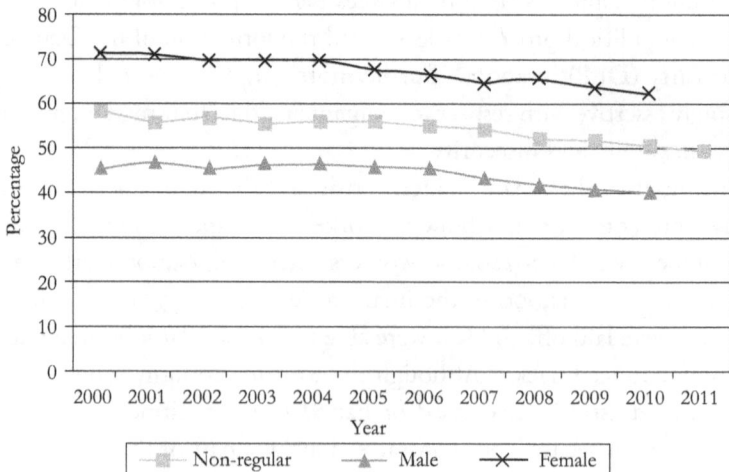

FIGURE 6.1 Non-regular workers in Korea, by percentage

SOURCE: Korean National Statistics Office, *Additional Survey of Economically-Active Population (2012)*, http://kostat.go.kr/portal/english/news/1/1/8/index.board?bmode=read&aSeq=270955.

Another observable trend in rising contingent labor is its gender disparity. As shown in Figure 6.1, the gap between male and female non-regular workers is not closing. As of 2011, 40.2 percent of employed men held non-regular jobs while 61.9 percent of women with a job were in non-regular employment. The disproportional share of female labor in non-regular employment is further reflected in union data. Table 6.3 shows that only 2.8 percent of non-regular workers were unionized, accounting for 13.7 percent of overall union membership. The gap between the share of unionized male workers and that of female workers increased dramatically over twenty years. While the gap in 1985 was 15.5 versus 11.1 percent, by 2006 it had grown to 13.5 versus 5.3 percent.[37] These figures point out that while women are predominantly employed as non-regular workers, Korean unions primarily based on the regular labor force grossly under-represent women workers. This further implies that non-regular women workers are not only disadvantaged in the labor market (with lower wages, greater job insecurity, and lack of social safety protections), but also they are deprived of basic organizational representation to raise their socioeconomic grievances.

National unions, both the Federation of Korea Trade Unions (FKTU) and the Korea Confederation of Trade Unions (KCTU), have often been criticized for their inadequacy in organizing non-regular and female workers and for their failure to address workers' concerns about deteriorating working conditions and labor rights violations. However, the increasing fragmentation in the labor market poses a serious threat to the labor unions. Korean unions have traditionally been strong in large corporations in the manufacturing sector. However, the regular labor force has been declining, both in the shrinking manufacturing sector and the expanding service sector. This means that labor unions have been losing their organizational basis while the task of organizing fragmented non-regular workers has become formidable.

TABLE 6.3
Disparities in union representation (2010)

Total paid employees (15.3 million)	Regular workers (49.6%)	Non-regular workers (50.4%)
Unionization rates	21.6%	2.8%
Share in total union membership	86.3%	13.7%

SOURCE: Korean Statistical Information Service, http://kostat.go.kr/portal/english/index.action.

Union density that reached a peak at 18 percent of paid employees in 1989 has since been declining, stabilizing at around 10 percent in the 2000s.[38]

The wage differential is an obvious disadvantage dividing regular and non-regular workers. Non-regular workers, even if they perform the same labor, are paid on average 57 percent of a regular worker's wage.[39] In addition to lower wages and more employment insecurity, non-regular workers face substantial discrimination in the provision of basic social welfare programs (public pensions, health insurance, employment insurance, and retirement allowances).[40] Table 6.4 shows the disparity in coverage between regular and non-regular workers and between workers in large firms (with more than three hundred employees) and those in small firms (with less than three hundred employees). With the exception of health insurance, workers in non-regular jobs or in small firms are hugely disadvantaged in coverage of public pensions, employment insurance, and retirement allowances. Moreover, the effective coverage rate of the programs is significantly lower than the legally mandated rate because a considerable proportion of non-regular workers and workers in small businesses are not covered.[41]

Disparities between regular and non-regular workers are not limited to wages and job security. Rather, they extend to greater socioeconomic inequalities due to the drastically different coverage in the social safety net as the following section discusses. These changing labor market conditions also affected the middle class by shrinking its size. The size of the middle class reached its peak in 1993 with 74.6 percent of paid-employee households, but this number dropped to 62.4 percent in 2009.[42] The proportion of the middle-class income also decreased from 65.2 percent to 53.3 percent

TABLE 6.4
Effective coverage of social welfare programs (2008)

		Public pensions	Health insurance	Employment insurance	Retirement allowance
All paid employees		70.6	93.9	56.8	61.4
Type of employment	Regular	81.3	96.3	65.8	74.5
	Non-regular	49.8	89.4	39.2	35.7
Size of company	300 and over	96.4	99.2	78.0	93.7
	Below 300	67.3	93.4	54.1	57.2

SOURCE: Korea Labor Institute, "Strategies to Improve Employment Security," KLI Research Report 2009-04 (2009).

during the same period.[43] The rising proportion of non-regular workers and the shrinkage of the middle class represent the widening economic gap within the Korean population.

UNEMPLOYMENT AND COLLEGE GRADUATES

Another serious socioeconomic problem in post-1997 Korea has been the rising unemployment among college graduates. Korea's official unemployment rate is modest, at 3.7 percent in 2010, but the unemployment rate of the non–economically active population is relatively high, at 32.9 percent.[44] Among the non–economically active population of 16.4 million in 2010, 0.93 million were two-year college graduates and 2.95 million were four-year university graduates.[45] This means the share of college degree holders among the unemployed has risen from 11.2 percent in 2000 to 17.6 percent in 2010.[46] Furthermore, according to the Ministry of Education, Science, and Technology, the unemployment rate among the 498,000 college students who graduated in 2010 is 41.4 percent.[47] A survey of 194 four-year colleges regarding the unemployment rates of their graduates shows a significant gender gap, with 37.8 percent of male students and 45.0 percent of female students remaining unemployed after graduation.[48]

Korean youth are known for spending long hours at school and at extra tutoring sessions to excel in a succession of highly competitive tests until they enter college. As a result, since 2004 the rate of high school students advancing to college has been above 80 percent.[49] Moreover, because of the rapidly rising college tuition, a majority of students graduate from college with a burdensome amount of debt. A recent survey of college graduates found that 68 percent of them had an average debt of US$11,000 by the time of their graduation.[50]

Yet what awaits them after earning college degrees is fierce competition in the labor market where only a few are able to land decent jobs with livable wages and minimal security. The failure to create jobs for college graduates is attributable to Korea's economic structure that is heavily concentrated in a small number of chaebŏls. Large conglomerates with more than 1,000 workers employed 1 million workers (8.3 percent of all those employed) in 1998, but these figures had dropped to 0.8 million (6.7 percent of all those employees) by 2009.[51] Except for during a short period in 1999–2002 when small venture capital in the IT industry flourished and small businesses were able to absorb a significant number of college graduates, the predominance of a small number of chaebŏls has contributed to the shrinking job market for young Koreans.

Growing inequality has been the most acute social problem in post-1997 Korea. This is an alarming turn for the national economy that was once praised for achieving rapid growth with relative equality. As compared in Table 6.5, the Gini coefficient, one of the most widely used equality indexes, improved to 0.28 in 1996, but by 2010 it had deteriorated to 0.34. The gap in market income between the top 20th percentile and the bottom 20th percentile also deteriorated, from 4.01 to 7.74. Households that earn less than 50 percent of the median income rose from 7.8 percent to 12.0 percent during the same period. The ratio of workers paid below the minimum wage increased from 4.2 percent in 2000 to 11.5 percent in 2010.[52] By any standard, inequality in Korea has risen since the Asian financial crisis. In a broader comparative evaluation, too, Korea's ratio-of-earnings deciles are far above the average of other capitalist economies known as liberal welfare states, while Korea's polarization of earnings is widening faster than that of any other Organisation for Economic Co-operation and Development (OECD) countries.[53]

Socioeconomic inequality is exacerbated not only by the sheer increase in the market income disparity, but also by other forms of wealth. For instance, the Gini coefficient of nonfinancial assets (i.e., real estate, increased from 0.57 to 0.70 during the period from 1993 to 2005).[54] Furthermore, because the Korean welfare system is underdeveloped, the improvement from the market income Gini coefficient (0.34) to the disposable income Gini coefficient (0.31) is minimal, at 0.03. This indicates that government

TABLE 6.5
Growing inequality

Year	Gini coefficient	Ratio of 5th to 1st earnings deciles	Relative poverty[a]	Workers paid below minimum wage[b]
1996	0.28	4.01	7.8%	4.2% (for 2000)
2010	0.34	7.74	12.0%	11.5%

SOURCE: Korean Statistical Information Service, http://kostat.go.kr/portal/english/index.action.
[a]Relative poverty is calculated by the share of households that make less than 50% of the median income.
[b]The minimum hourly wage was set at US $1.7 in 2000 and US $4 in 2010.

intervention with social protection policies has minimal effects in correcting the income gap. Among the OECD countries, those known for their high spending on social welfare, such as Belgium, Germany, Sweden, and Denmark, all rank high in this regard by improving the correction between market income and final disposable income by more than 0.20.[55]

Although the administrations of Kim Dae-jung and Roh Moo-hyun introduced and expanded social protection policies, the development of the Korean welfare state lags behind the level of its economic affluence. Social expenditures remain at 7.9 percent of government spending (next to Mexico), the lowest among the OECD countries and much lower than the OECD average of 22.1 percent.[56] Korea does not only spend miserly on social welfare programs, but also the programs are premised on "earned" entitlement. This means that the welfare system is largely funded by the contribution of employers and employees, with minimal financial commitments by the government. The system also uses strict means-test and benefit criteria to determine the beneficiaries, leaving many of the most needy citizens unprotected by social welfare. Furthermore, Korea's high tax breaks and low taxation rates aggravate the already existing economic inequalities by favoring high-income earners and penalizing low-income groups.[57]

Socioeconomic Polarization and Its Implications for Korean Democracy

The growing disparities in the labor market and social protection are not only the outcomes of market forces, but also the creation of political decisions. Government intervention and public policy constantly shape how markets operate and what outcomes markets produce. In this sense, the structural changes that occurred in the economy and the labor market have significant implications for Korean democracy. The magnitude of the financial crisis in 1997 hastened the implementation of market deregulation policies without much serious deliberation on the socioeconomic consequences or binding social consensus among the contending interests. The representative democratic system in Korea has been deficient in counterbalancing the unilateral application of neoliberal policies and the preponderance of business interests.[58]

Although Korean democracy has made significant progress in terms of constitutional stability since the 1987 transition from decades-long authoritarian rule, the political system has often been characterized by a dominance of executive, especially presidential, power and chaotic political parties. On the one hand, Presidents Kim Dae-jung and Roh Moo-hyun both tried to establish a foundation for social protection programs, but they were limited in tackling the rising socioeconomic polarization. On the other hand, political parties have been slow to attend to distributional issues and social protection programs, at least until the recent elections. Korean parties were created from the top and have been led by individuals with presidential ambitions; they have been organizationally inchoate from repeated splits and mergers; they have lined up along regional ties instead of along programmatic differences; and the emergence of "left" parties to represent distributional issues has long been suppressed because of the North–South division and the deep-seated anti-Communist ideology in the South.[59]

However, the neoliberal changes in the Korean economy and the growing discontent among the working people who are facing increasing economic strains have begun to change the political arena. Polarization (*yanggŭkhwa*), social protection (*pokchi*), and economic democracy (*kyŏngje minjuhwa*) emerged as the dominant political agenda items in public discourse. Such a shift in public opinion to recognize the centrality of economic redistribution is well reflected in recent surveys. In a 2011 poll conducted by the East Asian Institute, 57 percent of the respondents indicated that redistribution is more important than growth.[60] This is a significant increase from 45 percent from a similar poll taken in 2006. Even the respondents who identified themselves as politically conservative showed a greater level of support for economic redistribution, from 34 percent in 2006 to 47 percent in 2011. Also, more than half of the respondents were affirmative about raising taxes and introducing a net-wealth tax.

As citizens' concerns deepened from procedural democracy to economic democracy, socioeconomic cleavages began to be galvanized in electoral contestations, and political parties were pressured to be more responsive to social protection policies. First, the DLP, a pro-labor party formed in 2000 to represent distributional issues, was able to advance to the National Assembly in 2004. The emergence of the DLP signaled an electoral possibility of a progressive agenda as well as programmatic competition among political parties. Second, with the 2008 inauguration of President Lee Myung-bak from the Grand National Party (GNP) and his conservative policy orientation, Korean voters began to clearly discern the policy effects of competing political alternatives.[61] Taking advantage of this political competition, the traditionally center-positioned Democratic United Party (DUP) moved to the left to respond to the growing grievances over economic polarization. Even the conservative party, the GNP (renamed the Saenuri Party under the leadership of Park Geun-hye) adopted a set of social welfare policies to appeal to changing Korean voters.

Korean political parties, once disparaged for their regionalist appeal and lack of a programmatic differentiation, have increasingly mobilized around the socioeconomic cleavages, especially the issue of polarization and social protection. Although the DLP was the first to articulate social protection policies, in recent electoral contestations both the DUP and the GNP have been competing along these cleavages. At its party caucus in October 2010, the DUP adopted "universal social protection" as a major part of its platform, and the GNP responded by advocating "selective social protection."

The 2010 local elections are viewed as a demarcation in Korea's post-democratization electoral contests where the central political cleavages were transformed from regionalism to social protection. The center and left parties (the DUP, the DLP, the Progressive New Party, and the People's Participatory Party) aligned against the conservative candidates from the GNP and the Liberal Progressive Party. The former advocated universal social welfare, including free school meals prepared with eco-friendly ingredients, free child care, public subsidies for college tuition, and welfare for the elderly. The conservatives were drawn into this discourse but they campaigned for selective and gradual application of social protections. The center-left coalition won various positions in the local competitions, demonstrating voter demand for expanded application of social welfare policies. The electoral results are summarized in Table 6.6.

The referendum that took place in August 2011 in the Seoul metropolitan area is another example that reveals the galvanization of socioeconomic cleavages in partisan competition. The 2010 Seoul local election created a split government, in which the mayor was from the conservative GNP, and representatives from the liberal DUP held a majority in the Seoul Metropolitan Assembly. The Assembly passed an ordinance to introduce free school meals, but the conservative mayor called for a referendum for selective free meals based on family income. The DUP strategically campaigned for a boycott of the referendum, arguing that the ballot misrepresented

TABLE 6.6
Local election results, 2010[a]

	← RIGHT . . . . POLITICAL PARTIES . . . . LEFT →					
Election	Grand National Party	Liberal Progressive Party	Democratic Party	Democratic Labor Party	Progressive New Party	Total seats[b]
Head of greater local government[c]	6	1	7	1	0	16
Members of greater local assembly	287 (252+35)	41 (38+3)	362 (330+32)	24 (18+6)	3	762 (678+84)
Head of lower local government	82	13	92	3	0	228
Members of lower local council	1,247 (1,087+160)	117 (95+22)	1,025 (871+154)	115 (90+25)	22	2,888 (2,512+376)
Superintendent of education	10			6		16

SOURCE: National Election Commission, www.nec.go.kr/engvote_2013/main/main.jsp.

[a]A mixed voting system is used in Korea's local elections. The first number in the parentheses indicates the number elected from single-member districts, and the second number indicates the number elected from the party list based on a proportional representation rule.

[b]The numbers may not add up to the total number of contested seats because several minor parties and independents are not included.

[c]Greater local governments are at the level of 7 metropolitan cities and 9 provinces; lower local governments are at the level of cities, districts, and counties (228 total).

the alternative policy options. The referendum failed to gain the required minimum turnout rate (33.3 percent of the electorate) and the mayor of Seoul resigned, taking responsibility for the failed referendum.

The centrality of social protection policies continued in the national legislative election in April 2012 and the presidential election in December 2012. While the conservative GNP turned out as the winner in both elections, it was obvious that debates on economic democracy defined the electoral contestations of competing parties. Both the DUP and GNP candidates advocated how to realize economic democracy, as stipulated in Article 119-2 of the Korean Constitution, into actual policy programs.

The electoral campaigns and contested policy issues in recent elections demonstrate that the rising concern for socioeconomic polarization has crucially affected the direction of partisan competition. Ironically, the unfortunate outcome of heightened economic disparity has pushed Korean democracy to make a substantial move from practicing procedural democratization to contemplating economic democratization for economic equity and social inclusion.

Conclusion

This chapter examined the socioeconomic transformations in post-1997 Korea by focusing on the neoliberal policies implemented by the government and the subsequent change in government–business relations. Corporations in Korea, especially the chaebŏl groups, have grown increasingly independent from government regulations and have successfully expanded to global markets. They continue to form the backbone of the Korean economy, with a growing dominance in market shares and brand-name products, both domestically and globally.

Yet beneath this seemingly successful adaptation of Korean business to the global market, Korean workers face widening socioeconomic polarization. The labor market has become increasingly fragmented and stratified, with a growing number of non-regular (mostly women) workers and a rising rate of unemployed youth (especially among college graduates). Underdeveloped social protection programs and limited coverage have exacerbated economic disparities, as is reflected in the various inequality indicators.

The genesis of this dichotomy between global ascendancy and domestic fractures lies in the imbalance between economic liberalization and democratic politics. Although the shocking impact of the financial crisis on the Korean economy hastened implementation of market deregulation policies, the representative democratic system in Korea was deficient in counterbalancing the rising dominance of business interests with collective social policies. Political parties have been slow to attend to distributional issues and to initiate social protection programs. Labor unions have remained organizationally parochial, barely able to defend their members' interests. Until the recent elections, political forces to collectively represent the grievances of the working people have been dispersed, if not divided.

The local elections in 2010, when universal social protection emerged as a central campaign issue, demonstrate how the changing socioeconomic landscape since 1997 has affected the reconfiguration of political cleavages and partisan competition. Both the legislative and presidential elections in 2012 continued to show how the Korean representation system is undergoing transformation to serve as an institutional arena in which socioeconomic grievances are articulated and resolved. Without timely political interventions, the growing inequalities will eventually pose a detrimental threat to Korea's economic viability and social cohesion.

Notes

1. By gross domestic product in purchasing power parity in 2010. See World Bank, at http://data.worldbank.org.

2. In fact, market liberalization in Korea did not begin in the post–financial crisis period. The formal origins of market liberalization can be dated back to President Kim Young-sam's *segyehwa* drive in 1994.

3. The independence of the central bank is one of the core neoliberal programs. Yet the effectiveness of this independence is controversial among economists and policy makers.

4. The opening of the capital market began under the Kim Young-sam administration in the early 1990s as part of its effort to be admitted to the Organisation for Economic Co-operation and Development, which ultimately was successful in 1996.

5. Stephan Haggard, *The Political Economy of the Asian Financial Crisis* (Washington, D.C.: Institute for International Economics, 2000), 151.

6. Bank of Korea, *Economic Statistics System,* http://ecos.bok.or.kr./ [in Korean].

7. Ibid.

8. Korea Export and Import Bank, *Overseas Direct Investment Statistics Yearbook 2010* (Seoul: Korea Export and Import Bank, 2010).

9. Ibid.

10. Sung-Hee Jwa, "A New Framework for Government-Business Relations in Korea," in *Korea's New Economic Strategy in the Globalization Era,* eds. O. Yul Kwon, Sung-Hee Jwa, and Kyung-Tae Lee (Cheltenham, UK: Edward Elgar, 2003), 85–97.

11. Haggard, *The Political Economy of the Asian Financial Crisis,* 151.

12. O. Yul Kwon, "Korea's Economic Policy Framework in the Globalization Era," in *Korea's New Economic Strategy in the Globalization Era,* eds. Kwon, Jwa, and Lee, 29–49.

13. *Hankyoreh shinmun* (Seoul), August 20, 2011.

14. Jong-Il You, "The Political Economy of Reforms in South Korea," unpublished manuscript, 2010.

15. International Telecommunication Union, "Broadband Korea: Internet Case Study," unpublished manuscript, 2009.

16. Ministry of Planning and Finance, *Government Expenditure Statistics,* www.mosf.go.kr [in Korean].

17. Seong-Hoon Park, "Transformative Capacity of the State and the Development of the Korean IT Industry," *Han'guk Sahoe* 9, no. 2 (2008): 145–168 [in Korean].

18. International Telecommunication Union, www.itu.int/ITU-D/ict/statistics.

19. Yong-Soo Park, "The Political Economy of the Chaebŏls' Globalization," *Korea-Germany Social Science Journal* 11, no. 2 (2001): 245–268.

20. Ibid., 250.

21. Ku-Hyun Jung and Dong-Jae Kim, "Globalization and International Competitiveness: The Case of Korea," in *Democratization and Globalization in Korea: Assessments and Prospects,* eds. Chung-in Moon and Jongryn Mo (Seoul: Yonsei University Press, 1999), 349–367.

22. Ho-chang Lee, *The Reorganization of Shop Floors and Labor Unions' Strategies* (Seoul: Federation of Korean Trade Unions, 1999), 6–24 [in Korean].

23. The essential feature of the labor law reforms in 1996 and thereafter was to increase labor-market flexibility, i.e., to facilitate hirings and dismissals and to allow for increased use of flexible labor (e.g., temporary workers, non-regular workers, dispatch workers). This is why the labor law reforms in 1996 led to the largest nationwide labor strike, co-organized by the Korea Confederation of Trade Unions and the Federation of Korean Trade Unions. When the Korea Confederation of Trade Unions agreed to a similar labor law amendment in 1998, the union leadership was brought down by a revolt from its rank-and-file members. Since then, it has not played a role in the government-led tripartite consultations.

24. Interbrand website, www.interbrand.com.

25. Don-Mun Cho, *The New Management Strategy and the Responses of Unions* (Seoul: Korean Confederation of Trade Unions, 1998) [in Korean].

26. *Chosun Ilbo,* at http://english.chosun.com.

27. *Samsung Electronic Sustainability Report 2012,* www.samsung.com/us/about samsung/sustainability/sustainabilityreports/download/2012/2012_introduction .pdf.

28. Hyundai website, www.hyundai.com.

29. Ibid.

30. "World Motor Vehicle Production OICA Correspondents Survey," http:// oica.net/wp-content/uploads/ranking-without-china-30-nov-12.pdf.

31. LG Electronics website, www.lg.com.

32. Ibid.

33. Yoonkyung Lee, *Militants or Partisans: Labor Unions and Democratic Politics in Korea and Taiwan* (Stanford, CA: Stanford University Press, 2011). Yet the DLP remains a small minority party in the 299-seat National Assembly. From 2004 to 2007 the party had ten lawmakers, and since 2008 it has had only five.

34. Lee, *The Reorganization of Shop Floors,* 28.

35. Yoonkyung Lee, "Divergent Outcomes of Labor Reform Politics in Democratized Korea and Taiwan," *Studies in Comparative International Development* 44, no. 1 (Winter 2009): 47–70.

36. As of 2010 Hyundai Automobile in Ulsan employed about thirty-one thousand regular workers and eight thousand non-regular workers. "Workers Lament Over the Stopped Assembly Line," *Hankyoreh* 21, December 21, 2010.

37. Ministry of Labor, *Annual Report on Trade Unions 2007* (Seoul: Ministry of Labor, 2007).

38. Ibid.

39. Ministry of Labor, *Labor Statistics,* http://laborstat.molab.go.kr [in Korean].

40. The average hourly wage for non-regular workers in 2009 was US$7.7, about 60 percent of the hourly wage for regular workers (US$13.0) (Korea Statistical Information).

41. Jae-jin Yang, "The Political Economy of the Korean Welfare State," unpublished manuscript, 2010.

42. The middle class is defined as households that make 50–150 percent of the median income. Samsung Economic Research Institute, "Changing Middle Class in Korea and Its Socioeconomic Implications," unpublished paper, 2010.

43. Ibid.

44. Korea Statistical Information Service, http://kosis.kr [in Korean].

45. Ibid.

46. Ibid.

47. Ministry of Education, Science, and Technology, http://academyinfo.go.kr [in Korean].

48. Ibid.

49. In 2010 the economically active population was estimated to be 24.4 million.

50. *Choongang Ilbo,* http://article.joinsmsn.com [in Korean].

51. Korea Statistical Information Service, http://kosis.kr [in Korean].

52. Ibid.

53. Yang, "The Political Economy of the Korean Welfare State."

54. Soo-yeon Lee, "Reasons for Growing Inequality," *Saesayŏn Newsletter* 175 (2009): 4–7 [in Korean].

55. OECD (Organisation for Economic Co-operation and Development), http://stats.oecd.org.

56. Yang, "The Political Economy of the Korean Welfare State."

57. Ibid.

58. Jang-jip Choi, *Democracy After Democratization* (Seoul: Humanitas, 2010) [in Korean].

59. Lee, *Militants or Partisans.*

60. Hankook Ilbo, www.hankooki.com [in Korean].

61. Examples of conservative policies introduced during the Lee government include the reduction of the income tax from 35 to 33 percent and the cut in the corporation tax from 22 to 20 percent. The upper 20th percentile of income earners benefited from 77 percent of the income tax reductions and the corporation tax cut went to the 415 top firms (0.1 percent of all corporations) (*Hankyoreh shinmun,* May 15, 2011).

SEVEN

Challenges for the Maturing Taiwan Economy

Wan-wen Chu

Introduction

Taiwan's outstanding economic performance in the postwar period, along with that of other East Asian countries, has been well recognized. The fact that Taiwan's democratic transition has been relatively smooth and peaceful has led some to call it a political miracle. The shine on these "twin economic and political miracles," however, has faded somewhat because of problems in subsequent development since the early 1990s.

Problems of transformation on the political front are probably easier to discern, considering that a former president is now in jail for life on charges of corruption. Problems in the economic sphere are not as apparent but nonetheless are present and substantial.

The slowing pace of economic growth is understandable, for Taiwan has become a maturing industrialized economy. There is, however, a sense of pessimism and a lack of direction in terms of future development, which is partly manifested in the near zero average growth rate of investment during the early 2000s (see Table 7.1 below). The recent global recession has significantly affected Taiwan and even brought a sense of gloom as the economy tumbled again after a brief recovery in 2010. The rapidly increasing degree of integration with the Chinese economy has posed not only political challenges, but also an economic policy conundrum, that is, how to reconcile political and economic goals. This China factor and the associated political uncertainty about Taiwan's future create great anxiety and dominate other issues, such as economic uncertainty and worsening income distribution.

Since the early 1990s, almost every policy that promoted, or rather merely accommodated, increasing integration with mainland China was likely to provoke political opposition. The Democratic Progressive Party (DPP) advocates political independence from China and hence has taken a stand against increasing economic ties with China. When in power during 2000–2008, the DPP government adopted numerous political postures to defy China, but, in terms of economic policy, it mostly acquiesced to the change. Its political postures, however, inevitably brought political instability and economic uncertainty, and made the situation unsustainable. Nonetheless, to this day, the DPP has yet to come up with a policy plan reconciling its conflicting political and economic aims. The post-2008 Ma government realized its election pledge to stabilize cross-strait relations by successfully signing the cross-strait Economic Cooperation Framework Agreement (ECFA) in 2010, which should be considered a breakthrough. However, its passage coincided with the occurrence of the global economic crisis. The expected beneficial effects of ECFA were drowned out by the impact of recession, and thus failed to provide a counterweight to the anxiety brought by political uncertainty. In the meantime, the lack of consensus on a vision for the future of Taiwan's economy, caused by this unresolved policy conundrum, reinforced economic pessimism during this severe recession. Because populist politics since the early 1990s have greatly reduced fiscal revenues and increased the fiscal deficit, the Ma government has had little room to maneuver to alleviate the stress. All these contributed to the continuous decline in President Ma's popularity after he managed to win reelection in early 2012.

This situation differs much from that in the pre-reform era, when developmentalism was supported by social consensus. The current lack of consensus, along with the democratization process, has greatly altered the workings of the developmental state that had been responsible for promoting the early postwar economic development.

This chapter will review the record of growth after the economic and political transformation in the late 1980s, examine how the developmental state has been transformed and how economic transformation has affected democratization, and discuss future challenges facing Taiwan.

Transformation of the Economy: Liberalization and Globalization

After the Plaza Accord in 1985, the East Asian tigers were forced to liberalize their economies. In addition to strong American pressure, internal economic forces—including the ballooning accumulated trade surplus and the resultant booms in the asset markets—necessitated great changes in the successful early postwar growth model. In a way, the success of the postwar export-promotion regime brought about its own demise.

Starting in the late 1980s, Taiwan began a simultaneous great transformation in its economic, political, and social spheres. External economic liberalization began in earnest in 1986. The government lessened foreign exchange controls and began to reduce tariff rates, remove non-tariff trade barriers, and phase out the tariff rebate program. The liberalization of domestic markets went in tandem with the pace of democratization. After the lifting of martial law in mid-1987, the government began to open up (to both foreign and local firms) various domestic markets, in which the number of operating licenses had previously been limited and more or less remained frozen since the early postwar period. Significantly, at the same time the government began to improve the cross-strait relationship by allowing citizens to visit relatives on the mainland for the first time. Privatization of state-owned enterprises began two years later. Thus, democratization, liberalization, and globalization went hand in hand within a short period. It should be stressed that this was a process of managed liberalization, even though the extent of its success can be debated.

Now, after more than twenty years since this transformation, Taiwan's economy has become more globalized and liberalized. I will first examine its overall economic record and then discuss various aspects of this transformation in more detail.

Overall Record

Major economic indicators for Taiwan are reported in Tables 7.1 and 7.2. There is no doubt that Taiwan's economic performance has been relatively good during 1991–2010. According to International Monetary Fund estimates, Taiwan's per capita gross domestic product (GDP) based on purchasing power parity in current international dollars was $9,854 in 1990 and $35,227 in 2010, a respectable 3.58-fold increase. Current International Monetary Fund estimates rank Taiwan in 2010 twenty-first in global

TABLE 7.1

Major economic indicators I, 1951–2010

Year	Real GDP	Population	GNP per capita	Gross capital formation	Industrial production	Exports	CPI
			AVERAGE ANNUAL GROWTH RATES OF				
1951–1960	8.1	3.6	4.5	14.1	11.9	22.1	9.8
1961–1970	9.7	3.1	6.8	15.4	16.5	26.0	3.4
1971–1980	9.8	2.0	7.7	13.9	13.8	29.5	11.1
1981–1990	7.6	1.4	6.8	7.3	6.2	10.0	3.1
1991–2000	6.3	0.9	5.3	7.5	5.1	10.0	2.6
2001–2010	**3.9**	**0.4**	**3.6**	**0.2**	**5.1**	**6.7**	**0.9**

SOURCES: Directorate General of Budget, Accounting, and Statistics (hereafter, DGBAS), http://eng.dgbas.gov .tw/mp.asp?mp=2;http://eng.stat.gov.tw/mp.asp?mp=5;andwww.dgbas.gov.tw/ct.asp?xItem=9522&ctNode=2857 [in Chinese]. Also, Council for Economic Planning and Development (hereafter, CEPD), *Taiwan Statistical Data Book* (Taipei: various years).

rankings of real per capita GDP, ahead of some advanced countries like the United Kingdom and France.[1] In contrast, at the same time Taiwan's nominal per capita GDP was only $18,603 in nominal U.S. dollars in 2010,[2] indicating a significant undervaluation of the exchange rate. This reflects the fact that Taiwan, to some extent, still relies upon its export-promoting growth model, which includes an undervalued exchange rate, a stable price level, a low tax rate, and a diligent workforce with long working hours.

The pace of overall economic growth has slowed down gradually. The average annual growth rate in the first three postwar decades was around 9.0 percent, but it dropped to 7.6 percent, 6.3 percent, and 3.9 percent in the following three decades, respectively. The decrease in industrial production was even more pronounced, declining from an average of 14.0 percent in the first thirty years to 5.1 percent in the early 2000s. This in itself is no cause for alarm, of course, because it partly reflects the fact that Taiwan's economy is maturing and the service sector is becoming more important, despite the influence of the two global shocks in recent years.[3]

However, Taiwan's economy performed less well in the 2000s than in the 1990s. There may also be local causes for this, besides the obvious differences in the global conditions in these two periods, such as the booming 1990s and the crisis-prone 2000s. In terms of sources of GDP growth, on average, the increase in domestic demand accounted for 111.0 percent of the

TABLE 7.2
Major economic indicators II, 1951–2010

Year	Real GDP per capita (US$)	Gross fixed capital formation as a % of GDP	Exports as a % of GDP	Trade balance (US$ millions)	GDP BY INDUSTRY (%)		
					Agriculture	Industry	Services
1952	213	11.3	8.0	–71	32.2	19.7	48.1
1960	164	16.6	11.5	–133	28.5	26.9	44.6
1965	229	17.0	19.4	–106	23.6	30.2	46.2
1970	393	21.7	30.4	–43	15.5	36.8	47.7
1975	978	31.3	39.9	–643	12.7	39.9	47.4
1980	2,385	30.7	52.6	78	7.7	45.7	46.6
1985	3,290	19.5	52.5	10,678	5.7	44.6	49.7
1990	8,124	23.1	44.5	12,639	4.0	38.9	57.0
1995	12,918	25.7	46.3	9,330	3.3	33.1	63.5
2000	14,704	24.4	52.2	11,218	2.0	30.5	67.5
2005	16,051	21.9	61.0	15,817	1.7	31.3	67.1
2007	17,154	21.5	70.3	27,425	1.5	31.4	67.1
2009	16,353	18.1	60.5	29,304	1.6	29.8	68.7
2010	18,503	21.1	71.3	23,364	1.6	31.1	67.2

SOURCES: DGBAS, at http://eng.dgbas.gov.tw/mp.asp?mp=2; http://eng.stat.gov.tw/mp.asp?mp=5; and www.dgbas.gov.tw/ct.asp?xItem=9522&ctNode=287 [in Chinese]. Also CEPD, *Taiwan Statistical Data Book* (Taipei: various years).

growth in the 1990s, and only 34.3 percent in the 2000s.[4] That is, in the 1990s, while the currency appreciated and the service sector was liberalized, there occurred more balanced and domestically oriented growth. In the first years of the 2000s, however, industrial exports became the engine of growth once again. Though the export sector exhibits the same pattern of declining growth as the overall economy, the share of exports in GDP, after declining during the 1990s, began to increase in the 2000s, reaching 71 percent in 2010, much higher than the previous peak of 55 percent in 1986 prior to the reforms. In the meantime, the trade surplus has continued to grow, reaching a new high in 2009.

This renewed external imbalance is partly caused by stagnation in domestic consumption and investment. In the 1990s, private consumption grew around 6.9 percent annually on average, a level even higher than that of the GDP. During the early 2000s, however, the rise in private consumption has averaged only 2.2 percent and consistently lagged behind the overall growth rate.[5] The contributing factors for sluggish consumption growth probably include a continuously declining population growth rate, worsening terms of trade, and a lack of consumer confidence, among others.[6] An even more alarming development is that the average annual growth rate of gross fixed capital formation, which was 14.4 percent in the first three postwar decades, dropped to 7.3 percent and 7.5 percent in the following two decades and turned near zero in the 2000s.

The reasons for this lack of investment growth are manifold. One is that the growth of the service sector, though robust after the liberalization in the 1990s, slowed significantly upon entering the 2000s. Another reason for this imbalance has been the mainly one-way flow of cross-strait capital and human resources, from Taiwan to the mainland, due to government restrictions. This flow has become more pronounced in the 2000s.

In sum, the overall growth record seems satisfactory, but it has been accompanied by great economic imbalances. The latter reflect the fact that the process of liberalization has been only partly successful and that transformation of the pre-reform developmentalist model is incomplete.

Globalization

After liberalization, the pace of globalization in terms of trade and investment accelerated, as expected. Table 7.3 shows the inward and outward

TABLE 7.3
Globalization

Year	INWARD FDI [a]		OUTWARD FDI, TOTAL		OUTWARD FDI, TO CHINA			
	Number of cases	US$ billions	Number of cases	US$ billions	Number of cases	US$ billions	Share in total outward FDI (%)	Average value per case (US$ millions)
1952–1990	5,772	13.3	873	3.1				
1991	389	1.8	247	1.8	237	0.2	9.5	0.7
1992	411	1.5	286	1.1	264	0.2	21.8	0.9
1993	323	1.2	9,395	4.8	9,329	3.2	65.6	0.3
1994	389	1.6	971	2.6	934	1.0	37.3	1.0
1995	413	2.9	535	2.4	490	1.1	44.6	2.2
1996	500	2.5	419	3.4	383	1.2	36.2	3.2
1997	683	4.3	8,785	7.2	8,725	4.3	60.0	0.5
1998	1,140	3.7	1,322	5.3	1,284	2.0	38.2	1.6
1999	1,089	4.2	516	4.5	488	1.3	27.7	2.6
2000	1,410	7.6	874	7.7	840	2.6	33.9	3.1
2001	1,178	5.1	1,225	7.2	1,186	2.8	38.8	2.3
2002	1,142	3.3	3,183	10.1	3,116	6.7	66.6	2.2
2003	1,078	3.6	3,941	11.7	3,875	7.7	66.0	2.0
2004	1,149	4.0	2,071	10.3	2,004	6.9	67.2	3.5
2005	1,131	4.2	1,368	8.5	1,297	6.0	71.1	4.6
2006	1,846	14.0	1,154	12.0	1,090	7.6	63.9	7.0
2007	2,267	15.4	1,057	16.4	996	10.0	60.6	10.0
2008	1,845	8.2	714	15.2	643	10.7	70.5	16.6
2009	1,711	4.8	660	10.1	590	7.1	70.4	12.1
2010	2,042	3.8	998	17.4	914	14.6	83.8	16.0
Sum	Sum	Sum	Sum	Sum	Sum	Sum	Average	Average
1991–2000	6,747	31.3	23,349	41.0	22,974	17.1	37.5	1.6
2001–2010	15,389	66.3	16,370	118.8	15,711	80.2	65.9	7.6

source: Adapted from Ministry of Economic Affairs (hereafter, MOEA), *Statistics on Overseas Chinese and Foreign Investment, Outward Investment, Outward Technical Cooperation* (Taipei: MOEA Investment Commission, various years).

[a]FDI = foreign direct investment.

flows of capital over time. Taiwan's outward foreign direct investment (FDI) began to grow after liberalization in the late 1980s. During the 1990s, however, inward and outward FDI was more or less balanced. That is, many foreign firms were lured by the attraction of the opening up of the market in Taiwan. In the 2000s, however, outflows totaled US$118.8 billion, which was almost a threefold increase from the 1990s and exceeded the inflows by 80 percent. Since this century began, Taiwan has become a net exporter of capital.

The most significant aspect of this development is that mainland China has become a dominant partner, resulting in increased integration in terms of trade, investments, and flows of human resources. As shown in Table 7.3, the share of Taiwan's outward FDI going to China averaged 37.5 percent during the 1990s and rose to 65.9 percent during the 2000s, exhibiting a clearly rising trend. The average size of FDI also increased significantly, implying the growing involvement of large-scale firms.

In addition to investments, China also became the major destination of Taiwan's exports. The share of Taiwan's exports going to China displayed an increasing trend (see Figure 7.1). Beginning from almost zero in the late 1980s, it continued to rise thereafter, exceeding that of the United States in 2001 and reaching over 30 percent in 2007. From the 1960s to the 1990s, the United States had been Taiwan's most important market. It should be noted that few people expected this dramatic shift when liberalization first began.

The trade relationship across the strait remains imbalanced, mainly due to Taiwan government restrictions. Taiwan maintains various trade restrictions exclusively vis-à-vis China. Both economies entered the World Trade Organization (WTO) around 2002. At the time there was a long list of goods that could not be imported from China to Taiwan. The list was not shortened until the two sides signed the ECFA in 2010. It is well understood that the Beijing government tolerates Taiwan's trade discrimination due to political considerations. As a result, Taiwan maintains a large trade surplus with China. Despite large fluctuations, China's share in Taiwan's total trade surplus has averaged around 174 percent from 1991 to 2010. It is true that part of this surplus is related to China's trade surplus with the United States; nonetheless, it entails increasing economic integration across the strait.

How important has this economic relationship been for China? Foreign direct investment from overseas Chinese has played a key role since China

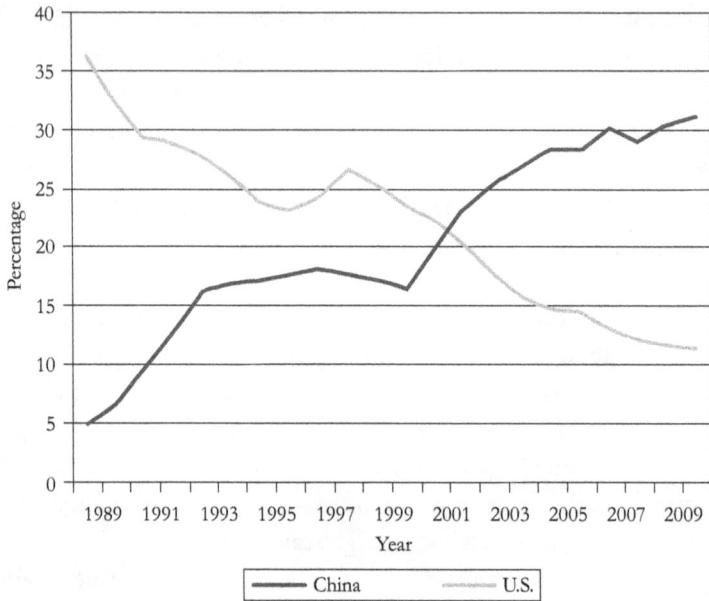

FIGURE 7.1 Exports to the U.S. and mainland China, as a percentage of Taiwan's total exports

SOURCE: Mainland Affairs Council, *Cross-Strait Economic Statistics Monthly*, no. 216, at www.mac.gov.tw/ct.asp? xItem=93930&ctNode=5934&mp=3.

opened its doors to FDI. Even though the amount of FDI from Hong Kong was much greater than that from Taiwan, FDI from Taiwan was more influential in the export-oriented manufacturing sector, especially in the information and communications technology (ICT) sectors. Furthermore, FDI from Hong Kong and Taiwan had a crucial influence during the 1990s, when foreign multinational firms stayed away from the mainland in the aftermath of the 1989 tragedy. The weight of FDI from Taiwan has declined as the Chinese economy has continued to grow, but it is still important in generating ICT exports from China and hence providing employment opportunities.

The importance of the cross-strait relationship for Taiwan is undeniable. Participation in the China boom has allowed Taiwan to maintain its own growth from the 1990s. By moving production to the mainland, Taiwanese firms have been able to greatly expand their scale of operations and hence have extended their life as subcontractors. The story of the ICT industry will be discussed in more detail later in this chapter.

At the same time, the cross-strait relationship continues to be a challenge. It goes without saying that reconciling the need to share in China's economic growth and to maintain political autonomy has been a core issue for Taiwan ever since the two sides resumed contact in the late 1980s. This remains a challenge even after signing the ECFA.

Shifts in Industrial Structure

Several industry trends are observable in Taiwan. Its exports mainly consisted of labor-intensive products in the earlier postwar period and technology- and capital-intensive products in the later period. Taiwan's exports came mainly from small and medium enterprises in the earlier period and from large-scale firms in the later period. During both periods, subcontracting has been the dominant business model. At present, the leading industrial enterprises in Taiwan are high-tech subcontractors and medium-tech upstream input producers. Very few large-scale firms have their own brands, and Taiwan's few global brands are mostly owned by non-major firms.[7] The recent unexpected success of HTC, a smartphone producer, can almost be considered an exception, the story of which will be discussed later.

Part of the reason why Taiwan has been able to maintain healthy growth in the postwar period is that its industry has been very adaptive. In other words, Taiwan has been able to find new growth industries as its comparative advantage has shifted. As a result, the manufacturing sector has not lost much ground in terms of the size of employment from 1991 to 2010, even though much of its operations moved offshore (see Table 7.4). Its total number of employees declined to around 2.4 million in 1990, and then fluctuated around 2.4–2.5 million during the last twenty years. Therefore, as shown in the Table 7.4, the average annual growth rate of employment in the manufacturing sector, though small, remained positive. The employment level of the service sector grew significantly during the 1980s and the 1990s, but slowed considerably in the 2000s. This is evidence that Taiwan still relies on its industrial sector to maintain growth and global competitiveness.

The industrial structure continued to change as Taiwan's comparative advantage shifted due to its own success. For example, in the early postwar period, the first leading sector was the textile and apparel industry. At the height of its influence, it accounted for over 23 percent of manufacturing

TABLE 7.4

Employment in industry, manufacturing, and service sectors

Year	Total	Industry	Manufacturing	Services
NUMBER OF EMPLOYEES (1,000 PERSONS)				
1974	—	1,705	1,475	—
1980	3,669	2,481	2,029	1,188
1985	4,342	2,881	2,492	1,462
1990	4,800	2,876	2,435	1,924
1995	5,762	2,998	2,398	2,764
2000	5,934	2,958	2,459	2,975
2005	6,201	2,933	2,479	3,268
2010	6,602	3,006	2,517	3,596
AVERAGE ANNUAL GROWTH RATE OF EMPLOYMENT (%)				
1974–1980	—	6.05	4.96	—
1981–1990	2.75	1.56	1.94	4.96
1991–2000	2.16	0.29	0.11	4.51
2001–2010	1.16	0.21	0.29	2.05

SOURCE: Calculated from data taken from DGBAS, http://win.dgbas.gov.tw/dgbas04/bc5/earning/ht456e.asp.

value-added in the early 1970s. As shown in Table 7.5, since then its share has continued to decline, reaching a mere 2 percent in 2010.

The last two columns of Table 7.5 display the changes in each sector's share in total manufacturing value-added during the 1990s and into the 2000s. The shift was more evenly distributed among sectors during the 1990s; for example, the declines in textiles and plastics were offset by the increases in chemicals, basic metals, and electronics. The more traditional or more labor-intensive industries gradually moved their operations overseas, especially to China.

In the 2000s, however, all sectors except electronics experienced decreases in their shares of total manufacturing value-added. The share of the electronics sector rose steeply from 26.85 percent in 2000 to 48.19 percent in 2010. Almost half of Taiwan's manufacturing activities are now concentrated in the one sector. In 1980 the share of the top three industries, in terms of size, accounted for only 40.86 percent of manufacturing. In contrast, that share accounted for 71.00 percent in 2010.

TABLE 7.5
Distribution of manufacturing value-added, 1980–2010 (%)

	1980	1985	1990	2000	2010	Changes 1990–2000	Changes 2000–2010
Food, beverages, and tobacco	7.85	8.44	6.79	7.08	4.23	0.29	-2.85
Textiles, apparel, and leather	18.74	17.49	12.55	6.02	2.08	-6.53	-3.94
Wood and furniture	2.65	4.31	2.61	1.04	0.31	-1.57	-0.73
Paper and printing	3.50	3.54	3.58	2.16	1.55	-1.42	-0.61
Chemicals and products	8.87	8.76	9.43	12.81	12.67	3.38	-0.14
Petroleum refining	7.99	5.32	4.80	2.29	2.29	-2.51	0.00
Rubber and plastics	8.37	9.80	9.36	4.63	2.57	-4.73	-2.06
Nonmetallic minerals	4.33	3.97	3.78	2.76	1.66	-1.02	-1.10
Basic metal	5.15	6.71	7.64	13.57	10.15	5.93	-3.42
Metal products	5.67	5.24	5.52	8.18	4.37	2.66	-3.81
Machinery	3.96	3.73	4.75	5.80	4.99	1.05	-0.81
Electrical and electronics machinery	13.25	13.80	18.58	26.85	48.19	8.27	21.34
Transport equipment	6.55	5.75	7.10	4.68	3.58	-2.42	-1.10
Miscellaneous	3.03	3.14	3.51	2.14	1.36	-1.37	-0.78

SOURCES: MOEA, *Industrial Production Statistics Monthly, Taiwan Area, R.O.C.* (Taipei, various years).

Electronics[8]

Taiwan has come to occupy a very important, though not quite visible, place in the global ICT industry.[9] Most of the successful second movers in Taiwan, however, have not pursued research and design (R&D)–intensive and own-brand strategies to catch up. Second movers expand by relying upon accumulated organizational capabilities based on subcontracting manufacturing, hence implying path dependence in development.[10] Thus, the strategy of choice for most has been upgrading subcontracting, cross-industry subcontracting, and then own-brand manufacturing (OBM), in that order. Among the structural factors affecting a firm's strategic choice, industrial policy has been crucial. South Korea has produced some successful global brands, supported by the state's national champion policy and long-term commitment to the *chaebŏl*. China has also adopted an ambitious national champion strategy. The fact that the government in Taiwan has never adopted a national champion strategy helps to partly explain the evolutionary path of Taiwan's second movers, and attests to the importance of industrial policy. Although HTC successfully established a global brand, other Taiwan ICT second movers (such as Acer and ASUS) either continue to be pure subcontractors or are struggling in an attempt to build up their own brands.

Table 7.6 lists some statistics on Taiwan's information technology (IT) hardware industry. Taiwanese firms have been able to participate in the growth of this global industry from the beginning, mainly through subcontracting. Though the sector enjoyed stable growth over the years and became the main behind-the-scenes producer, the speed at which it moved production offshore has been swift. In 1995, 72.0 percent of production still took place in Taiwan, but this dropped to below 50.0 percent in 2000 and had declined to a negligible 0.6 percent by 2009. In the meantime, an increasing portion of offshore production shifted to mainland China, reaching 95.0 percent in 2009. As noted above, moving production to China allowed Taiwanese firms to have access to an almost unlimited supply of cheap and efficient labor, allowing them to greatly expand their scale of operations. Thus, by 2009 the global market share of IT hardware products produced by Taiwan firms had probably reached its peak. The last column of Table 7.6 lists the global market share of Taiwanese firms for the most important IT product, the notebook PC. It increased from 52.5 percent in 2000 to 95.3 percent in 2009.

TABLE 7.6
Taiwan's IT hardware industry

Year	Value of production (Taiwan and offshore) (US$ millions)	Produced in Taiwan (%)	Produced in China (%)	Produced elsewhere (%)	Global market share of notebook PCs (%)
1995	19,543	72.0	14.0	14.0	27.0
1996	25,035	67.9	16.8	15.3	32.0
1997	30,174	62.6	22.8	14.6	n.a.
1998	33,776	57.0	29.0	14.0	40.0
1999	39,881	52.7	33.2	14.1	49.0
2000	47,019	49.1	31.3	19.6	52.5
2001	42,750	47.1	36.9	16.0	56.5
2002	48,435	35.7	47.5	16.8	61.2
2003	57,171	22.1	61.6	16.3	67.2
2004	69,664	15.6	71.2	13.2	72.4
2005	80,980	6.8	81.0	12.2	82.5
2006	89,656	3.6	85.4	11.0	86.2
2007	105,450	2.5	89.0	8.5	92.8
2008	110,251	2.5	89.0	8.5	92.4
2009	107,830	0.6	95.1	4.3	95.3

SOURCES: *Information Industry Yearbook*, various years (Taipei: Market Intelligence Center, Institute for Information Industry, various years).

Fortunately, Taiwan's second movers did move along the upgrading path stated above, from upgrading subcontracting to cross-industry subcontracting and then to OBM. As the growth of the global IT industry hit a plateau and the share held by Taiwanese firms reached a peak, the second movers entered other areas, especially communications and video products, and related parts and components. Therefore, despite the trend of moving production offshore in certain segments, total employment in the electronics sector did not decline from 1990 to 2010. Among the three electronics subsectors, only the more traditional electrical machinery subsector experienced a decline in employment. The decline in the average annual growth rate of employment in the ICT subsector reflects its maturing since the 1990s. The average growth rate of employment in the electronic parts and components subsector also shows a decreasing trend, but it still has maintained an average growth rate of 4.3 percent during the 2000s, contributing 2.3 percent to the entire electronics sector.

Several companies stand out as representative of Taiwan's electronics industry. Their development will be discussed briefly below to illustrate the growth of this very important industry.

An Unexpected Success Story—HTC

As noted above, very few successful second movers in Taiwan have their own brands. But an unexpected success story has emerged. HTC Corporation, a relative newcomer to Taiwan's IT sector, has made substantial progress in pursuing an OBM strategy. HTC was set up by a strong technical team that left Digital Equipment Taiwan in 1997.[11] It started out doing subcontracting own-design manufacturing (ODM) work by producing handheld devices, mainly personal digital assistants (PDAs), smartphones, and PDA phones. However, it began to build its own brand in mid-2006, reducing its reliance on ODM business to less than 10 percent of sales by the end of 2007. It brought out its HTC Touch phone series two weeks before Apple introduced its legendary iPhone in mid-2007. HTC brought out the first Google phone in cooperation with Google in 2008. Since then it has enjoyed spectacular growth, as touch-screen-based smartphones, especially Android-based phones, have become ever more popular. In April 2011 it was reported that HTC had overtaken Nokia in terms of market value.[12]

HTC did encounter difficulties when switching to the OBM mode, as its ODM customers, for instance Palm and HP, canceled orders. However, it was able to quickly make progress in the branding business, not only because of its superior technological capabilities and prior R&D investments, but also because it successfully entered into partnerships with various global communications service providers.[13] Thus, its business mode is still more of business-to-business rather than business-to-consumer, enabling it to ramp up its branding business quickly. In 2009, sales reached US$4.8 billion and its R&D ratio was 5.8 percent.[14] This is one of the few cases in which a Taiwan second mover successfully established its own brand within a relatively short time.

Taiwan's Ultimate Subcontractor—Hon Hai Precision Industry Company

Before HTC's rise, the two most important and representative companies in Taiwan's IT industry were Taiwan Semiconductor Manufacturing Company

(TSMC) and Hon Hai Precision Industry Company, both of which are sub-contractors, though of different sorts. Taiwan Semiconductor pioneered the business model of a specialized integrated-circuit foundry, and remains the world leader in this sector. Though it is a pioneer, in a sense TSMC is still a subcontractor, mainly providing production services.

The rise of Hon Hai has been extraordinary. Its upgrading strategy allowed it to become the ultimate subcontractor from the 1990s. It first established the groundwork by investing heavily in its core technology (molding) and institutionalizing its patent and knowledge management system. Before other companies did, it globalized its operations. Its timely and rapid expansion of production facilities in mainland China and elsewhere and its numerous mergers and acquisitions contributed to growth at an annual compound rate of almost 50 percent in the 2000s, with sales rising from US$0.5 billion in 1996 to US$47.0 billion in 2009.[15] In 2005 it became the largest company in Taiwan,[16] the largest exporter of China, and in 2010 number 112 on *Fortune*'s Global 100 list.[17] It also earned notoriety in 2010, when more than a dozen of its workers committed suicide in succession at one of its huge assembly factories in Dongguan, China.[18]

Hon Hai was set up in 1974, with initial capital of less than US$10,000, producing TV tuner knobs. It gained a place in Taiwan's IT industry by producing connectors in the 1980s. Since the early 1990s, however, its strategy has been to expand its subcontracting production services, in terms of both products and service functions, to as many areas as possible. In its own words, it is now a "provider of joint-design, joint-development, manufacturing, assembly and after-sales services to global Computer, Communication and Consumer-electronics ('3C') leaders," and its business model is a "vertically integrated one-stop shopping business model by integrating mechanical, electrical and optical capabilities."[19] It is an ultimate manufacturing services provider in the IT industry. Thus, from first starting out as a producer of connectors, it now also produces barebones computers, cell phones, notebook computers, digital cameras, and numerous IT components and accessories, all as a subcontractor.[20]

In sum, Hon Hai's strategy has been upgrading and cross-industry subcontracting on a grand scale. Actually, both Hon Hai and TSMC try their best to assure their customers that they will not cross the line to do branding. The story of how Hon Hai became Taiwan's largest company is indicative of trends in this industry in Taiwan.

Services: Managed Opening of the Domestic Market

Liberalization of the domestic market, especially the service sector, began in earnest in the late 1980s. This liberalization has both internal and external components: externally opening up to foreign investors, and internally allowing new domestic entrants in previously restricted markets. This is particularly important in the modern service sectors, such as finance, communications, transportation, and mass retailing.[21]

Regulation of foreign entries more or less followed the original developmental state model, that is, fostering local firms while opening up gradually to foreign competition. For example, when opening up telecommunications services, a former government monopoly, local entrants were encouraged to find foreign partners, but only as minority shareholders. The ceiling on foreign shareholding was later lifted, as their technology and managerial assistance became nonessential. Government restrictions on foreign investments in services during the early stages of the market opening permitted local firms to capture a second-mover advantage.[22]

In general, foreign firms have not played significant roles in Taiwan's industrial development. In Taiwan's most successful industry, electronics, foreign firms played an important role at the early stage, but it began to decline as local second movers took over and thrived. The foreign share in the sales of the top 500 manufacturing firms continued to decrease, from 17.4 percent in 1990 to 5.9 percent in 2009 (see Table 7.7).

In contrast, until the late 2000s the foreign share in services showed an increasing trend. At only 6.8 percent in 1990, it reached 18.6 percent in 2000, climbed to 25.4 percent in 2007, and dropped back to 19.3 percent in 2009. The foreign share in services in the 2000s exceeded that in manufacturing in any year. This is consistent with the general observation that, in terms of global competitiveness, Taiwan's manufacturing sector is superior to its services sector. Nonetheless, partly due to the government policy of managed opening, the level of foreign shares in services in Taiwan is still low compared to that in many other developing countries.

For the government to manage local entries was much more complicated, because it involved domestic politics and occurred during the democratization process. In general, most of the existing large-scale business groups tried to participate in some of the newly opened markets. The government showed a tendency to try to accommodate as many qualified applicants as

TABLE 7.7

Foreign share in the top 500 manufacturing and services firms, 1990–2009

Year	MANUFACTURING		SERVICES	
	Sales	Employment	Sales	Employment
1990	17.4	17.8	6.8	12.1
1991	17.1	16.0	9.5	13.3
1992	15.5	14.4	10.2	14.9
1993	16.3	15.6	9.8	16.5
1994	15.5	15.9	9.8	14.4
1995	15.9	15.0	11.3	15.5
1996	15.0	14.4	14.3	18.9
1997	15.0	13.5	13.6	13.4
1998	15.3	12.8	15.0	13.8
1999	14.7	12.0	16.6	15.3
2000	13.6	9.7	18.6	14.7
2001	10.9	9.3	16.7	15.8
2002	9.6	7.8	19.9	15.8
2003	9.4	10.6	20.4	15.7
2004	9.4	10.6	22.1	13.9
2005	9.0	12.1	24.4	15.1
2006	8.0	11.2	24.7	10.5
2007	7.3	12.0	25.4	10.7
2008	5.4	10.7	19.8	7.6
2009	5.9	11.4	19.3	5.5

SOURCE: China Credit Information Service, *Top 500: A Special Edition in Celebration of the 50th Anniversary of CCIS* (Taipei, 2011).

the situation allowed. For example, in 1991 the government announced that it would allow the establishment of new banks. Even after the government raised the entry threshold to initial capital of US$373 million dollars to limit the number of applicants, there were nineteen applications. The government finally approved fifteen applications, triple the originally planned five new banks. Each new bank was supported by one or more business groups. As can be expected, almost two decades later some of the new banks have been sold to or merged with other banks.

Other hotly pursued opportunities included entry into non-bank financial services, cable TV, electric power plants, mobile and fixed-line telecommunication services, high-speed rail, media, and so forth. In some sectors, the government had to restrict the number of licenses because of frequency or other limitations. As in the case of mobile phone services, after a round of intense lobbying, contestation, and deliberation, the government granted eight operating licenses to forty-two applicants.

One by-product of this round of internal liberalization is that the share of the business groups in economic activities has greatly increased, because the groups have been the main participants in the newly liberalized sectors. The ratio of sales of Taiwan's top 100 groups to GNP rose from 28.8 percent in 1981 to 54.0 percent in 1998.[23] Owing to regulatory changes in 1999, the business groups changed the way they file financial reports. Thus, the more recent statistics are not comparable to earlier series, and hence are not presented here. However, there is no doubt that this increasing trend has continued in the 2000s.

Considering that Taiwan's services lagged behind the manufacturing sector in terms of global competitiveness, the question arises as to whether Taiwan has been late in liberalizing its service sector. It is always difficult to answer a counterfactual question. However, it is fair to say that specializing in manufacturing has served Taiwan, and the other East Asian economies, quite well. The service sector cannot replace the manufacturing sector as the engine of growth in Taiwan, at least for now. What will probably matter in the future is how the two sectors perform in the China market.

Industrial Policy: The Transformation of the Developmental State

How has Taiwan's developmental state been evolving in response to the changes brought by democratization, liberalization, and globalization? In the past, the successful East Asian developmental state had several key components: The leaders had a strong political will to promote development; there was social consensus supporting the development policy; and the economic bureaucracy, with embedded autonomy, was capable and highly motivated.[24] All these components have undergone substantial changes from the late 1980s.

The following discussion is divided into three parts. The first discusses changes in industrial policy, in terms of whether and how the policy was able to accommodate the newly emerging social concerns. The second part examines whether the industrial policy still maintained its goal of furthering overall growth rather than particular vested interests. The third part explores changes in the guiding principles and influences of neoliberalism. Finally, we will look at how all these changes have affected Taiwan's vision for future development.

Broadening the Scope of Industrial Policy

In the earlier period of economic development, social concerns were severely suppressed. The authoritarian state ruthlessly eliminated the left, and suppressed political opposition and labor and student unrest. Within this environment, it was relatively easy to put development first in terms of the priority policy goals. As discussed above, the success of development brought about strong pressures for changes to the model.

The lifting of martial law in 1987 opened the flood gates. Various kinds of social movements flourished, including labor, student, women's, and environmental movements, among others. These presented new challenges to the policy makers and affected the economic policy process.

In the past, the economic bureaucracy had been in charge of promoting development, and the political leaders had ensured that development demands received priority. At a relatively low income level, there was consensus in support of development. The demands made by the newly emerged social movements, however, which were outside the usual economic sphere, presented difficulties for the economic bureaucracy. Coordination by higher offices was required to reconcile different demands within the various responsible ministries. The democratization process introduced a new type of political competition, and improving economic policy was not the focus of that competition. The new generation of political leaders did not necessarily have a strong motivation to attend to the difficult task of policy coordination, but that input was essential to reconcile the different demands, to broaden the scope of industrial policy, and to address the challenges in the new policy environment.

It was a painfully long and difficult process to reconcile the various social demands with economic development policies. This process has been ongoing since democratization began in the late 1980s. The economic bureaucracy was passive in responding to social demands, and the political leaders often failed to provide leadership because of the new rule of political competition. During the democratization process in Taiwan, political competition focused on political issues, such as ethnic identity and issues of nativism. Though this competition helped to bring about democracy peacefully, confrontation on identity issues inevitably made the political process partisan and divisive. This development was not helpful in terms of fostering rational debate on policy issues or forming consensus on policy options. Thus, transformation of the original developmental model has not been easy (see Table 7.8).

Pursuing Overall Growth

In the earlier postwar period, the success of industrial policy in the East Asian countries depended on the fact that the policy goal was to pursue overall growth rather than to foster advancement of particular vested interests. The requirements for promoting new industries had priority over those for protecting existing industries. This was easier to accomplish under an authoritarian regime which, for historical reasons, was determined to promote development.

Since democratization in Taiwan, have the political leaders demonstrated the same kind of resolve to put development first? The answer, arguably, is no. The strong political will of the earlier generation to promote development came from its historical legacy and experiences, and could not and need not be duplicated. Developmentalism is still influential, but it is no longer accepted as the undisputed priority goal.

There is no doubt that at this stage of development in Taiwan, the previous "development first" policy orientation needs to be modified. What should take its place? During the democratization process, has there emerged a new social consensus in terms of forming a vision for future development? The answer is mixed.

The democratization movement successfully established a new social discourse, which argued against the Kuomintang's (KMT's) authoritarian rule mainly on "ethnical" grounds, in addition to the usual issues of liberty and democracy. To deny the KMT's achievements in economic development, the discourse downplays the role of industrial policy, emphasizes the downside of development, and is essentially anti-development. It also advocates political autonomy from mainland China. In the meantime, the influence of developmentalism remains strong. Thus, the picture for the future remains complicated.

TABLE 7.8
Social indicators, 1952–2010

Year	Population (1,000 persons) (1)	Labor force participation rate (%) (2)	Unemployment rate (3)	LIFE EXPECTANCY (4)		Infant mortality (5)	Literacy rate (6)
				Male	Female		
1952	8,128	66.5	4.4	57.4	60.3	44.7	63.6
1960	10,792	62.4	4.0	62.3	66.4	35.0	78.7
1965	12,628	58.2	3.3	65.1	69.7	24.1	81.2
1970	14,676	57.4	1.7	66.7	71.6	16.9	87.6
1975	16,150	58.2	2.4	68.3	73.4	12.6	87.1
1980	17,805	58.3	1.2	69.6	74.6	9.8	89.7
1985	19,258	59.5	2.9	70.8	75.8	6.8	91.5
1990	20,353	59.2	1.7	71.3	76.8	5.3	93.2
1995	21,304	58.7	1.8	71.9	77.7	6.4	94.4
2000	22,216	57.7	3.0	73.8	79.6	5.9	95.6
2004	22,615	57.7	4.4	74.7	80.8	5.3	97.2
2005	22,690	57.8	4.1	74.5	80.8	5.0	97.3
2006	22,790	57.9	3.9	74.9	81.4	4.6	97.5
2007	22,867	58.2	3.9	75.5	81.7	4.7	97.6
2008	22,943	58.3	4.1	75.6	81.9	4.6	97.8
2009	23,016	57.9	5.9	76.0	82.3	4.0	97.9
2010	23,162	58.1	5.2	76.1	82.6	4.2	98.0

SOURCES:

1) DGBAS, http://eng.stat.gov.tw/mp.asp?mp=5; and www.dgbas.gov.tw/mp.asp [in Chinese].

2) CEPD, Taiwan Statistical Data Book, Taipei, various years.

3) DGBAS, http://eng.stat.gov.tw/mp.asp?mp=5; and www.dgbas.gov.tw/ct.asp?xItem=9522&ctNode=287 [in Chinese].

4) Ministry of Interior, http://sowf.moi.gov.tw/stat/year/elist.htm.

5) Ministry of Interior, http://sowf.moi.gov.tw/stat/year/elist.htm.

6) Health and Vital Statistics, 1995 and 2003 (Taipei: Department of Health).

The economic bureaucracy has a legacy from the developmental state period, and hence its institutional mission remains the promotion of development. However, as political leaders often put political considerations ahead of development concerns, the former model gradually eroded. Two main factors enter into the political considerations. One is the new social discourse, which is anti-China and anti-development. The other relates to pressures from short-term electoral competition, which tends to force politicians to seek slogan and quick-fix types of policy and to utilize public resources for partisan purposes. The short-term nature of the political competition does not help form a social consensus on a forward-looking vision of development.

This is not the place to delve into the influences of democratization in detail. It suffices to point out one alarming trend, among many, with consequences relating to development. Tax receipts (excluding social security contributions) as a ratio of GDP have been declining ever since the beginning of democratization. Since the early 1990s, political leaders have consistently advocated tax reductions. Thus, this ratio dropped continuously from a high of 20.0 percent in 1990 to 12.8 percent in 2011.[25] This has to be one of the lowest tax burdens in the world.[26] It also implies that the fiscal deficit as a percentage of fiscal revenue continues to increase, averaging −12 percent in the last ten years, despite occasional frantic selling off of government assets. This severely limits the government's ability to respond to the polarizing effects of globalization and neoliberalism. The effects of the latter will be dealt with in the following section.

On a comparison note: South Korea has fared better in this regard, in that its ratio of tax receipts to GDP showed no decreasing trend and remained around 20 percent in 2009, much higher than that of Taiwan.[27] This provided more resources for the Korean state to pursue industrial policies much more vigorously than Taiwan, and that also will be discussed later in this chapter.

Guiding Principle: The Developmental State versus Neoliberalism

Since the early 1990s, one of the pillars of Taiwan's new dominant social discourse has been neoliberalism. There are two main reasons for its rising influence. To deny the KMT any credit for successes during its period of authoritarian rule, the democratization movement denies the role of the developmental state in promoting economic development. Neoliberalism is not only consistent with this political logic, but also provides theoretical support to the opening up of previously restricted domestic markets. Furthermore, after becoming the economic orthodoxy in the United States in the 1980s, neoliberalism spread easily to Taiwan via the return of an entire generation of U.S.-trained economists. Since then, neoliberalism has dominated both the economy and society in Taiwan.

In the past, though the Nationalist (KMT) government suppressed the opposition, it adopted policies to widely spread the fruits of development so as to maintain the legitimacy of its rule. Thus, the income gap and the urban-rural divide were not serious in the earlier postwar period. Rule was both egalitarian *and* authoritarian.

Beginning in the late 1980s, liberalization and globalization went hand in hand with democratization in Taiwan. The old social contract, including government–business and capital–labor relations, under authoritarianism began to be dismantled. The old-style egalitarianism was gradually replaced by neoliberalism and populism.

The government bureaucracy in general has been affected by this neoliberal trend. It began to farm out various tasks, using open bidding to allocate projects and applying cost-effectiveness tests almost indiscriminately. This new mode of political competition also contributed to policy making becoming more short term and populist oriented. Moreover, the new neoliberal beliefs began to change the institutional mission of the economic bureaucracy. For example, in 2006 the chair of the Council for Economic Planning and Development, the government planning agency, announced that the government no longer needed to guide the direction of development.[28]

Unfortunately, this move toward laissez-faire occurred at a time when polarizing forces were intensifying. Figure 7.2 shows that the average annual growth rate of real wages began to decline after the liberalization of the late 1980s. The annual growth rate of real wages averaged around 5.0 percent during the 1960s and the 1970s, and 7.4 percent in the 1980s, indicating a more equal sharing of the fruits of growth. However, the rate dropped to 3.0 percent in the 1990s, and in the last ten years has edged even closer to zero.

Meanwhile, social movements often split along partisan lines rather than class lines. This helped reinforce the move toward neoliberalism. For example, the partisan split in the labor movement, along with the influence of neoliberalism, contributed to the failure of the social security campaign.[29]

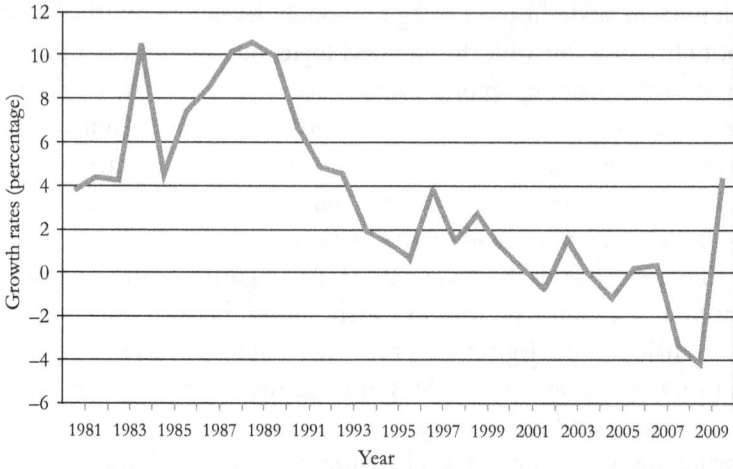

FIGURE 7.2 Average annual growth rates of real wages in industry and services, 1981–2010
SOURCE: Directorate-General of Budget, Accounting and Statistics, Taiwan, http://eng.dgbas.gov.tw.
NOTE: The nominal average wage data are taken from the DGBAS website (http://win.dgbas.gov.tw/dgbas04/bc5/earning/ht456e.asp) and are deflated using the consumer price index deflator.

Taiwan used to be one of the exceptional cases in which income distribution improved with growth; in other words, the ratio of the income share of the top quintile to the bottom quintile declined from 5.25 in 1965 to 4.17 in 1980. However, this ratio has shown an increasing trend since 1980 (see Table 7.9). It averaged 5.37 in the 1990s, but 6.39 in the 2000s. In fact, in the crisis year of 2009, if we disregard the equalizing effects of transfer payments, the ratio would have been 8.22.[30] In sum, income distribution has been worsening at an alarming rate. Even though social welfare expenditures have been increasing, the related policy-making process has been highly politicized and shaped by partisan concerns and election considerations. The anxiety caused by the so-called China factor has been politicized and only reinforced the partisan politics. This has not been helpful to establishing a rational social welfare system in Taiwan.[31]

The Effects of Economic Transformation on Democratization

Let us now turn the question around and ask how economic transformation has affected democratization. As stated above, economic liberalization began in earnest in the late 1980s, along with democratization. Even

TABLE 7.9

Changes in income distribution, 1964–2010

| Year | Gini coefficient | RATIO OF INCOME SHARE OF TOP 20% TO THAT OF BOTTOM 20% | |
		Without government transfers	With government transfers
1964	0.321	—	—
1970	0.294	—	—
1980	0.278	4.305	4.173
1990	0.312	5.525	5.183
2000	0.326	6.568	5.548
2005	0.340	7.447	6.036
2009	0.345	8.219	6.343
2010	0.342	7.719	6.194

SOURCES: Adapted from DGBAS, Executive Yuan, R.O.C., Survey of Household Income and Expenditure, various years, http://eng.stat.gov.tw/ct.asp?xItem=9725&ctNode=1598&mp=5.

though by that time the export-oriented part of the manufacturing sector had already participated in the global market for more than two decades, the rest of Taiwan did not fully join the globalized world until trade, capital flows, and travel restrictions were gradually lifted in the late 1980s. It cannot be stressed enough that a major element in Taiwan's globalization was the opening up of cross-strait relations with mainland China, which began at about the same time as the economic and political liberalization.

The effects of globalization are similar in most places and well known by now. As barriers to capital mobility are taken down much more rapidly than those of human flows, the economic policy space of the state becomes ever more limited. As freer trade brings in cheaper goods from elsewhere and intensifies competition among labor across borders, wage disparities become ever wider and the rate of unemployment often increases as well.

Moreover, WTO rules have limited the freedom of less-developed countries to adopt proactive industrial policies to promote industrialization. However, using science and technology policy to subsidize R&D is still allowed under WTO rules, because this is how the advanced countries compete among themselves. Having made sufficient progress so as to be able to participate in global technology competition, the East Asian tigers find themselves with more policy room than the less-developed countries and can follow the advanced countries in adopting competitive science and technology policies. Therefore, the state in Taiwan, by focusing on science and technology, has been able to change its policy framework and adapt to the new post-WTO environment.[32]

However, greater capital mobility and competition from imports after liberalization have imposed constraints upon the state's capabilities to regulate capital. The economic effects have become ever more evident with the intensification of globalization. Thus, as noted above, the local real wage level has not risen in the 2000s (see Figure 7.2). The extent of inequality in income distribution has also been increasing, especially during the recent financial crisis (see Table 7.9).

How have these developments affected democracy in Taiwan? Because outward FDI was a relatively new phenomenon in Taiwan in the early 1990s (Table 7.3), the trend created fears of a hollowing out of Taiwan's industries and put pressure on the government. The fact that a substantial share of the outward FDI was going to mainland China further complicated the matter, because the two sides across the strait had been staunch enemies since 1949. In addition, ever since the democratic movement gathered strength in the 1980s, it developed a nativist bent and became rather hostile toward mainland China. The combination of these factors influenced how political competition played out.

From the early 1990s, most politicians have tried to outcompete one another by remaining tough on China. In addition to their rhetorical provocations, they advocated policies to restrict economic exchanges, including the flow of trade, capital, and human resources, with China. But because the lure of the China economy was too great to resist, either as a manufacturing base or as an emerging market, the restrictive policy was difficult to enforce. However, it gave the government more reason to grant businesses extra favors to entice them to "stay" in Taiwan. This, coupled with greater capital mobility, put the government on the defensive when regulating capital. All these factors contributed to a government tilt toward business interests. As politicians competed to lower the various types of taxes since the early 1990s, the result was the continuous decline in the ratio of tax revenue to GDP.[33] Another consequence is that it has become more difficult to carry out rational and pragmatic discussions of economic policies, especially those relating to relations with mainland China.

Globalization and the policy tilt toward capital have resulted in stagnant wages and increasing income disparities. This distributional issue was eventually politicized, though with a particular twist. Instead of turning it into a class issue, the DPP took the lead in making it a populist issue, blaming China and the supposedly pro-China bias of the KMT. Rather than proposing a set of well-formulated social policies, the DPP made this into an election issue, advocating handouts to specific groups to solidify votes during elections. Thus, the making of the social welfare system, especially the pension system, was highly influenced by these election-period populist quick fixes.[34]

The same kind of political logic also led to changes in the government's regional and science park policies, with the guiding principle shifting from a developmentalist to a populist model.[35] In matters relating to education and human resources, it is clear that policies need to be more flexible and adaptable to the globalized environment. However, the DPP continues to oppose any policy measures that increase human inflow from the mainland. For example, because of its opposition, the number of mainland students allowed in remains small. These students also face various discriminatory measures applicable only to them, such as not being allowed to join the national health insurance plan or to obtain student assistantships.

Thus, the China factor has been a key element in Taiwan's transformation since the early 1990s. A major part of Taiwan's response to the globalization challenge consists of its adaptation to the emergence of a strong Chinese economy. The political process, so far, has not been able to deal well with this challenge. The DPP continues to oppose any policy accommodating to the increased economic integration, and is yet to face up to the question of how China fits into Taiwan's economic future. This question is rarely discussed openly, and hence there is no forward-looking blueprint on offer from either political party. Unlike the DPP, the KMT advocates peace and has signed ECFA, but it is afraid to offer any long-term proposals. Thus, the political competition tends to vilify China rather than to conduct rational and pragmatic discussions; hence, it is not conducive to drafting sensible economic policy.

Some Comparative Notes on Korea and Taiwan

Overall development patterns in Korea and Taiwan in the postwar period have been extremely similar. One area in which there has been a distinct difference, however, is with respect to policy on big business and national champions.[36] This difference was magnified after the recent economic transformation since the late 1980s. In Taiwan the Nationalist government had always placed priority on stability over growth, and hence shied away from pursuing a high-risk national champion strategy. It also tried to distribute favors more widely and not to align with any particular businesses. Lacking a firm long-term commitment from the state, most of Taiwan's leading firms were reluctant to pursue national champion or branding strategies. When the state began to promote an industrial deepening in the 1970s, that is, the import-substitution industrialization plan comparable to Korea's heavy and chemical industrialization plan, Taiwan's private firms were unwilling to undertake the projects.[37] As a result, state-owned enterprises substituted for the chaebŏl in undertaking the industrial deepening and there was more room for smaller firms. Institutional arrangements in Taiwan differ from those in South Korea because of different big business and national champion strategies.

How this long-term national strategy came about requires historical and sociopolitical explanations, which cannot be dealt with adequately here.[38] It should be noted, however, that nationalism continues to play a much stronger role in South Korea's industrial policy because it does not have Taiwan's troubling national identity issues. There is still a strong social consensus to pursue national glory in Korea, and that provides support for the ambitious industrial policy. As shown by Lee (Chapter 6 in this volume), the Korean government, along with the ever stronger chaebŏl, succeeded in forcefully pushing through the "Powerful Internet Nation" and the "Korean Wave" project from the 1990s. The government in Taiwan had made attempts in these same areas, but with less effort and cohesion and hence much less results.

This difference in development strategy has long-term implications in terms of industrial structure and income distribution, as evidenced by the transformations in the two economies since the 1990s. South Korea has been much more successful in establishing national champions,[39] but it pays a price for their success in terms of increasing local disparities, also as shown in Chapter 6 of this volume. By comparison, Taiwan's record of global ladder-climbing has been less spectacular, but there has been less of an increase in the degree of inequality in terms of industrial and income distribution than there has been in Korea. There is less concentration in Taiwan's industries, and its unemployment rate among college graduates and its gender gap are also somewhat lower.[40] This is only a matter of degree. Globalization and liberalization have led to stagnant wages and increasing inequality in both countries, as discussed above and in Chapter 6 in this volume.

The democratization process in Taiwan, unlike that in Korea, has been characterized by the dominance of ethnic or national identity issues and the lack of a prominent role by the political left in society. With respect to the impact of democratization on the economic transformation, it led to failure to form a coherent vision for Taiwan's economic prospects, which in turn meant less-ambitious industrial policies. Moreover, this also led to an increasing neoliberal influence within its social movements, especially among the political opposition during the democratization process. As discussed above, for historical and political reasons, the Nationalist party practiced a kind of authoritarian egalitarianism. With the lack of a left wing, the opposition movement threw out the baby with the bath water, so to speak, by opposing the ruling Nationalists in every way, including some of its paternalistic but nonetheless equalizing measures. The opposition party, the DPP, eventually resorted to neoliberalism and populism. As a result, unlike in South Korea, distributional politics have never been the focus of contention in Taiwan.

How does the impact of economic transformation on democratization differ in these two countries? Again, the national identity issue in Taiwan is distinct. Both economies have attained a high degree of integration with mainland China since the 1990s. Facing China's rise, South Korea has had fewer difficulties in reaching a consensus on pursuing an integration strategy. The successful chaebŏl have also been more globalized in their reach. However, firms in Taiwan have embraced China to a greater degree, even though the extent of their global reach has been less than that of Korean firms. The increasing economic integration with China poses great political challenges to Taiwan. Intertwined with ethnic issues, the issue of integration with China has dominated the political process and overshadowed all other areas since the early 1990s. It remains to be seen if Taiwan can resolve this crucial issue in the future.

Conclusion: Vision for Future Development

Taiwan's economy has performed relatively well since embarking on its great economic, social, and political transformation in the late 1980s. After two decades, industry continued to grow, and the unemployment rate remained at a moderate level. Although its labor-intensive production has moved offshore, its electronics industry persists in upgrading and expanding and maintaining its global competitiveness, thus becoming Taiwan's pillar industry. Integration with the Chinese economy has provided growth momentum and helped the second movers expand in scale. The legacy of the developmental state has meant that the external economic liberalization has been a managed affair, allowing local services to grow.

However, there remain many challenges. Overall growth relies on the old export-promotion regime, with an undervalued exchange rate and low wage levels. There are many imbalances in the economy. The lack of investment growth in the 2000s is probably related to the fact that the flow across the strait remains one way, that the growth of domestic consumption lags behind overall growth, and that the dominant industry, electronics, has encountered greater competitive pressures as it continues to upgrade. Although economic integration with China continues to grow, political debate persists in hindering rational policy planning. At the same time, globalization has also brought an unprecedented increase in the degree of inequality. The new rules of political competition have not been conducive to addressing these challenges.

Nonetheless, the democratic transition has been peaceful, and the framework of the developmental state has not been totally dismantled. But the conflict in political and economic direction remains unresolved, and the society has yet to face up to the crucial question of how to fit China into Taiwan's economic future. Thus, there is really no forward-looking development plan and a vision for future development. Hopefully, the ECFA will facilitate gradual normalization of economic relations across the strait. More important, if future political developments could promote more productive dialogue within Taiwan and across the strait, then there is a better chance that Taiwan will be able to formulate a new economic vision for its future development.

Notes

1. International Monetary Fund, World Economic Outlook Database, www .imf.org/external/pubs/ft/weo/2011/02/weodata/index.aspx.

2. From Council on Economic Planning and Development (CEPD), *Taiwan Statistical Data Book* (Taipei, 2012).

3. As stated above, Taiwan's GDP grew 3.9 percent on average in the 2000s. This figure is comparable to those of other East Asian economies, e.g., 4.1 percent for South Korea.

4. Calculated from Council on Economic Planning and Development (CEPD), *Taiwan Statistical Data Book* (Taipei, various years).

5. For example, looking at the sources of growth, in 1995, GDP grew 6.4 percent, of which private consumption contributed 3.3 percent and net exports 1.3 percent; while in 2007, GDP grew 6.0 percent, of which private consumption contributed 1.2 percent and net exports 4.6 percent. Council on Economic Planning and Development (CEPD), *Taiwan Statistical Data Book* (Taipei, various years).

6. Pei-yu Chen and Hui-Chi Tien, "Inquiry into Factors Affecting Taiwan's Real Effective Exchange Rate [Yingxiang Zhongchangqi Xintaibi Shizhi Youxiao Huilude Tantao]," *Quarterly Bulletin of Central Bank of Republic of China (Taiwan)* 34, no. 2 (June, 2012): 43–84.

7. Wan-wen Chu, "Can Taiwan's Second Movers Upgrade via Branding?" *Research Policy* 38, no. 6 (July 2009):1054–1065.

8. This electronics sector is defined as containing the ICT industry (which expanded from IT to include communications and video products), electronic parts and components, and electrical machinery.

9. Alice H. Amsden and Wan-Wen Chu, *Beyond Late Development: Taiwan's Upgrading Policies* (Cambridge, MA: MIT Press, 2003).

10. Chu, "Can Taiwan's Second Movers Upgrade via Branding?" 1054–1065.

11. HTC's current CEO, Peter Chou, has always emphasized HTC's debt to Digital Equipment, which was known for its innovative engineering culture; J. H. Huang, "Chou: Thanks to Compaq for Its Rejection [Chou Yung-Ming: Ganxie Campaq geide cuozhe]," *CommonWealth*, no. 400 (July 2, 2008). Though Digital Equipment folded in 1998, its influence shows up in an unexpected place.

12. Robin Kwong, "HTC Overtakes Nokia in Market Value," *Financial Times*, April 7, 2011, www.ft.com/cms/s/0/78586c86-6108-11e0-8899-00144feab49a .html.

13. J. H. Huang, "HTC's Chou: Godfather of Innovation Always Chooses the Toughest Task [HTC's Chou: Chuangxin Jiaofu Zhixuan Zuinan de Zuo]," *CommonWealth*, no. 388 (January 2, 2008).

14. From HTC's website, www.htc.com/www/investor.aspx.

15. From Hon Hai's website, www.honhai.com.tw/Investors_En/Financial _Information.html?index=1.

16. "*CommonWealth's* Taiwan's Top 1000 Companies [yiqianda zhizaoye paihang]," *CommonWealth* (May 9, 2007).

17. Global 500, *CNNMoney*, April 2010, http://money.cnn.com/magazines/ fortune/global500/2010/full_list/index.html.

18. "Sociologists and other academics see the deaths as extreme signals of a more pervasive trend: a generation of workers rejecting the regimented hardships their predecessors endured as the cheap labor army behind China's economic

miracle." David Barboza, "After Suicides, Scrutiny of China's Grim Factories," *New York Times*, June 6, 2010.

19. From Hon Hai's website, at www.honhai.com.tw/GroupProfile_En/ BusinessPhilosophy.html. The company's name in China is Foxconn Technology Group. It calls this business model "eCMMS," which stands for e-Enabled Components, Modules, Moves, and Services.

20. H. Y. Chang et al., *A Legend of Three Hundred Billion: Terry Kuo's Hon Hai Empire* [Sanqianyi Chuanqi: Kuo Taiming de Honhai Diguo] (Taipei: Common-Wealth Magazine Press, 2002).

21. This section draws from Wan-wen Chu and Chia-yu Hung, "Business Groups in Taiwan's Post-liberalization Economy [Ziyouhua yu Jituanhua de Qushi]," *Taiwan: A Radical Quarterly in Social Studies* 47 (September 2002): 33–83; and Amsden and Chu, *Beyond Late Development.*

22. Amsden and Chu, *Beyond Late Development*, 151.

23. Ibid., 121.

24. Chalmers Johnson, *MITI and the Japanese Miracle: The Growth of Industrial Policy, 1925–1975* (Stanford, CA: Stanford University Press, 1982); and Peter Evans, *Embedded Autonomy: States and Industrial Transformation* (Princeton, NJ: Princeton University Press, 1995).

25. Taken from the Ministry of Finance's website, at www.mof.gov.tw/public/ Data/statistic/Year_Fin/100電子書/htm/33080.pdf [in Chinese]. This tax-to-GDP ratio excludes social security contributions.

26. Ibid. According to the Organisation for Economic Co-operation and Development, Revenue Statistics, 2012, at www.oecd.org/ctp/tax-policy/revenue statistics2012edition.htm, among its rich member countries, the ratio of tax revenue (including social security contributions) to GDP averaged 34.0 percent in 2011, with Mexico's 19.7 percent the lowest. The comparable figure for Taiwan is 18.4 percent in 2010.

27. Ibid.

28. S. Y. Chuang, "The Evaporated CEPD [Zhengfalede Jingjianhui]," *CommonWealth*, no. 346 (May 10, 2006). In the past, CEPD staff had to report on the current economic situation to President Chiang Ching-kuo every two weeks. This practice was discontinued in 2000.

29. As a result, the Labor Pension Act followed the neoliberal principle and had few social security aspects. See Cheng-Liang Chen, "Failure in the Campaign for Social Security [Shehui Baoxian de Shibai]," *Taiwan: A Radical Quarterly in Social Studies* 79 (September 2010): 5–50.

30. From the *DGBAS 2010 Statistical Yearbook*, at http://eng.stat.gov.tw/ct.asp? xItem=9725&ctNode=1598&mp=5.

31. See Chen, "Failure in the Campaign for Social Security."

32. Amsden and Chu, *Beyond Late Development.*

33. As mentioned above, the ratio of tax revenue as a percentage of GDP has been declining steadily from the early 1990s and reached 11.9 percent in 2009, one of the lowest rates in the world.

34. Chen, "Failure in the Campaign for Social Security"; Meei-shia Chen, "The Analysis of the Historical Development of Marketization and Medicalization of the National Public Health System in Taiwan [Taiwan Gonggong Weisheng Tixi Shichanghua yu Yiliaohua de Lishi Fazhan Fenxi]," *Taiwan: A Radical Quarterly in Social Studies* 81 (March 2011): 3–78.

35. Jinn-yuh Hsu, "The Spatial Encounter Between Neoliberalism and Populism in Taiwan: Regional Restructuring Under the DPP Regime in the New Millennium," *Political Geography* 28, no. 5 (June 2009): 296–308; Jinn-yuh Hsu, "State Transformation and Regional Development in Taiwan: From Developmentalist Strategy to Populist Subsidy," *International Journal of Urban and Regional Research* 35, no. 3 (May 2011): 600–619.

36. See Tun-jen Cheng "Political Regimes and Development Strategies: South Korea and Taiwan," in *Manufacturing Miracles: Paths of Industrialization in Latin America and East Asia,* eds. Gary Gereffi and Donald L. Wyman (Princeton, NJ: Princeton University Press, 1990); and Chu, "Can Taiwan's Second Movers Upgrade via Branding?" 1062–1064.

37. In these projects, the state solicited but failed to obtain participation from private firms. Thus, for example, China Steel, a state-owned enterprise, undertook the integrated steel project, while semipublic firms, United Microelectronics and TSMC, were set up mainly with state funds to undertake the electronics projects. See Chu Wan-wen, "The Effects of Taiwan's Industrial Policy: A Preliminary Evaluation [Taiwan Chanye Zhengce Chengxiao de Chubu Pinggu]," *Taiwan: A Radical Quarterly in Social Studies* 42 (June 2001): 67–117.

38. One of the reasons could be that the Nationalists believed that their failures in economic policies, which caused hyperinflation and widespread discontent right before they were driven out of the mainland by the Chinese Communists in 1949, contributed greatly to their defeat. See Wan-wen Chu, "The Origin of Taiwan's Postwar Development: Colonial and Chinese Republican Legacy Reconsidered," manuscript, 2011. For example, *The Economist*'s survey on Taiwan, published on November 5, 1998, is titled "In Praise of Paranoia," praising the paranoid state of the Nationalist government.

39. Chu, "Can Taiwan's Second Movers Upgrade via Branding?" 1062–1064; see also Chapter 6 of this volume.

40. DGBAS, *Social Indicators 201* (Taipei, 2011), 96–115.

PART FIVE

Social Welfare Policy

EIGHT

Democratization and Health Care
The Case of Korea in Financing and Equity

Sangho Moon

Introduction

The welfare regimes in East Asia may have different characteristics from those in Europe that are examined by Esping-Anderson in the *Three Welfare Capitalisms.*[1] Following efforts to determine whether there might be different welfare regimes in Western Europe—other than Esping-Anderson's liberal, conservative, and social democratic regimes[2]—the same question has been asked of East Asia with reference to its *productivist* or *developmental* welfare system.[3] The welfare regimes in the East Asian countries such as the Republic of Korea (hereafter Korea) and Taiwan, as Holliday argues, can be understood as *productivist* in the sense that "all state policies are subordinate to economic or industrial priorities."[4] In slightly different terms, the East Asian welfare regimes may be called *developmental* because policy makers in the East Asian region tended to set "economic growth as the fundamental goal, with social policy being one of the instruments for its attainment."[5] In particular, the East Asian welfare regimes are to be described as having low or medium social security expenditures, high social investment, low coverage rates for pensions, high individual welfare loading, high family welfare responsibility, more extensive gender discrimination in salaries, and medium to high welfare satisfaction.[6] In the past, most scholarly attention focused on the economic miracles of the developmental welfare system. Less attention was paid to social or economic redistribution. A change in social policy or in the welfare system in the East Asian countries was more likely to be interpreted in the context of economic development rather than paying sufficient attention to equitable growth.

However, there have been dramatic changes since the Asian financial crisis (AFC) of 1997. Most scholars do not refute that a process of "multiple transitions," directly or indirectly related to the economic distress from the AFC, required the East Asian countries to develop a new social policy paradigm.[7] Nevertheless, the processes of the multiple transitions experienced by the East Asian countries have been diverse. The multiple transitions in the East Asian context after the AFC include "democratic transition," "an aging society," "a change in the welfare regime," "economic globalization," and "legal-institution building."[8] Others have noted the growing number of "informal-sector workers"[9] and "social polarization"[10] as notable factors in the economic transition.

I think it is worth mentioning Walker and Pellissery's nine "giant challenges" here, five of which resemble problems prevalent in Europe sixty years ago: want, squalor, poor health, unemployment, and inadequate education.[11] The four others—inequitable growth, discrimination, corruption, and an aging population—reduce the effectiveness of the policies targeted on the former five challenges. Although Korea and Taiwan are characterized by cultural diversity, they seem to share the same experience in the context of social policy. First, Korea and Taiwan did not seem to recognize sufficiently the adverse impacts of the giant challenges on the political and social orders in the course of sustained economic development. Second, Korea and Taiwan reacted to the giant challenges mostly through the political process of democratization. Third, Korea and Taiwan faced similar social challenges after the AFC, such as an aging society and a widening gap in income inequalities,[12] by focusing on government-initiated redistributive social policies. The AFC and the subsequent economic downturn intensified such government efforts.

As part of East Asia, Korea is an interesting area for research on social policy. As in Taiwan (see Chapter 9), Korea enjoyed rapid economic growth and industrialization, which ultimately led to unbalanced growth that caused social disorder and discrimination against disadvantaged groups in society. Social policy in response to the possibility of social disorder in Korea, however, did not attempt to fundamentally solve the social problems; rather, it sought to avoid the troubles temporarily, seemingly based on the principle "development first, distribution later." Referring to this passive attitude taken by past authoritarian regimes in Korea from 1960 to 1987, Shin and Shaw suggest that Korea was an authoritarian *developmental* state with a residual, "competition-compatible" form of social policy.[13] In a similar context, Huck-ju Kwon describes the nature of the Korean welfare system during that period as part of a politics of "legitimization" under the military rule.[14]

Democratic transition after July 1987, followed by the first direct presidential election in seventeen years in December 1987, was an important turning point for Korean social policy. During the period of the Roh Tae-woo government (1988–1992) and thereafter the Kim Young-sam government (1993–1997), a number of social security programs were implemented, including National Health Insurance (NHI), which was universalized by 1989.

In response to external pressures from economic globalization, the Kim Young-sam government advocated a Korean welfare model, which emphasized principles of conservative welfare: the role of the family, a partnership between the public and private sectors, development of human capital, and avoidance of dependency on the state.[15] In line with the conservatism of the Roh Tae-woo government, the Kim Young-sam administration spent only a small proportion (5.2 percent) of gross domestic product (GDP) on social welfare. With mandatory private social benefits, the ratio of public expenditures to total welfare spending remained low, indicating that the government significantly relied on the private sector for the provision of social benefits.[16] Thus, the role of the Roh Tae-woo and Kim Young-sam governments during the period 1988–1997 in terms of social welfare can best be described as a regulator rather than a provider.

The newly inaugurated Kim Dae-jung government (1998–2002) explored a new welfare system, the so-called productive welfare system, which stressed that welfare could be instrumental to the rise of economic productivity, similar to the active labor-market policy in the Scandinavian countries.[17] Productive welfare regards social protection and economic growth as overarching policy goals. One of the impressive changes in productive welfare or social investment under the socialistic rules of the Kim Dae-jung government (1998–2002) and the Roh Moo-hyun government (2003–2007) was the increase in the public share of expenditures on social benefits. Welfare responsibilities gradually moved from the private sector (i.e., private companies and the family) to the public sector (i.e., government and social entities). As a result, unlike in Hong Kong,[18] public expenditures on social welfare increased dramatically in Korea from 3.4 percent of GDP in 1996 before the AFC and the inauguration of President Kim Dae-jung to

7.6 percent of GDP in 2007, with the intention of strengthening the social security net.[19]

The purpose of this study is to determine the relationship between Korean democratization and health care, both historically and empirically. The health data from the Organisation for Economic Co-operation and Development (OECD) in 2010 and yearly data from the National Health Insurance Corporation (NHIC) are used to document the role of democracy in health financing.

This chapter also explores whether or not expanded budgets for institutionalized programs guarantee a real welfare state that is perceived by the participants as sufficient and equitable. For instance, income-related disparities in health care may be a challenge to the recent health democracy in Korea. To address this issue, a quantitative analysis is performed later in the chapter, based on a sample from the 2009 Korean Health and Nutrition Survey.

Health Democracy[20]

AUTHORITARIAN RULE AND THE INTRODUCTION OF LIMITED NHI, 1962–1987

The Korean health-care system has developed dramatically over the past half century. The most remarkable achievement in its evolution was the adoption of universal health insurance in 1976. However, the Korean case suggests that social provisions were not introduced for purely democratic reasons. As in the case of many social provisions under authoritarian military rulers in Eastern Europe and Latin America, there is insufficient evidence in the history of Korean health care of demand mobilization, either by citizens or by political parties representing the grassroots.[21] National Health Insurance was first considered in 1962 and was introduced by the military government in 1976. The introduction of NHI, the purpose of which was to support economic development, was the result of many rounds of debates over the previous ten-year period; Korea's polity score in the Polity IV Project during this period (1962–1987) was equal to level zero, indicating a non-democratic polity, as compared to a threshold of level six for democratic rule.[22]

Before 1976, when the military government was considering the introduction of NHI, less than 10 percent of the population had health insurance and per capita income was less than US$800 per month.[23] The idea of NHI was first conceived after the military coup d'état in 1961. The government delegated the project to the Committee for Social Security (CSS), a study group of bureaucrats from the Ministry of Health and Social Affairs (MHSA) and scholars interested in equity in social policy.[24] The health plan proposed by the CSS, however, was rejected by the Supreme Council for National Reconstruction, the highest decision-making body under the military government, because it was felt that the plan would become a financial burden on the administration.[25]

In 1976, however, the revised Medical Insurance Act, allowing NHI to cover industrial workers, was put into effect. The basic idea of NHI was similar to what the CSS had proposed in 1962, mandating compulsory medical insurance for employees and their dependents in large corporations with more than five hundred workers. In a financial sense, the nature of NHI was to gradually and incrementally expand coverage through private initiatives. The private initiatives were intended to work with a number of medical insurance societies, which independently collected insurance premiums, determined benefits, accumulated reserves, and reimbursed providers.[26] Under the umbrella of NHI, it was mandated that each workplace could establish separate health funds, to which the employers and the employees would evenly contribute corresponding funds. The health funds would serve as "financial intermediaries" that channeled funds to the providers of health insurance to workers employed in large corporations.[27] Without managerial risks, however, the health funds lacked incentives to generate profits; thus in order remain financially healthy, medical services had to be managed efficiently.

The coverage of NHI was expanded to employees working in smaller firms through a series of government laws that required an incremental phase-in of eligibility criteria. During the expansion of coverage, it was remarkable that the Korean economy did not experience any major disruptions, nor any apparent harm to specific industries or any adverse impact on small firms.[28] During the period 1976–1989, the Korean economy enjoyed one of the highest growth rates among OECD countries, about 12.2 percent per year, making it possible to implement mandatory NHI smoothly and without resistance from the private sector.

Meanwhile, in about 1980, members of the CSS and officials from the MHSA began to develop the idea of integrating the multiple health funds into one national fund providing universal coverage to the entire population. They believed that such integration would be an effective step toward universal coverage of the uninsured population. However, this idea was unacceptable to the political elites, for reasons similar to the objections in 1962—the excessive financial responsibility that would be placed on the Chun Doo-hwan administration (1981–1987).[29]

The Chun Doo-hwan administration, which assumed power after a military coup d'état in 1979, was concerned about the possible political conflicts that an abrupt change in health policy might produce. Moreover, the government was not prepared to make a financial commitment to run an integrated health fund. As in President Park's government (1964–1979), economic development remained the primary policy objective in order to legitimize the regime. In a sense, President Chun's legitimization policy involved maintaining the status quo in social policy, and the welfare state was to be limited to within the functional minimum of a capitalist state.[30]

Even though a Medical Assistance Plan was introduced as an in-kind public transfer program to protect indigent families in 1979, equity in health care was not yet perceived as a policy goal. The issue of integration was not even put on the table in the policy arena. The CSS members, cherishing the value of equity from the integration of health funds, did not formulate an effective advocacy coalition. Furthermore, they rarely affiliated with political partners outside the government. The CSS was dismissed and the MHSA officials who had participated in the CSS were forced to resign after the failure of this round of debate.[31]

The absence of a linkage with influential positions in the government may be one of the factors contributing to the failure of the reform. The "institutional weakness" and the lack of a "coherent rationale" within the group probably also contributed to its demise.[32] Moreover, the importance of equity had not yet been sufficiently articulated within the coalition.

The main issue in the administrative and financial integration of health funds into one carrier was passed over to the next government. Because of the instability in Korean politics at the time, characterized by a political confrontation between the authoritarian government and the civil society promoting democracy, the issue was not seriously considered as part of the policy agenda. The political elites in the government during this period emphasized economic policy and economic development at the expense of social policy. As a result, the informal group of health experts lobbying for universal health coverage through the integration of health funds was unable to develop into a full-fledged advocacy coalition. Furthermore, they did not find legitimate space in the political arena to debate the issue of health equity.

Despite the difficulties in pursuing the full integration of NHI, eligibility was gradually expanded. The initial coverage of industrial workers in large firms with more than five hundred employees as of 1977 was extended to cover employees in medium-sized firms with at least sixteen workers in 1982. Private employers were supposed to pay half of the premium for their employees. Over 30 percent of Korean citizens were thus covered by these industrial health funds. Government employees, school employees, and pension beneficiaries, constituting about 10 percent of entire population, had been enrolled in the government health funds of NHI since 1979. The government contributed by evenly splitting the premium. Meanwhile, about 10 percent of the entire population received Medical Aid, the government medical assistance program for those living in medical facilities, those unemployed persons relying on family assistance, and the medically needy population facing high medical expenses.

However, non-salaried employees, constituting more than 50 percent of the voters, remained uninsured because their employers did not cover their insurance premiums. Grievances over such exclusions from insurance coverage placed political pressures on the candidates running in the presidential election in December 1987. The elimination of the gap in insurance coverage thus became an important issue in the campaign, representing a giant step toward health democracy after the 1987 election.

DEMOCRATIZATION, UNIVERSALIZATION, AND AN ADVOCACY COALITION
FOR INTEGRATION, 1988–1997

The democratic campaign after July 1987, followed by the first democratic presidential election in two decades in December 1987, represented an important transition in Korean democracy. Polity IV scores evaluating the democratic transition showed significant progress as the Polity score increased from zero in 1986 to seven in 1988, thereby crossing the threshold for the introduction of democracy.

Democratization had an impact on the health-care system in a variety of ways that necessitated institutional changes in NHI. In the political battle to define the nature of the transition from authoritarian rule to democracy in 1986, the Chun Doo-hwan government, in an acknowledgement of non-salaried workers' grievances over their exclusion from NHI, announced its intention to expand health insurance coverage. Facing political pressures regarding the expansion of coverage, candidate Roh Tae-woo was forced to accept the idea of universal health care in his campaign. His 1988 pledge for universal health insurance called for covering industrial workers in firms with only five employees. By 1988–1989 the extension of coverage to rural and urban self-employed workers eliminated the preexisting coverage gap. This is evidence that over the years Korean democratization put health issues on the policy agenda and that universal coverage was achieved through political progress in democratization.

However, there still remained contentious debate—in particular between the power elites in the Roh Tae-woo government (1988–1992) and members of the advocacy coalition that supported integration (i.e., the CSS and the former MHSA officials)—over the issue of creating a single insurer to manage and finance health funds. During the presidential campaign, the advocacy coalition for integration was able to gather strength by affiliating with grassroots organizations representing more than 220 residential health funds of non-salaried employees: farmers, urban informal-sector workers, the self-employed, the unemployed, and the elderly.[33] The coalition worked effectively to prepare a common platform with the grassroots organizations that sought to achieve equity in health and redistribution of income.[34] According to Kwon, the coalition successfully articulated four main positions: "to integrate all health funds into one National Fund to widen the pooling of risk; to ensure access of low-income groups to health services; to increase the horizontal equity of health insurance contributions; and to increase the efficiency of health insurance administration."[35]

Until then, more than 350 health funds had developed a variety of financial statuses. Most industrial health funds enjoyed a surplus, whereas the residential health funds were more likely to struggle with financial deficits. Thus, the horizontal inequity problem became an important issue when paying contributions: Even people with the same income were supposed to pay different contributions depending on their types (i.e., industrial or residential) of health funds. Members of residential health funds typically paid more per capita than members of industrial funds, even at the same level of income, because of the weak fiscal conditions of the residential health funds.[36]

The rationale for integrating all health funds into one national fund, therefore, was acceptable to the public because it seemed to be an effective way to improve horizontal equity in financing by removing inequitable contributions and to enhance vertical equity in the utilization of services by widening the pool of risk to protect the needs of the low-income population regardless of their level of contribution.[37]

Meanwhile, those who opposed integration claimed that the integration of health funds would remove competition from the health insurance market. However, the fact that the 350 funds existing at the time (which were already controlled by government) could not play a role as an effective competitor in the health insurance market raised serious questions about the effectiveness of this argument. Second, those who opposed integration expressed concerns about possible imprudent utilization of health services by patients under one fund. They predicted that, under one national fund, there would be a moral hazard because patients would be less concerned about the fiscal conditions of the national fund. But this idea was often refuted because under the fee-for-service system, multiple health fund insurers also had no power to control the patients' moral hazard in utilizing health services.[38]

By a slim majority, upon the initiative of the opposition parties, a health insurance bill for gradual integration passed in the National Assembly in early 1989. But the bill was vetoed by President Roh Tae-woo in March 1989.[39] The government's position was that integration of health insurance funds violated private property law. President Roh believed that integration only benefited the low-income groups and that the upper- and middle-income families, the conservative supporters of Roh's administration, would end up being the losers in such a system. As the successor to incumbent President Chun Doo-hwan, President Roh was not prepared to accept principles of equity and redistribution.[40]

Conflicts among policy elites continued over the issue of integration during the following period of conservative statism (1990–1997), but stalemate ensued, dragging on without any breakthrough until the introduction of legislation for the Health Insurance Law in 1999. The Health Solidarity Coalition successfully mobilized the society to win popular support for the legislation. Expert activism continued to narrow the knowledge gap between elite policy makers and social groups through policy sharing and learning, thereby raising the policy-making profile of the actors in the social movement.[41] The goal of the coalition was equity in health and redistribution in finance.[42] The policy instrument to achieve this goal was the pooling of coverage of the different income groups into one national fund. According to Kwon, efforts to build an advocacy coalition progressed comprehensively until the legislation for the Health Insurance Law was introduced finally in 1999:

> In 1994, the Korean Federation of Trade Unions and the Citizens' Coalition for Participatory Democracy spearheaded the formation of a Coalition for the integration of NHI, which included 77 social pressure groups and maintained close contact with the opposition party. It had a clear link with the previous Association of Social Security Studies in terms of its core members. The coalition also represented a considerable part of the progressive political forces in Korea, and placed strong pressures on the government. The advocacy coalition concentrated its efforts on building social support for integration, since it realized that only upon a political decision were the pros and cons of integration to be revealed.[43]

Examining external economic circumstances may provide a useful perspective for understanding the Health Insurance Law legislation of 1999. It is clear that NHI had benefited from the economic growth during the previous two decades. From the launch of NHI through the mid-1990s, there had been no significant financial issues in the running of the program. Economic growth remained robust until the 1997 AFC. Hence, the financial implications of integration did not affect the debate until the economic crisis.

The AFC had an adverse impact not only on the Korean economy but also on its health-care system. The economic downturn led to the highest rate of unemployment in recent history. The sizable and growing deficit in NHI was reported to the Korean National Assembly in 1997. To deal with this deficit, the representatives in the National Assembly sought a way to reform the system. In an effort to enhance its administrative efficiency, the National Assembly agreed to enact a health insurance bill, which would integrate government and residential health funds but leave industrial health funds as they were.[44] Because a majority of voters learned about the bill through the Health Solidarity Coalition, there were political pressures on the parties, resulting in passage of the bill in January 1999.

DEEPENING DEMOCRACY, INTEGRATION, AND THE EXPANSION OF BENEFITS, 1998–2012

After the AFC, in the 1997 presidential elections the conservative Kim Young-sam was replaced by Kim Dae-jung, a long-standing opponent of conservative politicians since the Park Chung-hee regime (1964–1979). The Polity IV Project evaluated the political transition as an advance in democracy by scaling up the Polity score from seven to eight. The political transition influenced Korean social policy in three respects.

First, the economic crisis and political regime shift altered the social-welfare policy goals. Social policy was no longer perceived as an instrument supporting economic growth. Instead, the goal of social policy was to institutionalize a system of social protection against economic insecurity.[45] Because the economic crisis demonstrated that the traditional regulatory model for social welfare was no longer effective in coping with economic adversity, the Kim Dae-jung administration began to explore a new welfare model, the so-called *productive* welfarism, to strengthen the social security net for those in need through active labor-market intervention and a minimum living standard guarantee.[46]

The emphasis on social policy goals resulted in increased government expenditures on social-welfare programs. Welfare loading and responsibility moved from the private sector (i.e., private companies and families) to the public sector (i.e., government and social entities). This made it possible to implement the integration reform incrementally rather than to curtail the public commitment to health care, even in the midst of economic downturn.

Second, the deepening democracy changed the decision-making policy networks. The election of Kim Dae-jung to the presidency meant that his National Congress for New Politics party and his policy staff replaced the bureaucrats of the previous governments who had dominated the policy cycle in health care. In their stead, the previously inactive social movements helped promote social-welfare programs.[47] Some policy elites who spearheaded the advocacy coalition for integration rose to leading positions in the Ministry of Health and Welfare. Their mission was to complete the integration reform by merging, both administratively and financially, the residential health funds into one national fund. According to Kwon, the impressive role of the Health Solidarity Coalition in completing this mission was both timely and effective:

> President Kim Dae-Jung convened a tripartite committee of the government, business and trade unions to push through economic reform with social consensus. The advocacy coalition, which supported a full integration of the NHI, put the issue on the committee's agenda. Some members of the coalition also participated in the Transition Committee for the New Government. President

Kim appointed a former bureaucrat, who had been dismissed by the Chun government because of his support for integration, to be the Minister of Health and Welfare. This means that the advocacy coalition for integration and equity had a hold on key decision points. [48]

Third, deepening democracy changed policy perspectives on social welfare. The democratization progress worked as a means to force the policy elites and ruling-class political representatives to accept welfare-state arrangements.[49] The policy paradigm tended to lean toward generalized welfare rather than selective welfare, which not only emphasized redistribution but also sought productivity. By equating "productivity" and "social rights," Korea was now at the stage of becoming a productive welfare state that no longer relied on a hierarchical priority between economic and social policies and that recognized the dynamics of economic development as manifested within "social rights."[50] Policy elites in the Kim Dae-jung administration understood that social policy would contribute to the growth of the national economy and that economic growth in turn would require further social-policy reforms.[51]

The idea of productive welfarism strengthened the position of those policy elites arguing for an expansion of the state role in social-welfare programs. Thus, even under the adverse impact of the macroeconomic conditions, Korean social expenditures on health care grew (as illustrated in the next section), unlike the case in neighboring East Asian countries such as Hong Kong.[52] Korean reformers at the time found it difficult to roll back the state role.

In addition to the integration reform of health care to achieve equity and efficiency in the health system, in 2000 the Kim Dae-jung government embarked on another major reform—to separate drug prescriptions by physicians and drug dispensing by certified pharmacists in an effort to improve pharmaceutical safety. An early evaluation of this separation reform reveals that the overuse of prescription antibiotics was reduced significantly.[53] However, the separation reform gave rise to prolonged doctors' strikes since, by removing the doctors' margins from the sale of pharmaceuticals, their economic interests were threatened. To placate the protesting doctors, medical reimbursement fees were raised by 41 percent. [54] But the resultant rising health expenditures led to an increase in premiums, thereby adding to the patients' burdens.

After the separation reform, total health expenditures increased by 42 percent, from US$36.2 billion in 2000, the first year of the reform, to US$51.4 billion in 2003. This represents an average annual growth rate of

14.0 percent, much higher than the annual growth rate of 9.9 percent during the 1995–2000 periods. Per capita health expenditures rose by 39.3 percent from US$771 in 2000 to US$1,074 in 2003, indicating an annual increase of 13.1 percent, compared with an annual increase of 11.1 percent from 1995 to 2000.[55]

On the revenue side, NHI had three funding sources: contributions imposed on the taxable incomes of wage and salary earners, government subsidies, and contributions from residence-based members, with adjustments based on property, sex, age, and the number of family members. To manage the National Health Fund, the NHIC was established in July 2003, the first year of the Roh Moo-hyun government (2003–2007), representing completion of the financial integration of all health funds.

Roh Moo-hyun, political successor to incumbent president Kim Dae-jung, had to focus policy efforts on the NHI fiscal stabilization because of the growing deficit over the period 1997–2002. The NHI Financial Stabilization Act of 2002, imposing a special tax on cigarettes, successfully resolved the deficit, resulting in a surplus during the Roh Moo-hyun administration. However, by 2007 the deficit had returned and financing the program continued to be a major health policy issue during the Lee Myung-bak government (2008–2012).

Health-Care Financing

Korean health expenditures have been characterized as relatively low in terms of per capita spending but relatively high in terms of growth. Extended eligibility and benefits in the NHI program over the past three decades have contributed to the rising expenditures. Korea is expected to face even greater challenges from increasing health costs because of its aging population. Using data from the NHIC, in the following we will examine the evolution of the balance in the NHI budget.

Table 8.1 shows the trends in the NHI financial balance. The balance has been deteriorating since 1997, suffering from a continuing annual deficit up to 2002. In 2001, the financial deficit reached its highest level at US$ 1.9 billion (KW 2,178 billion). In response to the deficit, the Financial Stabilization Act enacted in January 2002 required that the government subsidize the NHIC by generating a stable revenue flow from the collection of the newly established tobacco tax.[56] Although by 2003 there was a surplus in

TABLE 8.1
Annual balance of NHI funds, 1984–2010 (unit: billions of Korean won)

	1984	1985	1986	1987	1988	1989	1990	1991	1992
Revenue	555	639	800	950	1,339	1,812	2,432	3,269	3,774
Expenditure	538	648	642	753	1,089	1,585	2,164	2,491	2,970
Balance	–3	–7	158	197	250	227	268	778	804

	1993	1994	1995	1996	1997	1998	1999	2000	2001
Revenue	4,199	4,711	5,614	6,631	7,554	8,230	8,892	9,828	11,928
Expenditure	3,464	3,971	5,076	6,464	7,795	8,788	9,610	10,744	14,106
Balance	735	740	538	167	–241	–558	–718	–916	–2,178

	2002	2003	2004	2005	2006	2007	2008	2009	2010
Revenue	14,305	17,467	19,408	21,091	23,263	25,270	28,901	31,182	33,561
Expenditure	14,798	15,972	17,331	20,146	22,944	25,554	27,541	31,185	34,860
Balance	–493	195	2,077	945	319	–284	1,360	–3	–1,299

SOURCE: National Health Insurance Corporation, *Statistical Yearbook*, various years (Seoul).
NOTE: Only reflecting cash flow surplus and excluding NHIC-holding asset values.

the annual balance of the NHIC owing to the subsidy, the growth in health expenditures, incurred by expanded benefits from 2003 to 2006, resulted in another deficit by 2007. Thereafter, with the exception of an unexpected surplus in 2008, the balance in the National Health Fund remained weak.

The reasons for the deficit can be attributed to overutilization of services, claimed to be the result of the fee-for-service system to reimburse physicians. To prevent this overutilization of services, high co-payments and more uncovered services were proposed. As a result, physicians tended to provide more uncovered services with higher margins than covered services with lower margins,[57] and patients tended to see the most profit-oriented physicians who provided the most sophisticated care, even for mild symptoms.[58] The NHIC's responsibility to control health-care costs resulted in a tightening of the review process for the utilization of services. It was recommended that in order to improve the health-care system, consumers would need to receive quality care at reasonable rates and providers would need to be allowed reasonable margins to foster investments in medical facilities and technology.

SOURCES OF PAYMENT

Table 8.2 and Figure 8.1 present the sources of payments contributing to the national health system over the past twenty-nine years. The ratio of social security financing to total health expenditures rose sharply, from 13.2 percent in 1980 to 42.5 percent in 2008, whereas the ratio of out-of-pocket (OOP) payments continually declined. Considering that other sources of payment (government subsidies, corporate contributions, and private insurance) did not change significantly during this period, one can conclude that social security financing basically replaced patients' direct payments.[59] The amount of public health financing, including social security payments and government subsidies, continually increased, from 23.2 percent in 1980 to 55.4 percent in 2008. This implies that public health social protection was strengthened in order to reduce the financial burdens on patients.

The proportion of private insurance financing in total health expenditures quadrupled during the period. The high rates of uncovered or inadequately covered services seem to have played a role in the growing ratio of private health insurance to total health expenditures. Increased national income and advanced medical technologies might also have contributed to the growth of private insurance by driving patients to pursue high-tech medical care through private insurance coverage.[60]

TABLE 8.2
Sources of payments for the Korean health-care system, 1980–2008 (%)

	1980	1981	1982	1983	1984	1985	1986	1987	1988	1989
Government	10.0	9.2	8.1	8.1	7.9	7.7	8.5	8.9	9.4	9.1
Social Security	13.2	13.4	17.5	20.9	24.1	25.2	22.6	22.6	24.3	25.2
Out-of-pocket	72.8	73.7	68.4	65.6	62.8	61.1	64.1	63.3	60.5	60.2
Private insurance	0.8	0.8	0.8	0.9	1.1	1.2	1.4	1.6	1.6	1.9
Corporation	3.2	3.0	5.2	4.6	4.1	4.8	3.5	3.5	4.1	3.6

	1990	1991	1992	1993	1994	1995	1996	1997	1998	1999
Government	9.0	9.3	8.6	8.5	8.0	8.0	8.6	9.2	9.6	10.8
Social Security	30.5	27.6	27.4	28.2	27.5	30.1	32.2	33.8	38.2	37.5
Out-of-pocket	55.5	57.6	57.2	56.1	53.1	52.9	50.5	47.8	43.4	43.4
Private insurance	1.9	2.0	2.0	2.2	2.5	2.6	2.5	3.0	4.0	3.4
Corporation	3.1	3.5	4.7	5.0	8.8	6.5	6.1	6.1	5.0	4.9

	2000	2001	2002	2003	2004	2005	2006	2007	2008	
Government	10.2	10.3	10.5	9.9	10.4	11.7	12.5	12.8	12.9	
Social Security	38.3	44.1	42.6	41.8	42.0	41.4	42.6	42.4	42.5	
Out-of-pocket	42.3	37.3	38.7	39.4	38.2	38.5	36.9	35.5	35.0	
Private insurance	4.3	3.4	3.3	3.6	3.4	3.4	3.3	3.9	4.4	
Corporation	4.9	4.8	5.0	4.8	4.6	4.6	4.3	4.8	4.7	

SOURCE: *OECD Health Data 2010* (Paris: OECD, 2010).

NOTE: Ratio of government subsidies (GS), social security schemes (SSS), out-of-pocket payments (OOP), private health insurance (PI), corporate contribution (CC) to total health expenditures (THE).

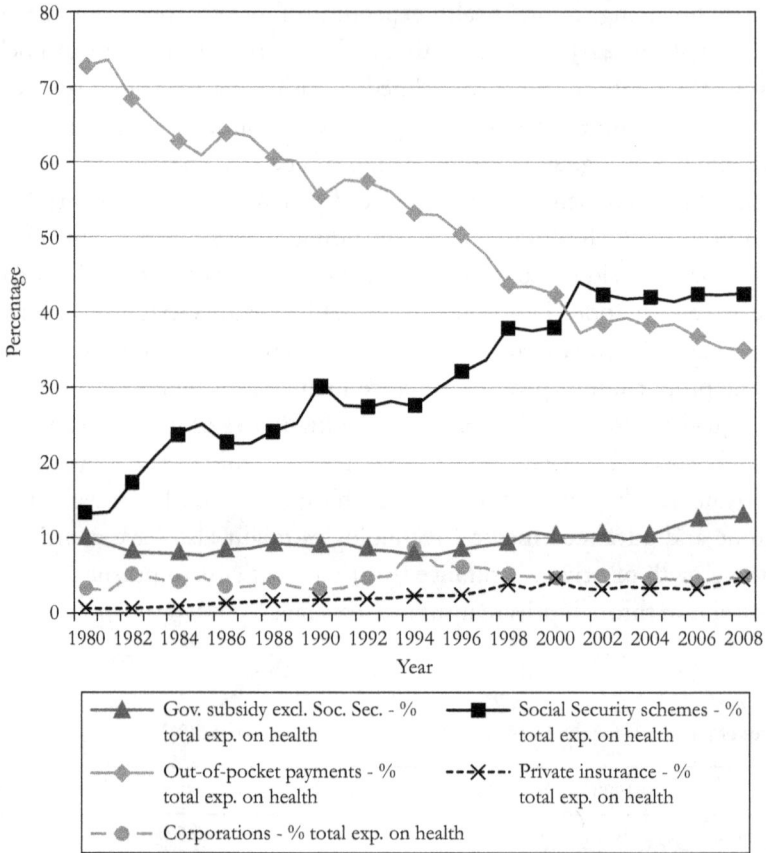

FIGURE 8.1 Sources of financing for the Korean Health System, 1980–2008
SOURCE: *OECD Health Data, 2010.*

Because the Korean NHI program began with low premiums for the insured and stringent government funding, the range of in-kind benefits was limited, leaving many medically indispensable services excluded from the benefit package. As a result, a variety of common services remained either uncovered or inadequately covered by the NHI plan. This may account for the relatively high ratio of OOP spending by Korean patients.[61] However, when NHI eligibility was extended to the entire population, the NHI plan imposed relatively high rates of cost sharing, even to receive covered services, because the health authorities were concerned that a comprehensive national plan might lead to a moral hazard in the utilization of health services. The cost-sharing scheme is still an important NHI tool to mitigate the burden of financing health care by encouraging beneficiaries to be price-sensitive in their use of services. Hypothetically, the cost-sharing rule could improve the financial stability of the NHIC in Korea, but in practice fulfillment of patient demands for health care will be a prerequisite to achieving such cost savings.

Completion of universal coverage within one decade is commendable. But such an achievement should be treated with caution. The coverage rate for medical services within the NHI is low compared with the OECD countries,[62] and continual progress is needed to eliminate the unmet healthcare needs of the disadvantaged population. Meanwhile, the expansion of benefits must be monitored to avoid heavy cost increases.

In terms of health financing, there are still several areas where performance might be improved. First, the high share of uncapped OOPs (35 percent in 2008) raises concerns about both the equity of financing and service use. The NHI insurance premium rates have not been raised sufficiently to finance the expanded benefits and the increased utilization after the health reform of 2000. A financially stable revenue mechanism has not yet been established to keep the growth of health expenditures on a sustainable path.

With respect to controlling health-care costs, two consumer-side schemes have been implemented: 1) enforced referrals from general physicians to tertiary providers for patients to receive specialized care, and 2) high co-payments to discourage the use of expensive and medically unnecessary treatments.

Academic evaluations constantly reveal that the effects of such demand-side cost controls have been limited. Experiences from the 1997–2002 health-care financial crisis suggest that health-cost policy in the absence of supply-side monitoring is not effective. Thus, an idea of payment reform, such as adopting a prospective payment scheme, has been suggested by scholars to maintain the financial viability of the system.

With respect to supply-side controls, for a long time the NHIC's cost-containment policy relied on maintaining low physician reimbursements. However, these price controls were challenged toward the end of the 1990s. In particular, after the physicians' strikes in the aftermath of the separation reform of 2000, it was argued that price regulation without considering the physicians' earnings structure might adversely affect the quality of care.

The Kim Dae-jung administration (1998–2002), acknowledging the need to control providers, conducted several pilot programs, such as the Diagnosis-Related Group (DRG) reimbursement scheme. The outcomes of the pilot programs were encouraging: There was less spending under the DRG system than under the fee-for-service system, as fees for services provided by hospitals and physicians in the former are set by the government.[63] However, the government failed to enact the DRG reimbursement system for the entire NHI system because of fierce opposition from providers, medical professionals, and hospitals. Therefore, few cost-containment programs have been implemented in Korea. The fixed-fee scheme was the most effective government regulation on providers, but it was rapidly abandoned in the face of the unexpected strikes by physicians.[64] Thus, the lack of regulation on the supply side, associated with universal NHI coverage to all citizens, led to rising health-care costs.[65] Furthermore, the rising health costs were primarily shifted to the consumers, as they faced greater payroll deductions for insurance premiums.

In summary, the large share of private health financing of total health expenditures (about 44.1 percent of total health-care expenditures in 2008) and the high cost-sharing by patients in Korea seem to be consequences of the weak monitoring of the fee-for-service payment system and of limited increases in NHI premiums despite continued expansion of coverage and covered benefits.[66]

NEW CHALLENGES TO HEALTH DEMOCRACY

Korea has developed a unique health-care system. The NHI universal coverage was prepared with low health-care costs. Patients were allowed to choose providers, and there was a relatively good network of public primary-care facilities.[67] However, the recent health democracy has exposed the Korean health-care system to new challenges: an aging society and income-related health disparities. Appropriate policy responses may be required for better performance and sustainable growth of the national health system.

AN AGING SOCIETY

The aging of the population is one of the major reasons for the rise in health-care costs. National forecasts indicate that Korea will soon be one of the most aged countries in the world. The proportion of elderly over the age of 65 increased from 3.1 percent in 1970 to 10.2 percent in 2010, and it is predicted to reach 20.8 percent in 2028 and 38.2 percent in 2050.[68]

An aging society tends to be associated with increasing health-care costs. The literature shows that elderly health-care requirements are more expensive than non-elderly health-care requirements. International empirical evidence supports that there is a positive correlation between "proximity to death" and rising health costs.[69] In particular, end-of-life health care has been documented to place huge financial burdens on society. As a result, Korea is likely to be vulnerable to NHI financial deficits because of its aging population. A study of the Korean age-expenditure profile from 1991 to 2003 reveals that a disproportionately large share of resources was spent on elderly health care. This suggests that health spending in Korea will continue to grow as the population ages.[70]

Table 8.3 and Figure 8.2 show the NHI ratio of elderly beneficiaries to the entire population, in comparison to the ratio of elderly health spending to national health expenditures from 2003 to 2010. The ratio of elderly health spending was 31.6 percent in 2010, an increase of 49.1 percent from the 21.2 percent in 2003. Per capita expenditures on the elderly rose from US$1,080 (KW 1.24 million) in 2003 to US$2,412 (KW 2.77 million) in 2010, implying an average annual growth rate of 17.5 percent—much higher than the 14.7 percent per capita annual growth rate of national health expenditures for *all* age cohorts.

Figure 8.3 illustrates the trend in annual NHI per capita health expenditures by age cohort between 2003 and 2010. Health costs were relatively high for infants and children under age 14, whereas costs were relatively low for youth under age 24. Health costs began to increase for the middle-aged population, and then rose rapidly in later years. Furthermore, during the 2003–2010 periods the rate of increase in per capita health costs for the elderly increased each year, implying that medical treatment for the elderly was becoming more expensive over time as compared to that for their non-elderly counterparts.

As a policy response, the issue of intergenerational allocation of medical resources needs to be addressed, possibly by imposing "reasonable" premiums on the wealthy elderly receiving family benefits from their children. In a technical sense, procedural standardization may be required for end-of-life care services. The scope of benefits for end-of-life care needs to be readjusted to deal with the rising costs of elderly health care.

TABLE 8.3
NHI expenditures for elderly health care, 2003–2010

		2003	2004	2005	2006	2007	2008	2009	2010
Beneficiaries (unit: 1,000 persons)	Total	47,103	47,372	47,392	47,410	47,820	48,160	48,614	48,907
	Elderly (65+)	3,541	3,748	3,919	4,073	4,387	4,600	4,826	4,979
	Percentage (%)	7.5	7.9	8.3	8.6	9.2	9.6	9.9	10.2
Expenditures (unit: billion kW)	Total	20,742	22,506	24,862	28,410	32,389	34,869	39,339	43,657
	Elderly (65+)	4,401	5,137	6,073	7,350	9,119	10,737	12,346	13,785
	Percentage (%)	21.2	22.8	24.4	25.9	28.2	30.8	31.4	31.6

SOURCE: National Health Insurance Corporation, *Statistical Yearbook,* various years (Seoul).

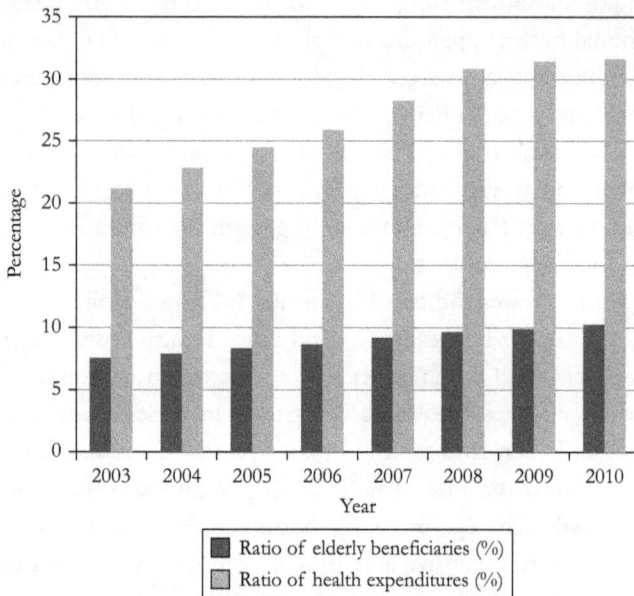

FIGURE 8.2 NHI expenditures for elderly health care, age 65+

SOURCE: National Health Insurance Corporation, *Statistical Yearbook,* 2003–2010, http://stat.kosis.kr/nsieu/view/tree.do?task=branchView&id=350_350_35006_35006_01*MT_OTITLE&hOrg=350 [in Korean].

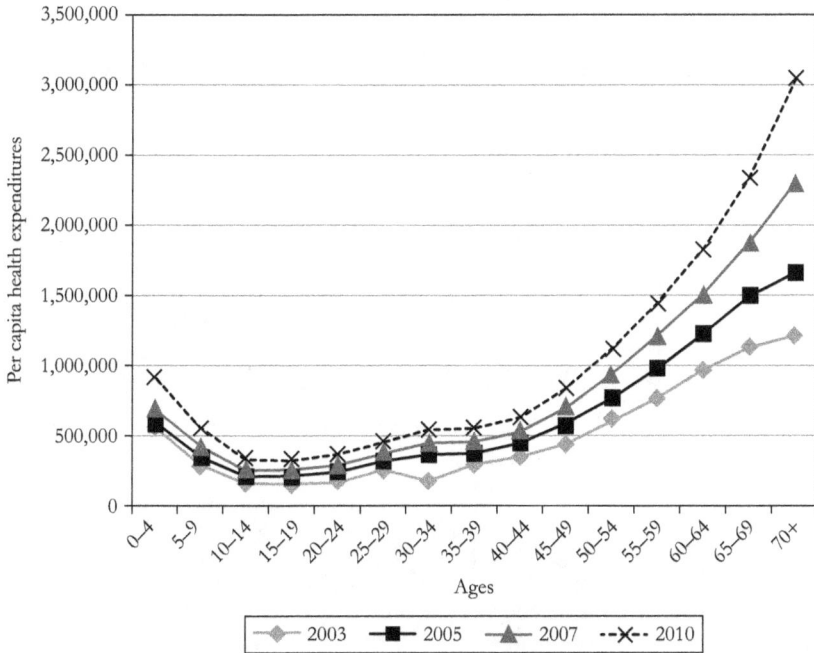

FIGURE 8.3 NHI per capita health expenditures, age cohorts (unit: Korean won)
SOURCE: National Health Insurance Corporation, *Statistical Yearbook* (various years), www.nhic.or.kr/portal/site/main/MENU_WBDDG0202/ [in Korean].

INCOME-RELATED HEALTH DISPARITIES

Occupational structural changes after the AFC had an adverse impact on the equal distribution of income. The market-income-based Gini coefficient, measured from a nationally representative sample of Korean families with two or more members, rose from 0.268 in 1997 to 0.325 in 2010, indicating a deterioration in the equal distribution of income after the economic crisis.

Since income inequality is associated with the distribution of accessibility to health care, the unequal distribution of income often leads to inadequate service utilization by the lower-income groups. This tends to cause a widening gap in health and health care between the higher- and lower-income groups. International evidence reveals that unequal socioeconomic status, or social polarization, is highly correlated with disparities in the use of health services as well as in health itself.[71]

Table 8.4 shows the health-care disparities between two income groups: the higher 20 percent and lower 20 percent cohorts. The self-reported

TABLE 8.4

Health status and health service utilization, 2008 (%)

	LOWER 20% INCOME (N = 2,255)			HIGHER 20% INCOME (N = 2,019)		
	Total	Elderly (N = 1,077)	Non-elderly (N = 1,078)	Total	Elderly (N = 102)	Non-elderly (N = 1,917)
OVERALL HEALTH						
Self-reported health	2.94^D (1.07)	2.66^C,E (1.08)	3.20^F (0.99)	3.57 (0.85)	3.22^F (1.03)	3.59 (0.83)
Illnesses during past 2 weeks	39.2^D (0.49)	51.7^C,E (0.49)	27.5^F (0.45)	18.0 (0.39)	30.2^F (0.46)	17.4 (0.38)
Sick days during past 2 weeks	4.24^D (6.08)	6.11^C,E (6.65)	2.48^F (4.87)	1.41 (3.69)	3.19^F (5.56)	1.31 (3.54)
MENTAL ILLNESS						
Depression	18.5^D (0.39)	17.7 (0.38)	19.5^F (0.40)	8.6 (0.28)	17.3^f (0.38)	7.9 (0.27)
Suicide attempt during past 1 year	7.6^D (0.27)	5.4^c (0.23)	10.8^F (0.31)	1.8 (0.13)	0 (0)	2.0 (0.14)
Suicide impulse during past 1 year	26.5^D (0.44)	30.6^e,C (0.46)	22.4^F (0.42)	10.5 (0.31)	18.6^F (0.39)	10.0 (0.30)
Stress perception	29.7 (0.46)	27.1^C,E (0.45)	32.8^f (0.47)	27.1 (0.45)	15.5^F (0.36)	28.0 (0.45)
Unmet needs during past 1 year	28.1^D (0.45)	28.3 (0.45)	27.8^f (0.45)	22.9 (0.42)	19.8 (0.40)	23.1 (0.42)
OUTPATIENT VISITS DURING PAST 2 WEEKS						
Number of visits (frequency)	0.84^D (1.60)	1.12^C (1.81)	0.58^F (1.34)	0.48 (1.05)	1.16^F (1.69)	0.45 (0.99)
Have not been to a doctor	60.4^D (0.49)	49.9^C (0.50)	70.2 (0.46)	71.2 (0.45)	44.9^F (0.50)	72.6 (0.45)
Have been to a doctor 1–2 times	30.1^D (0.46)	36.5^C (0.48)	24.0 (0.43)	26.3 (0.43)	41.8^F (0.50)	23.7 (0.43)
Have been to a doctor 3 or more times	9.5^D (0.29)	13.6^C (0.34)	5.7^f (0.23)	4.1 (0.20)	13.3^F (0.34)	3.7 (0.19)

INPATIENT VISITS DURING PAST 1 YEAR

	(1)	(2)	(3)	(4)	(5)	(6)
Number of visits (frequency)	0.14^D	0.16^{C}_{e}	0.11_f	0.09	0.09	0.09
	(0.42)	(0.47)	(0.38)	(0.31)	(0.35)	(0.31)
Have not been an inpatient	88.7^D	$86.6^{C,e}$	90.6_f	92.4	92.9	92.3
	(0.32)	(0.34)	(0.29)	(0.27)	(0.26)	(0.27)
Have been an inpatient once	9.7^D	$11.2^{c,e}$	8.0	6.8	5.1	6.9
	(0.30)	(0.32)	(0.28)	(0.25)	(0.22)	(0.25)
Have been an inpatient 2 or more times	1.6^d	2.2^c	1.1	0.8	2.0	0.8
	(0.13)	(0.15)	(0.10)	(0.09)	(0.14)	(0.09)

PRESCRIPTION DRUGS DURING PAST 2 WEEKS

	(1)	(2)	(3)	(4)	(5)	(6)
Number of refills (frequency)	0.54^D	0.65^C	0.44^F	0.36	0.71^F	0.34
	(0.92)	(0.99)	(0.84)	(0.68)	(0.96)	(0.66)
No refills	64.3^D	58.6^C	69.7^F	73.2	54.1^F	74.2
	(0.48)	(0.49)	(0.46)	(0.44)	(0.50)	(0.44)
1–2 refills	31.2^D	35.5^C	27.2_f	25.2	39.8^F	24.4
	(0.46)	(0.48)	(0.45)	(0.44)	(0.49)	(0.43)
3 or more refills	4.4^D	5.8^C	3.1^F	1.6	6.1_f	1.4
	(0.21)	(0.24)	(0.17)	(0.13)	(0.24)	(0.12)

PREVENTIVE CARE SERVICE

	(1)	(2)	(3)	(4)	(5)	(6)
Routine checkup during past 1 year	53.6^D	57.8^C	48.7^F	64.1	57.3	64.6
	(0.50)	(0.49)	(0.50)	(0.48)	(0.50)	(0.48)
Abdominal exam during past 1 year	24.1^D	25.7^c	22.2^F	28.2	22.9	28.6
	(0.43)	(0.44)	(0.42)	(0.45)	(0.42)	(0.45)
Liver cancer exam during past 6 months	9.4^D	9.2	9.7^F	17.9	10.4^f	18.5
	(0.29)	(0.29)	(0.30)	(0.38)	(0.31)	(0.39)
Colon cancer exam during past 2 years	20.9	22.4_f	19.2_f	22.1	20.8	22.2
	(0.41)	(0.42)	(0.39)	(0.42)	(0.41)	(0.42)
Cervical cancer exam during past 1 year (females)	24.6^D	19.6^C	30.6^F	38.4	12.5^F	40.5
	(0.43)	(0.40)	(0.46)	(0.49)	(0.33)	(0.49)
Breast cancer exam during past 1 year (females)	29.2	28.0^c	30.6	31.2	16.1^F	32.4
	(0.46)	(0.45)	(0.46)	(0.46)	(0.37)	(0.47)

SOURCE: *Korean Health and Nutrition Examination Survey (KHANES)*, Wave 4 (2009).

NOTES: 1 = Very Bad; 2 = Bad; 3 = Average; 4 = Good; 5 = Very Good. The reported values are the percentages of respondents who answer positively to the respective questions. The corresponding standard deviations are in parentheses. Superscript uppercase letters (A, B, C, D, E, and F) denote the statistical significance of the mean equivalence test between the groups at $p < .01$; superscript lowercase letters (a, b, c, d, e, and f) denote $p < .05$; subscript lowercase letters denote $p < .1$. The significance results are indicated only at the first result. For example, if a result in column A is significantly different from a result in column D, the letter D (upper or lower case, superscript or subscript, depending on the p value) will appear alongside the result in column A, but the letter A will not appear alongside the result in column D.

health was significantly different between the two groups. Measured on a five-point scale, the self-reporting by the lower-income group indicated that they were less healthy than their higher-income counterparts. Similarly, among both the elderly and non-elderly populations, low-income earners were found to have experienced more sick days in the previous two weeks than the high-income earners. Overall, low-income earners on average reported 4.2 sick days during the previous two weeks, whereas high-income earners reported only 1.4 days.

Mental illness was found to be more prevalent among low-income groups. Particularly among the non-elderly population, those with low incomes were significantly more vulnerable to depression than those with high incomes. In addition, the percentage of individuals who had felt suicidal impulses and had attempted suicide was significantly higher among the lower-income group. Moreover, both the elderly and non-elderly members of the lower-income group indicated a much higher perception of stress than their counterparts in the higher-income group.

With respect to health-care utilization, the percentage of unmet needs for medical care was higher among the lower-income population. On average, 28.1 percent of the low-income population reported that during the past year they had not received adequate medical care, whereas only 22.9 percent of the high-income population said they had unmet needs. In response to questions about the reasons for their unmet needs, about 50.4 percent of the low-income population who felt there were unmet needs attributed them to "financial unaffordability," whereas 32 percent of their high-income counterparts selected "time conflicts" as the greatest barrier to receiving adequate care.

The two income groups also differed in terms of their utilization of outpatient and inpatient care services and prescription drugs. More frequent visits and refills were reported by members of the lower-income group for all three services, with the non-elderly low-income group particularly prone to utilizing more services than their high-income counterparts.

One routine checkup and five cancer tests were examined to measure the utilization of preventive health services. Because preventive care services are not fully covered by NHI, members of the higher-income group found it more feasible financially to receive preventive medicine, and thus they had had more regular routine health checkups and abdominal and cervical cancer tests during the past year. High-income earners were also more likely to have received liver cancer exams during the past six months, although among the elderly population the difference was not statistically significant.

In summary, utilization of health services, including inpatient and outpatient visits and pharmaceutical refills, was more frequent among the lower-income groups, implying that a good deal of accessibility to services is guaranteed to people with limited resources. Policy efforts are still needed, however, to improve unmet health-care needs. The unmet needs of the low-income population are higher than those of their high-income counterparts due to their inability to afford high-cost medical treatments. From a policy standpoint, the relatively low ratio of covered services, compared with other OECD countries, seems to be responsible for the income-related disparities in unmet needs.

In terms of preventive medicine, high-income people were more regular users of preventive services than their low-income counterparts. This may be due to the high costs of such services, since NHI does not fully cover cancer exams and routine health checkups. The higher-income groups also seemed more likely to perceive the value of health, thereby contributing to their more frequent use of preventive medicine.

Furthermore, this study reveals that individuals in the low-income population on average rated their health lower, experiencing more illnesses, sick days, depression, suicidal impulses or attempts, and perceptions of stress, compared with their wealthy counterparts. Overall, six out of seven health indicators showed that the health condition of people with limited resources was worse than that of people with relatively abundant resources. It thus can be concluded that even after the health-care reform, income-related disparities in Korea still contribute to health-condition differences.

Enhanced public health programs to reduce the income-related disparities in health and health care are urgently needed to eliminate both unmet medical-care needs and health gaps between the two income groups. However, a populist free in-kind medical aid to the entire population, as recently raised by the political parties, will not provide a viable solution to the issue of inequity in health because it is neither financially feasible nor socially sustainable. Excessive redistribution through extremely progressive premiums would result in resistance to paying high contributions among plan holders, leading to a permanent deficit in the national health funds. Furthermore, in light of the growing NHI deficit associated with the aging population, the idea of providing free medical care to the entire the population in order to win electoral votes will not produce a desirable political outcome.

Korean democratization over the past three decades has increased public health expenditures and raised concerns about health-care equity. Democratization allowed for a health reform that integrated over 350 independent medical groups. But increasing health costs and disparities in health care remain an urgent issue for the nascent democracy. Moreover, as in Taiwan (see Chapter 9), the aging population in association with rising end-of-life medical costs is a significant challenge to health financing. Income-related health disparities, intensified by the widening income gap between the higher 20 percent and lower 20 percent income groups, also raise questions about the effectiveness of the integrated health reform that sought equity and redistribution. Further policy evaluation based on evidence is needed to monitor feedback and to reshape the future health system.

Notes

1. Gosta Esping-Andersen, *The Three Worlds of Welfare Capitalism* (Princeton, NJ: Princeton University Press, 1990).

2. Christopher Pierson, *Beyond the Welfare State? The New Political Economy of Welfare* (London: Polity Press, 1991); Stephan Leibfried, "Towards an European Welfare State? On Integrating Poverty Regimes into the European Community," *Social Policy in a Changing Europe*, ed. Zsuzsa Ferge and Jon Eivind Kolberg (Frankfurt am Main, Germany: Campus Verlag, 1992), 245–280; Francis G. Castles and Deborah Mitchell, "Identifying Welfare State Regimes: The Links between Politics, Instruments and Outcomes," *Governance: An International Journal of Policy, Administration, and Institutions* 5, no. 1 (1992): 1–26; Alan Siaroff, "Work Welfare and Gender Equality: A New Typology," *Gendering Welfare States*, ed. Diane Sainsbury (London: Sage, 1994), 82–100; Maurizio Ferrera, "The 'Southern Model' of Welfare in Social Europe," *Journal of European Social Policy* 6, no. 1 (1996): 17–37; Diane Sainsbury, *Gender, Equality, and Welfare States* (Cambridge: UK: Cambridge University Press, 1996); Duncan Gallie and Serge Paugam, "The Experience of Unemployment in Europe: The Debate," *Welfare Regimes and the Experience of Unemployment in Europe*, ed. Gallie and Paugam (Oxford, UK: Oxford University Press, 2000), 1–22.

3. Ian Holliday, "Productivist Welfare Capitalism: Social Policy in East Asia," *Political Studies* 48, no. 4 (2000): 706–723; Kwong-leung Tang, *Social Welfare Development in East Asia* (New York: Palgrave, 2000); Aurel Croissant, "Changing Welfare Regimes in East and Southeast Asia: Crisis, Change, and Challenge," *Social Policy & Administration* 38, no. 5 (2004): 504–524; Huck-ju Kwon, "An

Overview of the Study: The Developmental Welfare State and Policy Reforms in East Asia," in *Transforming the Developmental Welfare State in East Asia* (Basingstoke, UK: Palgrave Macmillan, 2005), 1–23; Yeun-wen Ku and Catherine Jones Finer, "Developments in East Asian Welfare Studies," *Social Policy & Administration* 41, no. 2 (April 2007): 115–131; Yih-Jiunn Lee and Yeun-wen Ku, "East Asian Welfare Regimes: Testing the Hypothesis of the Developmental Welfare State," *Social Policy & Administration* 41, no. 2 (April 2007): 197–221; Sony Pellissery and Robert Walker, "Social Security Options for Informal Sector Workers in Emergent Economies and the Asia and Pacific Region," *Social Policy & Administration* 41, no. 4 (August 2007): 401–409.

4. Holliday, "Productivist Welfare Capitalism."

5. Huck-ju Kwon, *The Welfare State in Korea: The Politics of Legitimation* (Basingstoke, UK: Palgrave Macmillan, 1999); Kwon, "An Overview of the Study: The Developmental Welfare State and Policy Reforms in East Asia"; Huck-ju Kwon, "Transforming the Developmental Welfare State in East Asia," *Development and Change* 36, no. 3 (May 2005): 477–497; Ian Gough, "Globalization and Regional Welfare Regimes: The East Asian Case," *Global Social Policy* 1, no. 2 (2001): 163–189.

6. Lee and Ku, "East Asian Welfare Regimes," 197.

7. Joseph Wong and Tun-jen Cheng, "Introduction to Social Policy in Asia," *American Asian Review* 21, no. 2 (2003): 23–24.

8. Peter S. Heller, "Aging in Asia: Challenges for Fiscal Policy," *Journal of Asian Economics* 10, no. 1 (Spring 1999): 37–63; Nelson Wing-sun Chow, "New Economy and New Social Policy in East and Southeast Asian Compact, Mature Economies: The Case of Hong Kong," *Social Policy & Administration* 37, no. 4 (August 2003): 411–422; Wong and Cheng, "Introduction to Social Policy in Asia"; Richard J. Estes, "Asia and the New Century: Challenges and Opportunities," *Social Indicators Research* 82, no. 3 (2007): 375–410.

9. Pellissery and Walker, "Social Security Options for Informal Sector Workers in Emergent Economies and the Asia and Pacific Region."

10. Po-Fen Tai, "Social Polarisation: Comparing Singapore, Hong Kong and Taipei," *Urban Studies* 43, no. 10 (2006): 1737–1756.

11. Robert Walker and Sony Pellissery, "Giants Old and New: Promoting Social Security and Economic Growth in the Asia and Pacific Region," *International Social Security Review* 61, no. 2 (April–June 2008): 81.

12. Nick Manning, ed., *Social Problems and Welfare Ideology* (Aldershot, UK: Gower, 1985).

13. Chang-sik Shin and Ian Shaw, "Social Policy in South Korea: Cultural and Structural Factors in the Emergence of Welfare," *Social Policy & Administration* 37, no. 4 (August 2003): 335.

14. Kwon, *The Welfare State in Korea*, 37–43.

15. Ministry of Health and Social Affairs, "The Development Strategy of Social Welfare Policy Preparing for the 21st Century," July 26, 1994.

16. Dong-Myeon Shin, "Financial Crisis and Social Security: The Paradox of the Republic of Korea," *International Social Security Review* 53, no. 3 (2000): 85.

17. Dae Jung Kim, *DJ Welfarism: A New Paradigm for Productive Welfare in Korea* (Seoul: Office of the President, Presidential Committee for Quality-of-Life, 2000), 9.

18. Eliza E. W. Lee, "The Politics of Welfare Developmentalism in Hong Kong," *Transforming the Developmental Welfare State in East Asia*, ed. Huck-ju Kwon (Basingstoke, UK: Palgrave Macmillan, 2005), 132.

19. Organisation for Economic Co-operation and Development, *OECD Health Data 2010* (Paris: OECD Press, 2010).

20. Many authors mention that advocacy coalitions have contributed to the achievements of Korean health democracy. The advocacy coalition argument maintains that health reform in Korea was not a simple policy response to economic downturns but an outcome of dynamic policy process with advocacy coalitions, which had long been arguing for social equity in public health policy. See Soon-yang Kim, "Dynamics in the Healthcare Policy Formation: Understanding the NHI Integration Reform through the Advocacy Coalition Framework," *Journal of the Korean Association for Policy Studies* 15, no. 3 (Fall 2006) [in Korean]; Huck-ju Kwon, "Advocacy Coalitions and Health Politics in Korea," *Social Policy & Administration* 41, no. 2 (2007): 148–161; Seung-ki Paik, "A Comparative Study on the NHI Integration Reform with the Advocacy Coalition Framework: The Case of Korea and Taiwan," *Korean Public Administration Review* 44, no. 4 (Winter 2010) [in Korean]; Joseph Wong, *Healthy Democracies: Welfare Politics in Taiwan and South Korea* (Ithaca, NY: Cornell University Press, 2004). The detailed information and descriptions in the section are drawn from the perspectives of the authors, including Gerald F. Anderson, "Universal Health Care Coverage in Korea," *Health Affairs* 8, no. 2 (1989): 24–34; Gyu-Jin Hwang, *Pathways to State Welfare in Korea* (Burlington, VT: Ashgate Publishing Ltd., 2006); Soon-yang Kim, 2006; Huck-ju Kwon, 2007; Sangho Moon and Jaeun Shin, "Performance of Universal Health Insurance: Lessons from South Korea," *World Health & Population*, no. 2 (2007): 95–113; Seung-ki Paik, 2010; and Joseph Wong, 2004, in illustrating the development of the Korean health-care system and the role of the advocacy coalitions.

21. Stephan Haggard and Robert R. Kaufman, *Development, Democracy, and Welfare States: Latin America, East Asia, and Eastern Europe* (Princeton, NJ: Princeton University Press, 2008).

22. Polity IV Project indices were used as guideposts of democratic transformation. The Polity Project conceptual scheme examines "concomitant qualities of democratic and autocratic authority" in governing institutions rather than discreet and mutually exclusive forms of governance. This perspective envisions a spectrum of governing authority that spans from fully institutionalized autocracies through mixed, or incoherent, authority regimes (termed "anocracies") to fully institutionalized democracies. The Polity Score captures this regime authority spectrum on a 21-point scale, ranging from –10 (hereditary monarchy) to +10 (consolidated democracy). The Polity scores can also be converted to regime categories: The Polity IV Project recommends a three-part categorization of *"autocracies"* (–10 to –6), *"anocracies"* (–5 to +5, with three special values of –66, –77, and –88), and *"democracies"* (+6 to +10)," www.systemicpeace.org/polity/polity4.htm.

23. Anderson, "Universal Health Care Coverage," 24–34.

24. Hong-bong Cha, "The Development of Medical Security System in Korea," *National Medical Security,* ed. Lee D. (Seoul: Nanam Publishing, 1992) [in Korean]; Wong, *Healthy Democracies,* 45.

25. Soon-yang Kim, "The Political Dynamics of Policy Networks and Advocacy Coalitions in South Korea's Healthcare Policymaking: The 20 Years Debate to Inaugurate a Single-Payer System," *Korean Journal of Social Welfare Studies* 42, no. 4 (Winter 2011): 78.

26. Anderson, "Universal Health Care Coverage," 27.

27. Soonman Kwon, "Healthcare Financing Reform and the New Single Payer System in the Republic of Korea," *International Social Security Review* 56, no. 1 (January 2003): 67.

28. Anderson, "Universal Health Care Coverage," 27.

29. Kim, "Dynamics in the Healthcare Policy Formation," 9; Kwon, "Advocacy Coalitions and Health Politics in Korea," 151–152.

30. Kwon, *The Welfare State in Korea,* 10.

31. Jae-kwan Kim, *Analysis of Arguments About Medical Insurance Policy in Korea* (Seoul: Sungkyunkwan University Press, 1992), 62 [in Korean].

32. Kwon, "Advocacy Coalitions and Health Politics in Korea," 153.

33. Kim, "The Political Dynamics of Policy Networks and Advocacy Coalitions in South Korea's Healthcare Policymaking," 93.

34. Paik, "A Comparative Study on the NHI Integration Reform with the Advocacy Coalition Framework," 243; Wong, *Healthy Democracies,* 93.

35. Kwon, "Advocacy Coalitions and Health Politics in Korea," 155; Paik, "A Comparative Study on the NHI Integration Reform with the Advocacy Coalition Framework," 243.

36. Kim, "Dynamics in the Healthcare Policy Formation," 11.

37. Soon-yang Kim, "The Formation and Role of Advocacy Coalitions in the Health Policy Process: The Case of NHI Integration and Separation Reforms in Korea," *Journal of the Korean Association for Policy Studies 19,* no. 2 (Summer 2010): 21 [in Korean].

38. Suk-jo Won, "A Study on the Ideological Background of the NHI Integration Reform," *Social Welfare Policy 17* (2003): 41–49 [in Korean].

39. Paik, "A Comparative Study on the NHI Integration Reform with the Advocacy Coalition Framework," 241.

40. Kwon, "Advocacy Coalitions and Health Politics in Korea," 156–157.

41. Wong, *Healthy Democracies,* 95.

42. Kim, "Dynamics in the Healthcare Policy Formation," 11.

43. Kwon, "Advocacy Coalitions and Health Politics in Korea," 156.

44. Paik, "A Comparative Study on the Integration Reform in the Advocacy Coalition Framework," 241; Kim, "Dynamics in the Health Care Policy Formation," 18.

45. Haggard and Kaufman, *Development, Democracy, and Welfare States,* 224.

46. Kim, *DJ Welfarism,* 9.

47. Hwang, *Pathways to State Welfare in Korea,* 160.

48. Kwon, "Advocacy Coalitions and Health Politics in Korea," 158; Hong-yun Lee, "A Comparative Analysis of Policy Makers: The Kim Young-Sam and Kim Dae-Jung Governments" (Seoul: Sungkyunkwan University, 2000) [in Korean].

49. Claus Offe, "Democracy Against the Welfare State? Structural Foundations of Neoconservative Political Opportunities," *Political Theory* 15, no. 4 (1987): 509.

50. Hwang, *Pathways to State Welfare in Korea,* 163.

51. Kim, *DJ Welfarism,* 9.

52. Haggard and Kaufman, *Development, Democracy, and Welfare States,* 243; Eliza E. W. Lee, "The Politics of Welfare Developmentalism in Hong Kong," 132.

53. Soonman Kwon and Michael R. Reich, "The Changing Process and Politics of Health Policy in Korea," *Journal of Health Politics, Policy, and Law* 30, no. 6 (December 2005): 1003–1025.

54. Organisation for Economic Co-operation and Development, *OECD Health Data 2010.*

55. National Health Insurance Corporation (NHIC), *Statistical Year Book* (Seoul: NHIC Press, 2010) [in Korean].

56. Yoo and Moon, "Evaluating Performance of Finance Stabilization Program for National Health Insurance," *Korean Journal of Policy Study* 16, no. 3 (2006) [in Korean].

57. Soonman Kwon, "Achieving Health Insurance for All: Lessons from the Republic of Korea," Extension of Social Security (ESS) Working Paper No. 1 (Geneva: International Labour Office, 2002).

58. Anderson, "Universal Health Care Coverage."

59. Sangho Moon, "Evaluating Recent Advances in Financial Reform in the Korean Health Care System," presented at the 3rd International Seminar of the Sustainable Urban Development Institute (Seoul: Sungkyunkwan University, 2008).

60. Moon and Shin, "Performance of Universal Health Insurance," 1–19.

61. Ibid.

62. Sangho Moon, "Evaluating Recent Advances in Financial Reform in Korean Health Care System."

63. Kwon, "Achieving Health Insurance for All."

64. Jong-chan Lee, "Health Care Reform in South Korea: Success or Failure?" *American Journal of Public Health* 3, no. 1 (January 2003): 48–51; Kwon and Reich, "The Changing Process and Politics of Health Policy in Korea."

65. Han-joong Kim, Woojin Chung, and Sang-gyu Lee, "Lessons from Korea's Pharmaceutical Policy Reform: The Separation of Medical Institutions and Pharmacies for Outpatient Care," *Health Policy* 68, no. 3 (June 2004): 267–275.

66. Moon and Shin, "Performance of Universal Health Insurance."

67. World Health Organization, *The World Health Report: Health Systems: Improving Performance* (Geneva, 2000).

68. Bureau of Statistics, *Long-term Population Projection in Korea* (Government of the Republic of Korea, November 2006) [in Korean].

69. Andreas Werblow, Stefan Felder, and Peter Zweifel, "Population Aging and Health Care Expenditure: A School of 'Red Herrings'? *Health Economics* 16, no. 10 (2007): 1109–1126; Sally C. Stearns and Edward C. Norton, "Time to Include Time to Death? The Future of Health Expenditure Predictions," *Health Economics* 13, no. 4 (April 2004): 315–327; Meena Seshamani and Alastair Gray, "Ageing and Health-care Expenditure: The Red Herring Argument Revisited," *Health Economics* 13, no. 4 (2004): 303–314.

70. Byongho Tchoe and Sang-Ho Nam, "Aging Risk and Health Care Expenditure in Korea," *International Journal of Environmental Research and Public Health* 7, no. 8 (August 2010): 3235–3254.

71. Paula A. Braveman et al., "Socioeconomic Disparities in Health in the United States: What the Patterns Tell Us," *American Journal of Public Health* 100, supplement 1 (April 1, 2010): S186-S96; Erick Messias, "Income Inequality, Illiteracy Rate, and Life Expectancy in Brazil," *American Journal of Public Health* 93, no. 8 (August 2003): 1294–1296; Laura E. Montgomery, John L. Kiely, and Gregory Pappas, "The Effects of Poverty, Race, and Family Structure on US Children's Health: Data from the NHIS, 1978 through 1980 and 1989 through 1991," *American Journal of Public Health* 86, no. 10 (October 1996): 1401–1405.

NINE

The Aging Society and Social Policy in Taiwan

Wan-I Lin

Introduction

A slower rate of population aging is characteristic of most developed countries, with the exception of Japan, which took twenty-four years (1970–1994) to move from a gray society (with an aging rate of 7 percent) to an aged society (with an aging rate of 14 percent), and only another twelve years to become a super-aged society with an aging rate of 20 percent.[1] By contrast, it is estimated that it will take sixty-nine years (1944–2013) for the population in the United States aged 65 and older to increase from 7 percent of the population to 14 percent, something that took 115 years (1865–1980) in France.[2]

Other East Asian countries are following Japan and experiencing extremely rapid demographic aging, although because of their lower starting point, the total proportion of older people will not reach worrying levels for some time. Taiwan is also on the road from an aging society to an aged society. It will take twenty-four years for it to become an aged society (1993–2017), and only another eight years thereafter for it to become a super-aged society (2017–2025).[3] South Korea is expected to accomplish the shift even more rapidly, in eighteen and eight years, respectively (see Chapter 7).[4]

With population aging a global phenomenon, the U.N. General Assembly has put forth a number of key policy recommendations. The Vienna International Plan of Action on Aging, endorsed by the U.N. in 1982, was the first international instrument designed to guide the formulation of global policies and programs on aging and to strengthen the capacities of governments to deal with the issue effectively. The plan included sixty recommendations in the following areas: health and nutrition, protection of elderly consumers, housing and the environment, family, social welfare, income security, and employment and education.[5] The following will focus on three critical aspects of the aging society in Taiwan: pension reform, health insurance reform, and long-term care.

This chapter begins by looking at patterns of population aging in Taiwan. It then moves to examine political contestation and social welfare development in Taiwan in order to provide a framework for understanding Taiwan's social policies on aging. The following section maps out the different kinds of related politics and policy making that are observed in combination with the political competition. Finally, the chapter discusses long-term care, an ongoing urgent issue in Taiwan, and presents some tentative conclusions.

Population Aging in Taiwan

Taiwan became an aging nation in 1993. By 2012 the share of people over age 65 had increased to 11.08 percent of the population, and it is expected that by 2014 the post–World War II baby boomers will reach old age. By 2017 Taiwan will become an aged society, and by 2025 the elderly segment of the population will account for one-fifth of the entire population (see Figure 9.1).

Four factors are contributing to the rapid aging in Taiwan.[6] The first is the migration from mainland China to Taiwan after the Chinese Civil War. After the Kuomintang (KMT, also known as the Nationalist Party) lost control of mainland China to the Chinese Communist Party, more than one million immigrants, including public servants, soldiers, traders, and others, left China with their families for Taiwan; by the 1990s most of these people were over the age of 65.

The second factor is the prospect of the post–World War II baby boomers entering old age between 2014 and 2028. Starting in the 1950s, after a peak in 1951, at 3.84 percent, population growth remained at about 3.5 percent per year. The population increase during this period will account for the major share of Taiwan's aged society in the near future.

The third factor is the rapid decrease in the gross birth rate that began in the early 1960s when the Taiwan government began to implement family planning policies. During the following three decades, the population growth rate fell in two waves. The first wave was between 1963 and 1972, when it

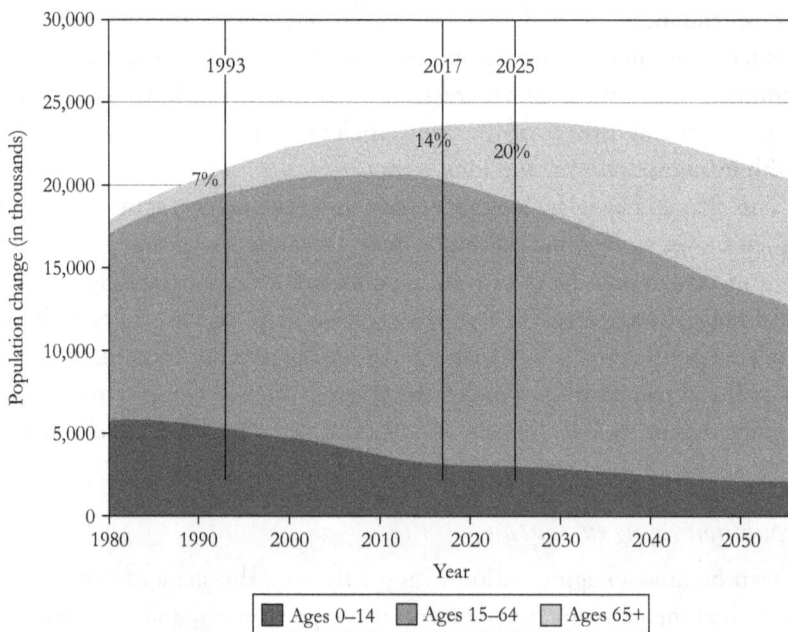

FIGURE 9.1 Population change in Taiwan, 1980–2050

SOURCE: Council for Economic Planning and Development, "Taiwan Population Projections: From 2008 to 2056," www.cepd.gov.tw/encontent/m1.aspx?sNo=0001457.

declined dramatically from 2.96 percent to 1.94 percent. However, thereafter the number of newborns increased from 369,022 in 1973 to 425,125 in 1976, as the post–World War II baby boomers reached childbearing age. Thus, from 1976 to 1985, the government promoted a second wave of family planning policies to stem the increase in newborns. The population growth rate after 1976 began to slide, down to 1.2 percent in the 1980s and further down to 0.8 percent in the 1990s. Analysis of the fertility rates of childbearing-age women (aged 15–49) indicates that a total fertility rate (TFR) of 1.72 was maintained from the early 1980s to the early 1990s. Thereafter, the TFR declined rapidly, to 1.4 by 2001 and to 0.895 by 2010, which is much lower than that in most advanced industrial countries. When this second wave of baby boomers reaches old age in 2041, the share of the population over age 65 will have increased to 30 percent.

The final factor is the substantial increase in longevity. In 1991 life expectancy at birth in Taiwan averaged 71.8 years for men and 77.2 years for women. By 2011 life expectancy at birth for men had risen to 75.98 years and for women to 82.65 years. By 2025 the numbers are projected to be 78.62 years for males and 85.57 years for females. Predictably, the number of very old people will continue to increase, accounting for a larger share of the total population.

Political Contestation and Social Welfare Development

Pluralist theories of the democratic process recognize that individuals form coalitions or interest groups that represent their common concerns, and that these groups attempt to influence government policy in a variety of ways.[7] In Western industrial democracies, welfare-state analyses have pointed to the continuing role played by political parties, which promote distinct interests based on historically rooted assumptions about class and milieu relations.[8] Strong left-wing parties, particularly the social democratic parties allied with the trade union movements, have been shown to have a positive effect on welfare-state expenditures and increasing redistribution.[9] Christian democratic parties, or center-left coalitions, have also been shown to have a positive effect on welfare-state expenditures, but primarily for transfer payments and with less redistributive impact.[10]

In Taiwan, neither of the two major political parties, the KMT or the Democratic Progressive Party (DPP), is a left-wing party.[11] The major supporters of the KMT are public employees, mainland Chinese, capitalists, and the urban middle class, whereas the major DPP supporters of Taiwan independence are farmers, the working class, middle-class doctors, and intellectuals. In a comparison of the counties and cities governed by the two major political parties, the differences are obvious. The areas governed by the KMT are mainly located in the central and northern urban areas of Taiwan, where the high-tech and service industries are highly developed, whereas the areas governed by the DPP are mainly located in central and southern Taiwan that are characterized by rural agricultural villages and traditional industries. The DPP attaches importance to the welfare of laborers, farmers, the disabled, women, and aboriginals, whereas the KMT puts more emphasis on the welfare of public employees and farmers.[12] It is well recognized that the DPP is more supportive of income redistribution policies.[13] Nevertheless, it is not a working-class-based left-wing political party.

In terms of welfare ideology, the KMT is generally conservative,[14] although this may change during electoral competition in order to minimize electoral losses.[15] However, it is impossible for the KMT to abruptly promote systemic and progressive social policies in place of the clientelist model of welfare that it has supported since the KMT government retreated to Taiwan in 1949. Nevertheless, the political democratization in Taiwan since the late 1980s has changed the institutional structures to a certain extent. The implementation of policies triggered by the civil sectors contributed to "ten golden years" of social welfare in the 1990s.

Although the class nature of the two parties is not very clear, there are significant differences between them with respect to national identity. Supporters of the DPP prefer Taiwan independence, or a sovereign independent-oriented status quo, whereas supporters of the KMT prefer reunification, or a fuzzy one-China policy. The difference between the two is also significant in terms of public policies, leading to the unique phenomenon of democracy in Taiwan. Therefore, in order to win the majority of votes, the KMT may have to support increased social welfare expenditures to maintain its ruling party advantage.

The KMT governments have adopted three strategies in response to the advocacy of social welfare by the opposition and by various social groups: blocking, obfuscation, and overruling. If electoral pressures are not great and the party need not compromise its positions, the KMT has generally been successful in blocking the social welfare policies proposed by the DPP in the Legislative Yuan because of its majority. However, if they have faced heavy pressure from social groups and have not been willing to compromise their positions, they have attempted to blur the focus by means of manipulating information. If they are aware that they will lose some seats or votes on account of their rejection of such pressures, as a countervailing force they tend to increase the amount that they will pay to curry favor with specific constituencies to win extra votes.[16]

Since the early 1990s, Taiwan incrementally entered a post-authoritarian era, and in 1996 the citizens participated in their first direct election for president. The voters increasingly vote for the party or politician who supports popular policies, such as old-age pensions; as a result, politicians or would-be reformers who want to be elected argue on behalf of social welfare policies. In other words, the underlying principle in policy-making guidelines is to avoid an electoral loss. Hence, the political purpose, rather than the actual content, has become more important in policy making, and support for social welfare has become a focus of the political controversy. In order to win more votes, the focus of social policies is their immediate political benefits rather than their sustainable development. In such cases the financial burdens of the various social policies are generally left to the next generations.[17]

National Pension Reform: Integration or Differentiation

In 1993 the elderly constituted 7.02 percent of the population in Taiwan. The country was on its way to becoming a gray society, facing all of the accompanying pressures of an aging population. At that time, 3.79 percent of citizens over age 15 and under age 65 participated in military insurance or government employee insurance, 53.98 percent participated in labor insurance, and 0.26 percent participated in private school faculty insurance. However, 32.16 percent of the citizens were not covered by any social insurance scheme that provided old-age benefits. These citizens were mainly housewives, farmers, fishermen, the elderly, the disabled, and the self-employed. Furthermore, the proportion of the elderly relying on their children was decreasing, from 65.8 percent in 1986 to 48.3 percent in 1996.[18]

Rudimentary Old-Age Assistance

The first Legislative Yuan candidate to propose old-age pensions, Su Huan-chih of the DPP in Tainan County in 1992, won the election with the support of the elderly in rural villages. In the 1993 eleventh county magistrate by-election in Penghu County, DPP candidate Kao Chih-peng advocated providing about US$100 per month in old-age benefits. With the support of people living in fishing villages, he too won the election. The increasing political pressure forced the KMT government to promote its Living Allowance for the Low-Income Elderly (LALIE) policy in July 1993, entitling those who were over age 65 and whose average household income was 1.5 times less than the poverty line to obtain old-age assistance of US$200 per month per person.

The DPP formally proposed the establishment of a welfare state during the legislative elections at the end of 1992 based on advocacy by Wan-I Lin, the author of this chapter. Tsai Han-hsien, Director of Social Affairs of the Ministry of the Interior at the time, recalled, "We advised the KMT government to propose a policy direction, because citizens were unable to compare good policies with bad policies if there was no policy direction."[19] In fact, the KMT did respond to this request. First, it condemned the old-age benefits policy of the DPP for its irresponsibility, financial burdens, and failure to exclude the wealthy from the welfare rolls. Second, the KMT promoted the LALIE. In 1993, a task force for planning a national pension scheme was established, and by the end of the year a draft on national pension insurance was proposed.[20]

However, the premier of the Executive Yuan, Hau Pei-tsun, opposed the idea of a welfare state. In his second policy address to the Legislative Yuan in 1992, he stated: "In the future, Taiwan will not become a welfare state." His basic proposition was that "everyone should be responsible for their own living, and only the disadvantaged who cannot take care of themselves, such as farmers, fishermen, the disabled, and the mental patients, need support from the government." This opinion was shared by most of the liberal economists, who suggested that conditions in the advanced countries that promoted social welfare, such as Sweden, Germany, and the United Kingdom, were declining, and that Taiwan should not follow in their footsteps.[21] Hau Pei-tsun argued that "social welfare is a social affair," and "three generations living under the same roof is the best model of social welfare."[22] Tsai Han-hsien, however, disagreed, arguing that "the idea of three generations living under the same roof can be encouraged. But it cannot be a policy because it would be impossible to implement."[23]

In September 1993 the DPP supported the establishment of an old-age pension action coalition. In the county and city magistrate elections at the end of the year, all the DPP candidates advocated old-age benefits and promised that every elderly citizen would receive US$167 in old-age pensions per month. On January 22, 1994, sixteen legislators, including Su Huan-chih, in an attempt to implement the DPP's old-age pension policy, drafted the Provisional Act to Provide an Old-Age Allowance and submitted it to the Legislative Yuan for review. Predictably, the KMT blocked it without mercy.

The KMT government had not planned to promote a national pension insurance plan. However, because of increasing political pressures, it loosened the eligibility requirements for the LALIE and increased coverage from the original 1.5 times the poverty line to 2.0 times the poverty line, thereby increasing the number of eligible senior citizens.

During the provincial governor and county/city magistrate elections in 1994, the DPP promised an old-age benefit whereby every senior citizen would obtain US$167 per month beginning July 1, 1994. In contrast, James Soong, the KMT provincial governor candidate, advocated a further loosening of the restrictions on eligibility for the living allowance. In terms of this issue, the difference between the KMT and DPP was selectivity versus universality.

In 1994, the DPP proposed a new National Pension Insurance Act in yet another attempt to implement its old-age pension policy. However, once again it was blocked by the KMT. At the same time, the Taipei City mayor, Chen Shui-bian of the DPP, promised to provide old-age pensions to the elderly. Despite opposition by KMT councilmen who constituted the majority in the City Council, six months of old-age allowance, and then an additional one-month allowance, were granted in March 1996. However, the old-age allowance was terminated in 1997, leaving only a disability allowance.

In order to win the votes of farmers, the KMT passed the Provisional Act to Grant a Welfare Allowance to Elderly Farmers on May 19, 1995, based on a proposal by DPP legislators. The act was promulgated and implemented on May 31, 1995. Elderly farmers were thus entitled to US$100 per month per person.

Beginning January 1, 1995, in order to cash the election check of James Soong, the KMT government again loosened the eligibility restrictions for the LALIE. Any senior citizen over the age of 65 whose average household income was 1.5–2.5 times less than the poverty line could now obtain a living allowance of US$100 per month.

Also in January 1995, the KMT government issued a national pension planning report. However, it did not intend to approve old-age pension legislation. In 1996, the first presidential election was held in Taiwan. The DPP candidate, Peng Ming-min, was no match for KMT candidate Lee Teng-hui, who was a Taiwanese, and Peng lost by a large margin. As expected, Lee Teng-hui and Lian Chan won 54.00 percent of the votes, Peng Ming-min and Frank Hsieh won 21.1 percent, and the two other independent candidates won 24.9 percent. Therefore, the KMT did not feel compelled to advocate an old-age pension in its major policies. During the county/city magistrate elections in 1997, because the DPP candidates consistently supported old-age benefits, some KMT candidates, such as the magistrate candidates in Hsinchu County, followed the trend.

However, because the KMT, which constituted the majority in the Legislative Yuan, did not support pension legislation, the local governments successively ended the allowances owing to budget constraints. In 1998 the KMT government completed phase I and phase II of its planning report on old-age pensions. A national pension program was viewed as one part of social insurance, as distinguished from military insurance, public employee insurance, or labor insurance. In 1999 the DPP proposed the Basic Pension and Supplementary Pension System, whereas the KMT proposed the National Basic Pension System.

Universal Old-Age Allowance

During the presidential elections in 2000, one of the social welfare policy proposals of Chen Shui-bian, the 333 Settling Project, proposed granting US$100 per person per month to those over age 65 before implementing a national pension policy. Thereafter, the DPP government, which came to power in May 2000, proposed a national pension insurance system (Project A), a balanced fund system (tax system) (Project B), amended versions of a social insurance system (a combination of Project A and Project B), and the integration of national pension insurance with the personal retirement savings accounts.

To carry out President Chen's policies, the Executive Yuan drafted the Provisional Act Granting an Old-Age Welfare Allowance in 2000 and submitted it to the Legislative Yuan for review. Other versions were also submitted, including one from the KMT (Huang Ming-hui, Cheng Lung-shui) and one from the People First Party (PFP, led by James Soong). In proposing their own versions, the opposition parties were attempting to interfere with the legislation. However, the KMT and PFP were fully aware that opposition to the DPP's universal Old-Age Welfare Allowance would be detrimental to their electoral success. Thus, they intended to loosen the eligibility requirements to cover their supporters and at the same time to blur the focus of the old-age allowance.

The expenditure race in the various versions of the old-age allowance resulted in citizen protests and ultimately forced the ruling party and the opposition parties to suspend a review of the allowances. The DPP had intended to implement a national pension system on January 1, 2001. In fact, the probability that it would be implemented was low because DPP party members had not yet reached a consensus on the issue. Furthermore, the KMT used tactics to fight the legislation in order to achieve its own political objectives.

In 2001 the Executive Yuan drew up a budget of US$0.6 billion to grant an old-age allowance in the following year. On January 18, 2002, the Legislative Yuan reached a resolution and approved the budget to grant the allowance. However, only when the legislation was completed would the allowance be granted. Moreover, aboriginal legislators requested that the age restrictions for aboriginals be reduced to 55 years.

In April 2002 the DPP proposed three types of national pensions, namely, a tax-funded system, a savings insurance system, and a social insurance system. At the third National Social Welfare Forum held by the Ministry of the Interior that convened in May 2002, social welfare nongovernmental organizations (NGOs), together with social welfare scholar Wan-I Lin, opposed the personal savings insurance system proposed by the DPP and supported a social insurance system. It was clear that the DPP was supporting liberalism over social democracy, even though Chen Shui-bian had been influenced by British scholar Anthony Giddens during the election and had proposed a new middle way.

Beginning in January 2002, all people over age 65 who were not public employees, and laborers and aboriginals who were over age 55, could obtain an old-age allowance of US$100 per month. In response to the resolution reached at the third National Social Welfare Forum, the DPP government proposed a social insurance system for the National Pension Plan to keep up with the old-age allowance. On May 22, 2002, the Provisional Act Granting an Old-Age Welfare Allowance was passed.

In order to fulfill the promises made during the election, the government increased the number of elderly receiving an old-age allowance to 210,000 on June 5, 2003, and increased the annual budget by US$250 million. In other words, elderly citizens who already received old-age benefits of less than US$100 from public employee insurance, military insurance, and labor insurance were now also entitled to an old-age allowance, thereby eliminating the occupational differentiations in the old-age allowance.

In 2003 the DPP government's draft on national pension insurance, the KMT's draft on national pension insurance, and the draft on a provisional act for a national pension (a tax system plus an occupational pension) proposed by Shen Fu-hsiung were all submitted to the Legislative Yuan for review. However, none of these drafts were approved. In 2005 the DPP government's draft on national pension insurance (Pan-Green version), the KMT's draft on a national pension (Pan-Blue version), and the basic national pension proposed by the Pan-Purple coalition (trade unions and disadvantaged groups) were resubmitted to the Legislative Yuan. It was clear that as long as the almost universal old-age allowance was available, there was less urgency to improve an old-age pension system because there was less political pressure from the voters.

However, financial pressures were building. The number of elderly receiving the three old-age allowances (i.e., the LALIE, the old-age farmer welfare allowance, and the old-age welfare allowance) increased from 1.279 million in 2002 to 1.490 million in 2003. If the number of veterans receiving government care benefits (106,000) and the number of disabled citizens receiving living subsidies (70,000) were included, as many as 1.67 million senior citizens (79.8 percent of the total) were receiving various types of old-age allowances. In 2004 a budget of US$818 million was drawn up for the old-age allowance, an increase of US$187 million compared to the previous year. A budget of US$1.07 billion was drawn up for the old-age farmer allowance, an increase of US$297 million. The total budget for these schemes, amounting to US$1.89 billion, accounted for 19.8 percent of the central government's social welfare expenditures,[24] thereby putting pressure on the DPP government to accelerate integration of the different versions of the national pension.

In February 2005 the Executive Yuan established the national pension work circle, led by Minister without Portfolio Fu Li-yeh, an associate professor of social welfare at National Chengchi University. The purpose of this group was to design a pension system for laborers to replace the lump-sum system that had been in effect since 1950. Thereafter, the Ministry of the Interior drew up a draft National Pension Act, according to the planning directions of the national pension work circle, and on December 9, 2005, it was submitted to the Executive Yuan for review. Social welfare NGOs associated with Wan-I Lin also aggressively developed a plan for national pension insurance with a guaranteed pension.

In January 2006 the Draft on National Pension Action, namely, a mini labor pension system for the elderly, the disabled, and survivors, covering maternity, sick, and funeral benefits, was approved by the premier of the Executive Yuan, Frank Hsieh, just before he was relieved of office. After Su Tseng-chang took up this official post on January 25, 2006, he asked for advice from various interest groups in order to build a consensus. In February 2006 social welfare NGOs opposed the DPP government's draft because it did not focus on resolving the chaos in the old-age benefits system. Instead, they proposed a civil version of the draft on national pension insurance, integrating labor pensions and other various old-age allowances. They intended to resolve the chaos and uncertainty in the current old-age allowances, and simultaneously to propose a solution to the lack of a pension system for labor and farmer insurance.

National Pension Act

The premier of the Executive Yuan, Su Tseng-chang, invited Wan-I Lin to join his cabinet and to serve as Minister without Portfolio, responsible for coordination of policies concerning social welfare, education, labor, health, youth, aboriginals, and veterans. On July 27–28, 2006, the Executive Yuan convened the Taiwan Economic Sustainable Development Forum, which included in its social security outline the establishment of a national pension system. Among its final twelve conclusions was a provision to cover all citizens by 2007.

On September 20, 2006, the DPP government proposed the Mega Warmth Social Welfare Program, covering four major issues: reducing the gaps between country and city and between rich and poor, enhancing care for the elderly, responding to the declining birthrate, and promoting national health. This packaged social welfare plan consisted of twelve major projects. In terms of enhancing care for the elderly, the projects included promoting the National Pension Act and providing labor pensions and long-term care projects. In order to promote the legislation, the DPP government established the Project for Promoting a National Pension System. It amended the draft on the National Pension Act formerly approved by the Executive Yuan, and included the consensus about national pensions reached during the Taiwan Economic Sustainable Development Forum. The integration of the relevant allowances and their linking up with other social insurance schemes became a priority. The goal was to ensure that various old-age allowances of similar natures but with different objectives could be integrated into a universal old-age pension. To get around the differences among the systems, it was necessary to concurrently amend the Labor Insurance Act to change the lump-sum payments for the elderly, the disabled, and survivors into an annuity system.

Minister without Portfolio Wan-I Lin played a leading role in the planning of the National Pension System. A total of thirteen meetings were held between November 1, 2006, and May 1, 2007. The (Draft) National Pension Act was submitted to the Legislative Yuan for review on May 10, 2007. However, on February 10, 2007 (Chinese New Year), President Chen Shui-bian invited DPP public officials to participate in a Coherence and Progress of the New Year meeting at the Great Roots Forestry Spa Resort in Sanhsia Township, Taipei County. President Chen indicated that, in response to the coming legislative and presidential elections in 2008, the Executive Yuan was prepared to increase the old-age farmer allowance by an additional US$33 per month. Based on his political sophistication, President Chen Shui-bian predicted that the KMT candidate, Ma Ying-jeou, would make a similar proposal. It went without saying that these two politicians shared the same ideas about using old-age farmer allowances to win the votes of the farmers. In fact, as long as one party proposed it, the other had to make a similar proposal; otherwise, the farmers might suggest that the party could not take care of them. Thus, in order to win the election, the two parties spared nothing to make more capital and policy commitments. Therefore, aging policy became an inevitable battlefield during the campaign.

An increase in the amount of the old-age farmer allowance was no longer news. In the run-up to the presidential election, the contest between the two parties became extremely fierce. The DPP government intended to increase the amount of the old-age farmer allowance, and neither the KMT nor the PFP opposed it for fear of losing votes. With a consensus reached among all the political parties, on December 17, 2003, the Legislative Yuan approved an increase in the monthly old-age farmer allowance, from US$100 to US$133. Moreover, members of fishermen associations were also included, even though they were already covered by labor insurance. To avoid any controversies, the three parties pledged, in all sincerity and seriousness, that the amount of the allowance could only be adjusted once every five years.[25] However, in the following year the Legislative Yuan failed to keep its promise.

The elections on December 3, 2005, for county/city magistrates, county/city councilors, and town mayors were all extremely competitive. KMT legislators had proposed an amendment to the old-age farmer allowance in order to increase the amount of the allowance; DPP legislators were afraid that this would affect the results of the election and thus agreed with the proposal. Although the DPP lost the election, on December 15 the amendment was approved in the Legislative Yuan. The amount of the allowance was increased to US$167 per month per person. This US$33 increase added US$0.2 billion to the annual budget. It was impossible to arrest the continuous increases in old-age farmer allowances as long as the political parties sought to win votes by spending public money.

On April 14, 2007, KMT party chairman Ma Ying-jeou held discussions with fishermen and farmers in Hsinchu and Taichung. He advocated an increase in the amount of the old-age farmer allowance, indicating that as long as the KMT won the election in 2008, the US$167 allowance for fishermen and farmers would be increased to US$200. President Chen Shui-bian's prediction seemed to be fulfilled. The vicious competition between the two major parties had transformed the old-age pension allowance into a tool to win votes.[26]

At that time, Minister without Portfolio Wan-I Lin and Minister of the Directorate-General of Budget, Accounting, and Statistics Hsu Chang-yao both opposed the increase in the allowance and suggested that such electoral manipulations would destroy the planned National Pension System. This view was supported by Premier Su Tseng-chang. Thereafter, the National Pension System Planning Team of the Executive Yuan completed a study titled, "The Influence of Increases in the Amount of the Old-Age Farmer Allowances on National Pensions," and requested that President Chen Shui-bian place priority on the National Pension Act legislation. Furthermore, social welfare NGOs indicated that they opposed any increase in the old-age farmer allowance. President Chen Shui-bian conceded, announcing, "If the National Pension Act is not approved in July, the amount of the old-age farmer allowance will be increased by US$33."

However, approval of the National Pension Act was a difficult task, as the KMT held the majority in the Legislative Yuan and opposed many of Chen Shui-bian's initiatives. In addition, Ma Ying-jeou supported an increase in the amount of the old-age farmer allowance.

At that time, it was proposed that the monthly old-age pension be US$253. First, if the old-age farmer allowance were to be increased to US$200, the difference would be minor (US$53), which might result in the lack of any incentive to support this social insurance plan. Second, the national pension was designed to incorporate the old-age farmer allowance. The transition period (twenty-five years) in the original design had to be extended to thirty-two years to protect the vested interests of elderly farmers. Further estimations revealed that if the old-age farmer allowance were to be increased by US$33, the basic amount of the national pension would also have to be increased by US$33. Therefore, it would be necessary to increase the budget. In the first ten years, the annual budget would be US$2.62 billion. In the next ten years, it would be increased to US$4.9 billion, and ten years later it could be as much as US$15.30 billion. Third, in 2006 the allowances for the 732,000 elderly cost US$1.37 billion. If the allowances were to be increased by US$33 per person, the government would have to increase its budget by US$293 million per year. Furthermore, it would be unfair to adjust the old-age farmer allowance and not adjust other old-age benefits.

With the cabinet reshuffling on May 20, 2007, Premier Chang Chun-hsiung agreed with implementation of an increase in the old-age farmer allowance, and the Presidential Office and Executive Yuan reached a consensus. The Executive Yuan decided to increase the old-age farmer allowance by US$33. Meanwhile, the amount of the national pension specified in the draft National Pension Act submitted to the Legislative Yuan on May 10 was also increased.

Under the premise that the two parties both supported an increase in the old-age farmer allowance, the National Pension Act was rapidly approved on July 20, 2007, and the fifteen-year plan for the National Pension System was put into place. Citizens, including elderly farmers who were not covered by other social insurance schemes, would be covered by the National Pension System. Various other old-age allowances were abolished. The National Pension Act represented a significant improvement in the old-age pension system. However, a labor pension system had still not been approved.

The KMT government, after winning the presidential election and in order to fulfill its promise to increase the old-age farmer allowance, separated the old-age farmer allowance from the national pension. This amendment was approved by the KMT-controlled Legislative Yuan on July 18, 2008. As a result, farmers were no longer insured under the National Pension Plan. Thus there was a significant decrease in the number of citizens participating in the National Pension Plan that went into effect on October 1, 2008. In addition, because labor pension benefits were also increased, some self-employed citizens and part-time workers, who had originally intended to participate in the National Pension Plan, changed their minds and decided to participate in the labor insurance, resulting in an uncertain future for the National Pension Plan.

As expected, by the end of 2010 the number of citizens participating in the National Pension Plan was 3,895,034, significantly fewer than at its peak in January 2009 (4.27 million). After the labor pension system was implemented in January 2009, many citizens changed their insurance enrollment under the labor insurance.

As predicted, prior to the presidential and legislative elections in early 2012, there were discussions among the KMT legislators to raise the amount of the old-age farmer allowance. At the same time, DPP's legislator Chen Ming-wen (Chiayi County) also proposed to raise the amount of the old-age farmer allowance by US$33, at the DPP Central Standing Committee meeting on July 20, 2011. Such was the proposal provided by the DPP legislators of the Legislative Yuan. The KMT-dominated Procedure Committee of the Legislative Yuan made its first objection on September 13, 2011, but because of the supreme guiding principle to win the election, it changed its position on the issue after ten days and allowed the proposal to proceed directly to the second reading. Meanwhile, the KMT legislators in the agriculture-dominated counties placed increasing pressure on the KMT, requesting support. Thus, announcements were made by President Ma Ying-jeou on October 18, 2011, stating that the old-age farmer allowance and the eight other categories of welfare subsidies would be adjusted according to the consumer price index every four years.

After conversion, the pension for elderly farmers merely increased by US$10.50, with the wealth-exclusion clause incorporated. The KMT legislators from the agriculture-dominated counties harshly criticized the proposal, demanding that the subsidies be raised to US$333. During this period the KMT declined the DPP's invitation regarding the amendments to the Welfare Allowance to Elderly Farmers four times. However, unwilling to risk losing the presidential election, the KMT government reached a consensus on a drastic change in policy on November 17 after a confidential discussion with the KMT legislators. President Ma Ying-jeou announced that the old-age farmer allowance would be raised by US$33, and that the eight other categories of welfare subsidies would be dramatically increased, from 16.67 percent (the increased amount of pension for elderly farmers) to 33.27 percent (the long-overdue adjustment in a one-time adjustment). The estimated number of beneficiaries reached 2,252,900, with an additional budget increase of US$460 million annually. In addition, the subsidies for elderly farmers reached US$1.48 billion in 2012, accounting for 40 percent of the Council of Agriculture's total budget in 2012.

However, the KMT claimed that raising the elderly farmers' monthly pension was an attempt to establish a system that would be adjusted according to the consumer price index every four years. Asking political figures not to resort to the campaign tactic of raising elderly farmers' subsidies would have entailed holding them to a high moral standard while under the pressure to win an election. Considering the DPP presidential candidate Tsai Ying-wen as an example, during her term as the Vice Premier of the Legislative Yuan in 2007, not only did she object to the proposal of President Chen Shui-bian to increase the monthly subsidies for elderly farmers by US$33, but also she expressed her opposing view with an anti-tax protest. However, in July 2011, as DPP Chairman and a presidential candidate, she denied her previous commitment and resorted to the campaign tactic of raising elderly farmers' subsidies by US$33. Nevertheless, such a preemptive tactic did not win the presidential election for Tsai Ying-wen. The vicious political competition that involved using the elderly farmers' monthly pension as a bargaining chip in the election did not guarantee winning the election. Conversely, the promised subsidies resulted in a continuing budget deficit for the government and made integrating the pension system even more difficult.

Income-Related Labor Pension Reform

Labor insurance was introduced on March 1, 1950, and an old-age benefit was provided through a lump-sum payment. In response to appeals for a labor pension, in 1993 there was an attempt to design a labor pension system, triggered by the planning of the National Pension Plan. However, because the National Pension Plan was not approved immediately, the labor pension system was postponed.

Although a retirement annuity was stipulated in the Taiwan Labor Standards Act enacted in 1984, many employers were unwilling to allocate money to the pension fund. Data from 1999 indicate that less than 8 percent of employers were contributing to the fund, and less than 18 percent of laborers could draw retirement benefits.[27] As a result, workers began calling for labor retirement annuity reform. However, it was unclear whether the government would implement a personal savings account system or a supplementary pension system. Because labor groups mainly preferred a supplementary pension system with defined benefits, during the discussions over labor pension reform there were conflicts between labor groups and the government. It was not until the DPP government convened the Economic Development Advisory Conference in 2001 that laborers, employers, and the government reached agreement on concurrent implementation of three systems: a personal savings account system, a supplementary pension system, and other portable pension systems. However, in 2004 the system included in the Labor Pension Act that was approved by the Legislative Yuan was a personal savings account with defined contributions and a commercial annuity, instead of a supplementary pension system.

A labor retirement pension in Taiwan is a mandatory pension, requiring employers to allocate 6 percent of the employees' monthly salaries to the retirement pension savings account. The account is portable, as it is transferred with the employee. The Labor Pension Supervisory Board manages the employer contributions to the fund.

The labor retirement pension personal savings account system exempts the government from the financial burdens of premium sharing, and also allows the government to avoid the financial burdens of old-age pension systems with defined benefits. Moreover, it alleviates the stress caused by a rapidly aging population and potential intergenerational conflicts. However, the income redistribution effect of the Labor Retirement Pension Plan is minimized.

During discussions on the Labor Retirement Pension Act in September 2000, the DPP's Council of Labor Affairs submitted the planned Labor Insurance Pension System to the Legislative Yuan for review. By November 2001, the Control Yuan censured the Executive Yuan for its delay in establishing the labor insurance pension.

In May 2002, in addition to requesting expedited approval of the National Pension Plan, a resolution from the third National Social Welfare

Forum requested expedited approval of the labor pension system. Between May 2003 and December 2004, the Legislative Yuan reviewed the Labor Insurance Pension System several times. However, the system was not approved due to differing opinions regarding the contribution rates.

To coordinate with the planning for the National Pension System, under the supervision of Minister without Portfolio Wan-I Lin, the DPP government concurrently submitted the National Pension Plan and the amendment to the Labor Insurance Act (labor pensions) to the Legislative Yuan for review on May 10, 2007. To avoid differences in benefits between the National Pension Plan and the Labor Pension Act, National Pension Plan payments were to be equivalent to those received by employees from the Labor Insurance Act.

After the change in the ruling party on May 20, 2008, the Legislative Yuan rapidly approved the amended Labor Insurance Act and put it into effect on January 1, 2009. However, the annual benefit rate for workers was increased to 1.55 percent, whereas the rate in the National Pension Plan remained at 1.30 percent. Therefore, laborers without fixed employers began to change their national pension insurance to labor insurance by joining occupational groups, thereby blocking the development of the National Pension Plan. Moreover, because the annual benefit rate was increased, the pension income replacement rate for laborers with thirty years of seniority would be 69.5 percent (including 46.5 percent from the labor insurance pension and 23.0 percent from the retirement pension) (see Figure 9.2), thereby protecting the economic security of laborers. However, the premium rate was not based on actuarial calculations, and thus the financial deficits in the Labor Insurance Fund were exacerbated.

These policies with high benefits and low premiums have been implemented for some time. According to an estimation by the Council of Labor Affairs, by 2026 the amount in the Labor Insurance Fund will be insufficient to cover the various claims. If the premiums are not increased or the benefits not reduced, the government will need to allocate additional funds. In fact, the phenomenon of low premiums and high benefits exists in the case of public employee insurance funds as well, and the deficits have had to come out of the government budget. To date, US$10 billion has been allocated. This is another case of improving benefits so as to win votes but without regard to damaging the system.

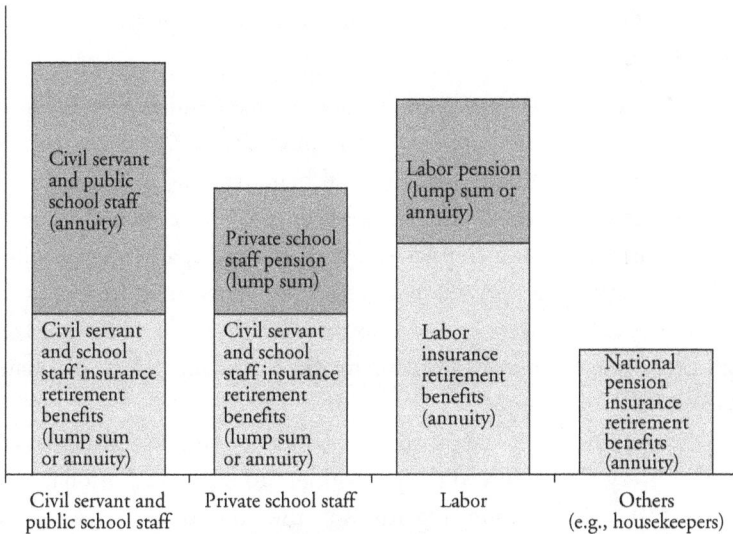

FIGURE 9.2 Old-age pension systems in Taiwan

In October 2012 questions regarding the labor insurance budget deficit were again posed. The laborers were worried about the bankruptcy of the Labor Insurance Fund and not being able to receive their pensions, and demanded the same insurance benefits as those of civil servants and teachers, implying that the government would finalize and issue a pension benefit guaranty. All of the political parties feared offending the laborers and agreed to amend the Labor Insurance Act, thereby incorporating the commitment of a pension benefit guaranty into the act. Unless the government lowered the pension benefit or raised the contribution rates, the substantial budget deficit regarding the Labor Insurance Fund could not be resolved. However, if the government would have lowered the pension benefit, the laborers would have protested unless the pension benefit for military personnel and civil servants and teachers was lowered accordingly. Furthermore, the income replacement rates for the military personnel insurance and civil servant and teacher insurance have been 20 percent higher than that of laborers for a long time. However, military personnel, civil servants, and teachers, who were loyal supporters of the KMT, would have protested against the measure to lower the income replacement rates for them. The KMT would have accounted for the pressure of winning the election, which would have complicated the upcoming pension reform.

The Second-Generation National Health Insurance Reform:
A Half Measure

To ensure that the health-care needs of low-income families were being met, the Health Insurance for Low-Income Households Scheme was launched in 1990. By the end of 1994, ten medical benefits had been put in place. Approximately 59 percent of citizens were entitled to receive medical benefits under various social insurance schemes. However, a further 41 percent (8.6 million people), comprised mainly of children, the unemployed, housewives, and the elderly, were excluded as beneficiaries of these schemes, even though there was a high demand for medical care and a lack of financial means among these groups.

The ever-increasing pressure to establish a universal health insurance scheme for every citizen forced the government to expedite National Health Insurance (NHI) integration, regardless of the potential obstacles. Similar to the case in Korea with the development of universal health insurance after democratization at the end of 1980s (see Chapter 8), Taiwan's NHI was fully developed after a comprehensive reelection of the legislature. On August 9, 1994, the NHI Act was promulgated. On January 1, 1995, the Bureau of National Health Insurance was established, and on March 1, 1995, the NHI program commenced.

Unlike the financial management of the Korean NHI that is controlled by 350 health funds (even though to a certain degree they were already controlled by the government) (see Chapter 8), Taiwan's NHI is managed by the Bureau of National Health Insurance. Since 1995, the government has successfully provided affordable, high-quality health care to the people of Taiwan. Currently Taiwan's single-payer social insurance scheme has received widespread international praise. At the end of 1995, its first year of implementation, the enrollment rate reached just over 92 percent of the entire population. By 2000 the enrollment rate had increased to over 96 percent. And by 2002, with the inclusion of military personnel, the enrollment rate exceeded 98 percent, indicating that the NHI program had almost attained universal coverage.

As in the case of Korea,[28] because of rising health-care needs and low co-payments, both the frequency and total expenditure of elderly NHI use greatly surpassed that of adults and children. By 2010, 10.6 percent of the beneficiaries were over the age of 65. Their benefits accounted for 29.0 percent of outpatient medical expenses and 43.5 percent of inpatient medical expenses, including co-payments.

The NHI continues to be plagued by difficulties.[29] Since 1998 it has encountered financial deficits because the income from insurance premiums failed to meet annual expenditures. For instance, after implementation of the program, the average outpatient visit and length of hospital stay per person per year in Taiwan increased by 1.4 and 1.6 times, respectively. From 2001 to 2011, insurance premium income increased by 4.9 percent, but insurance expenditures increased by 5.5 percent during the same period (see Figure 9.3).

To enhance the overall competitiveness of the rapidly expanding healthcare industry, providers in Taiwan have been required to almost double investments after implementation of the NHI program.

The various premium payments and increasing out-of-pocket medical expenses paid by the insured exacerbated the program's problems. The fee structure for NHI premium payments and premium rates had originally been designed based on an individual's occupation, and in consideration of the payment systems in the existing social insurance programs, namely, the government employee insurance, the labor insurance, the military insurance, and the farmers insurance. However, the fairness of this system was widely questioned.

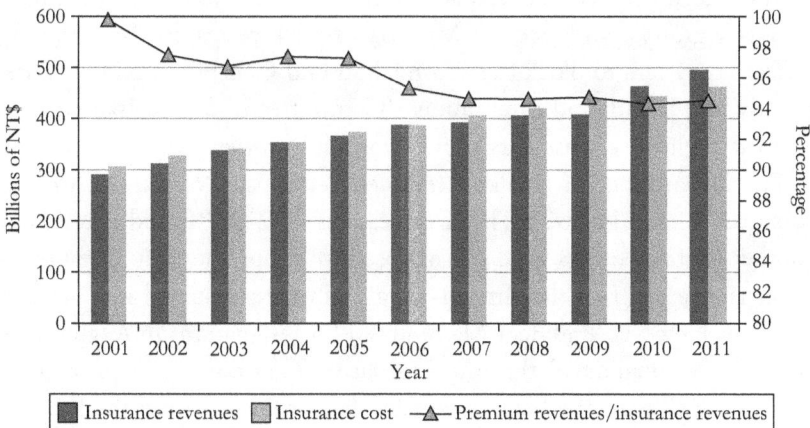

FIGURE 9.3 Financial status of the BNHI (on accrual basis; unit: New Taiwan dollars)

SOURCE: Bureau of National Health Insurance, Department of Health, *Statistics & Surveys*, www.nhi.gov.tw/English/webdata/webdata.aspx?menu=11&menu_id=296&webdata_id=1942&WD_ID=296.

In 2002, national health expenditures in Taiwan amounted to US$19.48 billion, an increase of US$8.85 billion compared to the amount in 1994, 65 percent of which came from out-of-pocket expenses paid by the insured. Because the out-of-pocket expenses increased so dramatically, many citizens refrained from seeking medical attention.

To manage the financial deficits and standardize the contributions paid by citizens, the DPP government established the Second-Generation National Health Insurance Planning Task Force on July 1. The aim was to review the payment structure, to make improvements in the existing system, and to suggest policies for future implementation. The ultimate goal was to build a fair, efficient, high-quality NHI system to ensure the well-being of all citizens.

In 2005, the Planning Task Force proposed the Second-Generation NHI to the Executive Yuan, and in 2006 a new draft NHI amendment was delivered to the Legislative Yuan for review. However, the major opposition party, the KMT, rejected the amendment.

Because of difficulties similar to those experienced in the 1990s, in 2010 the KMT, two years after it came to power, was forced to re-propose the Second-Generation NHI. However, within the KMT consensus could not be reached regarding the revised proposal. The Ministry of Finance argued that because the information on household gross income was inaccurate, there was no basis for calculating the premiums. In contrast, the Department of Health was confident that it could collect and audit the premiums. Advocacy groups cautioned the Ministry of Finance against using the imperfect tax system to block the reformed Second-Generation NHI. Consequently, the Health and Environment Committee in the Legislative Yuan retained twenty-six controversial provisions in its review.

The Department of Health attempted using party operations to help swing the vote in its favor. The KMT caucus, however, found that a large number of its members were still opposed to raising the insurance premiums. As a result, Health Director Yang Chih-liang resigned in March of that year. However, President Ma returned his resignation. In August 2010 President Ma mandated that the Legislative Yuan convene a provisional council. Until then the Legislative Yuan had still not passed the Second-Generation NHI bill, and had requested that the Executive Yuan propose a new Second-Generation NHI amendment. Finally, the provisional council confirmed a temporary resolution based on President Ma's requirement that

Chairperson Wang hold party negotiations by December 7, 2010, to complete the amending of the law.

In the process of the amendment, the position of the opposition party, the DPP, was to advocate a return to the 2006 version of the Second-Generation NHI. It did not support the KMT version of the Second-Generation NHI that ultimately was defeated due to internal opposition within the KMT.

The Department of Health proposed a new amendment on November 26, adding the concept of virtual income, which meant that people who did not have any income would still be required to pay a premium based on a basic wage. This new virtual income presented a new point of contention: Pensioners would not have to pay NHI premiums, whereas the unemployed and housewives would be required to pay the basic wage premium. To minimize the disputes, KMT legislators overruled the Second-Generation NHI amendment that imposed a fee based on total household income, and instead passed the reformed NHI on January 4, 2011.

Premium collection in the amended NHI uses a two-track system. The first track sustains the original purpose of the scheme, and it is divided among fifteen groups of contributors (including inmates). On this track, the contribution rate forming the basic premium was reduced from 5.17 percent to 4.91 percent. The second track allows for bonuses, executive business income, dividends, interest, and other additional income, and it is levied at 2 percent. However, this only solves the problem for those in higher income brackets because their premiums are relatively low. This sparked new debate regarding the fairness and complexity of the premiums.

However, with the Supervision Committee and the Medical Expenditure Negotiation Committee jointly responsible for making NHI financial decisions, health-care management and financial information will be more accessible and will require closer community supervision.

Long-Term Care Insurance: Who Benefits?

In response to the aging of the population, at the beginning of 1998 Vice Premier Liu Chao-shiuan consulted with Wan-I Lin to initiate planning for a long-term care system. A Symposium on Care for the Elderly was held in the Department of Sociology of National Taiwan University, with support from the National Science Council, in May 1998.[30] One of the purposes of the symposium was to investigate Japan's golden ten-year plan. The symposium concluded by urging the Executive Yuan to approve a three-year Pilot Project for the Establishment of a Long-Term Care System. Moreover, in 1998 the Executive Yuan also approved the Project for Enhancing Care for the Elderly (amended in 2002). The purposes of these projects for the elderly were to enhance home care, promote physical and psychological health, ensure economic security, and improve social participation.

In 2001 the economic growth rate began to decline. Against the background of an increasing unemployment rate and the need for long-term care for the elderly, on May 11 Premier Chang Chun-hsiung of the Executive Yuan introduced the Program for Development of the Care Services Industry. The program was approved by the Executive Yuan on January 31, 2002, and specific measures in the projects were amended on March 12. This program was included in the National Development Plan for 2008. It explicitly defined service providers as "nonprofit groups and profit-making enterprises jointly investing in the care services industry" and initiated increases in both the welfare and profits of long-term care services in Taiwan.

In order to provide community care, the Ministry of the Interior promulgated the Project for the Establishment of Community Care Sites in 2005 to encourage establishment by local governments and social groups. The services provided by community care sites included home visits, telephone contacts, consultations and referral services, meals-on-wheels services, and health promotion. At the end of 2009, a total of 1,589 care sites had been established in various cities and townships, and the project had become the major mechanism for a community mutual-aid system. However, after the change in the ruling party in 2008, the number of community care sites did not increase significantly.

In order to promote and coordinate interdepartmental long-term care projects in Taiwan, the Social Welfare Promotion Committee of the Executive Yuan established the Long-Term Care System Planning Team on April 27, 2005. Discussions were held between the central government and local governments in order to comprehensively understand the opinions of local governments and civil nonprofit organizations regarding this issue.

As noted above, the DPP government proposed the Mega Warmth Social Welfare Program on September 20, 2006. This ten-year long-term care plan was highlighted in the Flagship Plan, indicating the importance of long-term care. In March 2007 the Executive Yuan approved a long-term care plan called the Ten-Year Long-Term Care Plan in Taiwan, modeled after Japan's Golden Plan. It was expected that the establishment of a long-term care system in Taiwan would be completed within ten years by spending US$2.72 billion from the national budget.

During the presidential election in 2008, KMT candidate Ma Ying-jeou included in his campaign two policies related to long-term care: 1) the introduction of old-age care insurance; and 2) the introduction of legislation for long-term care insurance within four years. Ma Ying-jeou's team ignored the ongoing development of long-term care systems and instead intended to abruptly transform the systems into long-term care insurance. However, the KMT's ideas regarding long-term care systems were inconsistent.

To fulfill President Ma's campaign policies, in December 2008 the premier of the Executive Yuan, Liu Chao-shiuan (former vice premier in 1998), designated the Council for Economic Planning and Development, the Department of Health, and the Ministry of the Interior to initiate planning of a long-term care insurance system. The Long-Term Care Insurance Planning Team was established by the Department of Health in order to promote the planning.

Premier of the Executive Yuan Liu Chao-shiuan announced on January 21, 2009, that the draft on the Long-Term Care Insurance Act would be proposed by the end of 2009 and would be submitted to the Legislative Yuan for review. In order to fulfill President Ma's campaign promises, it would be prepared in 2010 and implemented in 2011. On February 4, 2009, Wan-I Lin, opposing the abrupt implementation of any long-term care insurance, wrote in the *China Times*: "Long-term care insurance cannot be implemented in a hurry." Elderly welfare NGOs also strongly opposed the long-term insurance because it provided insurance but no services. On February 11, 2009, Premier Liu Chao-shiuan met with Wan-I Lin at the Executive Yuan. Premier Liu was persuaded to further deliberate the long-term care insurance, as various items had not yet been prepared, such as the service delivery system, the care management system, a caregiver training system, information management, and immigrant caregivers management, among others. It was therefore necessary to slow down the introduction of long-term care insurance. A Ten-Year Long-Term Care Plan was proposed rather than hastily introducing long-term care insurance.

The Long-Term Care Promotion Team of the Executive Yuan convened its first meeting on June 29, 2009, to report the results of the preparations for long-term insurance. Chairman, Minister without Portfolio Tsai Hsung-hsiung indicated the importance of convening such forums in order to solicit opinions from the various stakeholders and social welfare groups.

Although the Executive Yuan ordered that Department of Health invite the Ministry of the Interior to participate in the Long-Term Care Insurance Preparation Team in July 2009, as well as in the drafting of the Long-Term Care Insurance Act, progress seemed to be slowing down. To avoid questions about failure to carry out President Ma's campaign promise with respect to long-term care, the Executive Yuan requested that the Department of Health draft a Long-Term Care Services Act, to replace the Long-Term Care Insurance Act, as the legal basis for promoting a long-term care system. In fact, there were sufficient legal provisions in the Senior Citizens Welfare Act, the People with Disabilities Rights Protection Act, and the Nursing Practice Act, to be used as the legal basis for promoting long-term care, which facilitated approval of the Ten-Year Long-Term Care Plan by the Executive Yuan.

The Department of Health introduced the draft on the Long-Term Care Services Act for review. However, because it was uncertain if the management of immigrant care givers could be included, the conclusion of the review was delayed. Finally, the draft was completed and submitted to the Legislative Yuan for review in March 2011. It was clear that the KMT government was attempting to raise the stakes in the race for long-term care and was attempting to blur the focus.

On January 25, 2011, premier of the Executive Yuan, Wu Den-yih, indicated that it was necessary to divide the development of a long-term care system into several stages. The legislation for the Long-Term Care Services Act had to be completed first, followed by establishment of a long-term care delivery system and then an insurance system. Obviously, Ma Ying-jeou's proposal to introduce long-term care insurance within four years was not considered.

According to estimations of the Ten-Year Long-Term Care Plan, there were approximately 245,551 senior citizens requiring long-term care in 2011. If people with severe disabilities (117,033) were also included, there would be 362,584. A total of 10.50 percent of the elderly population required long-term care, including 11.25 percent of the disabled (1.55 percent of the total population).

There were 1,053 long-term care institutions in Taiwan in 2011, including 408 nursing homes and 18 veteran care homes, with a total of 96,030 beds, of which 73,435 were in use—a utilization rate of 76.47 percent covering 2.94 percent of the elderly population. Therefore, approximately 30 percent of the disabled elderly required residential care (based on an estimated disability rate of 10 percent).

Immigrant caregivers were introduced in Taiwan in 1993 to provide long-term care. At the end of 2011, there were 195,726 foreign caregivers in Taiwan employed by families or residential care institutions to act as caregivers for the elderly and the disabled. They mainly came from Indonesia and Vietnam. These foreign caregivers replaced family caregivers for the elderly and those with severe disabilities. They were not required to receive skills training for long-term care or to learn the local language, and their cultural compatibility was not taken into consideration. Since the urgent need for family long-term care could not be met by the services provided by the government, the regulations on labor conditions for foreign caregivers were flexible, and these workers were not protected by the Labor Standards Act. Foreign caregivers often did not get holidays and they were frequently asked by their employers to engage in other housework, such as washing clothes, cooking meals, cleaning, taking out the garbage, and child care. Some foreign caregivers had to do additional work at their employers' enterprises, but most still only received their basic wages. However, if the problems of the immigrant caregivers are not solved in Taiwan, it will be difficult to promote any long-term care insurance.

The KMT eagerly promoted long-term care insurance as part of its political contestation with the DPP. However, it did not understand the content and progress of the Ten-Year Long-Term Care Plan developed by the DPP. It criticized the DPP for its disregard of state affairs during its eight years of rule. However, the KMT neglected to review the DPP's policy achievements and initiated new policies thoughtlessly. It was well known that the KMT would have to repay enterprises for helping it win the election, so it abruptly attempted to implement policies related to long-term care since this is a profitable sector for the aging enterprises. The KMT was open to having the long-term care services provided by profit-seeking enterprises. However, it ignored that the objective of long-term care insurance was not to solve economic problems, but to respond to the aging of the population, and that the beneficiaries should be the elderly and their family caregivers. The creation of business opportunities was only an added value.

Conclusions

Taiwan is a relatively new democracy. In addition to the KMT, whose long existence was established under an authoritarian regime, the DPP—its primary opposition party—was established in 1986 and was elected to govern Taiwan from 2000 to 2008. Meanwhile, the people in Taiwan became increasingly familiar with the campaign tactics involved, using votes to fight for their rights and welfare. In the post-authoritarian era, the KMT could not rely on the army, police, and the dissemination of ideologies to control the people as they did in the martial law period. After the lifting of martial law, laborers and farmers realized that they did not have as much welfare allowances, retirement payments, or old-age benefits, and became increasingly discontented with the KMT.

The KMT understood that it would be difficult to continue its policies unless the restive laborers and farmers were mollified. Furthermore, the DPP has claimed that the KMT is representing the interests of farmers, laborers, and the advantaged. Although the proposition by the KMT did not correspond to the party's mainstream ideology, the KMT's main strategy in competing against the DPP gradually focused on improving social welfare policies. Thus, the National Health Insurance Policy was passed in 1994, the Welfare Allowance to Elderly Farmers was implemented in 1995, the Living Allowance for Elderly People Act was promulgated in 2002, the National Pension System was passed in 2007, and the Ten-Year Long-Term Care Plan was passed in Taiwan in 2007. In addition, the monthly allowance for elderly farmers was raised four times, each time increasing by US$33.

All of the above measures indicated that the KMT would rather change policy than lose elections. The KMT was loath to offend its loyal supporters, who were military personnel, government employees, and teachers. Thus, the KMT was reluctant to improve the benefits of laborers and farmers, and was unwilling to cut the benefits of military personnel, government employees, and teachers. By using high benefits, low contribution rates, and low tax rates to please voters, the competition between the two parties increased the country's budget deficit. Such is the reason for financial crises in new democracies.

The aging of the population and the extremely low birthrate have further aggravated the problems that Taiwanese society faces. Politicians in Taiwan must deal with these difficult issues. The political competition between the two parties has been obvious in the introduction of old-age pension policies and the establishment of a long-term care system. Although KMT supporters, such as enterprises and public employees, are more conservative politically, the KMT still has to compete with the DPP to win the votes of those who support social welfare. Since 1992, the DPP has never held a majority in the Legislative Yuan. Therefore, support from the KMT has been required to pass social welfare–related legislation. The legislative process for the old-age pension system is indicative of the predicament of the DPP.

After failing to block the DPP policy, the KMT has had to support it. In response to pressure from public opinion and voters during election campaigns, the KMT has occasionally cooperated with the DPP, such as with respect to the National Pension Plan, the labor retirement pension, and the Labor Pension Insurance Plan. At the same time, the KMT has intended to promote its own political interests through its support of these policies. Increasing the amount of the allowances is a common and cheap approach used by the political parties in Taiwan. But in terms of overall national interests, it is a high-cost political game. In fact, promotion of long-term care insurance can also be considered part of this game. However, if the service delivery system is incomplete, citizens will not enjoy adequate long-term care services even though they are required to pay the premiums for this insurance.

When there is keen competition among the parties for the ruling position in the government, it becomes impossible to argue about social welfare policies rationally and systematically, and such policies may be detrimental to the establishment of institutions. The dark future of the National Pension Plan, the accelerated bankruptcy of labor insurance, and the slow progress in the establishment of a long-term care service system are all by-products of the vicious political competition. There is thus an urgent need to impose more public pressure so as to change this situation; otherwise the politicians will destroy every potentially good social policy.

Notes

1. Chikako Usui and Howard A. Palley, "The Development of Social Policy for the Elderly in Japan," *Social Service Review* 71, no. 3 (September 1997): 360–381.

2. Robbyn R. Wacker and K. A. Roberto, *Aging Social Policies: An International Perspective* (London: Sage Publications, 2010).

3. Wan-I Lin, "The Coming of an Aged Society in Taiwan: Issues and Policies," *Asian Social Work and Policy Review* 4, no. 3 (2010): 148–162.

4. Sung-won Kim, "Social Changes and Welfare Reform in South Korea: In the Context of the Late-Coming Welfare State," *International Journal of Japanese Sociology* 18, no. 1 (November 2009): 16–32.

5. Wacker and Roberto, *Aging Social Policies.*

6. Lin, "Coming of an Aged Society"; Wan-I Lin and Shin-Yi Yang, "From Successful Family Planning to the Lowest of Low Fertility Levels: Taiwan's Dilemma," *Asian Social Work and Policy Review* 3, no. 2 (June 2009): 95–112.

7. Ian Gough, "Theories of the Welfare State: A Critique," *International Journal of Health Services* 8, no. 1 (1978): 27–40.

8. Evelyne Huber, Charles Ragin, and John D. Stephens, "Social Democracy, Christian Democracy, Constitutional Structure, and the Welfare State," *American Journal of Sociology* 99, no. 3 (November 1993): 711–749; Martin Seeleib-Kaiser, Silke Van Dyk, and Martin Roggenkamp, *Party Politics and Social Welfare: Comparing Christian and Social Democracy in Austria, Germany and the Netherlands* (Cheltenham, UK: Edward Elgar, 2008); and Kees van Kersbergen, *Social Capitalism: A Study of Christian Democracy and the Welfare State* (London: Routledge, 1995).

9. Francis G. Castles, *The Impact of Parties: Politics and Policies in Democratic Capitalist States* (London: Sage Publications, 1982); Alexander Hicks and Duane H. Swank, "On the Political Economy of Welfare Expansion: A Comparative Analysis of 18 Advanced Capitalist Democracies," *Comparative Political Studies* 17, no. 1 (1984): 81–119; Alexander Hicks and Joya Misra, "Political Resources and the Growth of Welfare in Affluent Capitalist Democracies, 1960–1982," *American Journal of Sociology* 99, no. 3 (1993): 668–710; Alexander Hicks, Joya Misra, and Tang Nah Ng, "The Programmatic Emergence of the Social Security State," *American Sociological Review* 66, no. 3 (June 1995): 329–349; Evelyne Huber and John D. Stephens, "Political Parties and Public Pensions: A Quantitative Analysis," in *Power Resources Theory and the Welfare State: A Critical Approach,* eds. Julia S. O'Connor and Gregg M. Olsen (Toronto: University of Toronto Press, 1998), 98; Evelyne Huber and John D. Stephens, *Development and Crisis of the Welfare State: Parties and Policies in Global Markets* (Chicago: University of Chicago Press, 2001); Torben Iversen and John D. Stephens, "Partisan Politics, the Welfare State, and Three Worlds of Human Capital Formation," *Comparative Political Studies* 41, no. 4–5 (2008): 600–637; Walter Korpi, "Power, Politics, and State Autonomy in the Development of Social Citizenship: Social Rights During Sickness in Eighteen OECD Countries Since 1930," *American Sociological Review* 54, no. 3 (1989):

309–328; W. Korpi and Michael Shalev, *Strikes, Power, and Politics in the Western Nations, 1900–1976* (Stockholm: Institutet för social forskning, 1980); and Walter Korpi, "Social Policy and Distributional Conflict in the Capitalist Democracies: A Preliminary Comparative Framework," *West European Politics* 3, no. 3 (1980): 296–316.

10. Van Kersbergen, *Social Capitalism*; Castles, *The Impact of Parties*; H. L. Wildavsky, "Leftism, Catholicism, and Democratic Corporatism: The Role of Political Parties in Recent Welfare State Development," in *The Development of Welfare States in Europe and America,* eds. Peter Flora and Arnold J. Heidenheimer (New Brunswick, NJ: Transaction,1981), 345–382; John D. Stephens, *The Transition from Capitalism to Socialism* (Chicago: University of Illinois Press, 1986); and Gøsta Esping-Andersen, *The Three Worlds of Welfare Capitalism* (Princeton, NJ: Princeton University Press, 1990).

11. W. I. Lin, *Social Welfare in Taiwan: Historical and Institutional Analysis* (Taipei: Wu-Nan Book Inc., 2012) [in Chinese].

12. W. I. Lin and H. S. Yeh, "Social Movement and Social Policy in Taiwan: The Case of the Disadvantaged Group Movement," *Journal of Social Work* 2 (1992): 137–156 [in Chinese].

13. Kate Y. T. Wang, "Why Do People Support a Redistributive Social Welfare Policy? Review and Revision of Self- Interest," unpublished paper, 2011 [in Chinese].

14. Lin, *Social Welfare in Taiwan.*

15. Paul Pierson, *Dismantling the Welfare State? Reagan, Thatcher, and the Politics of Retrenchment* (New York: Cambridge University Press, 1994); and Jane Jenson, "Changing the Paradigm: Family Responsibility or Investing in Children," *Canadian Journal of Sociology* 29, no. 2 (Spring 2004): 169–192.

16. John Kenneth Galbraith, *The New Industrial State* (Princeton, NJ: Princeton University Press, 2007).

17. W. I. Lin, "Review and Prospects for the Development of Social Welfare in Taiwan Since the 1990s," *Community Development Quarterly* 109 (2005): 12–35 [in Chinese].

18. Lin, *Social Welfare in Taiwan.*

19. J. C. Lee, ed., *Professor Tsai Han-Hsien and His View of Social Welfare* (Taipei: Song-hui Publishing Co., 2004) [in Chinese].

20. W. I. Lin, "A Discussion of the KMT's Opinions on Social Welfare," in *Social Welfare in Taiwan: Public Views* (Taipei: Wu Nan Book Inc, 1995) [in Chinese].

21. Ibid.

22. Ibid.

23. Lee, ed., *Professor Tsai Han-Hsien and His View of Social Welfare.*

24. Lin, "Review and Prospects for the Development of Social Welfare."

25. Lin, *Social Welfare in Taiwan.*

26. Ibid.

27. Ibid.

28. Ibid.

29. Department of Health, "Overview of the National Health Insurance Reform" (2004) [in Chinese].

30. Lin, *Social Welfare in Taiwan.*

PART SIX

Nationalism, Regionalism, and Global Trends

TEN

Influencing South Korea's Democracy
China, North Korea, and Defectors

Katharine H. S. Moon

What kind of impact will China's rise have on the political systems and institutions, especially democracy, of its neighboring states? The question of domestic impact rarely attracts serious thought, whereas policy debates and scholarship on geopolitical implications—for instance, hegemony, balance of power, arms race—abound, especially in the United States. However, the question is both intellectually and politically pressing, since a great power can have major influence over domestic political ideologies and norms, as well as patterns and habits of governance, in its region or sphere of influence. American power since the end of World War II projected a global "will to democracy" even as U.S. policy during the Cold War failed to support democratic movements in a consistent way. Moreover, the evolution of and experimentation with democracy and civil society in the United States, from the movements for civil rights and women's rights to human rights at home and abroad, became ideals and goals that many around the world have sought to emulate or adopt. In Asia, the United States had a direct influence on the creation of constitutions and democratic values among citizens, even if the allied state did not always abide by them (e.g., in authoritarian South Korea, the Philippines, and Taiwan until the late 1980s).

Scholars and analysts who focus almost exclusively on the relations among great powers neglect or dismiss the agency of smaller states. This chapter emphasizes the fact that the countries that neighbor China are not passive chess pieces simply to be acted upon by China or the United States. Especially with respect to Japan and South Korea, China is dependent on its wealthier neighbors for its continued economic growth. Even North Korea, which long should have prostrated itself before China, given its multiple weaknesses and need for Beijing's help, has never been pliant, and as Chinese economic ties with North Korea grow, mutual dependence will also increase.

Unlike Taiwan, whose postwar political origins and identity are inseparable from mainland China's and were established as its antithesis, South Korea has existential distance from the People's Republic of China (PRC) as well as political legitimacy, a governance structure, and an ethno-national consciousness that counterbalance China's influence. As for China, it seeks, first and foremost, stability and the status quo on the Korean peninsula. With respect to the future of democracy on the Korean peninsula, China is less of a looming question than North Korea and inter-Korean relations. The balance that the two Koreas strike "between the forces of integration and disintegration"[1] is the key to the future of democracy on the peninsula. Integration and fragmentation within South Korea's democracy, especially as new actors such as defectors from the North seek political equality and participation, are endogenous challenges that Koreans must face. If the process of reconciliation and reunification between the two Koreas ever comes to a head, democracy on the peninsula will confront a severe test of survival and direction. And this process would present serious dilemmas for Chinese leaders.

First this chapter discusses China's options and intentions regarding domestic politics in the Republic of Korea (ROK, or South Korea) and the Democratic People's Republic of Korea (DPRK, or North Korea) and emphasizes stability and self-restraint as the most realistic policy goals. With regard to the Koreas, China seeks amicable relations with both and continued lucrative economic interactions with the South. The tensions between China and the two Koreas, which challenge and constrain Beijing's actions, will also be discussed. The discussion then turns to domestic politics within South Korea and the public's views of China, with a focus on the role of a new and growing interest group—defectors from North Korea—in influencing inter-Korean relations and China's relationship with both Koreas. Many of the defectors, based on their often harrowing experiences making their way into or out of China—which included surviving in fear and degradation for years in a country that refuses to recognize them as legitimate refugees and has threatened to deport them to North Korea—have negative and suspicious perceptions of China. If their influence grows in South Korean politics, they could complicate China's relations with the ROK and the DPRK. Should inter-Korean tensions intensify, or should unification occur without political and economic preparation on both sides, democracy on the peninsula could experience greater levels of ideological division, regional factionalism, and procedural dysfunction in the short to medium term. Rather than external influence on South Korean democracy, internal and inter-Korean factors will weigh more heavily.

Chinese Power Versus Influence

Would an authoritarian and communist China become a political model that its neighbors would want to emulate? Most likely not, since many of China's Asian neighbors—particularly Japan, South Korea, the Philippines, Mongolia, possibly Vietnam and even Myanmar/Burma—and of course, Taiwan—either have thriving democracies or are experimenting with political liberalization. David Kang's emphasis on learning from Asia's past to foresee Asia's future with China as its hegemon may not hold true in this respect: The legitimacy of Chinese values and governance practices and their adoption by China's neighbors in the pre–modern era[2] do not apply today.

Conversely, would a rising China adopt democracy promotion as a foreign policy? The obvious answer is no. First, there is no realistic chance of China becoming a genuine democracy any time soon unless irrationality were to rule and the political establishment obliterated itself and ushered in economic and social chaos. China expert Harry Harding puts it bluntly:

> It is, in fact, highly unlikely that China will become a truly democratic political system, and moreover a democratizing Middle Kingdom may well be overwhelmed by the nationalistic sentiments that are part of China's contemporary political culture, and that the present Communist government has deliberately cultivated. Even if we arbitrarily and optimistically assign a 50 percent probability to each of these outcomes, over the next decade or so, that means that the chances of a Chinese regime that is both democratic and cooperative would be no more than 25 percent. Those are not the best of odds. Nor are these odds of true democratization within our ability to change.[3]

Like Richard Bush (in Chapter 11 of this volume), this author believes that China is not a revisionist power but rather a country that "is still relatively weak and needs both time (a period of decades) and a peaceful international environment" to pursue its modernization project and that its actions by and large accord with international norms and diplomatic behavior. On a practical level, China's internal politics and the daily challenges of governing and transforming a huge and complex society deter any serious experimentation with democratization. The challenges also obviate against military adventurism in the region. Changes in leadership, individual wealth acquisition, consumption, as well as regional disparities, local uprisings, corruption in the public and private spheres, and generational change that eventually might engender louder calls for political liberalization and inclusion may outweigh or disable whatever regional geopolitical ambitions Beijing may have. Developmental success, stagnancy, and regression all are possibilities and could deplete political resources and constrain policy options for China's leaders. Fareed Zakaria warns that the "stability and peace of the post-American world will depend, in large measure, on the balance that China strikes between the forces of integration and disintegration."[4]

If regional stability is essential to China's internal development and stability, how far would Chinese foreign policy go to maintain control in the neighborhood and keep other powers, such as the United States, Japan, and Russia, at bay? Would China, as the epicenter of Asia and the region's preponderant power, inevitably seek to influence the domestic politics of its neighbors in order to make the region safe for authoritarianism, particularly its own, and thereby preserve Communist Party leadership and internal social stability? Aaron Friedberg believes strongly that a democratic Asia surrounding China is at worst a threat to the latter's internal political interests and at best an obstacle to its regional dominance:

> Even as it grows stronger and, in certain respects, more self-confident, the Communist Party continues to dread ideological contamination. For the moment, with the exception of Mongolia, China does not share a readily passable border with a fully functioning democracy. . . . Pliant, like-minded states along its borders are far more likely to help Beijing deal with this danger than flourishing liberal democracies with strong ties to the West. The desire to forestall "peaceful evolution" at home gives the regime another compelling reason to want to shape the political development of its neighbors.[5]

But compulsion toward regime change among its neighbors is neither necessary nor beneficial for China's development or growth as a great power. There is no reason to assume that as the economic structure and processes change, the political structures and processes will stay stagnant in China, no matter how much its leaders try to forestall "peaceful evolution." Moreover, China's own dynamism will likely depend on the dynamism and competition generated by its democratic neighbors.

We can pose a related question: Would Beijing seek to abet its authoritarian form of governance in neighboring countries? North Korea would be the obvious candidate as a border-sharing communist neighbor with a repressive government. But Pyongyang's severe economic and political strangulation of its people can actually destabilize the society and possibly create security and economic crises on China's borders. Rather than assist Pyongyang in cracking down even more on its society, Chinese authorities have tried for years to persuade North Korea to tone down its unproductive form of authoritarianism and attempt economic reform, to ease up on its ultra-aggressive internal rule and hostile acts toward the outside world. Some Chinese elites' resistance to unconditional support for North Korea has been apparent throughout the 2000s, as the Kim Jong-il regime exploded nuclear devices, launched rockets, and engaged in other dangerous actions. According to Scott Snyder and Joel Wit, "[a]n increasingly vocal minority of Chinese specialists" have urged "starkly tougher measures in response to North Korea's 'brazen' act [October 2006 nuclear test], including reining in the Kim Jong-il regime or promoting alternative leadership in Pyongyang."[6]

The unknown possibilities of inter-Korean relations—massive migration flows into neighboring countries, including China; conflict and violence between the two Koreas; peaceful and gradual reunification that could strengthen the collective Korean nation; or a sudden and urgent reunification dilemma that would demand immediate economic and other assistance from neighboring countries—make the peninsula a dangerous hot potato to play around with. Since late December of 2011, the question of whether Kim Jong-un can and will consolidate power, maintain stability within North Korea and with other powers, and prevent a military coup or regime collapse remains an unknown. Given the shared border between the DPRK and the PRC, any instability, chaos, or violence on the peninsula promises significant problems that the Chinese would find hard to avoid. Obviously, China has no self-interested reason for raising the issue of political reform or democratization in North Korea, but it does have an interest in helping Pyongyang reduce economic deprivation and political oppression so as to avoid a regime collapse or other catastrophe, as well as to deflect international opprobrium as the North's patron.

Andrei Lankov warns that a crisis on the peninsula that neither the South nor the North is able to contain "will create a temptation for China to get involved."[7] However, I would emphasize that given the current burden of governing its own large and unwieldy population and a highly nationalistic North Korean public, along with the formidable presence of U.S. and ROK troops and military facilities in South Korea (and Japan), China is not going to take dramatic steps to alter or control domestic politics in the DPRK. A survey of Korean and Chinese views about bilateral relations, published in 2012 by the East Asia Institute in Seoul, found that nearly 70 percent of the Chinese respondents understand that a military clash between South and North Korea is one of the major "potential factors that could threaten Chinese security and national interests ten years in the future."[8]

Lankov admits the undesirability of Chinese intervention, since Beijing would have to take on a large economic burden that "will not be popular with the Chinese public who believe that there are much better uses for this money."[9] Especially after the North Korean hostage-taking of Chinese fishermen in May 2012, Chinese citizens have been expressing their rancor against North Korean ingratitude. Emblematic of such sentiments is one by microblogger "Qingxiaomingchu" who posted on the popular website Sina Weibo: "Why is China still taking care of little North Korea??? Why feed a stray dog"?[10] Even Chinese censors have loosened up on criticism against North Korea, permitting reports and opinions that question Beijing's "special treatment" of North Korea.[11]

Additionally, China's rising power and oft-assumed leverage over Pyongyang would serve as reasons for self-restraint, lest the world expect China to do more than it is ready or willing to do for Northeast Asian security or have efforts amount to failure. Finally, the Chinese leadership has long emphasized the principle of respecting sovereignty, especially at the U.N. Security Council, and may keep its chopsticks to itself and not poke around in others' internal affairs.

As for South Koreans, the majority (69.0 percent) view Chinese intervention in support of the North in the case of an inter-Korean crisis as likely and hold negative views of Chinese intervention if there were a regime crisis in Pyongyang (64.3 percent).[12] Generally, any strengthening of the relationship between China and North Korea is considered a negative development (68.0 percent).[13] Given that South Koreans are suspicious of Chinese influence on and support of Pyongyang and believe that Chinese are generally opposed to the unification of the peninsula,[14] they are vigilant about Chinese actions and inactions. In this kind of political environment, the Chinese need to be extra cautious about dealing with the DPRK, since South Korea and other countries in the region do not systematically separate Chinese intentions and policy from those of North Korean leaders.

Despite the fact that North Korea is in a client position with China as the patron in international relations parlance, the latter's influence is limited. North Korea obsessively safeguards its sovereignty and self-interest even with its economic and political dependence on its larger neighbor. Pyongyang has been performing the same act for about two decades, cozying up to Beijing through state visits and exchange of advisors, showing some interest in adopting some forms of Chinese economic reforms but never implementing them in any substantive or sustained manner. And although Chinese capital and technology are coveted goods (about 66 percent of the 305 foreign investments in the DPRK come from the PRC), North Korea takes as much advantage of China as possible. Kim Jong-un is reported to have claimed that his country's mineral resources "are being sold off too cheaply" to the Chinese and is demanding higher prices for its iron ore.[15]

The Xiyang Group, a Chinese conglomerate that had invested US$40 million in mining operations in North Korea, had sought to produce iron powder (needed for steelmaking) from its North Korean operations at half the price of Chinese production costs. Since October 2012 the Chinese have had their teeth kicked by their client; Kim's government seized the iron ore mine, evicted Chinese workers with North Korean armed guards, and accused Xiyang of not having fulfilled its investment obligations. Xiyang officials described its experience in North Korea as a nightmare and blamed the North for mastering the Chinese technology and then breaking the contract and kicking the company out.[16]

There indeed is mutual need and therefore ample room for contention between the patron and client. The Chinese see economic opportunities in the DPRK and have established a strong foothold in North Korea for mineral and metals acquisition. They also draw from the cheap and plentiful labor reserves in its poor neighbor as Chinese labor costs increase and grow less competitive internationally. Both governments made a deal in 2012 to move about "40,000 seamstresses, technicians, mechanics, construction workers and miners to work in China on industrial training visas."[17]

Liaoning and Jilin provinces in northeastern China have tied their economic fates to that of the DPRK, "bank[ing] on trade with North Korea as a central part of their development plan (about half of the Chinese investors in North Korean joint ventures come from these two provinces)."[18] Jilin in particular has "invested billions of yuan in infrastructure to create an economic corridor from Changchun, running across the border, and ultimately linking China's lease on a pier at North Korea's port city of Rajin."[19] Zhiqun Zhu emphasizes: "Should North Korea fail, the catastrophe would hit Beijing in the heart and the northeast in the wallet."[20] This echoes Shelly Rigger and Toy Reid's observation regarding Chinese localities' dependence on investment and trade with Taiwan, which Richard Bush mentions in Chapter 11. Whether or not North Korea's and Taiwan's contributions to the Chinese economy can thwart any intention by Beijing to push its political will toward either country is unknown. But the two smaller states can muster up leverage of their own.

That Pyongyang is a pain in China's side is indisputable. It is an economic drain on Chinese resources, and WikiLeaks documents in 2010 revealed that some Chinese leaders consider North Korea a "spoiled child" and "no longer . . . a useful or reliable ally."[21] But North Korea might also consider China a pain in its side. Apparently, anti-China sentiment is palpable among North Korean elites. They discern Chinese national interests in its dealings with and regarding the DPRK and fear "living as a slave of China."[22] As for China, leaders and scholars know that Pyongyang is impossible to control and can leave China in the dark out of expedience. As a Chinese academic puts it, China "has 'lost face again and again' over the past decade in its dealing with North Korea."[23] The growth of China's power is real and so is the wariness and distrust of China by the one Asian country with the oldest alliance, a shared Communist legacy, and extreme need. That China would be able to influence the domestic governance and public opinion of other regional neighbors to its liking, at the desired times, is not a likely prospect.

China's Stakes in a Stable Korean Democracy

At this time, China has compelling reasons for maintaining favorable relations with both Koreas. Its economic ties with the ROK are formidable.

From 1992, when diplomatic normalization commenced, to 2010, bilateral trade increased by thirty times, from US$6.37 billion to US$207.00 billion. A year later, the total was US$240 billion, surpassing South Korea's aggregate trade volume with the United States and Japan.[24] The two countries exceeded their target of US$200 billion by 2012 earlier than hoped, and are poised to meet their next target of US$300 billion by 2015.[25] In terms of annual flows, South Korea became the leading foreign investor in China in 2002 with US$1.72 billion, which rose to US$4.00 billion by 2010.[26] But by 2011 South Korea's investment figures slipped back to US$2.55 billion, behind Japan's US$6.35 billion and Singapore's US$6.33 billion. Nevertheless, even at the lower amount, South Korea was on par with the United States (US$2.99 billion) and ahead of the United Kingdom (US$1.61 billion), Germany (US$1.14 billion), and France (US$802.00 million).[27] On a per capita and gross domestic product basis relative to the wealthier (and in some cases more populous) co-investors, South Korea's portion would be more significant than the gross dollar amount suggests. Conversely, in 2010 China was the largest provider of a trade surplus among all of South Korea's trade partners, totaling US$32.5 billion.[28] In January 2012 China and the ROK agreed to start formal negotiations for a free trade agreement, which is expected to have a greater impact on the Korean economy than the ones it has with the European Union and the United States. A free trade agreement with China is projected to produce a 2.72 percent increase in gross domestic product, compared to a 1.00 percent and a 0.56 percent increase through the European Union–South Korea Free Trade Agreement and the United States–Korea Free Trade Agreement, respectively.[29] Korean exporters of automobiles, textiles, and petrochemicals, which wield power and influence in business and politics, will be the main beneficiaries.

Between a democracy like South Korea and a non-democracy like China, economic cooperation and a growing web of connections have facilitated closer relations between peoples and between states. Robert Sutter recalls South Koreans' prediction in 1996 that ten years from then, China would become South Korea's "closest partner" (47 percent versus 24 percent selecting the United States) and that, according to a 2000 media survey, 52 percent of those surveyed predicted that "China would be the most influential Asian power" by 2006; "few chose the United States."[30] In the public opinion survey published by the East Asia Institute in 2012, 75.6 percent of

Korean respondents believed that China will have superseded the United States as the "global leader" in ten years' time.[31]

Opposition to the policies of the George W. Bush administration, the tragic deaths of two South Korean girls by a U.S. armored vehicle, and near-unilateral decisions regarding the reduction and redeployment of U.S. troops in South Korea in the 2000s certainly influenced public opinion against the United States. Nevertheless, China's relatively new friendship with South Korea is a reality based on economic, geopolitical, and cultural ties. The popularity of Korean pop culture in China is sky high, and people-to-people contacts have skyrocketed since the opening of diplomatic relations in 1992. In 2011, 6,410,000 Chinese and Koreans visited each other's country, compared to 130,000 in 1992, and "a total of 130,000 people currently participate in student exchange programs (64,000 Chinese students in Korea and 68,000 Korean students in China)."[32]

Pragmatism brought both countries to the friendship table in the early 1990s, and pragmatism continues to guide the relationship. South Koreans view China as their largest market for exports and a neighbor they can use as leverage against any heavy-handed behavior by the United States. The growing power and presence of China in the region and the world means the ROK can keep both great powers guessing and play them off each other. For China, South Korea serves as an anti-Japan ally, given both societies' highly sensitive reactions to the history and legacy of Japanese imperialism. Japan is the most disliked nation in China and South Korea. A democratic Korea ensures that its vibrant civic groups and Internet activism keep the flames of anti-Japanese sentiment alive, whereas authoritarian Korea under Park Chung-hee and his military successors tried to keep a lid on nationalistic excesses that went against government policy. Furthermore, South Korea's rapid recovery from the Asian financial crisis and its economic dynamism contrast sharply with Japan's stagnation. South Korean capitalism also serves as a motivating force for Chinese economic innovation and growth.

In tandem with economic cooperation is economic competition between Seoul and Beijing.[33] Jae-ho Chung describes the eruption of the "garlic war" in the summer of 2000, noting that the "pace, magnitude, and the aftershock of the trade dispute were felt so intensely."[34] The Koreans slapped high tariffs on Chinese imports of frozen or pickled garlic, while the Chinese took only six days to place a complete ban on imports of important

Korean industrial products, mobile handsets, and polyethylene. (Retaliatory tariffs would have been the customary first response).

By 2004, as soon as ROK had outpaced Japan as the world's leading shipbuilder, South Koreans were "already looking over their shoulder at China, which ha[d] embarked on a path toward becoming the largest shipbuilder by 2015."[35] A Korean businessman characterized China as the "chaser," with Korea the "chased," working harder and harder to keep its lead.[36]

In 2005 Shanghai Automotive Corporation, China's largest car manufacturer, bought controlling stakes in South Korea's Ssangyong Motor Company. By 2009 both countries' deepening economic ties began "falling apart in acrimony and criminal investigations."[37] With declining sales and conflict with its Chinese investors, Ssangyong declared bankruptcy early that year, and China got a taste of the willfulness and unruliness of labor and the media in the ROK. About a thousand workers in the plant went on strike for seventy-seven days by seizing the factory and planning for an armed defense against riot police. At one point nearly a thousand autoworkers from nearby plants, such as KIA Motors, joined in the demonstration as a gesture of solidarity, as did three thousand members of the Korean Metal Workers Union. Ssangyong seems to have intended a gradual reduction of the Korean plant and a transfer of operations to the PRC, but given that Shanghai Auto had majority stakes in the company, the "combative labor unions and some South Korean commentators" cast the Chinese company as a villain that "siphoned off Ssangyong's technology, reneged on promises to invest, and dumped the company when the market turned sour."[38] Even though Shanghai Auto's interpretation differed, the end result was the collapse of the joint venture and "a black eye for China."[39]

In another case, Chinese BOE Technology Group bought HYDIS of South Korea in 2003, only to let it go bankrupt in 2006. In both instances, with South Korean workers being laid off and their companies in shambles, South Korean resentment and suspicions of China's intentions grew; they feared that China was buying up Korean companies to "steal" their technology with little or no return for Korean investors and workers.

In the Ssangyong case, the Lee Myung-bak government came down heavy-handed with repressive measures, including two thousand riot police, lawsuits against almost two hundred strikers, the labeling of labor's advocates as North Korean sympathizers, and the use of a helicopter to spray tear gas to stop the protests of strikers who were positioned on the roof of a building.

This was the first violent labor engagement in South Korea in quite a while—since the riotous days of the democracy movement in the 1980s—and the government response was harsh, not because the Lee administration valued the Chinese business relationship or sought to bend to the PRC's norms of labor control, but because Lee's government and party, *Hannara dang* (Grand National Party), was establishing its hard-line policies.

South Korea's maintenance and nurture of democracy, or backing away from it, depend on the ideological orientation of its political leadership. Lee Myung-bak took regressive steps during his tenure by narrowing political freedoms and popular participation, and by pursuing an authoritarian style of governance; while his predecessors, Roh Moo-hyun and Kim Dae-jung, broadened political space and encouraged civic activism, especially for liberals. But whether the leadership is conservative or liberal, the continued existence and use of the National Security Law, which gives the executive extraordinary prerogatives to safeguard national security against North Korean encroachment, influence, and those in South Korea who are deemed to pose a threat to the ROK, compromise the country's democratic future.

It remains to be seen whether the conservatism of Park Geun-hye, daughter of the authoritarian president Park Chung-hee, is hard-line and supportive of a labor and political environment in South Korea that accommodates Chinese business preferences. Her father's eighteen-year rule involved egregious cases of human rights abuse and political repression of society despite the country's dependence on the military, economic, and political support of the United States. And he openly defied attempts by American human rights groups, media, and political leaders to press for political reform and cease human rights violations. He snubbed former president Jimmy Carter's call for democracy and human rights and gave him less than red-carpet treatment upon his state visit to Seoul in 1979. What is clear, given Korea's history of state–society relations, is that regardless of the hegemonic power in the region, national politics colors the texture and strength of democracy.

Currently and for the foreseeable future, nationalism will play a role in influencing domestic public opinion and leaders' options in both democratic South Korea and authoritarian China. There are a number of issues that could flare up, from the trafficking of North Korean women into the PRC for commercial sexual slavery and forced or fraudulent marriage to Chinese farmers, to the increased reliance of South Korean society on Chinese nationals (mostly of Korean descent) as low-wage workers, domestics, and "foreign brides," many of whom have been mistreated or abused by Koreans. Since the normalization of relations, masses of Korean Chinese have come to South Korea with hopes of earning high incomes and enjoying reunions with long-lost kin, only to have their hopes be dashed by the Korean society's suspicion of and discrimination against them. Among the numerous Chinese migrant workers in Korea who have kept small businesses alive during an era of labor shortage in the poorer and less desirable sectors of the economy, thousands have been unpaid for work completed, or had their pay delayed, their travel documents withheld, and medical expenses for treating broken limbs and burns that occurred on the job not covered by their Korean bosses. Conditions and legal protections have improved since the 1990s, but discrimination and neglect continue in addition to periodic official threats of deporting undocumented migrants.[40]

A potent issue that hangs like a shadow in Sino–Korean relations is the territorial contention over the ancient kingdom of Koguryŏ (37 BCE–668 CE). In the early 2000s, Chinese academics and government officials provoked Korean ire by claiming as Chinese the ancient land of Koguryŏ, which lies in the northern half of the Korean peninsula. One Korean academic saw sinister signs in China's strategic ambitions in East Asia: "its real objective is to establish China's pre-eminence"[41] on Korean soil. Given these and other issues of contention, China has ample evidence that South Korean nationalist sentiment is ever present and could easily be ignited, should activists or the ROK government fan the flames against China. Given the national sensitivity of both Koreas and Pyongyang's obsession with any violation of its sovereignty, the Koguryŏ issue would invite some kind of North–South cooperation in protesting China's claims if China were to press them aggressively.

Additionally, many South Koreans and North Korean defectors take great offense at China's policy of repatriating North Korean border crossers back to the DPRK. Activists have decried the policy and held protests in front of the Chinese Embassy in Seoul. The South Korean media and Internet users have regularly posted articles or comments that lambast Chinese brutality toward the North Koreans. South Korea officially views the border crossers as refugees, while China views them as illegal economic migrants. With the growing number of North Korean defectors in South Korea, issues can become more complicated as the new residents vie for jobs with Chinese nationals and harbor resentment against China for the often frightening and dehumanizing experiences that they had endured (and that their relatives continue to endure) as border crossers and migrants in and through China.

Defectors and Democracy

During the early 2000s, the number of North Koreans arriving in the South rose exponentially. As of 2013, about twenty-three thousand defectors were living in the ROK. The progressive or left-leaning administrations of former presidents Kim Dae-jung and Roh Moo-hyun limited the defectors' ability to speak publicly and participate in politics and policy making. After all, many of them had voted with their feet and rejected the DPRK as their home while the two leaders pursued a policy of generous engagement with Pyongyang. Defectors were caught in the delicate inter-Korean dance performed and were discouraged from generating negative energy that might jeopardize the courtship.

Yet since the first decade of the 2000s, South Korea's political arena has been adjusting and opening up to the North Korean defector-newcomers at a faster pace than one might have expected. Given the decades of hostility and mistrust toward North Koreans, this is a noteworthy development and reflects the diversification and deepening of democracy and civil society in the South. Former North Koreans increasingly have become a unique identity and interest group, and they have received significant financial and social services support from both the Roh Moo-hyun and Lee Myung-bak governments to integrate them into the larger society. Electoral politics has also become an important channel for their interests. This development can be good for the future of democracy on the peninsula, helping to legitimate, acculturate, and integrate newcomers into South Korea's political system and process. Also, it can prevent the former North Koreans from remaining on the fringes of society and accumulating grievances that could grow into bigger problems.

Conversely, increasing numbers of politically active defectors can complicate politics within South Korea and with North Korea and China. As the number of new arrivals grows each year and individuals establish themselves in South Korean life, defectors become increasingly conscious of the need to assert their sociopolitical identities and agendas. Their desire to become politically active and their capacity to articulate and assert their demands and opinions as ROK citizens grew robust after the coming to power of the conservative Lee Myung-bak administration in 2008. The journal *Sisa* described this scenario as "fish finding water," meaning that the former North Koreans' political activism flourished. They created and consolidated organizations, brought public attention to their areas of concern, and deepened their influence and stake in South Korean politics.[42] They framed their political participation as essential to the national security of the ROK, claiming that they were indispensable to any true understanding of North Korean politics and people. They also have asserted that their assessments and interpretations of Pyongyang's policies are critical to the formulation of sound ROK policy toward the DPRK. On March 28, 2008, twenty-eight out of thirty-three defector organizations formed a federation (*T'alch'ongnyŏn*) in order to consolidate their power and influence. One aim was to pass a defectors protection act in the National Assembly; another, to destroy North Korean missiles.[43]

As the political climate for defectors improved with the Lee presidency, some from the North have mobilized for political office. In 2010 Yun Sŭngil ran as a preliminary candidate in the Grand National Party but failed to win the nomination. He ran again for the 19th National Assembly election in spring of 2012 with a different party affiliation. The desire to hold political office is not only a male prerogative; Lee Ae-ran, the first defector to hold a Ph.D. in South Korea and later a university lecturer, ran for a proportional representation seat through the Displaced People's Security Party in the 2008 election. She failed to be elected.[44]

In April 2012, Cho Myŏng-ch'ŏl became the first defector to gain a seat in the National Assembly. He was elected to office as a member of the Saenuri party through the proportional representation process. He had held the highest-ranking government position among all defectors, having been appointed in June 2011 as head of the Education Center for Unification, which is affiliated with the Ministry of Unification.[45] In 2011 he stated that the ROK government "must not make it seem as though the ultimate goal is cooperation and better ties (with North Korea)." Rather, "[o]ur ultimate goal has to be taking down the North Korean system and achieving reunification."[46] This kind of hard-line approach toward the DPRK is not compatible with the accommodationist approach of the PRC, and if Cho's kind of thinking were to dominate South Korean politics, relations between Beijing and Seoul would certainly grow strained.

In addition to civil society groups and political candidates, a small number of former North Korean elites have entered government service. Under the auspices of the Ministry of Unification, thirty-eight defectors were temporary workers in local and central government offices by the end of 2011 as part of a program intended to expand employment positions for defectors.[47] According to *Yonhap News*, nineteen other defectors worked in the Ministry of Unification, the Seoul metropolitan government, the Inchŏn city government, and the Kyŏnggi provincial government.[48] Defectors also are employed at the National Intelligence Service on North Korea–related issues. These numbers will most likely grow in the future, along with their influence in interpreting issues and advising policy.

Inter-Korean tensions since the sinking of the *Ch'ŏnan (Cheonan)* and the North Korean shelling of Yŏnp'yŏng (Yeonpyeong) Island in 2010 have elevated the status of the defector-elites in the South. On March 26, 2010, the South Korean corvette-class ship *Ch'ŏnan* exploded and sank in the Yellow Sea, killing forty-six naval personnel and wounding fifty-six. A South Korean investigation composed of international representatives reported that the DPRK had used a submarine torpedo to destroy the ship; North Korea has denied this charge. Later, on November 23, 2010, the DPRK engaged in artillery bombings of Yŏnp'yŏng Island, which both Koreas claim, killing two South Korean marines stationed there and two South Korean civilians. The Yŏnp'yŏng incident was the first and only outright military exchange between the two Koreas since the cessation of hostilities in the Korean War, and it engendered an acute sense of political and military crisis in the Asian region and further strained inter-Korean relations. Through these crises, defector-elites have increased their importance as "translators" of North Korean military and political developments and intentions. They have advised the government, think tanks, and circulated their opinions in writing through conventional and online media.

After the *Ch'ŏnan* and Yŏnp'yŏng Island incidents, the South Korean public has taken a less optimistic view of the prospects for peace with North Korea, and general sympathy for the people of the DPRK has soured. Stephan Haggard cites a 2010 survey by the East Asia Institute and highlights the "dramatic increase in those willing to contemplate force" after the shelling of Yŏnp'yŏng Island:

> Following the sinking of the Cheonan, EAI researchers asked which of four options respondents favored, allowing them to choose multiple responses: take the issue to the UN Security Council; impose sanctions; sever North-South ties;

and undertake limited military retaliation. Only 28.2 percent favored limited military retaliation. *After the attack on Yeonpyeong Island, however, 68.6 percent of respondents were open to retaliation.*[49] [Emphasis added.]

Additionally, support for humanitarian aid plummeted after Yŏnp'yeong, with 57 percent advocating a minimization or reduction of aid, compared to 31 percent twelve months prior.[50]

South Koreans' attitudes toward North Korea are interactive and dynamic. Events are significant drivers. The same applies to China. Whether a pro-China or anti-China disposition dominates depends on the particulars at any given time. Before April 2004, when the Chinese Foreign Ministry deleted Koguryŏ from its official website on Korean history (and refused to respond to Seoul's requests to restore the information), a survey of Korean politicians revealed that 80 percent believed China was Korea's "most important trade and business partner."[51] But by the summer of 2004, a *Korea Herald* survey showed that almost 80 percent of the 237 National Assembly members (out of 299) who had responded now ranked the United States as "Korea's top priority in diplomatic as well as economic issues."[52] The fact that China has not acted tougher with North Korea in the aftermath of nuclear tests, rocket launches, and the 2010 incidents and has permitted North Korea to circumvent international sanctions makes South Koreans, including defectors, frustrated and angry. China's unwillingness to express unequivocal intolerance of North Korea's aggressive actions—nuclear tests, rocket launches, and the 2010 incidents—breeds dissatisfaction and distrust among South Koreans, including the defectors from the North. China gets identified with the misdeeds and affronts of North Korea.

South Koreans, especially the defectors, become angry over the mistreatment of North Korean border crossers into China and the periodic roundups and deportations to the DPRK. From the winter to spring of 2012, China's deportations of North Koreans in its territory and the threat to continue such actions attracted national political attention in South Korea and societal antipathy toward China. Human rights groups in the South, together with celebrities, politicians, and defectors, publicly protested Chinese deportations, even with hunger strikes in front of the Chinese Embassy in Seoul.[53] President Lee Myung-bak spoke out against Chinese treatment of border crossers, whom Beijing views as economic migrants rather than refugees. The ROK National Assembly passed a resolution in February

2012 demanding that China cease and desist from its forced deportations of North Koreans.[54] The Chinese government ceased that round of deportations after much pressure from the Korean government and North Korea's missile test in April 2012.

In 2005 Jae-Ho Chung stated that the possibility of South Korea becoming part of the Chinese sphere of influence in the long term exists but that South Koreans, even during their romance with China in the early 2000s, held "unabated reservations about China's intentions for the region," and any attempt by China to demonstrate an "imperial" attitude toward South Korea—a side effect of a new Sino-centric order—might "work as a crucial restraint on South Korea's exclusive reliance on China at the expense of the United States."[55] The interplay of Chinese actions and transformations in domestic politics and democracy on the peninsula will be key to understanding any connection between the rise of China and its influence on its neighbors. Beijing must balance its political and economic support of North Korea with timely and unequivocal chastisement or condemnation of aggressive actions by Pyongyang, while also balancing the need to protect its border, regional stability in its northeast region, and the safety and security of North Korean border crossers. It also needs to take care, given its desire for lucrative economic ties with South Korea, that it does not affront South Korea's national pride or provoke South Koreans with the mistreatment of their Northern kin. The balancing act required for stability and peace on the Korean peninsula requires skill, artfulness, and discretion from all the major parties involved.

Notes

1. Fareed Zakaria, *The Post-American World* (New York: W. W. Norton and Company, 2009), 88.

2. David C. Kang, *China Rising: Peace, Power, and Order in East Asia* (New York: Columbia University Press, 2007).

3. Harry Harding, "Beijing Through Rose-Colored Glasses: Why Democracy Cannot Tame China," *The National Interest* (digital version, July 13, 2011), http://nationalinterest.org/commentary/beijing-through-rose-colored-glasses-why-democracy-cannot-ta-5603.

4. Zakaria, 88.

5. Aaron Friedberg, *A Contest for Supremacy: China, America, and the Struggle for Mastery in Asia* (New York: Norton, 2011), 162.

6. Scott Snyder and Joel Wit, "Chinese Views: Breaking the Stalemate on the Korean Peninsula," *United States Institute of Peace Special Report 183* (Washington, D.C.: USIP, February, 2007): 1, www.usip.org/files/resources/sr183.pdf.

7. Andrei Lankov, "Chinese Interest on the Korean Peninsula and the Future of North Korea," *East Asia Institute Issues Briefing*, no. MASI 2012–02 (March 19, 2012): 2.

8. Jung-Nam Lee, "Faltering Korea–China Relations with the Emergence of the G2 Era," *East Asia Institute Security Initiative Working Paper 26* (October 2012): 13, 2013, www.eai.or.kr/data/bbs/eng_report/2012100511563436.pdf.

9. Lankov, 5.

10. Massoud Hayoun, "What China's Talking About Today: Getting Tough With North Korea," *The Atlantic Monthly*, April 7, 2012, www.theatlantic .com/international/archive/2012/05/what-chinas-talking-about-today-getting-tough-with-north-korea/257540/.

11. Brian Spegele, "North Korea Releases Chinese Fisherman," *Wall Street Journal*, May 20, 2012, www.globalpost.com/dispatch/news/regions/asia-pacific/china/120521/north-korea-releases-chinese-fishermen-ransom.

12. Jung-Nam Lee, 20–21.

13. Ibid., 22.

14. Ibid., 20.

15. Jane Perlez, "China–Korea Tensions Rise After Failed Venture," *New York Times*, October 20, 2012.

16. Ibid.

17. Barbara Demick, "China Hires Tens of Thousands of North Korea Guest Workers," *Los Angeles Times*, July 1, 2012; Kyung-hwa Song, "China Adjusts to Influx of Cheap North Korean Labor," *The Hankyoreh*, September 13, 2012, www .hani.co.kr/arti/english_edition/e_northkorea/551521.html.

18. Zhiqun Zhu, "The Sinking of the Cheonan, the Shelling of Yeonpyeong and China-North Korea Relations," *East Asian Policy* 2, no. 4 (2010): 18.

19. Ibid.

20. Ibid.

21. Simon Tisdall, "Wikileaks Cables Reveal China 'Ready to Abandon North Korea,'" *The Guardian* (U.K.), November 29, 2010, www.guardian.co.uk/world/2010/nov/29/wikileaks-cables-china-reunified-korea.

22. Sung Jin Lee, "Anti-Chinese Sentiment High Among North Korean Elite," *The Daily NK*, November 9, 2009, www.dailynk.com/english/read.php?num=5627&catald=nko2500.

23. Louisa Lim, "Hijacking Reveals Strains In China–North Korea Ties," *National Public Radio*, June 12, 2012, www.npr.org/2012/06/12/154774626/hijacking-reveals-strains-in-china-north-korea-ties.

24. Jung-Nam Lee, 1.

25. Dilip K. Das, "Reginal Implications of Korea–China FTA," *Korea Times*, January 27, 2012, www.koreatimes.co.kr/www/news/opinon/2012/01/137_103588. html; *Yonhap News*, "S. Korea's Trade Minister Stresses Need for FTA with China, January 29, 2012, http://english.yonhapnews.co.kr/business/2012/01/29/91/050200 0000AEN20120129000700320F.HTML.

26. *Chosun Daily*, "Korean Investment in China Dwindles," January 28, 2011, http://english.chosun.com/site/data/html_dir/2011/01/28/2011012801124.html.

27. "News Release of National Assimilation of FDI From January to December 2011," Invest in China (website), January 19, 2012, www.fdi.gov.cn/1800000121_49_2569_0_7.html.

28. *People's Daily Online*, "S Korea Posts Record High Trade Surplus in 2009," January 14, 2010, http://english.peopledaily.com.cn/90001/90778/90858/90863/68 69236.html.

29. Hongshik Lee et al., "Economic Effects of Korea–China FTA and Policy Implications," *Korea Institute for International Economic Policy*, December 30, 2005, www.kiep.go.kr/eng/publications/pub02_view.jsp?page=1&no=131931&sCate=013001&sSubCate.

30. Sutter, 158.

31. Jung-Nam Lee, 10

32. Ibid., 1.

33. "Koreans Look to China, Seeing a Market and a Monster," *New York Times*, February 10, 2004.

34. Jae Ho Chung, "From a Special Relationship to a Normal Partnership? Interpreting the 'Garlic Battle' in Sino–South Korean Relations," *Pacific Affairs* 76, no. 4 (Winter, 2003/2004): 550.

35. "Korean Shipbuilders See China's Shadow," *New York Times*, January 6, 2005, www.nytimes.com/2005/01/06/business/worldbusiness/06ships.html?_r=0.

36. Ibid.

37. "In Carmaker's Collapse, a Microcosm of South Korea's Woes," *The New York Times*, February 24, 2009.

38. Ibid.

39. Ibid.

40. Katharine H. S. Moon, "Migrant Workers' Movements in Japan and South Korea," in *Egalitarian Politics in the Age of Globalization*, ed. Craig N. Murphy (New York: Palgrave, 2002), 186–188.

41. *Korea Herald*, "Korea-China Ties: 12 Years Mark Gains but Challenges Loom," August 24, 2004, www.accessmylibrary.com/coms2/summary_0286 -13084693_ITM.

42. Nakin Chŏng, "*Chŏngch'i nŏmbonŭn talbuktanch'edŭl* [North Korean Refugees' Political Ambitions]," *Sisa Journal* [in Korean], May 13, 2009, www.sisapress.com/news/articleView.html?idxno=49111.

43. Chŏng, "*Chŏngch'i nŏmbonŭn talbuktanch'edŭl.*"

44. Ibid.

45. Ibid.; "North Korean Defector Appointed to Key Post in the South," *Chosun Ilbo* [English edition], June 8, 2011, http://english.chosun.com/site/data/html_dir/2011/06/08/2011060800665.html.

46. Hae-in Shin, "Better N.K. Ties Not Ultimate Goal," *Korea Herald*, July 6, 2011, www.koreaherald.com/view.php?ud=20110706000759.

47. "Only 20 N. Korean defectors work as public servants in S. Korea: lawmaker," *Yonhap News*, October 9, 2011, http://english.yonhapnews.co.kr/national/2011/10/09/4/0301000000AEN20111009000800315F.HTML.

48. Ibid.

49. Stephan Haggard, "Public Opinion in South Korea: The Effects of the Cheonan and Yeonpyeong Shelling," *Peterson Institute for International Economics*, February 15, 2011, www.piie.com/blogs/nk/?p=311.

50. Ibid.

51. *Korea Herald*, "Korea–China Ties."

52. Ibid.

53. British Broadcasting Company, "Seoul Urges China on North Korea Refugees," February 22, 2012, www.bbc.co.uk/news/world-asia-17123208.

54. Ibid., "South Korea Passes Resolution on North Korea Refugees," February 27, 2012, www.bbc.co.uk/news/world-asia-17187469.

55. Jae Ho Chung, "China's Ascendancy and the Korean Peninsula: From Interest Reevaluation to Strategic Realignment?" *Power Shift: China and Asia's New Dynamics*, ed. David Shambaugh (Berkeley: University of California Press, 2005), 162.

ELEVEN

China's Rise and Other Global Trends
Implications for Taiwan Democracy

Richard Bush

Introduction

In thinking about the future of democratic Taiwan in its changing East Asian neighborhood, some scholars have recalled Finland during the Cold War. Bruce Gilley is the most notable.[1] He explains that Finland, in 1948, in order to preserve its national independence and avoid becoming another Soviet satellite, made an agreement with the Soviet Union with three elements. First, Helsinki would not join alliances challenging Moscow or serve as a base for any country challenging Soviet interests. Second, in return, Moscow agreed to uphold Finnish "autonomy" and respect Finland's democratic system. And third, from 1956 to 1981, "Finland pursued a policy of strategic appeasement and neutrality on U.S.-Soviet issues and limited domestic criticism of the Soviet Union," a policy that the Finnish public supported.[2] Gilley notes that a "Finlandized" state is not a "client" or "puppet state." A Finlandized state voluntarily makes concessions to a larger neighbor in order to guarantee important elements of its independence. A client or puppet state does not have that freedom of action. A Finlandized state makes a calculated response to a situation of power asymmetry.

How might twenty-first-century Taiwan be an analogy for Cold War Finland? Gilley argues that Taiwan is a small but "internally sovereign" state. It is geographically close to a "superpower" with which it shares cultural and historical ties. It balances a "fierce sense of independence" with a pragmatic sense of the need to accommodate China's vital interests. Its current leaders understand the value of "integration" and the dangers of confrontation.

Obviously, there are differences between the two cases. The U.S. security commitment to Taiwan is more explicit than it was for Finland, and the People's Republic of China (PRC) military threat to Taiwan is more direct than the Soviet Union's to Finland. Still, Gilley believes that the essence of the analogy—that a small county abjures certain security options and limits domestic political parameters to preserve its fundamental security—may still apply. He concludes that Taipei has begun to move "in the direction of eventual Finlandization."[3] And he identifies a possible Finland bargain for the island:

- Taiwan would reposition itself as a "neutral power, rather than a U.S. strategic ally."
- It would thereby hope to calm Beijing's fears about being an obstacle to China's regional ambitions.
- It would refrain from "undermining the CCP's rule in China."
- Beijing would back down on its military threats, grant Taipei expanded participation in international organizations, and extend favorable economic and social benefits to the island.[4]

I have deep admiration for the way in which Finland adjusted the operation of its democratic system in order to preserve its national independence vis-à-vis the Soviet Union. Yet I also believe that a Finland analogy does not work regarding Taiwan (nor do I agree with Gilley's views that Finlandization would solve a strategic problem for the United States, but that is another issue). But his insight is a useful point of departure for this essay. The underlying issue is important, even pressing. China's rise—or more accurately, China's revival—as a great power is probably the most important development of the twenty-first century. Whether that transition is managed well or poorly will determine whether East Asia enjoys peaceful coexistence or is doomed to conflict. Taiwan and its people have a unique place in that process. There is a line of argument in China that holds that the nation's rise will not be complete until the century-plus history of disunion is brought to an end, with the reincorporation of Taiwan.[5] That is, China regards unification as fundamental to its rise. This ambition in turn presents Taiwan with some tough choices, and its democratic system will be the mechanism by which those choices are made. That the people of the island have sometimes been denied a say in decisions about their future course and have had to live with the consequences of decisions that others have made for them makes it imperative that new choices be made well.[6]

This essay inventories some of the ways in which the growth in China's power has or may affect the system by which authoritative choices are made on Taiwan. I assess the cause side of this relationship (China's rise) both generally and in ways that are more specific to Taiwan. The effect side must cover different elements of democratic politics on Taiwan, but the focus is on how choices might be distorted or constrained in ways that would not exist absent the China factor. My purpose is more to tease out aspects of the problem rather than provide a full and heavily documented exposition.

Conceptual Context: Power Transition

In getting an intellectual handle on China's revival and the challenges it poses for all of us, I find the interrelated rubrics of power transitions and the security dilemma to be particularly useful. To paraphrase Thucydides on the root cause of the Peloponnesian War: "The growth of the power of Athens, and the alarm which this inspired in Sparta—the leading power of the day, made war inevitable." To state the idea generally, international conflict is likely when regional and global power balances shift quickly, when a rising power challenges the status quo and the position of the state or states that guard the established order. The examples of Germany before World War I and World War II, Japan in the 1930s and 1940s, and the Soviet Union in the Cold War all come to mind.

Which, of course, raises the question: Might China some day challenge American preeminence in East Asia, if not the world? There is no question that China's power is growing and that is why some people in the United States, Japan, and Taiwan are getting a little bit excited. And, as I suggested, we should regard this rise as a revival, one that is driven by Chinese people's sense of past humiliation and an optimism and sense of historic responsibility to return their country and civilization to greatness.

It is worth noting that a rising power and the established power do not always descend into conflict. Great Britain accommodated to the rise of the United States about a century ago. Whether that is possible in China's instance is an interesting case, one that poses both an intellectual and a policy challenge. To go back to the analogy of Germany, will China's leaders over the long run tend to act like Wilhelm II or, God forbid, Adolf Hitler? Or will they end up like Helmut Kohl and Angela Merkel?

As for the intellectual challenge, scholars like Randall Schweller observe that it is not always easy to figure out the objectives of a rising power.[7] Is it limited in its goals? Or is it trying to fundamentally change the international order, what scholars call revisionist or revolutionary? Of course, countries do not go around advertising whether their objectives are revisionist or not, for obvious reasons, and sometimes they change their goals. So it is hard for established states and scholars to know.

Another question about a rising power, Schweller stresses, is its approach to risk. Is it risk-averse or not? To make the question even more interesting, the nature of the rising power's goals may be different from its approach to risk. *Revolutionary* states may take a lot of risks, and rising powers with *limited* goals may be risk-averse. That's what you would expect. But a state with limited goals may be willing to take lots of risks, and established powers may mistakenly view it as a revolutionary power. Conversely, a state that has long-term ambitions of overturning the system may be risk-averse, lulling the established powers into a sense of complacency. Great Britain under Neville Chamberlain made a bad mistake when it believed that Hitler had only limited aims. That only invites more aggression. But established powers can make the opposite mistake: concluding that a rising power with limited aims has revolutionary goals.

Analytically, these two cross-cutting variables dictate that rising powers have four modes for addressing the international system. Furthermore, established powers correctly assess which mode the rising power has adopted and have a choice of responses, ranging from preemptive war at one extreme and appeasement at the other. And assuming that established powers correctly assess the rising power's goals and propensity to risk, their response should be appropriate to the choices of the rising power. Preemptive war may be a proper response to a power with revisionist goals and an acceptance of risk. Engagement may be optimal for a rising power that has limited goals and is risk-averse. Moreover, an established power may have a mixed strategy. Hedging, which combines engagement with a degree of deterrence, is appropriate for a situation where the rising power has adopted limited goals in the medium term and takes few risks to achieve them, but whose long-term goals and behavior cannot be predicted with any confidence.

If one looks at China's external record since the beginning of the reform and opening-up period in 1979, it is hard to conclude that China is acting internationally like a revisionist power, a rising power intent on overturning the system. Instead, the Beijing regime assumes that China is still relatively weak and needs both time (decades) and a peaceful international environment in which to complete the modernization necessary to become a true great power. We see a policy set to provide both time and a peaceful context. On balance, Beijing has adhered to international norms rather than undermined them. It has supported the missions of international organizations rather than frustrated them. It advocates dialogue rather than engaging in brinksmanship. Although China's record is not perfect, and its behavior in 2010 and 2012 are exceptions to a generally positive rule, its leaders seem to understand that even if they were bent on a challenge to the international order, doing so in the near term would be stupid.

So it *appears* that China's fundamental approach combines limited goals and a cautious approach to risk. And most countries have responded as theory would predict, with a policy that emphasizes engagement and binding, in the hope that China's long-term goals will remain limited and constructive. Yet some uncertainty remains, particularly in light of China's behavior since 2010, particularly in the East Asian maritime domain. So China's neighbors and the United States hedge their bets, mainly by balancing behavior (China is hedging as well, because it too is uncertain).

Beijing's approach to Taiwan has not always been consistent with this norm of limited goals and aversion to risk. Its goal of ending the island's de facto independence on its terms is more revisionist in character than its objectives elsewhere (at least from the point of view of Taiwan people!). Moreover, when Beijing has concluded that it is facing a fundamental challenge to its interests (e.g., in 1995–1996, 2003–2004, 2007–2008), it has accepted more risk. When it has had confidence that trends are favorable and the door to unification remains open, however, it has displayed strategic patience.

As useful as power-transition and security-dilemma concepts are in understanding China's revival as a great power, I would add two more dimensions. On the one hand, these provide, if you will, a series of snapshots of the relative positions of the rising power and established ones. These should be supplemented with a "motion picture" that portrays in greater detail the interaction between China, on the one hand, and the United States and Japan, on the other, on a set of concrete issues such as Taiwan, the Korean peninsula, Iran, the global economy, and climate change. This interaction is intensive and continuous. Through its course, each side learns lessons about the other, and each draws conclusions—correct or incorrect—about the other's long-term intentions. Whether the interaction in these specific arenas is cooperative or competitive will define the trajectory of China's rise. On the other hand, it is important when considering power transitions to distinguish levels of the international system. China may not challenge the United States globally for a long time, but it is testing the United States in the PRC's home region of East Asia. Similarly, in the early twentieth century, the United States behaved one way in the international system as a whole and in another in its home hemisphere.[8]

TAIWAN'S RESPONSE TO CHINA'S REVIVAL

With this conceptual architecture in mind, where do we place Taiwan on the map of potential responses to China's reemergence? Taiwan does have issues at play with China that no other country does, and the essence of Ma Ying-jeou's grand strategy appears to be to build, as much as possible, an institutionalized, mutually beneficial relationship with China that increases the cost of coercion by the latter to such a high level that Beijing would never attempt it. Moreover, the Ma administration's approach looks similar to that of the United States and other countries of East Asia. It is a mixed strategy that combines:

- engagement and reassurance: rewarding the PRC for what it assumes are limited goals and doing nothing that might lead Beijing to take risks; and
- external balancing: reliance on the United States to come to its aid in the event that engagement fails and Beijing decides to take risks for revisionist purposes.

(Whether Taiwan's leaders and people conclude over time that this strategy has been successful is another question, one to which we will return.)

Some might say that the Ma administration's engagement has morphed into appeasement. I disagree. It has in no way granted Beijing the benefit it most seeks: Taiwan's agreement to resolve the fundamental dispute between the two sides on China's terms. And Ma does seek to bolster the island's international role and so reverse the marginalizing trend that began in the early 1970s.

Looking back, how should we assess the approach of the Lee Teng-hui and Chen Shui-bian administrations, especially their later phases? Each sought to put some limits on economic engagement with the Mainland. Each thought that these limits were necessary to keep Taiwan economically strong (internal balancing), but the targets of those limits (the business community) were able to circumvent them. Lee and Chen arguably each engaged in what we might call political preemption, promoting definitions of Taiwan's legal status that Beijing certainly judged to be a change in the status quo (as did the United States). Whether this preemption tendency stemmed from security-dilemma dynamics; whether it was politically motivated (true in both cases, I believe), it was still an effort to extricate Taiwan from a trap whose door was seen to be closing. Lee and Chen both pursued external balancing, and assumed that the United States would come to Taiwan's aid even if there was an element of entrapment.[9]

Conceptual Context: Democratic Development

There is a general sense that Taiwan's political system does not work terribly well. Unless we understand the source of that dysfunction, we may misunderstand how China's revival will affect and be affected by that system.

It is tempting to attribute the problems of Taiwan's democratic system to the idiosyncrasies of its leaders (Lee Teng-hui, Chen Shui-bian, et al.) or to the problem of divided government that existed from 2000 to 2008. If those attributions are correct, one might infer, the return of unified government and the rise of leaders with moderate views and temperament would solve the problem. But united government has not fostered a political paradise, and there has been something of a consensus that much of the political dysfunction was structural in origin.

That is, leaders, parties, politicians, and publics are operating, often in spite of themselves, in a democratic order that is only partway constructed and not yet consolidated. The behavior that we see may make sense for the individual actors in the system, but it is dysfunctional for the public at large and will likely continue until the democratic order is completely consolidated. Various institutional problems—semi-presidentialism, the legislature, the party system, the electoral system, and the mass media—work together in an interlocking way to reduce accountability, foster a zero-sum political psychology, promote policy deadlock, ensure suboptimal policy performance, and defer consensus on the rules of the game.[10]

A key measure of the effectiveness of the Taiwan political system is how the public evaluates its performance. Larry Diamond's paper for a 2010 conference in Taipei provides polling evidence relevant to this measure since the mid-1990s. Generally speaking, the Taiwan public has vacillated in its satisfaction regarding "the way democracy works." The share of those surveyed who were satisfied stood at 67.2 percent in 1996; fell to 53.4 percent in 2001; rose to 55.9 percent in 2006; and jumped to 68.6 percent in 2010.[11] The picture was mixed when it came to specific features of Taiwan's system, as summarized in Table 11.1.

On most measures, there is little or no change. The only exception is growing confidence in the control of corruption (but this may simply be that supporters of the Kuomintang (KMT) and other conservative parties (the "Blues") approve of corruption prosecutions against former officials of the Chen administration). More disturbing is the low share of those surveyed who believe that the system is responsive and that the legal system can hold lawbreaking officials to account.

The Legislative Yuan should have a key role in ensuring responsiveness, but Hawang Shiow-duan of Soochow University has identified a number of institutional features that act as constraints: lack of specialization and expertise in legislative committees; the role of the procedure committee in blocking consideration of bills; lack of transparency in the mechanism of inter-party negotiation on bills; and corruption and conflicts of interest among legislators. On the rule of law, Jacques de Lisle has confirmed the public perception that the politically powerful tend to win in sensitive cases.

TABLE 11.1
Specific measures of Taiwan's system performance

	2006	2010
Freedom	74.9	76.4
Competitiveness	56.4	58.6
Vertical accountability	46.4	48.2
Horizontal accountability	51.1	47.5
Rule of law	40.8	42.5
Control of corruption	45.8	56.1
Responsiveness ("to what people want")	35.8	38.5

SOURCE: Larry Diamond, "How Good a Democracy Has the Republic of China Become? Taiwan's Democracy in Comparative Perspective," presented to the INPR Conference: A Spectacular Century: The Republic of China Centennial Democracy Forums, Taipei, June 24–25, 2011, drawn from the Asian Barometer surveys (www.asianbarometer.org/).

NOTE: Vertical accountability refers to the people's power to change a government they don't like. Horizontal accountability refers to the ability of the legislature to check the executive.

Moreover, access to the system can be a problem, and judges and prosecutors are not always up to handling complex economic cases.[12]

There is clearly room for a systematic evaluation of the degree to which democratic consolidation has advanced since Ma Ying-jeou came to office. But my impression is that although Taiwan's balance of power and political atmosphere have changed since 2008, the fundamental dysfunction remains. The problems are mainly structural, and unless and until systemic solutions are devised for what are systemic problems, the dysfunction will continue and politicians will continue to perform according to the cues that the system creates. The losers will be the people of Taiwan, who are placed at a growing disadvantage vis-à-vis China. The winner is the government in Beijing.

The stakes regarding the health and quality of Taiwan's democracy are high. First of all, Taiwan's success or failure is important for democratization in general and for political change in China in particular. Second, China is not exactly a passive actor, since Beijing is promoting the idea that illiberal, technocratic regimes are more effective in achieving the goals that really matter, and that the systems in Taiwan and the Philippines are suffering a "democracy deficit"—meaning, democracies do not promote the common good. Third, there should be some compensation for the historical fact that decisions were made concerning the status of Taiwan and the fate of the people of Taiwan without consulting them. Fourth and finally, Taiwan faces daunting choices when it comes to reconciling the conflicting goals of the challenge of China and the challenge of security, economic prosperity, and social welfare in an era of globalized competition and flat government budgets. The people of Taiwan will have to live with their choices, perhaps forever, so it would be good if those choices are made well. But if the political system—the mechanism by which those choices are made—is defective, then the people's interests will not be well served.

If Taiwan pursues a mixed strategy toward China, moreover, one that combines engagement and balancing, it must command political support in order to be sustainable. Even in the best of circumstances, competing domestic constituencies and segments of the public will have conflicting views on what the appropriate combination is. And a dysfunctional political system (if that indeed is what Taiwan has) will be hard pressed to fine-tune a mixed strategy, whatever the combination of elements.

China's Revival and Taiwan's Choices: Specific Issues

China's revival as a great power will have some effect on Taiwan's democratic political system: the choices available to it; the choices that are actually made; and how those choices are made. The real or potential effects that come immediately to mind are deterrence of Taiwan independence, the multifaceted implications of Taiwan's dependence on the Chinese economy (e.g., united-front tactics; potential for economic coercion), a general decline in Taiwan's political resolve, and the implications of the one country, two systems (1C2S) formula. I examine each of these in turn, and find that at least some are less serious than they appear at first glance.[13]

DETERRING DE JURE INDEPENDENCE

Already, a more powerful China has likely negated the possibility of one ultimate option for Taiwan: that is, de jure independence. How seriously Taiwan's political leadership and a majority of its people ever contemplated that objective is subject to debate. More certain is the fact that PRC leaders *believed* that Lee Teng-hui was plotting separatism and acted to prevent it. Ironically, the time when Taiwan had the most freedom to pursue that objective—when Beijing was very weak and the United States was probably the most willing—was also the time that Chiang Kai-shek harshly repressed anyone who took the view that perhaps the island should be independent, as well as denying democracy.[14] By the 1990s when independence ideas could be discussed on the island and Lee Teng-hui was departing from KMT orthodoxy, China was already firmly ensconced in the U.N. and other international organizations and was becoming important to the global economy. Meanwhile the United States had long since taken its do-not-support-independence position. Although China was still relatively weak militarily, it created sufficient fear that conflict might erupt through accident or miscalculation that the United States opted to urge restraint on both Beijing and Taipei. So even the chance that the Chen Shui-bian administration might actually take clear and irreversible steps to independence was relatively modest. And in 2008, Taiwan voters signaled that they preferred a different approach.

Thus, Chinese deterrence worked in excluding one option, however remote it may have been. Conversely, one can make a good case that if Lee Teng-hui and Chen Shui-bian had not promoted the policies that they did, and in the ways that they did, the growth of China's *military* power might have occurred on a more gradual trajectory than it did. That is, the dynamics of Taiwan's democratic system in the late 1990s and early 2000s had its own impact on China's revival, by prompting a stronger People's Liberation Army deterrent against independence. This is not to fault those policies but to note that they did have an effect that continues until this day.

ECONOMIC ASYMMETRY

The growing size and centrality of the Mainland economy is the dimension of China's growing power that has most affected Taiwan. The Dengist policies of reform and opening up have presented Taiwan companies and the Taiwan economy as a whole with great opportunities. But they have also fostered fears about the political consequences of an economic orbit closer to the Chinese sun. Taiwan's political system has come up with a series of answers to this dilemma, one created as much by globalization as by China. But the dilemma cannot be avoided. We confine ourselves here to some of the more obvious of these political consequences.

UNITED-FRONT TACTICS

One political consequence of economic dependency has to do with those Taiwan people most instrumental in promoting cross-strait economic relations. It has been no secret that the PRC regards Taiwan business executives with operations in China (*taishang*) as a potential political resource, just as it regarded Hong Kong businessmen.[15] Second, people on Taiwan are aware of Chinese formulations. Beijing has not kept secret its hopes for using businessmen to steer politics (*yishang weizheng*) and manipulating economics to promote unification (*yijing cutong*). And this united-front approach takes institutional form in the Taiwan business associations that began forming in the PRC in 1990. They have links to the Taiwan Affairs Office of the State Council, its subordinate offices, and to local party and government units. The secretariats of the associations are drawn from those Chinese organizations. The issue is whether Beijing has actualized that potential and used *taishang* to further its goals within the Taiwan political system, as it successfully used their Hong Kong counterparts.

The assessment so far is "no." In one study, Shu Keng and Gunter Schubert conclude that *taishang* influence is rather weak. First of all, their business interests vary considerably; and forging a common position on a

fundamentally political issue, like how Taiwan should resolve the fundamental dispute with China, would be extremely difficult. More likely is a
consensus on changing or repealing Taiwan government policies that are
bad for business, a consensus that probably existed regarding the Chen
Shui-bian administration. Even if *taishang* could agree on the desirability of
unification, they lack the institutional channels through which to advocate
their preferences in Taiwan. (Anecdotally, it is said that *taishang* believe that
they would lose much of their preferential treatment from Beijing if unification happened.) The main ways that *taishang* influence the political process
is through their votes (if they are willing to return to the island to cast their
ballots) and through campaign contributions. On the former, they constitute only a small share of the electorate. On the latter, if reported campaign
contributions are any indication, corporations give to both major parties
and only modestly more to the KMT. Keng and Schubert conclude, "Even
if China tried to exert pressure or influence on Taiwan by making use of the
taishang, such a strategy would not work."[16]

Moreover Schubert, in another study based on extensive research among
Taiwan executives in China, found that *taishang* tend to have shifting identities depending on the circumstance. They may understand the gap between
Mainland and Taiwan society; remain interested in Taiwan's domestic politics; tend to support the KMT but maintain a low political profile; worry
more about ties with local government officials than with trends in national,
cross-strait politics; not believe that *taishang* can or should play a role in the
conduct of cross-strait relations; prefer to maintain the political status quo
and believe that, in the long term, economic integration will contribute to
both business success and resolving the China–Taiwan conflict.[17]

ECONOMIC SANCTIONS

China's leverage over Taiwan does not depend on using *taishang* as political
agents within the island's political system. Another way that Beijing might
exploit Taiwan's dependence on the Mainland would be to threaten to with-
draw the benefits of economic cooperation unless and until Taipei agreed to
negotiate on its terms. That is, it would use economic leverage to force onto
the Taiwan political agenda a fundamental choice between prosperity and
the political status quo.

As in the case of the utility of united-front tactics, analysts so far have
concluded that sanctions will not have their desired effect and may even

be counterproductive. Shelley Rigger and Toy Reid conducted a detailed analysis of the presence of Taiwan business operations on the Mainland and were struck by how much the affected Chinese localities had to lose by any PRC effort to exert political leverage. "Without Taiwanese investors," they write, "many of China's wealthiest provinces and cities would lose the crown jewels of their local economies, and China's exports, especially IT exports, would decline sharply. In other words, cross-strait economic interactions have given actors within China a strong interest in avoiding events that would disrupt those interactions." The only question is whether the local officials, who have the most to lose from sanctions or any other kind of coercion, have the influence in Beijing to dissuade those actors who would pursue coercion (and the will to exercise that influence).[18]

A 2007 RAND Corporation study concluded, among other things, that when it comes to economic sanctions, "political factors—in particular domestic politics within the initiating and target countries—usually have a greater impact on the initiator's ability to convert economic influence into political leverage. . . . Thus, China's growing capacity to inflict economic pain upon Taiwan has not automatically provided Beijing with . . . powerful political leverage."[19] How Taiwan leaders might respond to hypothetical Chinese sanctions would be a function of the domestic political pressure that the government would face. Sanctions could certainly produce a panic that might lead to the capitulation that China sought; Chinese missile tests in March 1996 created a run on the Taiwan stock and foreign-exchange markets. But economic coercion could just as well create anger and resistance on the part of the public.

SOVEREIGNTY

Democratic Progressive Party (DPP) leaders have regularly alleged that the Ma administration, in order to secure greater benefits from the Mainland economy, has sacrificed or otherwise undermined Taiwan's sovereignty. Regardless of whether the charge is justified by the reality of the situation, this is not a trivial issue. How Taiwan or the Republic of China (ROC) is or should be a part of China is the key sticking point for any mutually acceptable resolution of the fundamental dispute between the two sides. There is a broad consensus on the island that it is a sovereign entity (KMT and DPP presidents alike have repeated the mantra, "The ROC [or Taiwan] is an independent sovereign state"). Lee Teng-hui and Chen Shui-bian sought without success to get Beijing to accept the claim of sovereignty before they were prepared to negotiate on core issues (and Beijing insisted on its claims). Ma Ying-jeou has taken a different tack: Taipei will not insist on its claim if Beijing does not deny or reject it.

How does this issue affect the Taiwan political system? Sovereignty actually has different dimensions: whether a governing entity is a recognized member of the international system; whether and how it controls its borders; who or what controls the governing entity (who "rules within"); and Westphalian sovereignty, whether the governing entity has the right to rule within the territory under its jurisdiction (non-subordination). One problem with the sovereignty discourse on Taiwan and between Taiwan and China is a lack of clarity on which dimensions are being discussed. Certainly, it refers to Taiwan's role (or lack of it) in the international system, and that is probably the most likely understanding of the term. In my view, however, Westphalian sovereignty is as important as international sovereignty, if not more so. There will be no resolution of the cross-strait dispute unless the two sides address that issue in the medium and long terms. For the short term, the question is whether the Taipei government has in one way or another diminished its right to rule in the way it engages Beijing.

Based on an examination of the negotiations conducted so far, I conclude, first, that the Ma administration has *not* undermined the claim that the ROC is a sovereign entity. So far, the two sides have not challenged each other's core position on this issue, but rather have used the 1992 consensus as a basis for discussions and generally adopted the approach of "mutual non-denial." The 1992 consensus possesses elements of both agreement and disagreement, and Beijing and Taipei have opted in a tacit understanding to use the former and ignore the latter. Consequently, they have been able to expand the areas of cooperation. As one Taiwan scholar put it, "If either side sabotages the tacit agreement, the other side will do the same, and the relationship will therefore sour. . . . Only fools would like to tear it apart."[20]

Second, it appears that so far the Ma administration has been able to conduct its negotiations with Beijing on essentially a government-to-government basis, and that the "white gloves" of the Straits Exchange Foundation and the Association for Relations Across the Taiwan Straits are becoming increasingly nominal. Moreover, the PRC has accommodated to this trend. By sustaining cross-strait interactions on an intergovernmental basis, Taiwan has preserved the idea that it is a sovereign entity.

Third, the agreements negotiated concern matters that are usually in the purview of national governments. Essentially, it is PRC and ROC government agencies that will conduct this cooperation, and on a direct basis. To be sure, similar cooperation occurs between the Beijing government and the relevant agencies of the Hong Kong government under the aegis of the one country, two systems formula. That China and Taiwan have concluded economic agreements does not presage political outcomes but neither does it foreclose them. Beijing did not rule out a 1C2S outcome by accepting these agreements as written. But neither did Taipei do anything that undercut its claim of sovereignty, and the fact that officials of the ROC will be implementing these agreements with their PRC counterparts fortifies that claim.

Finally, at least some of these cross-strait agreements, at the same time that they sustain Taiwan's claim of Westphalian sovereignty, may also have positive implications for another dimension of sovereignty, by expanding Taiwan's role in the international system. That *may* be the promise of the Economic Cooperation Framework Agreement (ECFA), if Beijing is prepared to allow Taiwan to conclude free-trade-agreement–like arrangements with other countries and so permit its participation in the international system. (See below on how cross-strait relations can affect yet a third dimension: who rules in Taiwan.)

Of course, it is still early days in cross-strait relations. That expanding economic relations have apparently not undermined Taiwan's Westphalian sovereignty does not mean that future negotiations will also have a benign effect. After all, it appears that Beijing will insist on the one-China principle rather than the 1992 consensus for negotiations on political and security issues, with potential consequences for sovereignty matters.

SAPPING TAIWAN'S WILL

But perhaps sovereignty attrition, sanctions, and united-front tactics are unnecessary. Perhaps the cumulative effect of economic interdependence and growing military power will foster a political consensus on the island that 1C2S is the only choice. There again, choices are constrained.

This, after all, is China's hope and expectation. People in the PRC have their own ideas about the relationship between its power and Taiwan's system. Between the lines of Hu Jintao's December 31, 2008, statement of Taiwan policy is a specific logic chain:

- China's policies from 1979 create "a strong foundation and dependable safeguard for advancing the development of cross-Strait relations and realizing the peaceful reunification of the motherland."
- Taiwan identity (which has complicated China's quest for unification) has roots in Chinese culture and does not automatically foster separatism.
- There are people on Taiwan who misunderstand the Mainland and suspect its policies. Beijing can and should "undo such sentiments and counsel them with the greatest tolerance and patience." This includes the "Taiwan independence" adherents.
- Transforming the existing balance of sentiment on Taiwan will not be a quick process (the implementation of the policy of "peaceful development" would occur "for a long time to come"; resolution of legacy and new issues would occur "gradually").
- But China can be confident of the ultimate outcome.[21]

One reason for Chinese "strategic patience" is that the challenges facing Taiwan are daunting. Socially, Taiwan is a prosperous, well-educated, middle-class, demographically mature society with small families. Economically, some sectors have moved far up the economic and technology ladder, but in the service sector there are too many banks and too many people are employed in small, inefficient, family operations. In gross domestic product per capita, Taiwan approaches some of the countries of Western Europe. In some respects, it has a lot in common with South Korea.

Even if China did not exist, Taiwan would face tough choices if these socioeconomic trends continue. The most serious is the aging of the society. Fewer working people will be supporting a growing number of elderly, with all the costs that entails. The options appear to be increasing immigration (including from the Mainland), increasing taxes on those who are working, or reducing social services. (More employment of women does not seem to be an option, because they are already 45 percent of the employed labor force.[22]) If more social resources are directed to the elderly, that is likely to reduce the standard of living for everyone else. Would there have to be a choice between quality schools and quality care for the elderly?

Another choice has to do with preserving economic competitiveness. Taiwan has some outstanding companies, and the best of these have become solid links in the global supply chains connecting China's assembly and manufacturing operations with consumer markets in advanced countries. But we cannot assume that Chinese entrepreneurs and enterprises will remain content to play the role they have played since 1979. They will wish to move up the technology and value chain. What do Taiwan companies do then? Do they find new niches or get displaced? What is to be done to ensure that even as the number of working people of the island declines, they can find employment in well-paying jobs? How can Taiwan reduce the inequality between those who work in the advanced sectors of the economy and those who do not? Even if ECFA is relatively successful it will just keep Taiwan in the game and prevent more extreme marginalization. It will not totally answer the challenge of remaining competitive and assuring a high standard of living for Taiwan's residents.

Whatever choices Taiwan makes regarding its competing domestic priorities, there is another issue to address. That is, how will the leaders and people of the island balance the desire for a good standard of living for all citizens and the need to ensure external security? One thing we can be sure of is that the buildup of PRC military forces will continue. How much of that will worsen Taiwan's sense of vulnerability is difficult to know. Some of the People's Liberation Army's new capabilities will not have a Taiwan mission, directly or indirectly, but many will. Even if Taiwan's policy of accommodation quiets Beijing's fear of separatism, it is unlikely to negate the concern that China's leaders may feel driven at some point to pursue a policy of coercion. The constraints on Taiwan's national defense are well known. One is the transition to an all-volunteer army, which will require a transfer of resources from the category of military investment to that of personnel—unless the defense budget is increased significantly.

To compound these dilemmas among prosperity, social welfare, and security, the priorities of the government are fairly well established. They reflect what people in a society like Taiwan want—or reflect those desires as well as the political system processes them. But funding those choices will be increasingly difficult.

The danger is that Taiwan will seek to muddle through rather than face the choices that are looming. Most people lead fairly comfortable lives. There is no sense of crisis. The consequences of not acting are long term, whereas public choice takes place in the short term. In the resulting scenario, established trends continue, and three effects are not improbable. First, Taiwan's economy becomes less competitive globally (even if some companies hold their own), and the standard of living declines. Second, there is a suboptimal response to the challenge of caring for the elderly, so that both the working population and the elderly are unhappy. Third, Taiwan's military power continues to decline relative to the PRC's.

What is the effect of such an outcome on public consciousness, and on how Taiwan defines itself by 2025, for example? That is hard to say. Four presidential elections will have occurred, and few people who were alive at the time the ROC government moved to the island will still be alive.

I do not have the impression that average residents of Taiwan spend their time agonizing over whether they are Chinese, Taiwanese, or a mix—despite the efforts of pollsters to get them to do so. I expect that the average Taiwanese think most about whether their standard of living is better than that of their parents, whether it is getting better or worse for them, and how they are going to assure that their children will have a better life. These are the concerns, probably, that most shape their social identity.

That being the case, we may speculate that continuation of established trends will foster deeper doubt and disagreement about what Taiwan is and what it means. It may also lead to a decline in the public's sense of confidence—confidence about the future and about the competence of the island's institutions to address the dilemmas at hand. Already, we know, a large majority of Taiwan citizens have seen "deterioration in the capacity of the political system to deliver economic growth, social equity, and law and order."[23] Having a consensus on fundamental identity and a strong sense of confidence will be crucial to meeting the biggest challenge of all: Beijing's expectation, currently deferred, that unification should occur. It is not in Taiwan's long-term interests to negotiate from a position of perceived weakness.

THE ISSUE OF "HOSTILITY"

There is recognition in China that its growing military power is an impediment to a stable cross-strait relationship and resolving the fundamental dispute with Taiwan. And the proposed means of removing that impediment and fostering stability in the security realm is some sort of formal agreement to create "peace." Thus, Hu Jintao in his policy statement at the end of 2008 reiterated the PRC's appeal that, "On the basis of the one-China principle, [the two sides] formally end the state of hostility across the Strait through consultation, reach a peace agreement, and build a framework for the peaceful development of cross-Strait relations."[24] Some Mainland scholars go further and call the absence of political talks and a peace accord a "bottleneck" in the Taiwan relationship that has to be removed if progress is to be sustained.

Yet there was a curious logic in how these scholars explained why a peace accord was a difficult project, one that focused on how the Taiwan political system defined its choices. Thus, in a series of articles in 2009, Yu Keli, the director of the Institute for Taiwan Studies at the Chinese Academy of Social Sciences, argued that cross-strait relations remained a situation of "mutual hostility" that fostered a "shadow and suspicion resulting from mutual mistrust or even hatred remaining in the hearts of the compatriots on both sides of the Strait." For Yu, the greatest contributor to this hostility was the low level of mutual political trust, particularly with respect to the one-China principle (i.e., how Taiwan related to the state called China). Mistrust continued because, among other reasons, Taiwan independence sentiment persisted on Taiwan and the KMT was unwilling to constrain it.[25] Having set this premise, Yu drew a remarkable conclusion in a December 2009 essay: "Now, only if the Taiwan authorities resolutely and bravely lead Taiwan society to carry out radical reform, abandon the separatism of 'Taiwan consciousness,' . . . and restore the original meaning and remold the identity of Chinese culture, the Chinese nation, the Chinese and the motherland can the ghost of 'Taiwan independence' awareness lingering over Taiwan be fundamentally driven away . . . and the problems related to cross-Strait political differences and the consensus be naturally solved."[26]

In the 2009 debate over Taiwan policy, Yu had positioned himself at an ideological point on the Chinese policy spectrum. Other scholars—and the regime, it seems—do not share Yu's sense of urgency about pushing political talks. But Yu is not alone when it comes to the basic idea he has expressed. That is, Taiwan may have its concerns about what it would regard as manifestations of Beijing's hostility (i.e., its growing military capabilities), but the Mainland sees hostility in the form of the "ghost of 'Taiwan independence' awareness." Only if the Taiwan government is prepared to exorcise that ghost, in effect by altering Taiwan political culture in a more China-friendly fashion, will China be willing to reduce its own "hostility." In other words, Taiwan must discipline its democracy.

ONE COUNTRY, TWO SYSTEMS AND TAIWAN POLITICS

The Chinese expectation that Taiwan must be willing to narrow the parameters of political debate should not be surprising. What we know of the

PRC's long-term approach suggests that narrowing the political agenda is only the beginning.

To be sure, Chinese leaders have said relatively little about the subject. One exception was a talk that Deng Xiaoping had with American scholar Winston Yang in June 1983: "After reunification, as a special administrative region, Taiwan can adopt systems different from those on the mainland and enjoy privileges, which other provinces and autonomous regions may not share. The region can have the powers of a legislature, judiciary and final adjudication."[27] But at its core, the application of the formula to Hong Kong is not encouraging. For the underlying purpose of the Basic Law, the special administrative region's charter, is to deny real power to political forces whose intentions Beijing suspects. The nomination of the chief executive is tightly controlled through a selection committee made up predominantly of "patriotic" local figures, with the result that a leader of the Democratic Party (or any other figure whom Beijing mistrusts) cannot mount a competitive challenge to China's choice. And the system of functional constituencies for the election of members of the Legislative Council, plus the use of proportional representation for filling geographic seats, means that opposition parties can never win a majority.

If, hypothetically, Beijing were to take the same prudential approach toward a post-unification Taiwan, it would seek to engineer the political system in such a way that politicians like Lee Teng-hui and Chen Shui-bian and parties like the DPP could never come to power—unless, of course, they foreswore independence. And even then, it might erect high hurdles to such contingencies. Getting future Taiwan leaders to voluntarily rule out these political outcomes would certainly be harder than doing so in Hong Kong, if only because it would mean reversing a reality that has existed since the DPP became a serious competitor in Taiwan politics in the 1990s. Perhaps Beijing would not try. Perhaps under those circumstances (Taiwan acceptance of 1C2S), no political force on Taiwan would adopt a stance unfavorable to China. But that, of course, is the point. Political choices on Taiwan would be constrained, either because of self-abnegation by the island's political forces or Beijing's political engineering.

The various ways that China's growing power has or might affect the choices available to the Taiwan system present a mixed picture. China's robust deterrence against de jure independence has likely removed an option (if it was ever a serious option in the first place). The dangers of united-front tactics, economic coercion, and attrition of sovereignty through negotiations turn out to be less serious than some have thought (at least for now). But looming on the horizon in the 1C2S formula and Chinese discussions of "hostility" are intimations that Taiwan may have to further restrict its democracy if it is to achieve a more stable peace or to resolve the fundamental cross-strait dispute. And there is lingering anxiety that picking among the array of choices facing Taiwan is just too hard.

Finlandization Redux

This essay began with Bruce Gilley's idea that Taiwan may already have begun to model its relationship with China on that of Finland toward the Soviet Union during the Cold War (or at least the option exists). That choice would require significant shifts in Taiwan's external policies, particularly its relationship with the United States, and in how it operates its democratic system. I believe that the Finland and Taiwan cases are different enough that Taipei would never consider Finlandization as a serious option. Whereas the Soviet Union was happy with Finland's "strategic appeasement," China seeks more from Taiwan. Whereas the Soviet Union recognized that Finland was a full member of the international system (along with the East European members of the Warsaw Pact), there is no sign that Beijing is willing to reverse its campaign of over six decades to marginalize Taiwan. Hans Mouritzen, the leading scholar on Finlandization, comes to a similar conclusion: "My main objection to Gilley's analysis is that unilateral dependency is not a desirable project for any small power. It may be necessary for a nation to make the best out of a difficult situation, but no small power today will voluntarily discard a reasonable alliance option and limit its room to maneuver in the way Finlandization requires. Taiwan is already pursuing a détente policy in line with West Germany's Ostpolitik—which took place within NATO—but that should not be mistaken for Finlandization. Finlandization may eventually come to the Taiwan Strait, but only if an overburdened United States decides to reduce its future role in Asia, creating a wholly new regional environment."[28]

Even if we dismiss the strategy of Finlandization, we should not ignore aspects of the Finland example. That is, Finland did not rely solely on appeasement to ensure its national survival. Even as it eschewed the option of external balancing, it did not ignore the necessity of internal balancing.

This was most obvious in the political dimension: fostering a consensus that ruled out playing politics with foreign policy. It also worked to create a stable society and effective economy. It was, after all, pursuing a mixed strategy in meeting the challenge of a rising power.

We may apply this insight to Taiwan, which is pursuing a mixed strategy that combines engagement of China with some measure of external balancing. That approach will not be sustainable unless Taiwan also engages in its own internal balancing. Even if China did not exist, the imperatives of globalization would require it.

What should this internal balancing include? In my view, it should include the following elements:

- Enhancing economic competitiveness, not only through liberalization externally but through fostering innovation internally.
- Maintaining a sufficient military deterrent to discourage China from resorting to coercion either to prevent what it fears or to achieve what it wants, at least for the few weeks that the United States would need to fully intervene on Taiwan's behalf. (Taiwan should of course discourage Beijing through reassurance about its own goals, but it cannot rule out that China might choose coercion because of misperception and miscalculation of cross-strait trends.)
- Improving understanding within the elite and in the public at large about what it means to claim that Taiwan is a sovereign entity, particularly as it concerns cross-strait relations.
- Reforming the dysfunctional political system so that it is less focused on the distribution of benefits and denigrating the personal character of political leaders and more on facilitating objective, hardheaded choices regarding the island's future—as difficult as that may be in an environment of an aging population and flat budgets. To avoid those choices and the creation of a mechanism for making them well is also a choice, and a self-destructive one at that.

One more observation: Hans Mouritzen, in the passage cited above, warned that Taiwan Finlandization was more likely if the United States lost the will to provide security public goods in East Asia. This, I believe, is the key issue in how the entire region adjusts to the rise of China. The critical variable in determining whether China's global role will be threatening to the United States and to the countries of East Asia is the ability and the resolve of the United States to continue to play the kind of leadership role in the region it has played since World War II. If the United States continues to build its absolute power, even as the relative gap with China declines;

and if the United States is prepared to remain a resident Asian power, Beijing is likely to continue to accommodate to Washington. But that requires, more than anything, rebuilding the pillars of national power that made the United States the hegemon in the first place, including a healthy economy, sound government finance, a creative science and technology infrastructure, a first-class education system, and so on. That in turn depends on whether we can effectively address the dysfunction of our political system.

Notes

1. Bruce Gilley, "Not So Dire Straits: How Finlandization of Taiwan Benefits U.S. Security," *Foreign Affairs* 89 (January/February 2010): 44–60.

2. Ibid.

3. Ibid., 50.

4. Ibid.

5. See Alan M. Wachman, *Why Taiwan: Geostrategic Rationales for China's Territorial Integrity* (Stanford, CA: Stanford University Press, 2007), 29–30.

6. More theoretically, the topic also stands at the intersection between understanding politics at the level of the international system without regard to the domestic politics of the system's constituent units, and giving more weight to what happens within those units.

7. The discussion that follows is based on Randall Schweller, "Managing the Rise of Great Powers: History and Theory," in *Engaging China*, ed. Alastair Iain Johnston and Robert Ross (New York: Routledge, 1999), 1–32.

8. Jack S. Levy, "Power Transition Theory and the Rise of China," in *China's Ascent: Power, Security, and the Future of International Politics*, ed. Robert S. Ross and Zhu Feng (Ithaca, NY: Cornell University Press, 2008), 11–33.

9. All three administrations tried military internal balancing, to the extent that they either initiated or continued programs for an independent long-range precision-strike capability against the PRC.

10. Shelley Rigger, "The Unfinished Business of Taiwan's Democratic Democratization," in *Dangerous Strait: The U.S.-Taiwan-China Crisis*, ed. Nancy Bernkopf Tucker (New York: Columbia University Press, 2005), 43.

11. Larry Diamond, "How Good a Democracy Has the Republic of China Become? Taiwan's Democracy in Comparative Perspective," *A Spectacular Century: The Republic of China Centennial Democracy Forums: Conference Manual*, June 2001, 174. This data is from the Asian Barometer Survey.

12. See "Consolidating Taiwan's Democracy: Challenges, Opportunities, and Prospects," conference, March 22, 2006, Center for Northeast Asian Policy Studies, The Brookings Institution, www.brookings.edu/events/2006/0322taiwan.aspx.

13. Much of the rest of this section is based on my book *Uncharted Strait: The Future of China–Taiwan Relations* (Washington, D.C.: Brookings Institution Press, 2013).

14. On American flexibility, see for example the various proposals during the Kennedy and Johnson Administrations to keep the ROC in the United Nations, in Richard C. Bush, "The Status of the ROC and Taiwan, 1950–1972: Explorations in United States Policy," in *At Cross Purposes: US–Taiwan Relations, 1942–2000* (Armonk, NY: M. E. Sharpe, 2004), 85–123.

15. Christine Loh, *Underground Front: The Chinese Communist Party in Hong Kong* (Hong Kong: Hong Kong University Press, 2010).

16. Shu Keng and Gunter Schubert, "Agents of China–Taiwan Unification? The Political Role of Taiwan Business People in the Process of Cross-Strait Integration," *Asian Survey* 50 (March/April 2010): 303–304, 309 (cited passage). On campaign contributions, see "DPP Receives NT$179.6 Million Donation Last Year: Control Yuan," *Taiwan News* Online, September 1, 2010 (Open Source Center [hereafter OSC] CPP20100901968026).

17. Gunter Schubert, "The Political Thinking of the Mainland *Taishang*: Some Preliminary Observations from the Field," *Journal of Current Chinese Affairs* 39 (2010): 93–97.

18. Shelley Rigger and Toy Reid, "Taiwanese Investors in Mainland China: Creating a Context for Peace?" in *Cross-Strait at the Turning Point: Institution, Identity and Democracy*, ed. I Yuan (Taipei: National Chengchi University Institute of International Relations, 2008), 78–111; cited passage on p. 110. Chen-yuan Tung has concluded that "China has no economic leverage over Taiwan in terms of imposing economic sanctions and that Taiwan's vulnerability to such a scenario is almost non-existent." See Chen-yuan Tung, "Cross-Strait Economic Relations: China's Leverage and Taiwan's Vulnerability," *Issues and Studies* 39 (September 2003): 137–175; cited passage on p. 137. Also on Taiwan, see Steve Chan, "The Politics of Economic Exchange: Carrots and Sticks in Taiwan-China-U.S. Relations," *Issues and Studies* 42 (June 2006): 1–22.

19. Murray Scot Tanner, *Chinese Economic Coercion Against Taiwan: A Tricky Weapon to Use* (Santa Monica, CA: RAND Corporation, 2007), 135.

20. From summary of Lai Yue-chien, "1992 Consensus Favorable," *Lien-ho Pao*, January 6, 2010 (OSC CPP20110107086002).

21. "Join Hands to Promote Peaceful Development of Cross-Strait Relations; Strive with Unity of Purpose for the Great Rejuvenation of the Chinese Nation," Xinhua Domestic Service, December 31, 2008 (OSC CPP20081231005002). Alan Romberg concludes that Hu's policy is based on the "realization that it would take a long time to move to unification, and that in the meantime, the two sides needed to weave a fabric of relationships that could serve as the basis for ultimate

'reunification' on terms acceptable to both." See Alan D. Romberg, "Ma at Mid-Term: Challenges for Cross-Strait Relations," *China Leadership Monitor* 33 (Summer 2010):10, http://media.hoover.org/sites/default/files/documents/CLM33AR.pdf.

22. "Table 21. Important Indicators of Labor Force Status," *Statistical Yearbook of the Republic of China*, Directorate-General of Budget, Accounting and Statistics, Executive Yuan, R.O.C. (Taiwan), http://eng.dgbas.gov.tw/public/data/dgbas03/bs2/yearbook_eng/y021.pdf.

23. Yu-tzung Chang and Yun-han Chu, "How Citizens View Taiwan's New Democracy," in *How Asians View Democracy*, ed. Yun-han Chu, Larry Diamond, Andrew J. Nathan, and Doh Shull Shin (New York: Columbia University Press, 2008), 110–111.

24. "Join Hands to Promote Peaceful Development of Cross-Strait Relations."

25. Yu Keli, "The Two Sides of the Strait Should Look Squarely at the Issue of Ending the State of Hostility and Signing a Peace Agreement," *Zhongguo Pinglun*, August 2009 (OSC CPP20090805710007).

26. Yu Keli, "Promoting Political Relations Is the Only Way for the Two Sides," *Zhongguo Pinglun*, December 2009 (OSC CPP20091230710007).

27. "Deng Xiaoping's Six Conceptions for the Peaceful Reunification (1983)," webpage of the Embassy of the PRC in Latvia, May 8, 2008, http://lv.china-embassy.org/eng/zt/twwt/t251058.htm.

28. Hans Mouritzen, "The Difficult Art of Finlandization," *Foreign Affairs* 89 (May/June 2010): 131.

Index

Page numbers with "t" or "f" indicate material in tables or figures.

aboriginals (Taiwan): and DPP, 287; and identity politics, 119; and KMT, 113; legislative seats reserved for, 109t, 110; old-age allowance for, 293; and online social movements, 174

ABS (Asian Barometer Survey), 29, 62; on authoritarian rule, 43; on checks and balances, 31, 39–40 (40t); on democratic institutions, 43–46 (45f); on democratic legitimacy and satisfaction in East Asia, 13–16 (14f, 15t); on democratic quality, 50–53 (51t); on democratic supply/satisfaction with democracy, 47f, 48f, 49; on desire for democracy, 36–37, 48, 62; on essential characteristics of democracy, 31–33 (32f); on extent of democracy, 46–49 (48f); on non-democratic alternatives, 44f, 45f; on preference for democracy, 33–36 (34f, 35f), 38; on preference for democracy by age cohorts, 56–58 (56f, 58f); on rule of law, 40–41 (40t); on social pluralism, 40t, 41–42; on suitability and efficacy of democracy, 37–38; on trust in institutions, 53–55 (54f, 55f); on trust in institutions by age cohorts, 58–61 (59f, 60f)

Acer, 228

"actualizing citizens," 139

AFC (Asian financial crisis, 1997) and Korea: effects on health-care system, 262; "multiple transitions" following, 254–255; neoliberal labor reforms following, 191, 194, 201–202; recovery from, 328; rise in inequality following, 206, 273

affective orientation, 30–31, 33, 61

age cohorts: health expenditures for, 271, 273f; preference for democracy by, 56–58 (56f, 58f); trust in institutions by, 58–61 (59f, 60f)

aging society issues (Korea): age dependency ratios, 11–12 (12f); increasing health costs, 265, 270–273 (272tf, 273f), 277–278. *See also* socioeconomic/social welfare issues

aging society issues (Taiwan): age dependency ratios, 11–12 (12f); consequences of, 355; demographics of, 237t, 284–287 (286f), 310–311; distribution of insurance sources, 289; foreign caregivers, 311; National Pension Act, 295–300; old-age assistance in 1990s, 289–292; old-age assistance in 2000s, 292–295; old-age farmer allowance, 294, 296–300; voter support for old-age pensions, 288–289. *See also* socioeconomic/social welfare issues

NDRP (New Democratic Republican
Party), 74t, 76f, 77, 78t, 83
neoliberalism (Korea), 194–195, 201, 207–
208, 212n3
neoliberalism (Taiwan), 238–240 (240f),
245, 248n29
Netherlands, 140f, 197
networked public sphere, 138
New Democratic Republican Party
(NDRP), 74t, 76f, 77, 78t, 83
New Frontier Party. *See* Saenuri (New
Frontier) Party
New Korea Party (NKP), 74t, 76f, 78t, 79f,
80f, 82–84 (82f, 83f)
New Management Strategy, 198–199, 201
"new media," 19. *See also* digital media/
Internet
New Millennium Democratic Party. *See*
MDP (New Millennium Democratic
Party)
New Political Federation of People, 76f,
104n31
"New Taiwanese" concept, 121
NHI (National Health Insurance), Korea,
253–256; introduction of limited NHI
(1962–1987), 256–257; military government's introduction of limited coverage, 256; gradual expansion of coverage,
257–259; candidate Roh's universal
health insurance pledge (1988), 260;
universalization goal (1989), 255; Roh
vetoes health funds integration (1989),
261; effects of AFC (1997), 262–263;
Health Insurance Law (1999), 261–262;
separation reforms (2000), 264–265;
funding sources and financing trends,
265–270 (266t, 267t, 268f); aging society issues, 265, 270–273 (272tf, 273f),
277–278. *See also* equity in health care
(Korea)
NHI (National Health Insurance), Taiwan,
304–307, 305f
Nisbelt, Matthew C., 135
NKP (New Korea Party). *See* New Korea
Party (NKP)
non-regular workers/*pi chŏnggyujik*, 202–
204 (202f, 203t, 204t)

non-subordination, 353
norms and principles, support for regime,
30
norms and rules, 29–30, 31, 41
Norris, Pippa, 30, 137
North Korea, 16–17; China repatriation
of border crossers from, 331; defectors
from in South, 17, 332–336; favorability
ratings of by South Koreans, 95–97
(96t–97t); hostage-taking of Chinese
fishermen, 324; and identity politics,
88–95 (89t–90t, 93t–94t); industrial
training visas to China, 326; inter-
Korean summit (2000), 44–45, 57, 86;
labeled part of "axis of evil," 87; nuclear
program of, 86, 95, 323–333, 335; relations with China, 320, 323–326, 331;
satellite/rocket launches, 92, 335–336;
shelling of Yŏnp'yŏng Island, 334–335;
sinking of the *Ch'ŏnan*, 334; Sunshine
Policy toward, 71, 85–87, 91, 104n35;
trafficking of women to China, 330. *See
also* Koreas, relations between
Norway, 140f
NP (New Party), Taiwan, 107–110 (108t,
109t), 127t, 128t130

OBM (own-brand manufacturing), 228,
230
ODM (own-design manufacturing), 230
OECD health data, 256
official law-abidingness, 41
OhmyNews, 142–143, 149, 151
Oh Se-hoon, 97–98
Oh Yeon-ho, 143
old-age assistance. *See* aging society issues
(Korea); aging society issues (Taiwan)
old-age farmer allowance (Taiwan), 294,
296–300
one country, two systems (1C2S) formula,
354, 358–360
one-party rule, 31, 44f–45f, 113
online anonymity and lack of accountability, 138
"Open Taipei" campaign event, 173
Open Uri Party (URI), 74t, 76f, 79f, 80f,
88–91 (89t–90t)

The authorized representative in the EU for product safety and compliance is:
Mare Nostrum Group
B.V Doelen 72
4831 GR Breda
The Netherlands

www.ingramcontent.com/pod-product-compliance
Lightning Source LLC
Chambersburg PA
CBHW020451270326
41926CB00008B/563